INOUE PRESENTS

THE DUKE OF DEATH AND HIS MAID

2

CONTENTS

Chapter 15: What Happened Last Night

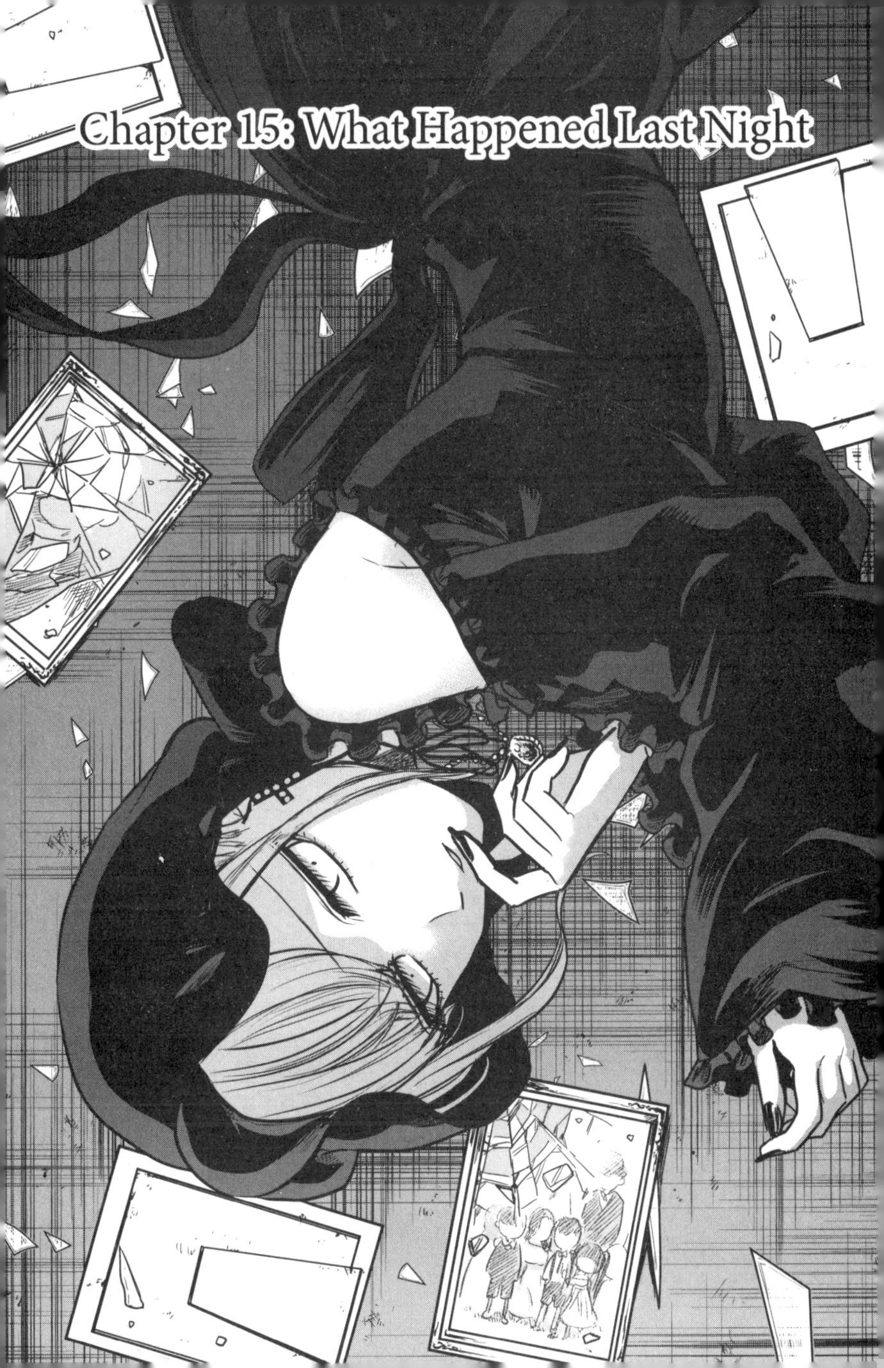

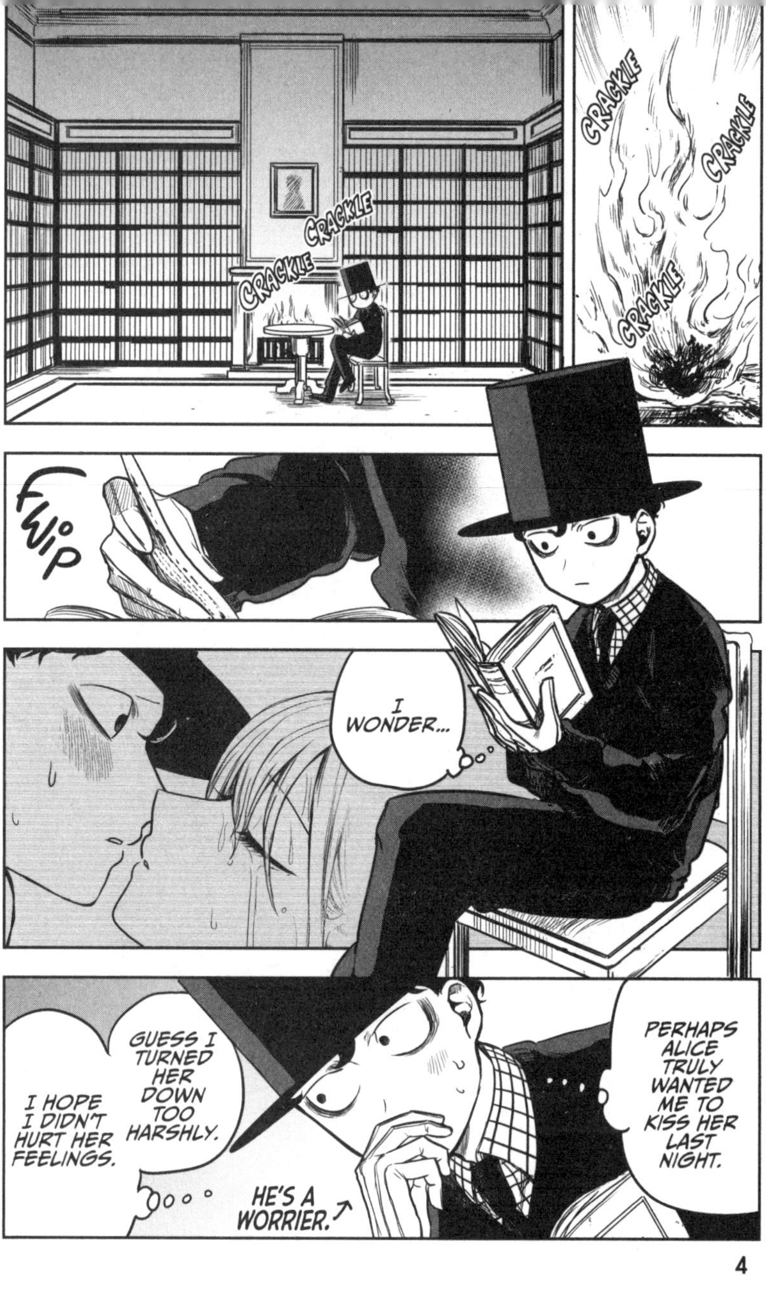
CRACKLE
CRACKLE
CRACKLE
CRACKLE
CRACKLE
FWIP
I WONDER...
PERHAPS ALICE TRULY WANTED ME TO KISS HER LAST NIGHT.
GUESS I TURNED HER DOWN TOO HARSHLY.
I HOPE I DIDN'T HURT HER FEELINGS.
HE'S A WORRIER.

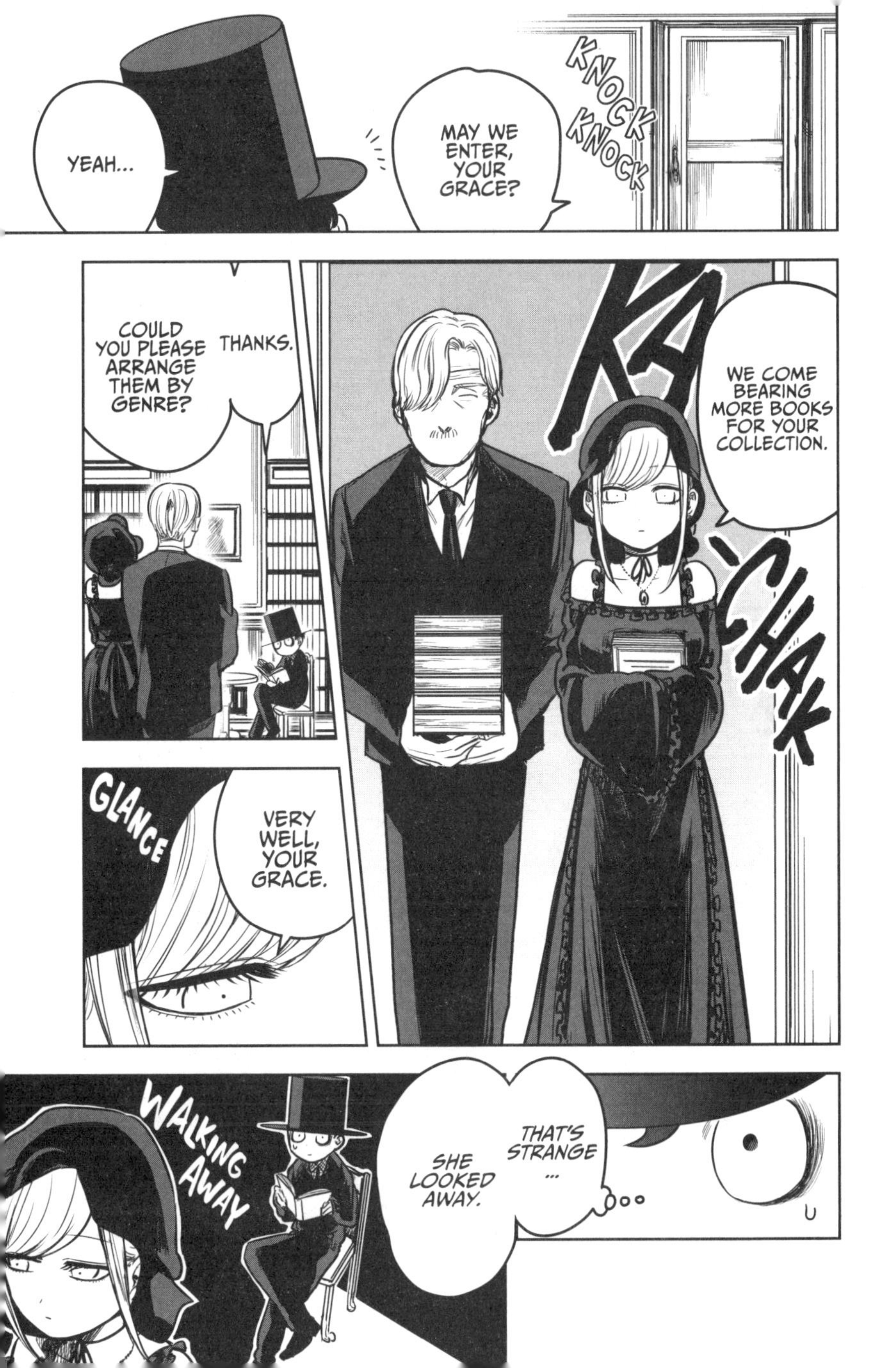
KNOCK KNOCK
MAY WE ENTER, YOUR GRACE?
YEAH...
KA-CHAK
WE COME BEARING MORE BOOKS FOR YOUR COLLECTION.
THANKS.
COULD YOU PLEASE ARRANGE THEM BY GENRE?
VERY WELL, YOUR GRACE.
GLANCE
THAT'S STRANGE ...
SHE LOOKED AWAY.
WALKING AWAY

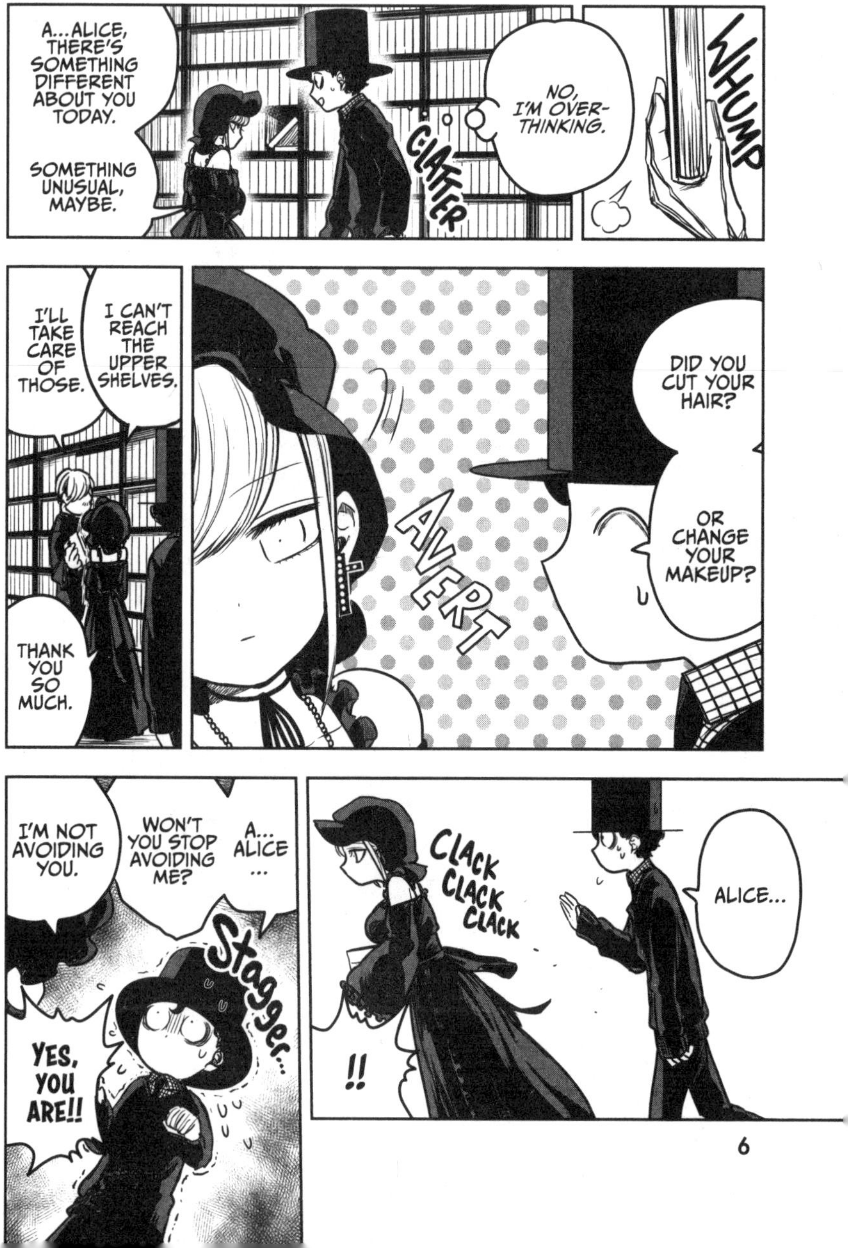
WHUMP
A...ALICE, THERE'S SOMETHING DIFFERENT ABOUT YOU TODAY.
SOMETHING UNUSUAL, MAYBE.
CLATTER
NO, I'M OVER-THINKING.
DID YOU CUT YOUR HAIR?
OR CHANGE YOUR MAKEUP?
AVERT
I CAN'T REACH THE UPPER SHELVES.
I'LL TAKE CARE OF THOSE.
THANK YOU SO MUCH.
ALICE...
CLACK CLACK CLACK
!!
A... ALICE ...
WON'T YOU STOP AVOIDING ME?
I'M NOT AVOIDING YOU.
Stagger...
YES, YOU ARE!!

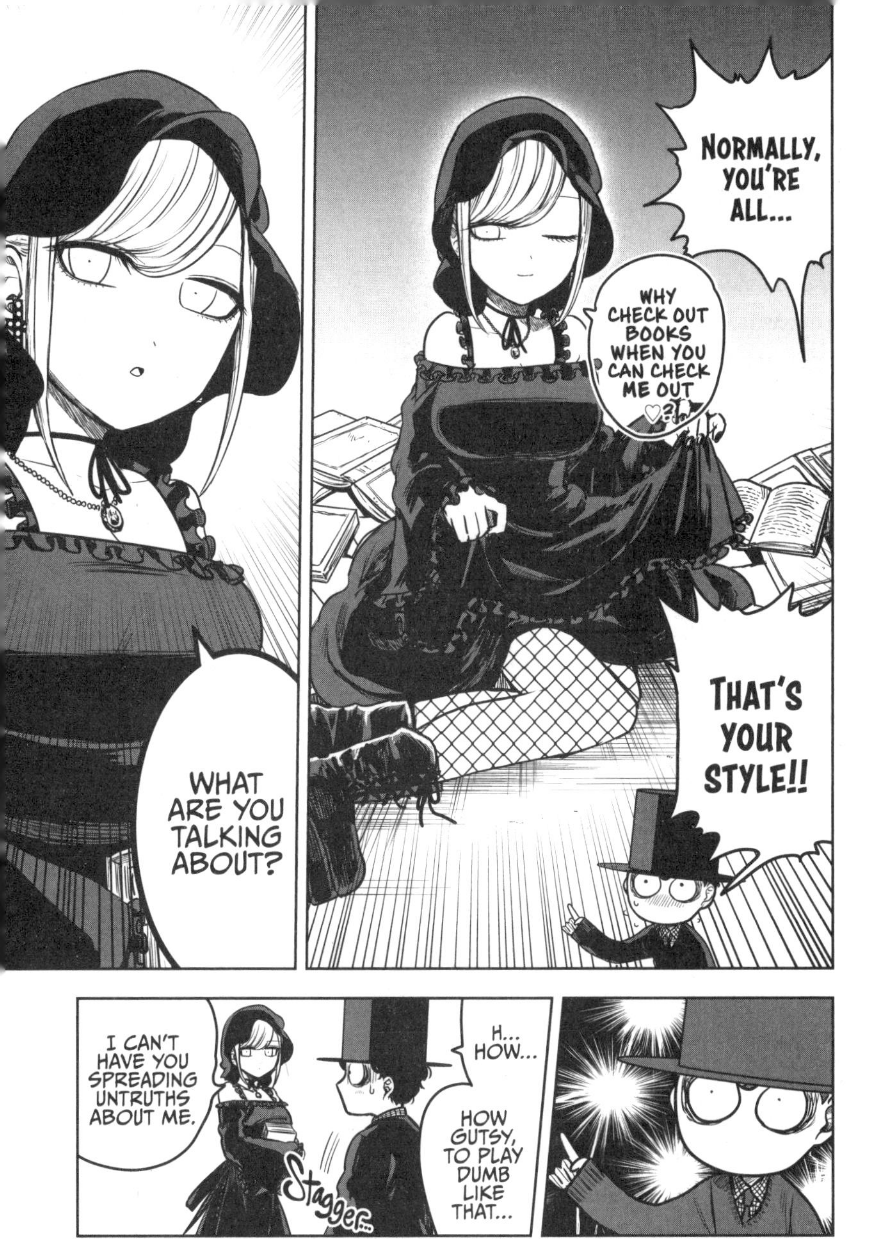
NORMALLY, YOU'RE ALL...
WHY CHECK OUT BOOKS WHEN YOU CAN CHECK ME OUT ♡
THAT'S YOUR STYLE!!
WHAT ARE YOU TALKING ABOUT?
H... HOW...
HOW GUTSY, TO PLAY DUMB LIKE THAT...
Stagger...
I CAN'T HAVE YOU SPREADING UNTRUTHS ABOUT ME.

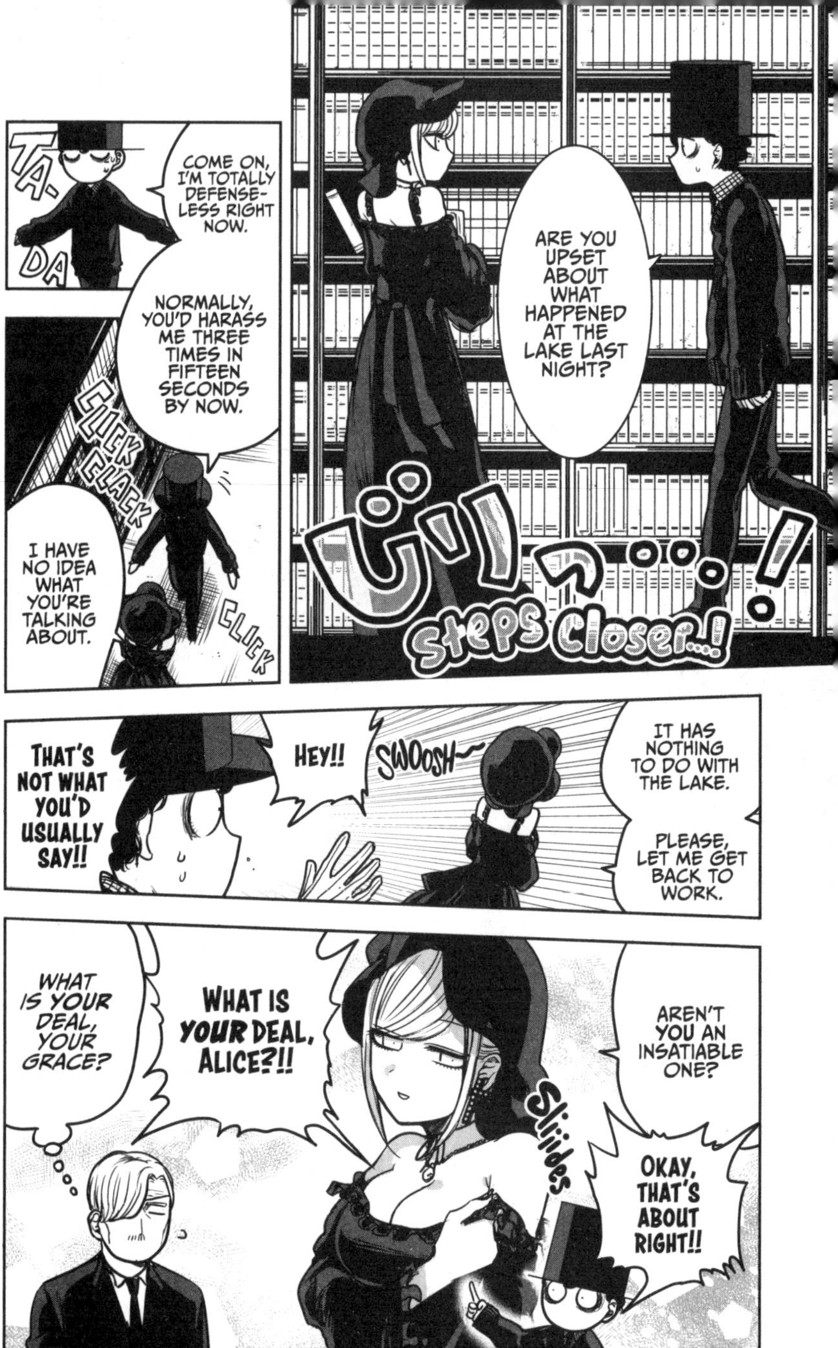
ARE YOU UPSET ABOUT WHAT HAPPENED AT THE LAKE LAST NIGHT?
ぴりっ...!
Steps closer...!
TA-DA
COME ON, I'M TOTALLY DEFENSE-LESS RIGHT NOW.
NORMALLY, YOU'D HARASS ME THREE TIMES IN FIFTEEN SECONDS BY NOW.
CLICK CLACK
I HAVE NO IDEA WHAT YOU'RE TALKING ABOUT.
CLICK
IT HAS NOTHING TO DO WITH THE LAKE.
PLEASE, LET ME GET BACK TO WORK.
SWOOSH~
HEY!!
THAT'S NOT WHAT YOU'D USUALLY SAY!!
AREN'T YOU AN INSATIABLE ONE?
OKAY, THAT'S ABOUT RIGHT!!
Sliiides
WHAT IS YOUR DEAL, ALICE?!!
WHAT IS YOUR DEAL, YOUR GRACE?

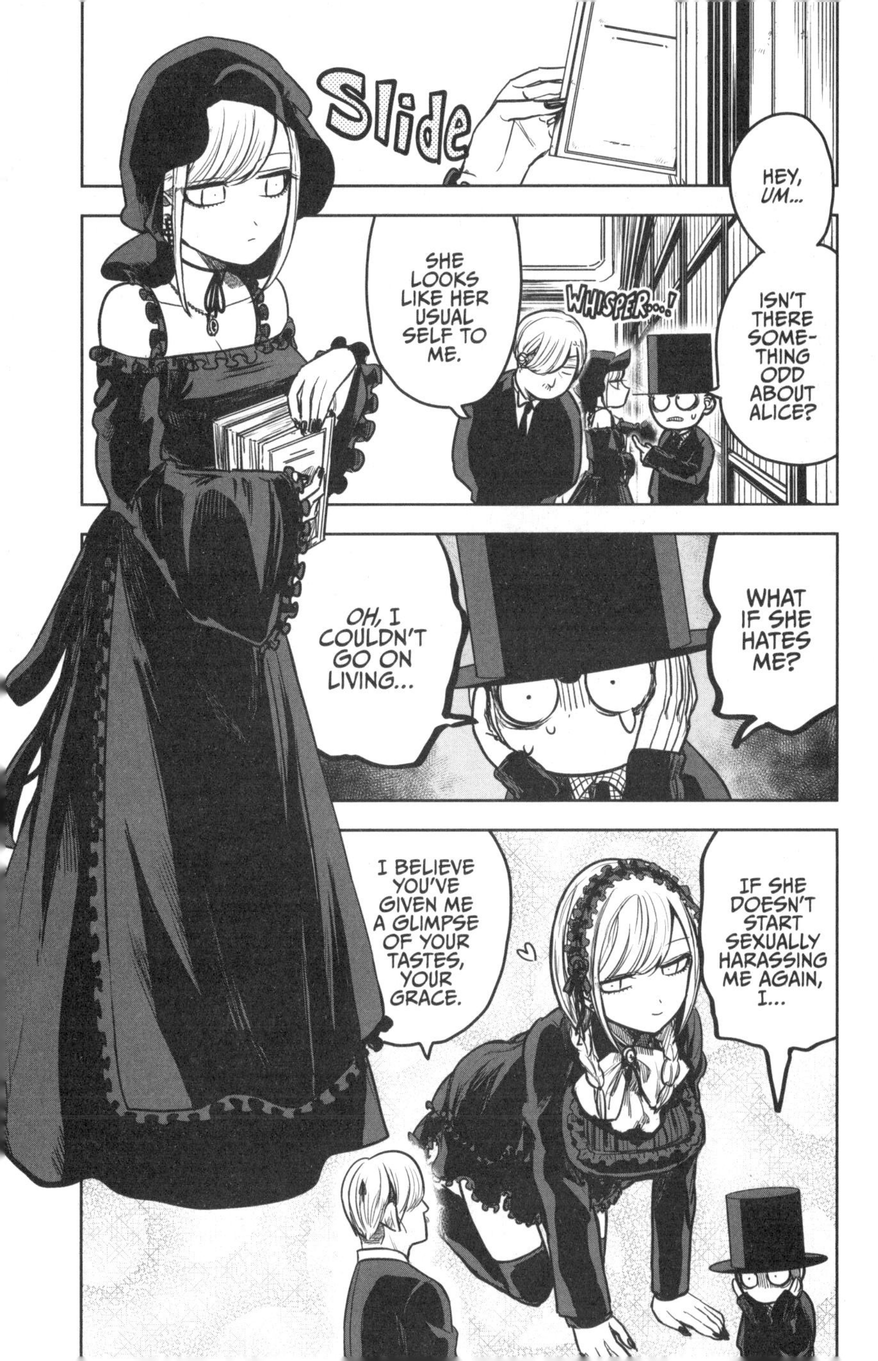
Slide
HEY, UM...
ISN'T THERE SOMETHING ODD ABOUT ALICE?
WHISPER...!
SHE LOOKS LIKE HER USUAL SELF TO ME.
WHAT IF SHE HATES ME?
OH, I COULDN'T GO ON LIVING...
IF SHE DOESN'T START SEXUALLY HARASSING ME AGAIN, I...
I BELIEVE YOU'VE GIVEN ME A GLIMPSE OF YOUR TASTES, YOUR GRACE.

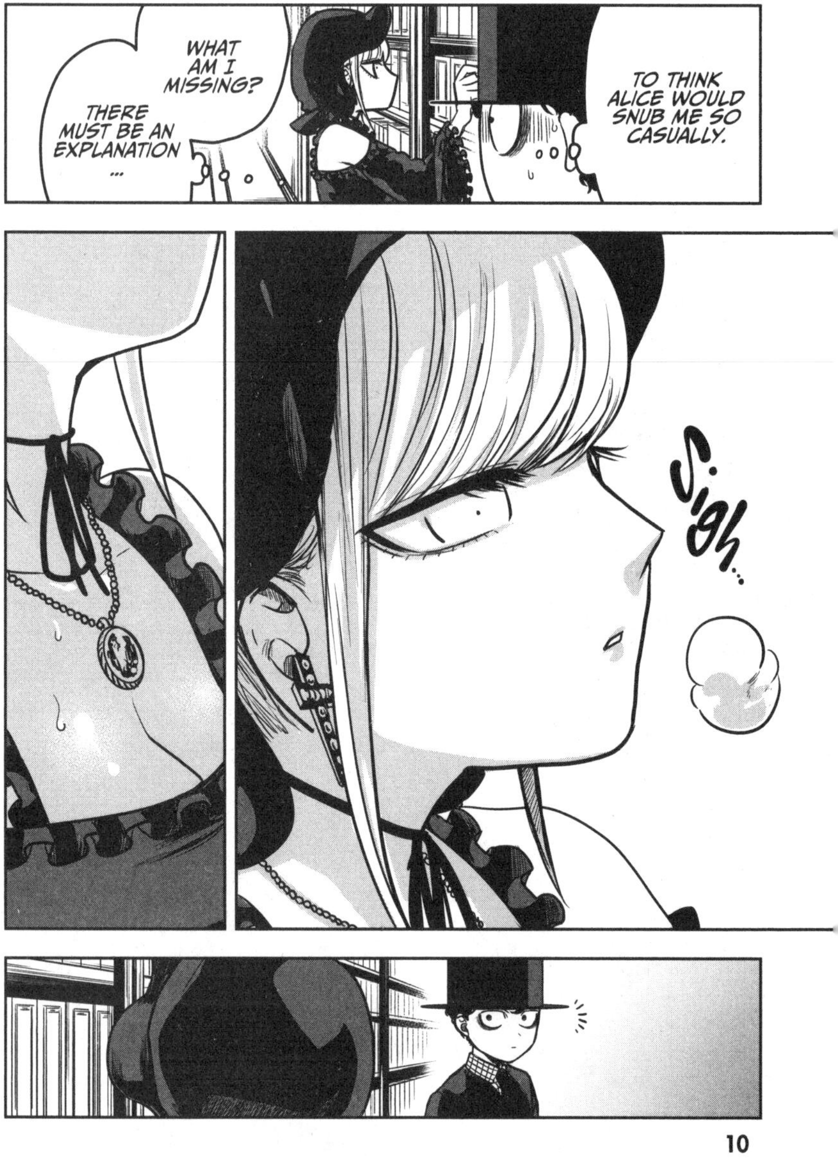
TO THINK ALICE WOULD SNUB ME SO CASUALLY.
WHAT AM I MISSING?
THERE MUST BE AN EXPLANATION ...
Sigh...

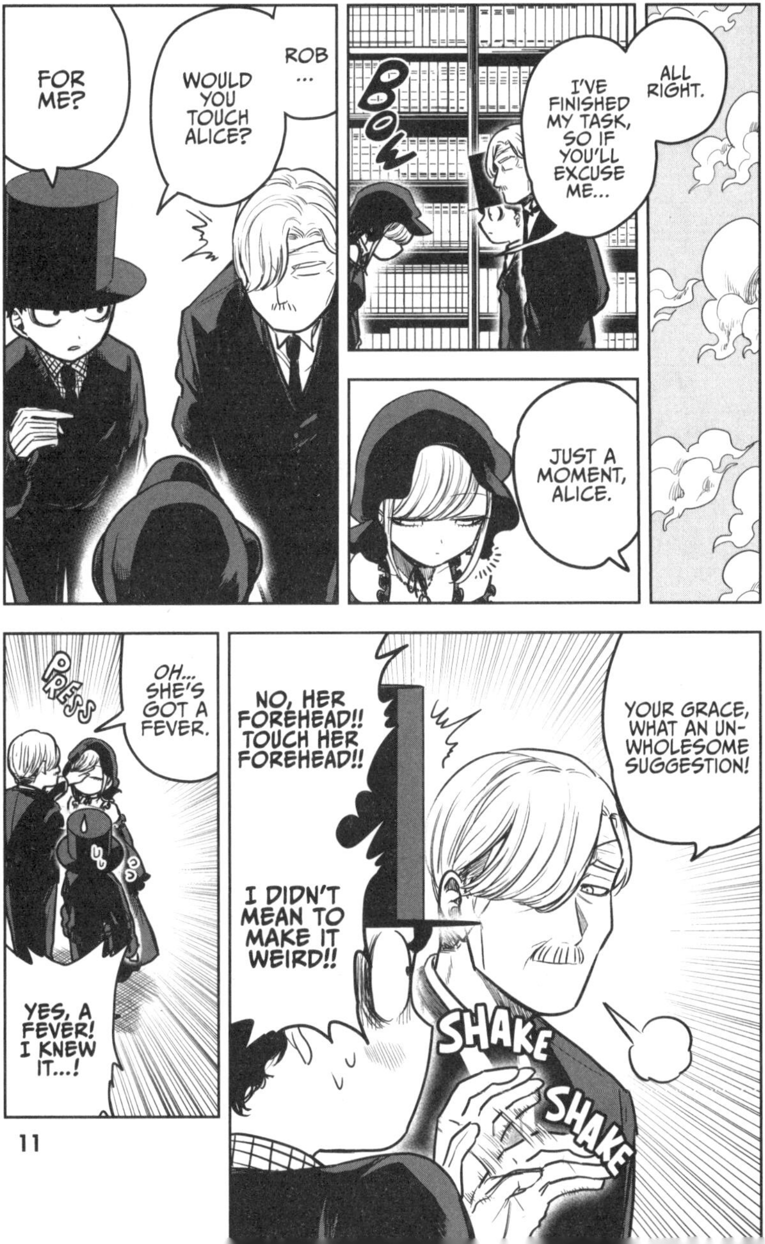
ALL RIGHT.
I'VE FINISHED MY TASK, SO IF YOU'LL EXCUSE ME...
BOW
JUST A MOMENT, ALICE.
ROB ...
WOULD YOU TOUCH ALICE?
FOR ME?
YOUR GRACE, WHAT AN UN-WHOLESOME SUGGESTION!
NO, HER FOREHEAD!! TOUCH HER FOREHEAD!!
I DIDN'T MEAN TO MAKE IT WEIRD!!
SHAKE
SHAKE
PRESS
OH... SHE'S GOT A FEVER.
YES, A FEVER! I KNEW IT...!

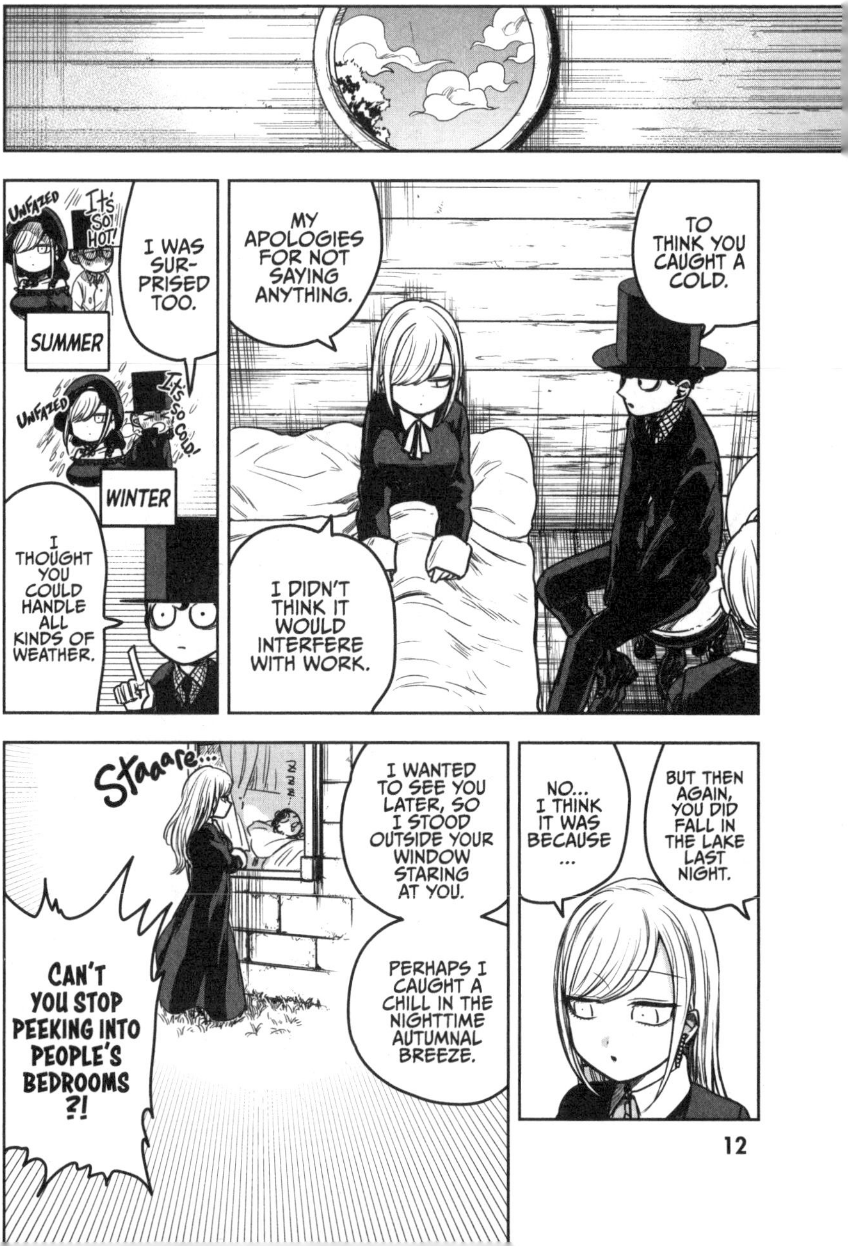
TO THINK YOU CAUGHT A COLD.
MY APOLOGIES FOR NOT SAYING ANYTHING.
I DIDN'T THINK IT WOULD INTERFERE WITH WORK.
I WAS SUR-PRISED TOO.
It's SO HOT!
UNFAZED
SUMMER
It's SO COLD!
UNFAZED
WINTER
I THOUGHT YOU COULD HANDLE ALL KINDS OF WEATHER.
BUT THEN AGAIN, YOU DID FALL IN THE LAKE LAST NIGHT.
NO... I THINK IT WAS BECAUSE ...
I WANTED TO SEE YOU LATER, SO I STOOD OUTSIDE YOUR WINDOW STARING AT YOU.
PERHAPS I CAUGHT A CHILL IN THE NIGHTTIME AUTUMNAL BREEZE.
Staaare...
CAN'T YOU STOP PEEKING INTO PEOPLE'S BEDROOMS ?!

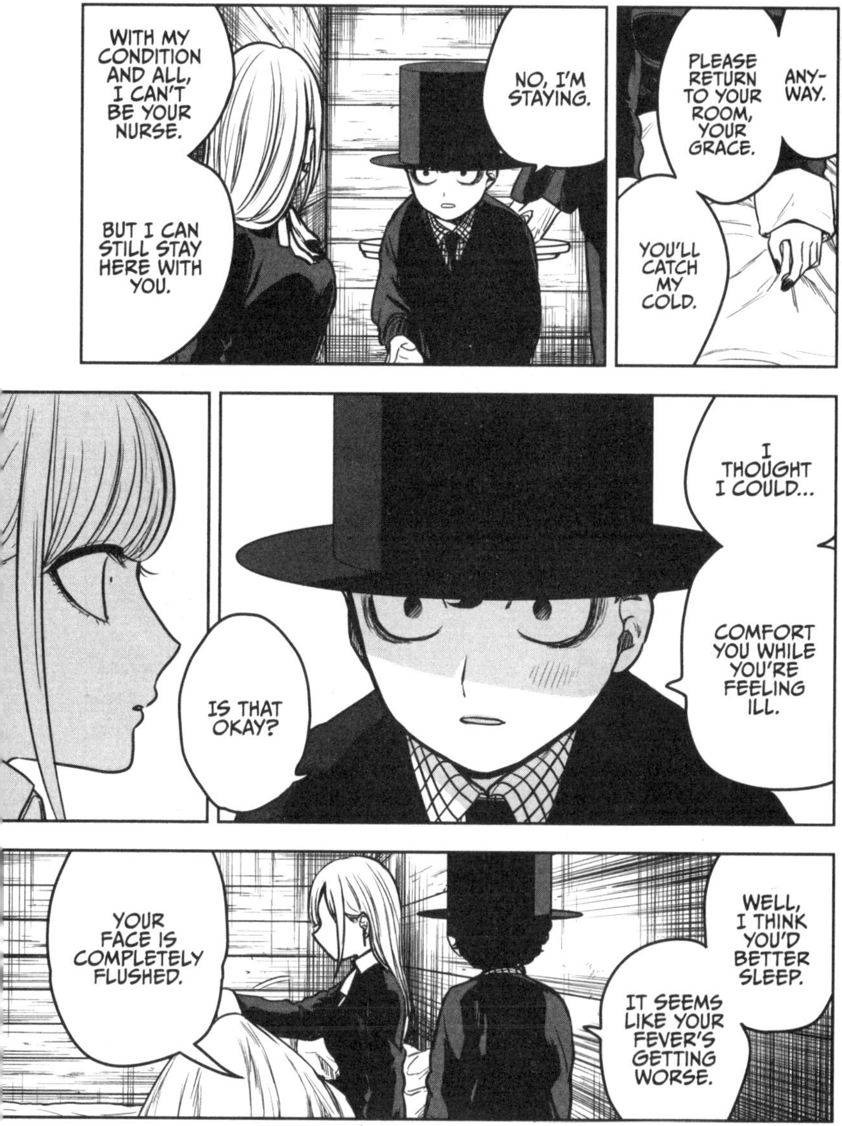
ANYWAY.
PLEASE RETURN TO YOUR ROOM, YOUR GRACE.
YOU'LL CATCH MY COLD.
NO, I'M STAYING.
WITH MY CONDITION AND ALL, I CAN'T BE YOUR NURSE.
BUT I CAN STILL STAY HERE WITH YOU.
I THOUGHT I COULD...
COMFORT YOU WHILE YOU'RE FEELING ILL.
IS THAT OKAY?
WELL, I THINK YOU'D BETTER SLEEP.
IT SEEMS LIKE YOUR FEVER'S GETTING WORSE.
YOUR FACE IS COMPLETELY FLUSHED.

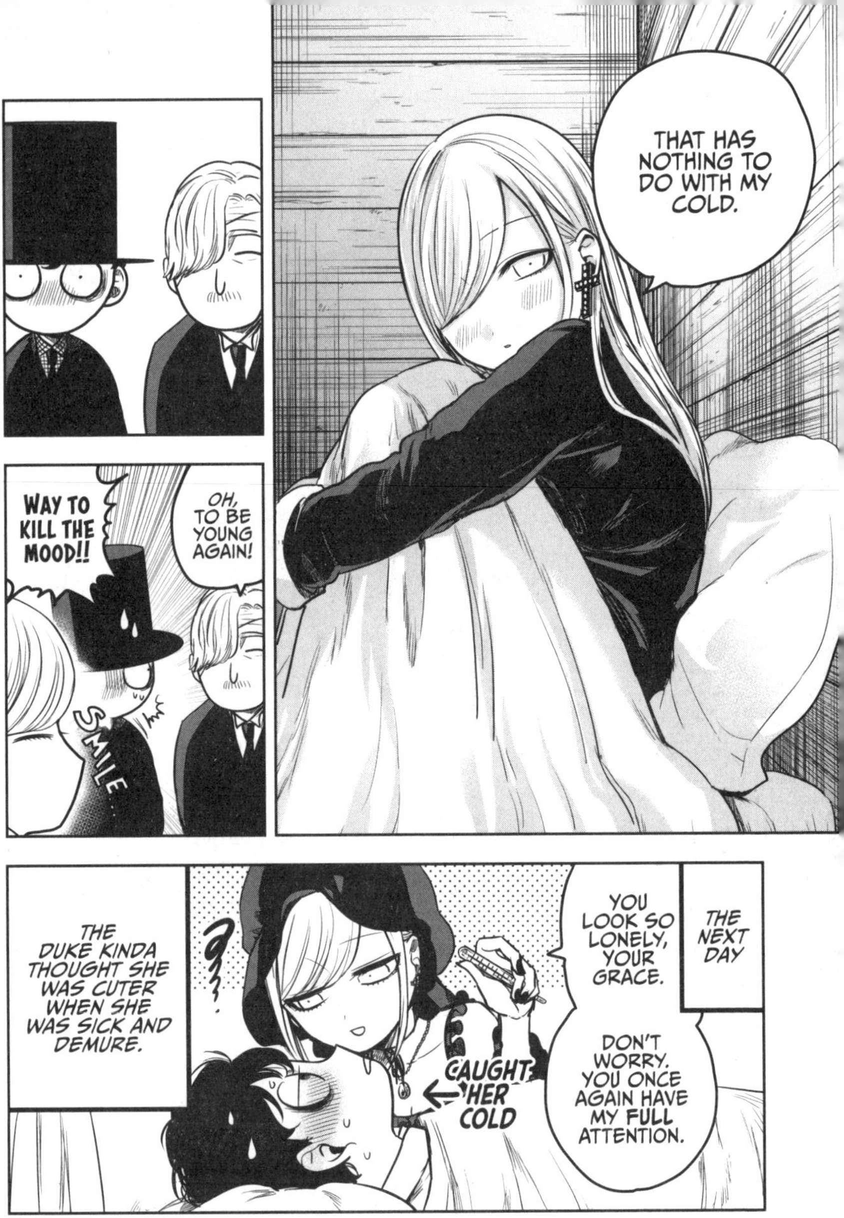
THAT HAS NOTHING TO DO WITH MY COLD.
OH, TO BE YOUNG AGAIN!
WAY TO KILL THE MOOD!!
SMILE...
THE NEXT DAY
YOU LOOK SO LONELY, YOUR GRACE.
DON'T WORRY. YOU ONCE AGAIN HAVE MY FULL ATTENTION.
CAUGHT HER COLD
THE DUKE KINDA THOUGHT SHE WAS CUTER WHEN SHE WAS SICK AND DEMURE.

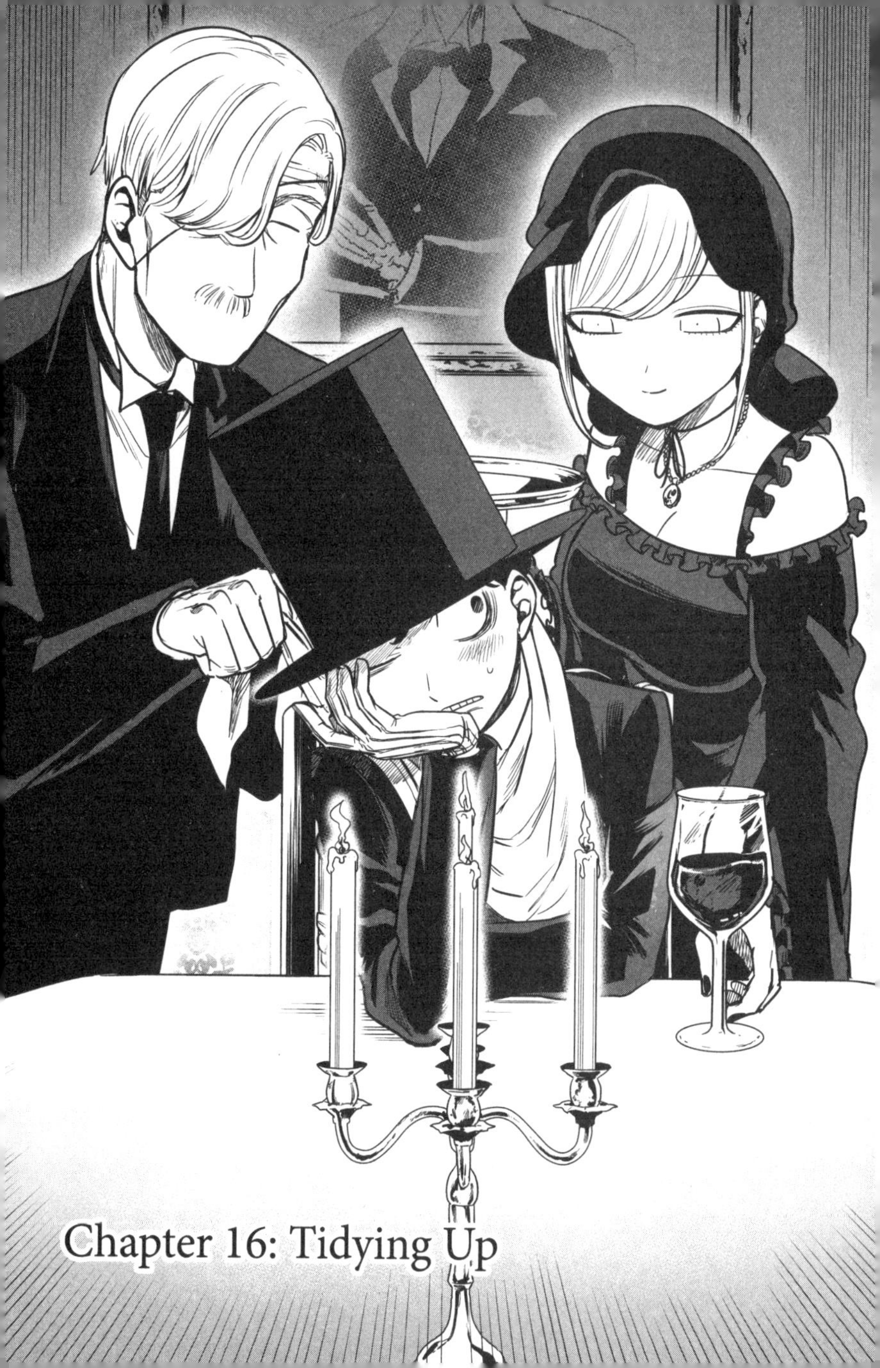

Chapter 16: Tidying Up

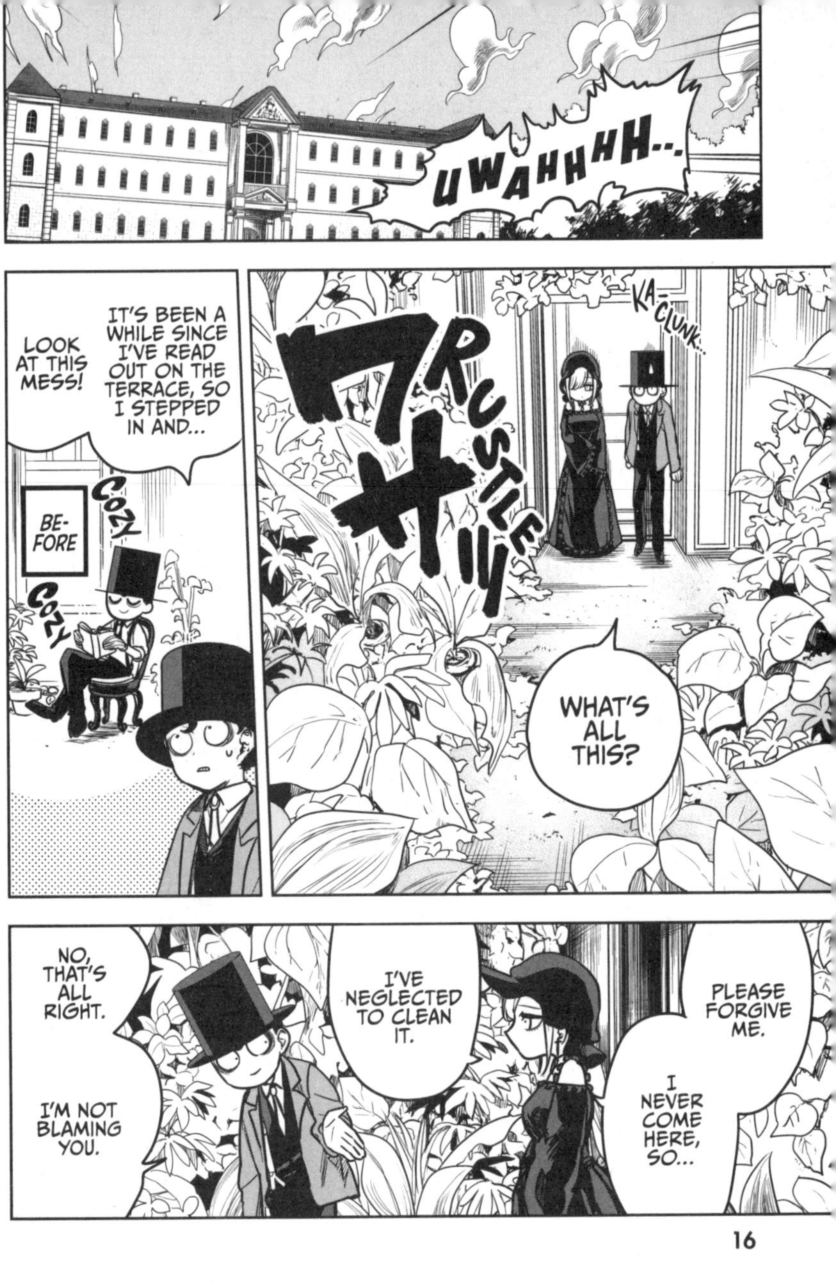
UWAHHHH...
KA-CLUNK...
RUSTLE
WHAT'S ALL THIS?
IT'S BEEN A WHILE SINCE I'VE READ OUT ON THE TERRACE, SO I STEPPED IN AND...
LOOK AT THIS MESS!
BE-FORE
COZY
COZY
PLEASE FORGIVE ME.
I NEVER COME HERE, SO...
I'VE NEGLECTED TO CLEAN IT.
NO, THAT'S ALL RIGHT.
I'M NOT BLAMING YOU.

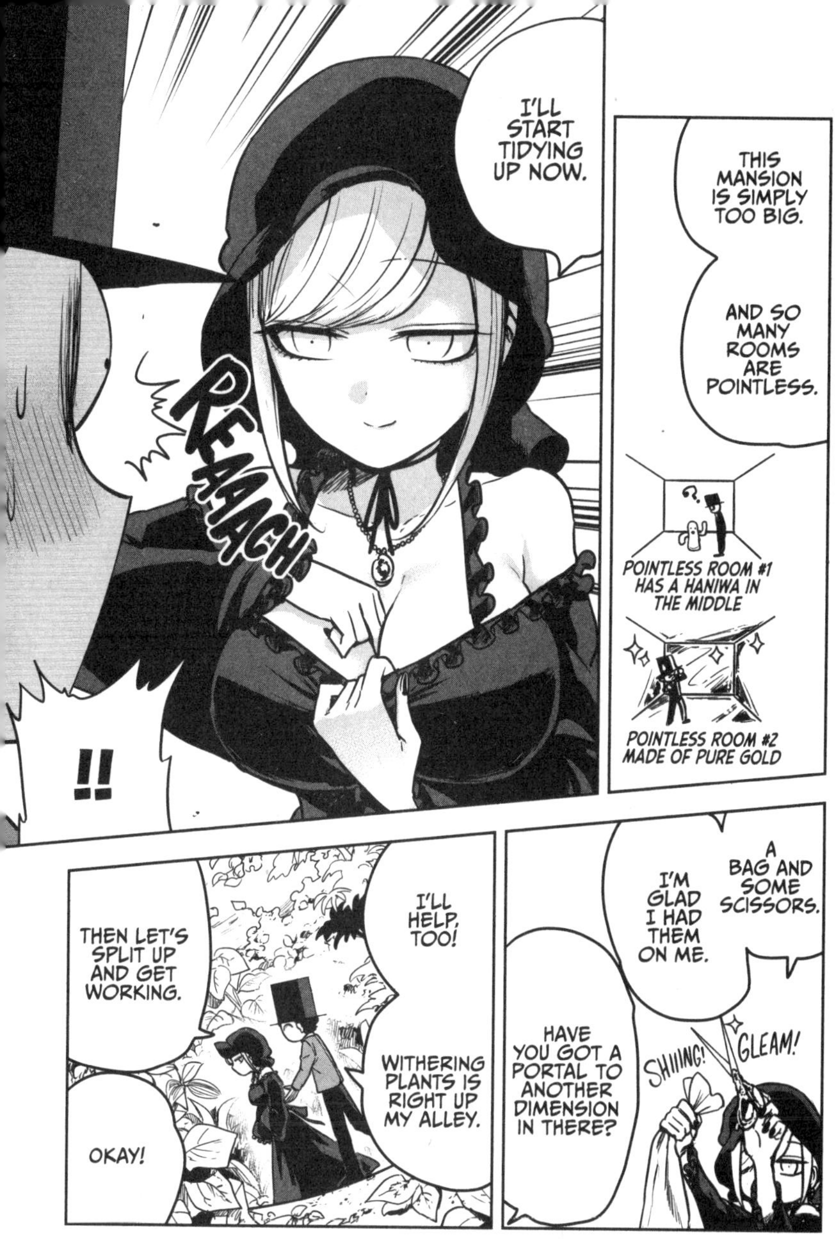
THIS MANSION IS SIMPLY TOO BIG.
AND SO MANY ROOMS ARE POINTLESS.
POINTLESS ROOM #1 HAS A HANIWA IN THE MIDDLE
POINTLESS ROOM #2 MADE OF PURE GOLD
I'LL START TIDYING UP NOW.
REAACH!
!!
A BAG AND SOME SCISSORS.
I'M GLAD I HAD THEM ON ME.
GLEAM!
SHIIING!
HAVE YOU GOT A PORTAL TO ANOTHER DIMENSION IN THERE?
I'LL HELP, TOO!
WITHERING PLANTS IS RIGHT UP MY ALLEY.
THEN LET'S SPLIT UP AND GET WORKING.
OKAY!

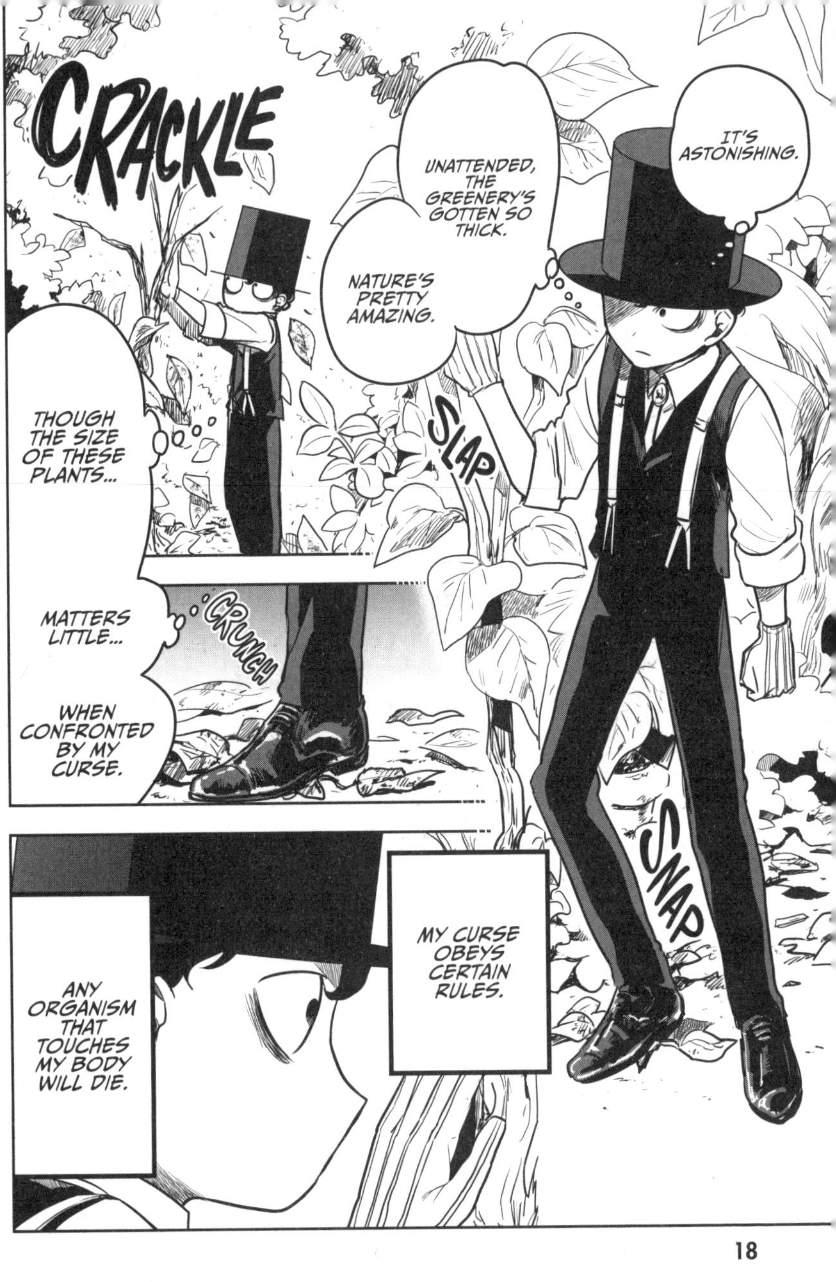
IT'S ASTONISHING.
UNATTENDED, THE GREENERY'S GOTTEN SO THICK.
NATURE'S PRETTY AMAZING.
SLAP
SNAP
CRACKLE
THOUGH THE SIZE OF THESE PLANTS...
CRUNCH
MATTERS LITTLE...
WHEN CONFRONTED BY MY CURSE.
MY CURSE OBEYS CERTAIN RULES.
ANY ORGANISM THAT TOUCHES MY BODY WILL DIE.

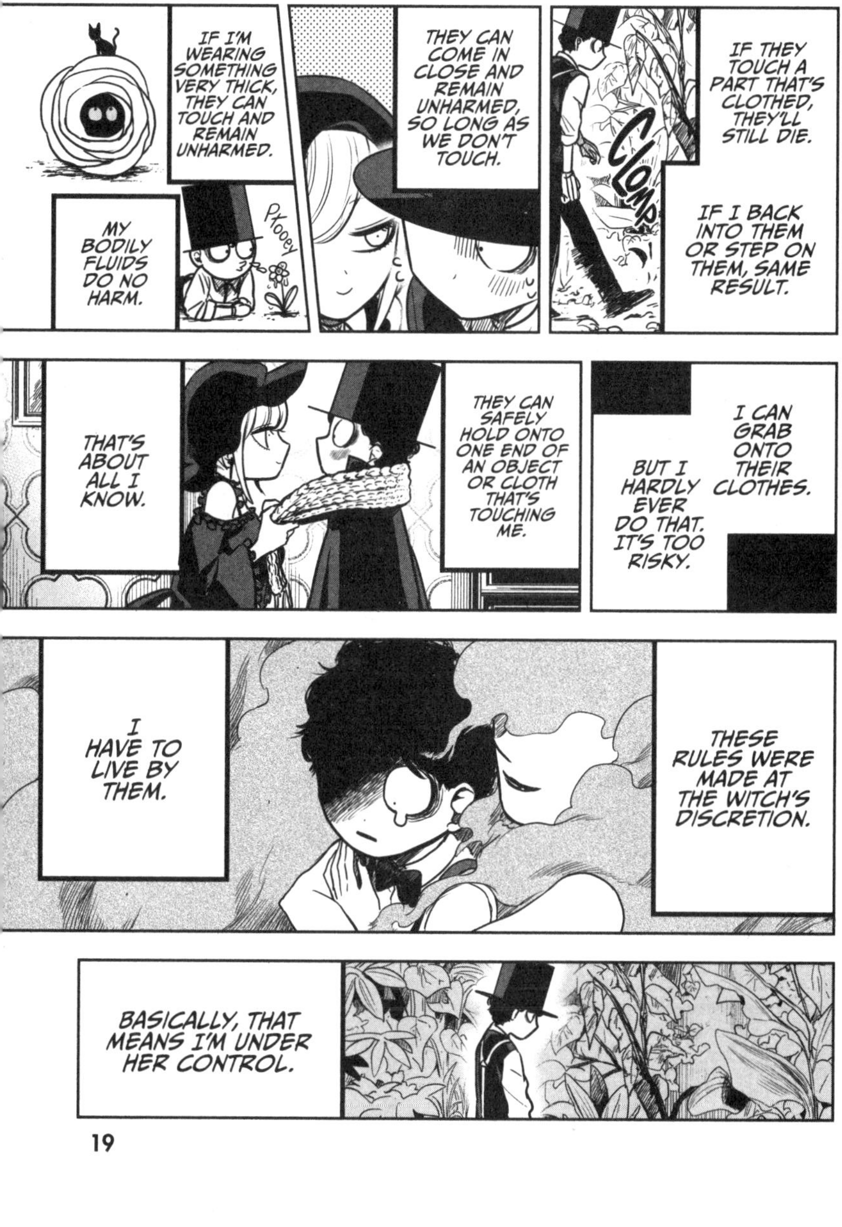
IF THEY TOUCH A PART THAT'S CLOTHED, THEY'LL STILL DIE.
CLOMP
IF I BACK INTO THEM OR STEP ON THEM, SAME RESULT.
THEY CAN COME IN CLOSE AND REMAIN UNHARMED, SO LONG AS WE DON'T TOUCH.
IF I'M WEARING SOMETHING VERY THICK, THEY CAN TOUCH AND REMAIN UNHARMED.
MY BODILY FLUIDS DO NO HARM.
PTOOEY
I CAN GRAB ONTO THEIR CLOTHES.
BUT I HARDLY EVER DO THAT. IT'S TOO RISKY.
THEY CAN SAFELY HOLD ONTO ONE END OF AN OBJECT OR CLOTH THAT'S TOUCHING ME.
THAT'S ABOUT ALL I KNOW.
THESE RULES WERE MADE AT THE WITCH'S DISCRETION.
I HAVE TO LIVE BY THEM.
BASICALLY, THAT MEANS I'M UNDER HER CONTROL.

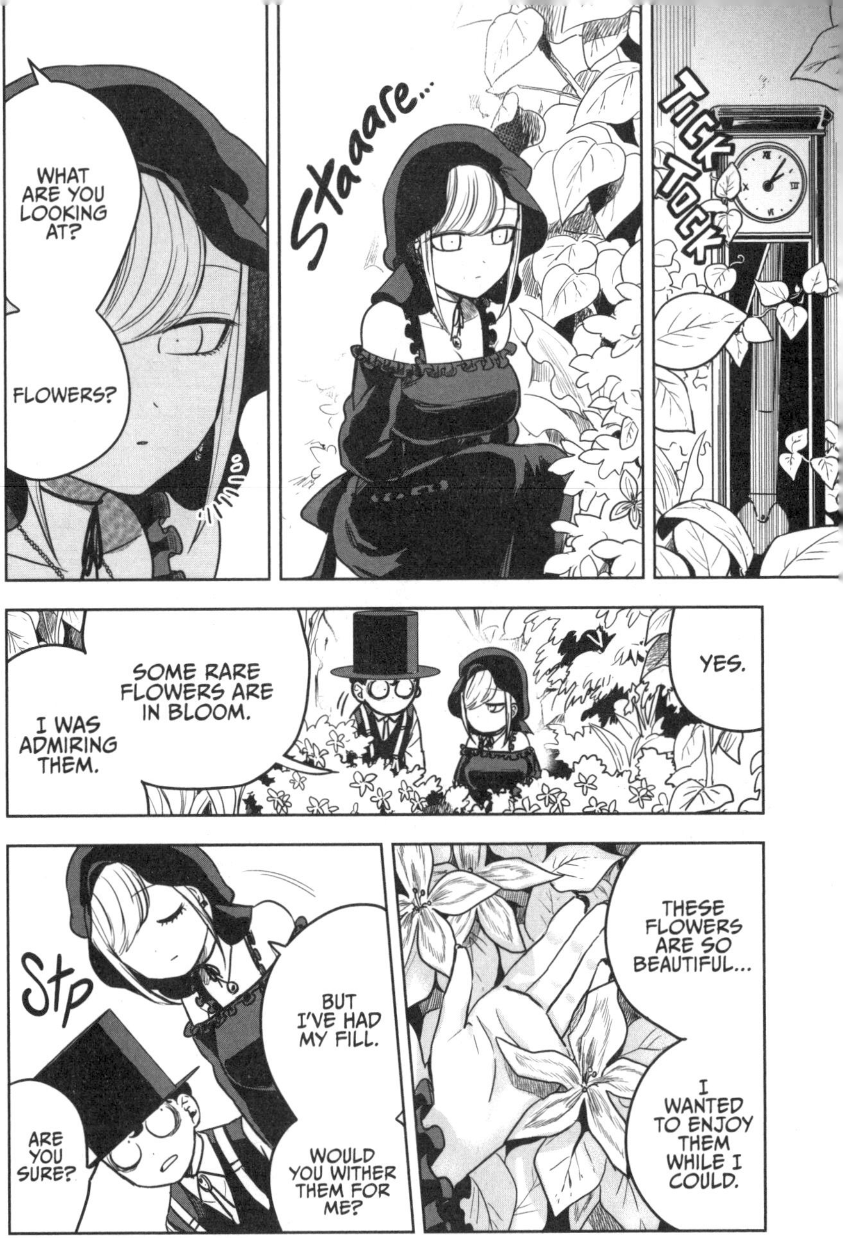
TICK TOCK
Staaare...
WHAT ARE YOU LOOKING AT?
FLOWERS?
YES.
SOME RARE FLOWERS ARE IN BLOOM.
I WAS ADMIRING THEM.
THESE FLOWERS ARE SO BEAUTIFUL...
I WANTED TO ENJOY THEM WHILE I COULD.
Stp
BUT I'VE HAD MY FILL.
WOULD YOU WITHER THEM FOR ME?
ARE YOU SURE?

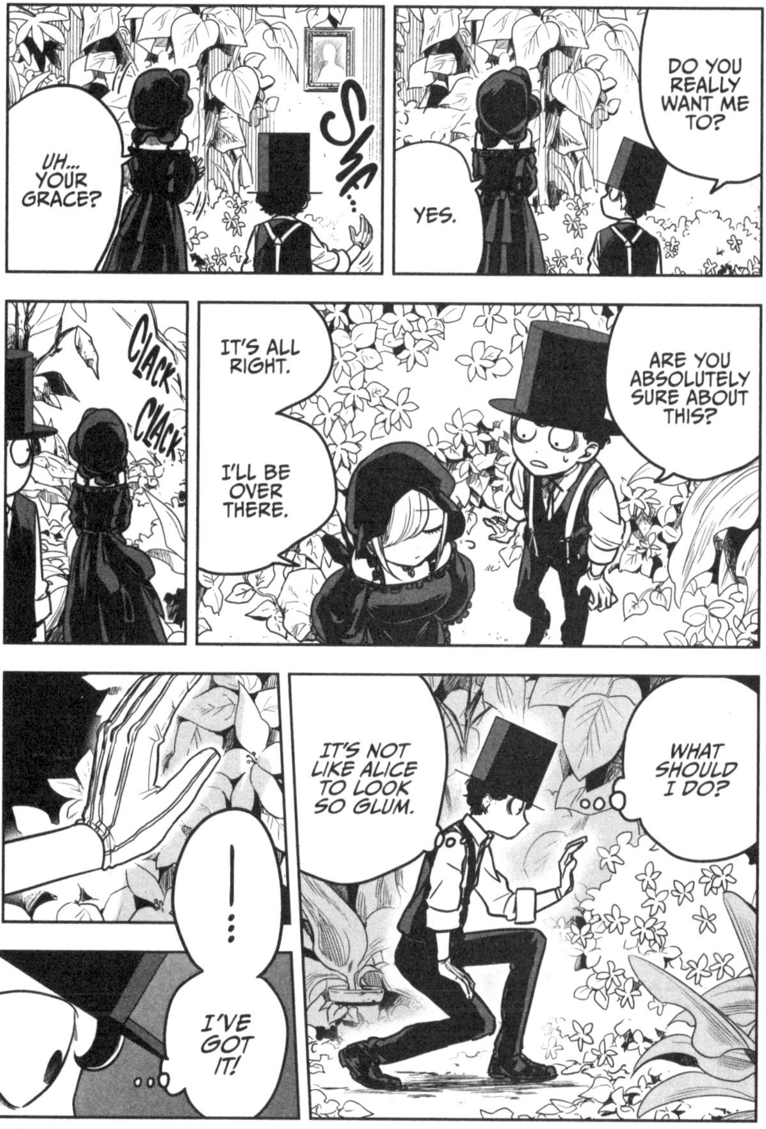
DO YOU REALLY WANT ME TO?
YES.
SHF...
UH... YOUR GRACE?
ARE YOU ABSOLUTELY SURE ABOUT THIS?
IT'S ALL RIGHT.
I'LL BE OVER THERE.
CLACK
CLACK
WHAT SHOULD I DO?
IT'S NOT LIKE ALICE TO LOOK SO GLUM.
!...
I'VE GOT IT!

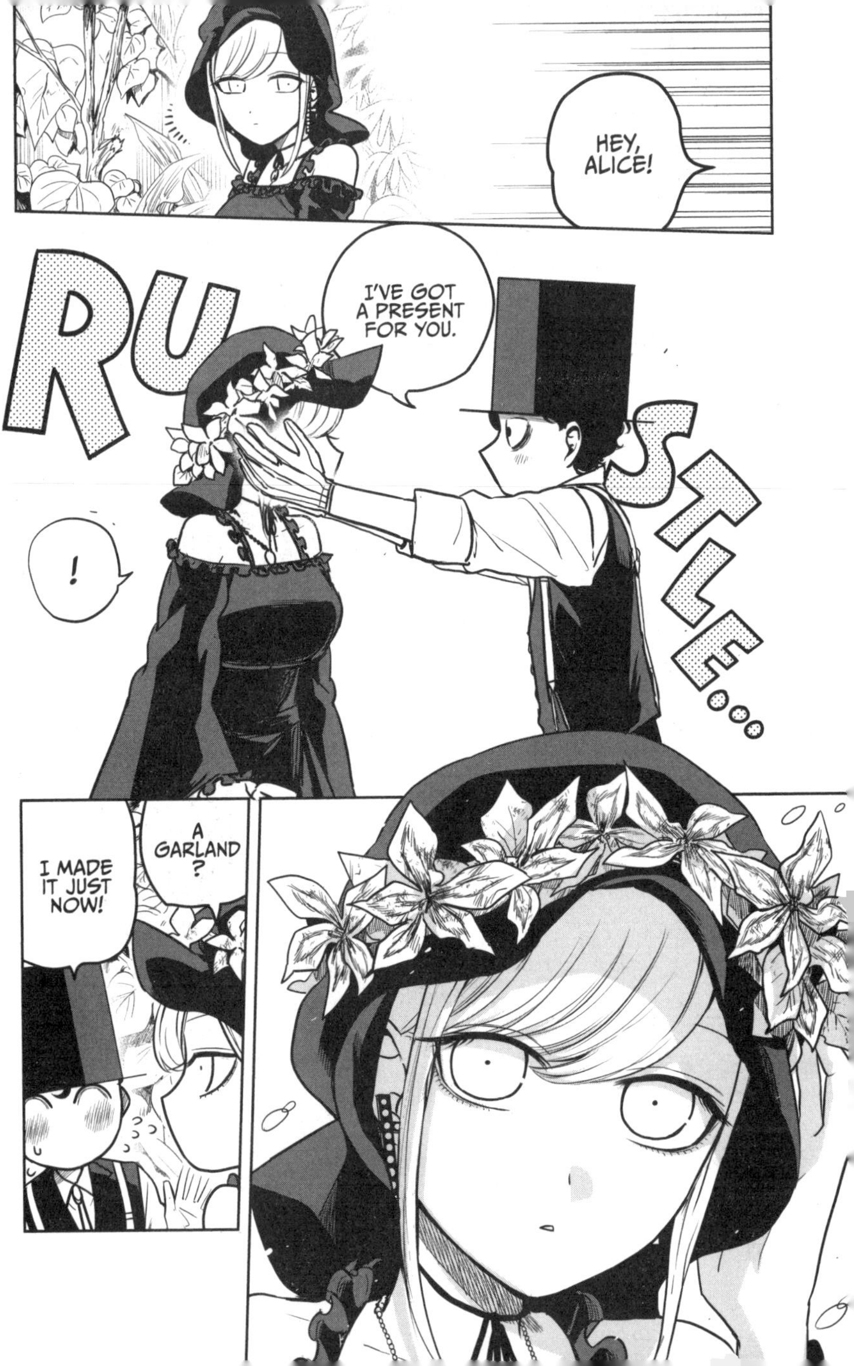
HEY, ALICE!
I'VE GOT A PRESENT FOR YOU.
RUSTLE...
!
A GARLAND?
I MADE IT JUST NOW!

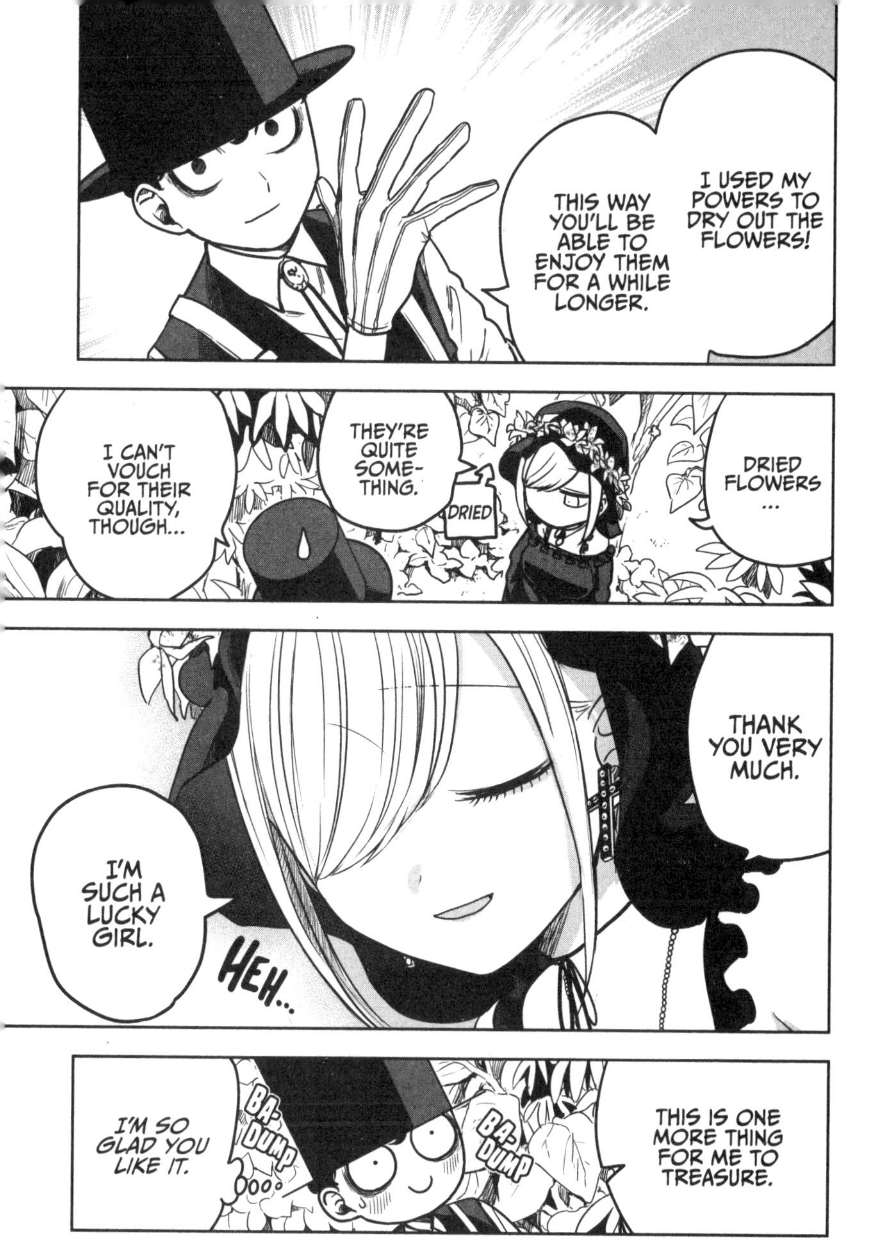
I USED MY POWERS TO DRY OUT THE FLOWERS!
THIS WAY YOU'LL BE ABLE TO ENJOY THEM FOR A WHILE LONGER.
DRIED FLOWERS ...
DRIED
THEY'RE QUITE SOME-THING.
I CAN'T VOUCH FOR THEIR QUALITY, THOUGH...
THANK YOU VERY MUCH.
I'M SUCH A LUCKY GIRL.
HEH...
THIS IS ONE MORE THING FOR ME TO TREASURE.
BA-DUMP
BA-DUMP
I'M SO GLAD YOU LIKE IT.

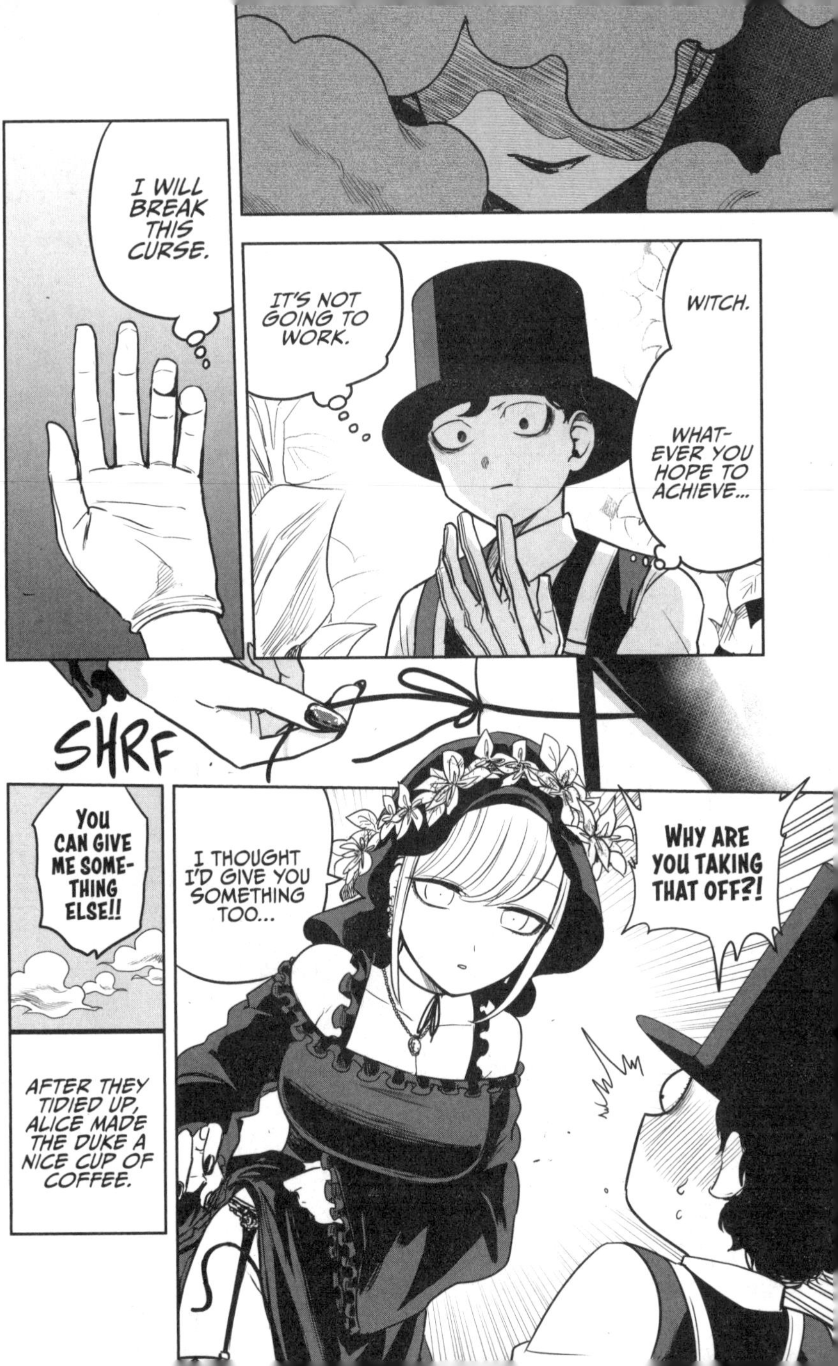
WITCH.
WHAT-EVER YOU HOPE TO ACHIEVE...
IT'S NOT GOING TO WORK.
I WILL BREAK THIS CURSE.
SHRF
WHY ARE YOU TAKING THAT OFF?!
I THOUGHT I'D GIVE YOU SOMETHING TOO...
YOU CAN GIVE ME SOME-THING ELSE!!
AFTER THEY TIDIED UP, ALICE MADE THE DUKE A NICE CUP OF COFFEE.

Chapter 17: Viola

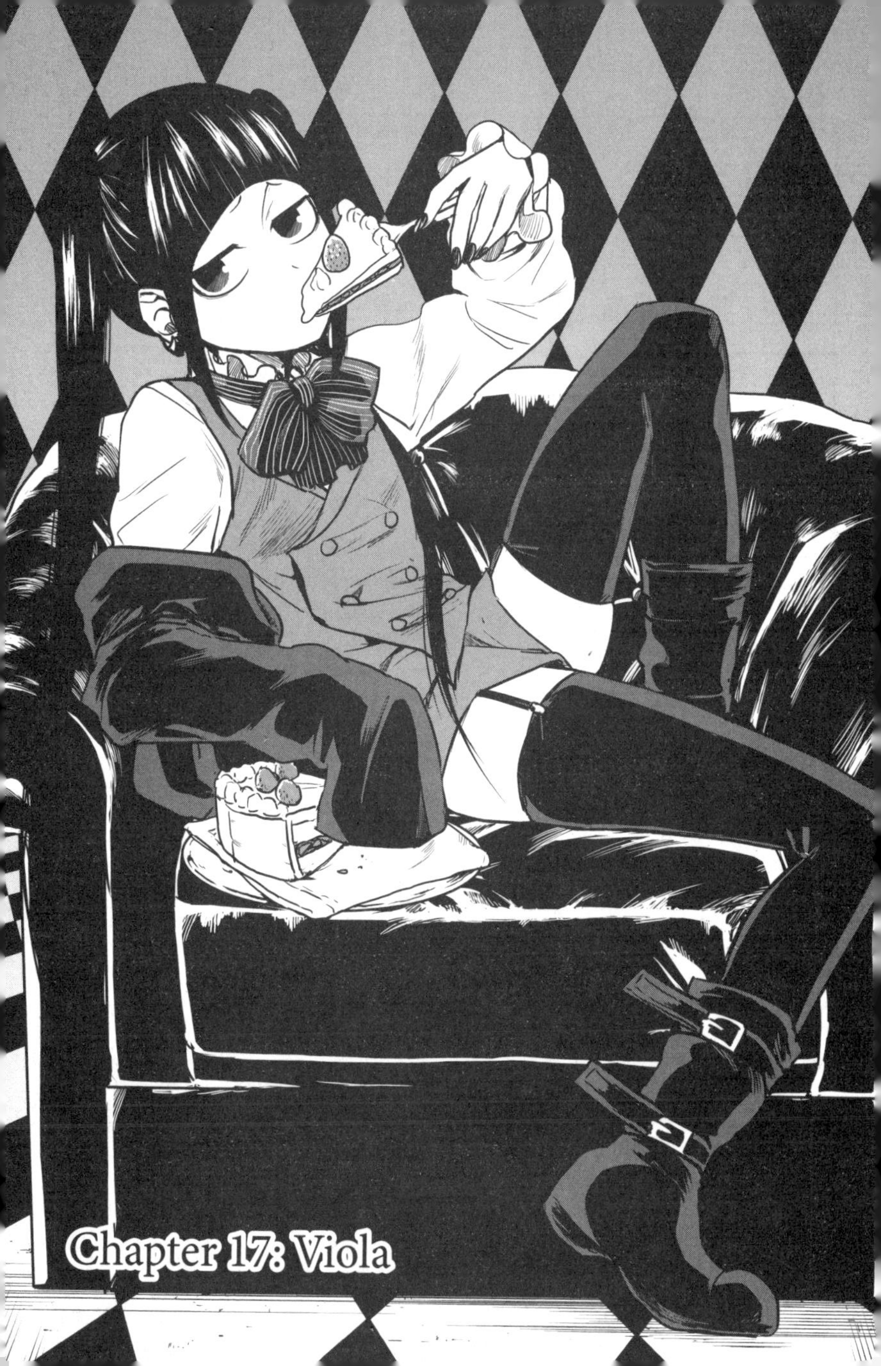

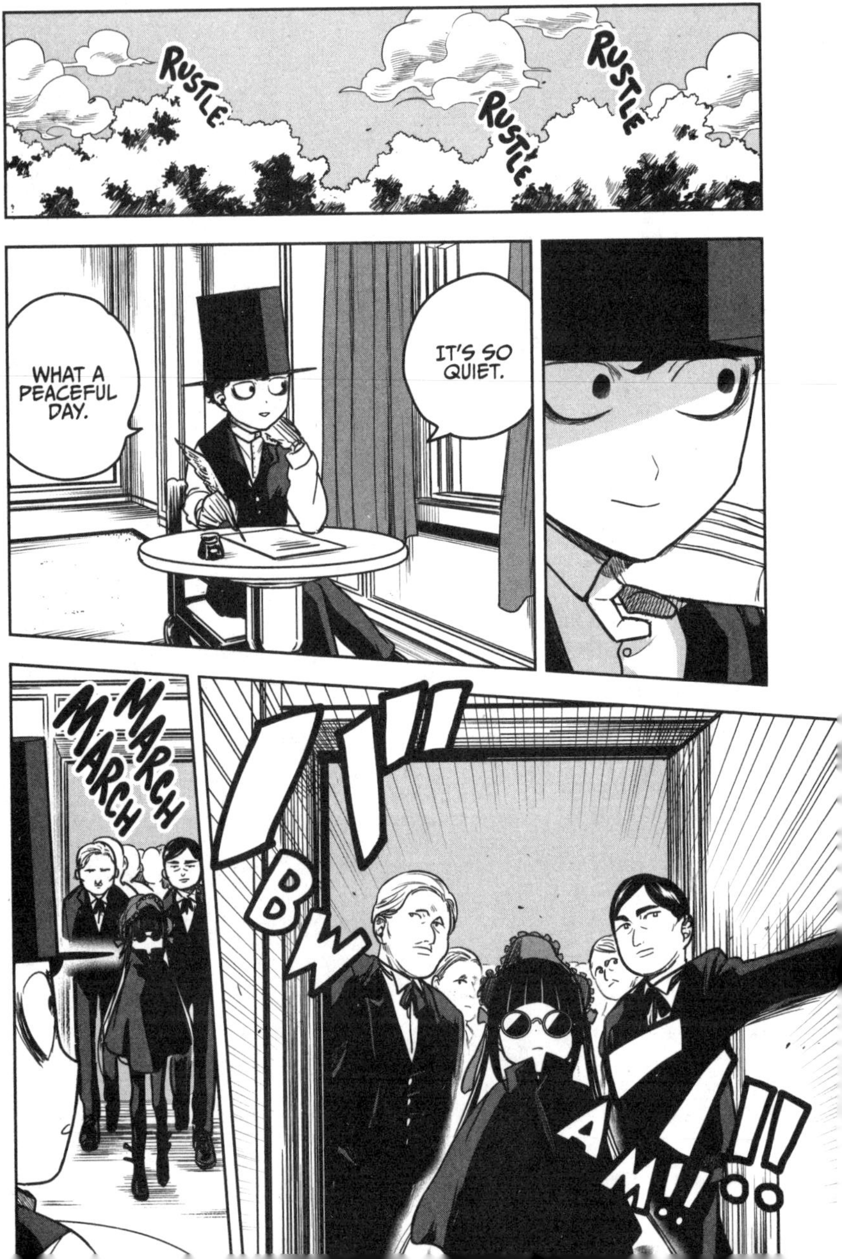
RUSTLE
RUSTLE
RUSTLE
IT'S SO QUIET.
WHAT A PEACEFUL DAY.
BWAM!!
MARCH
MARCH

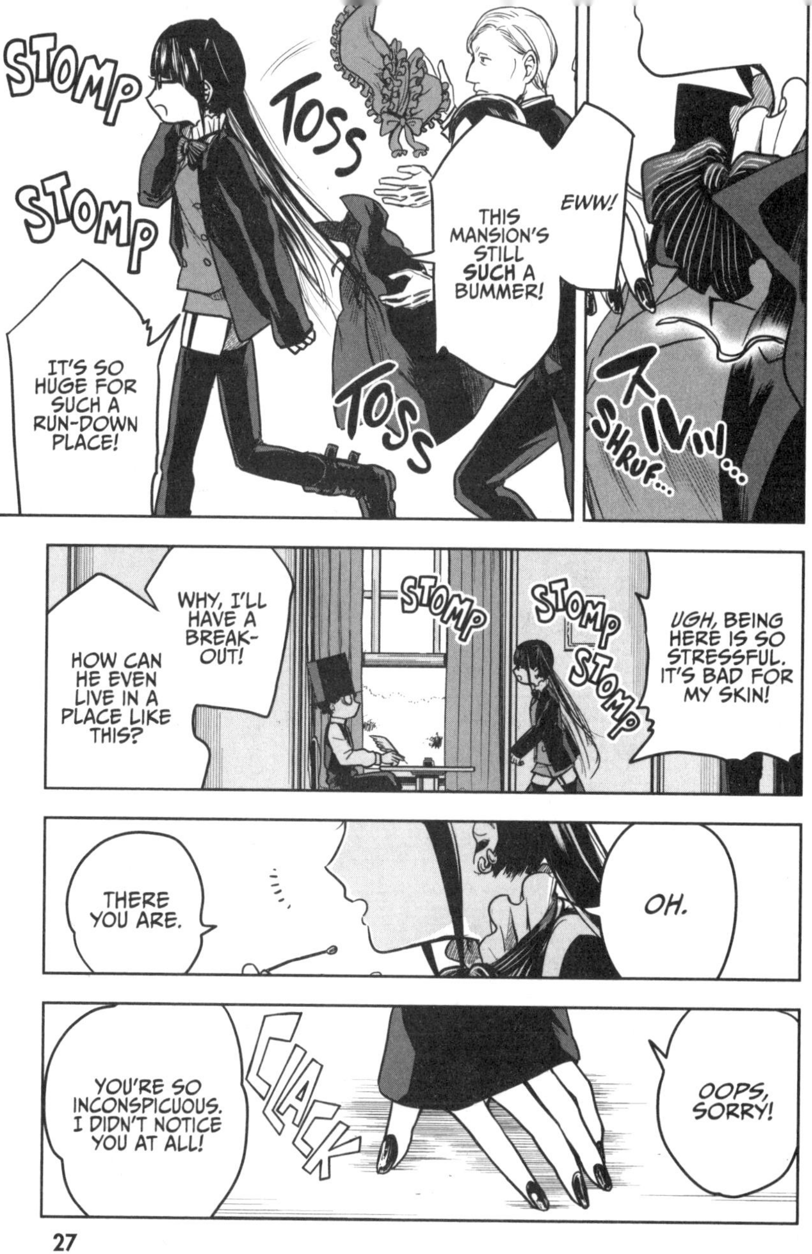
SHRUF...
EWW!
THIS MANSION'S STILL SUCH A BUMMER!
TOSS
STOMP
TOSS
STOMP
IT'S SO HUGE FOR SUCH A RUN-DOWN PLACE!
UGH, BEING HERE IS SO STRESSFUL. IT'S BAD FOR MY SKIN!
STOMP STOMP
STOMP
STOMP
WHY, I'LL HAVE A BREAK-OUT!
HOW CAN HE EVEN LIVE IN A PLACE LIKE THIS?
OH.
THERE YOU ARE.
OOPS, SORRY!
CLACK
YOU'RE SO INCONSPICUOUS. I DIDN'T NOTICE YOU AT ALL!

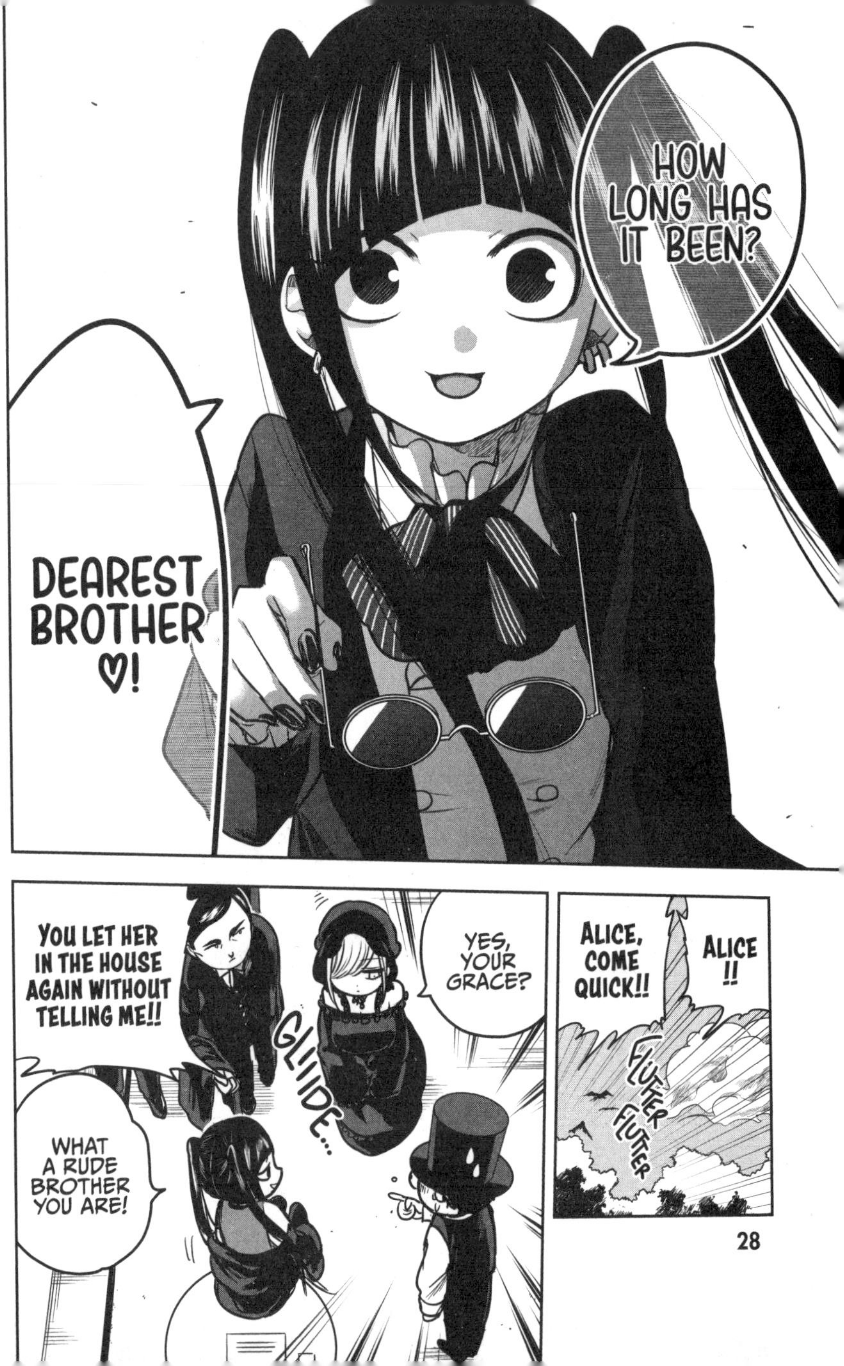
HOW LONG HAS IT BEEN?
DEAREST BROTHER ♡!
ALICE !!
ALICE, COME QUICK!!
FLUTTER FLUTTER
YES, YOUR GRACE?
YOU LET HER IN THE HOUSE AGAIN WITHOUT TELLING ME!!
GLIIIDE...
WHAT A RUDE BROTHER YOU ARE!

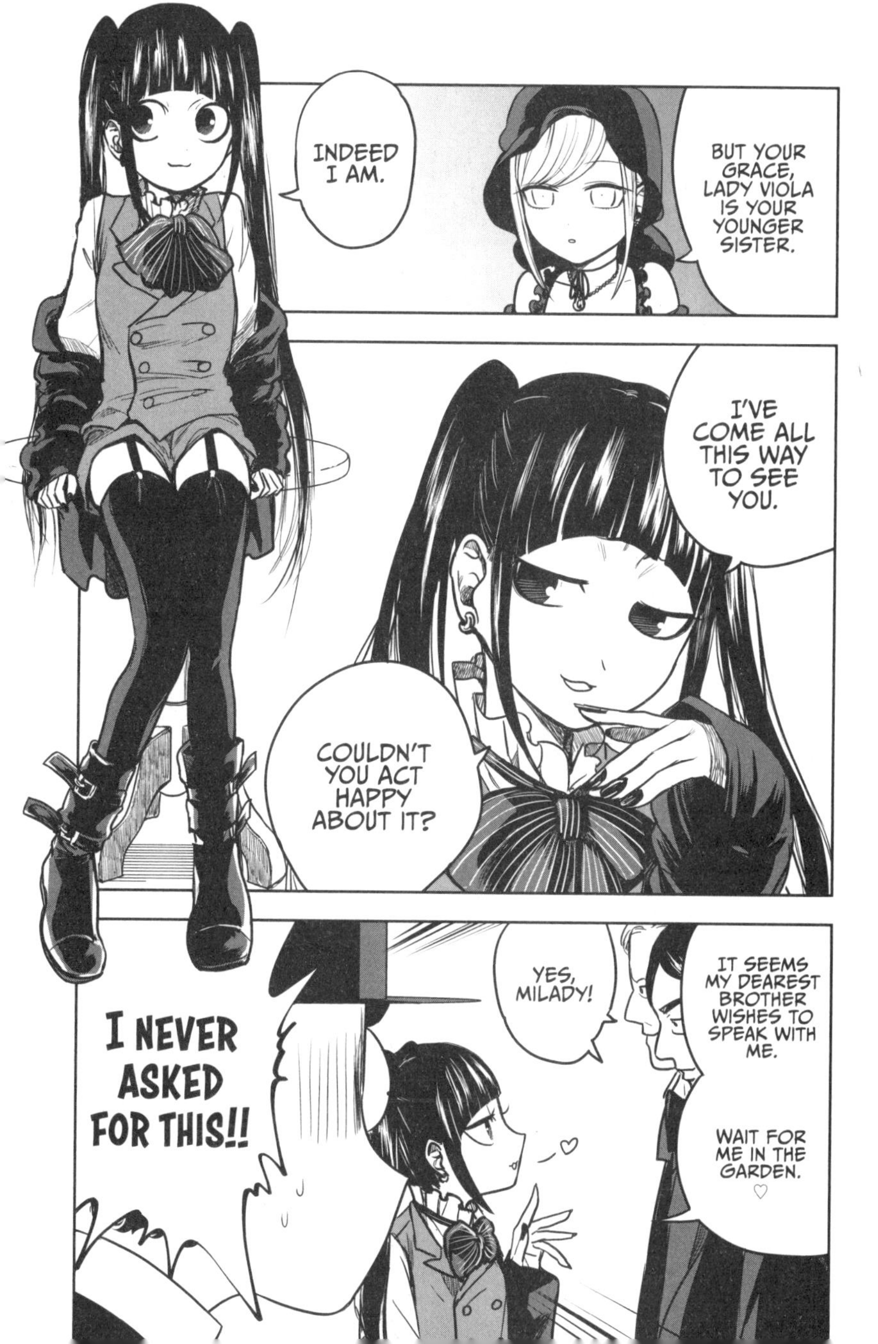
BUT YOUR GRACE, LADY VIOLA IS YOUR YOUNGER SISTER.
INDEED I AM.
I'VE COME ALL THIS WAY TO SEE YOU.
COULDN'T YOU ACT HAPPY ABOUT IT?
IT SEEMS MY DEAREST BROTHER WISHES TO SPEAK WITH ME.
WAIT FOR ME IN THE GARDEN. ♡
YES, MILADY!
I NEVER ASKED FOR THIS!!

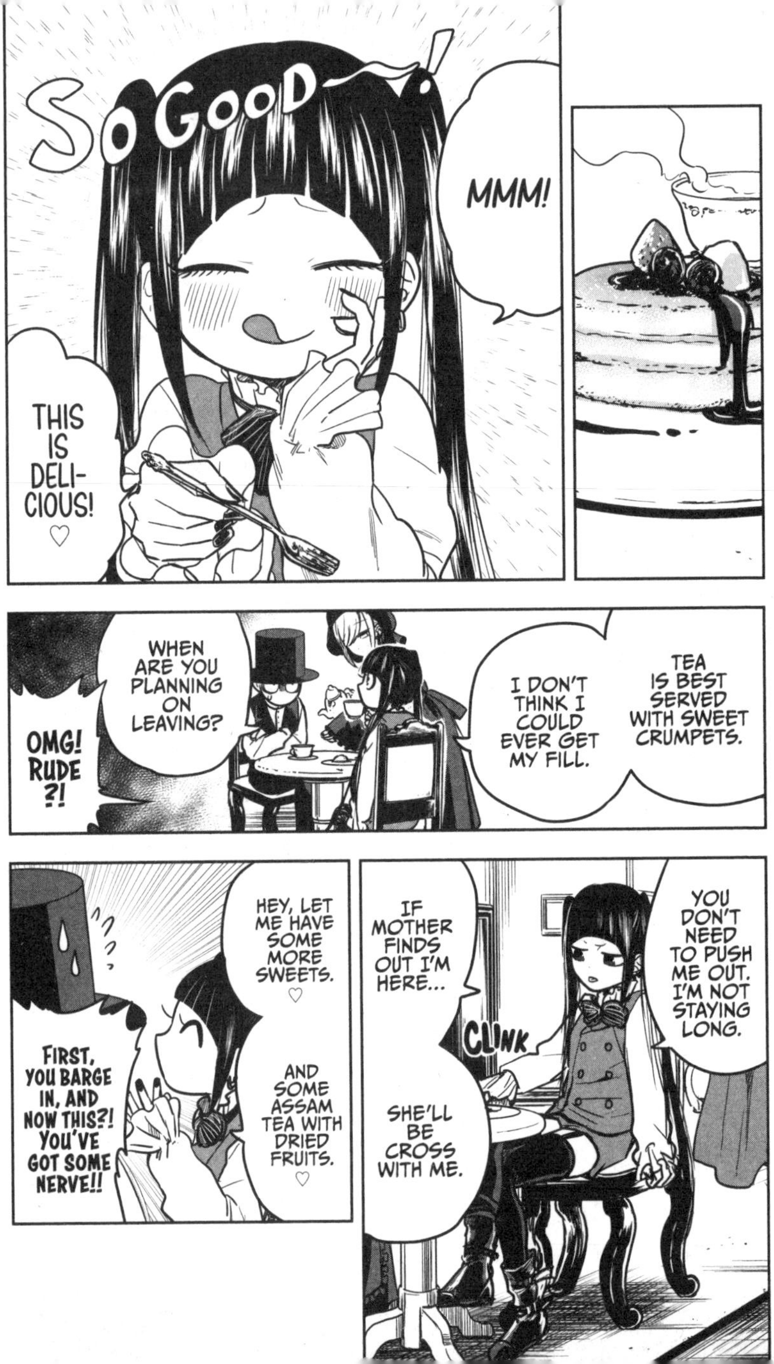
MMM!
SO GOOD~~!
THIS IS DELICIOUS! ♡
TEA IS BEST SERVED WITH SWEET CRUMPETS.
I DON'T THINK I COULD EVER GET MY FILL.
WHEN ARE YOU PLANNING ON LEAVING?
OMG! RUDE?!
YOU DON'T NEED TO PUSH ME OUT. I'M NOT STAYING LONG.
IF MOTHER FINDS OUT I'M HERE...
CLINK
SHE'LL BE CROSS WITH ME.
HEY, LET ME HAVE SOME MORE SWEETS. ♡
AND SOME ASSAM TEA WITH DRIED FRUITS. ♡
FIRST, YOU BARGE IN, AND NOW THIS?! YOU'VE GOT SOME NERVE!!

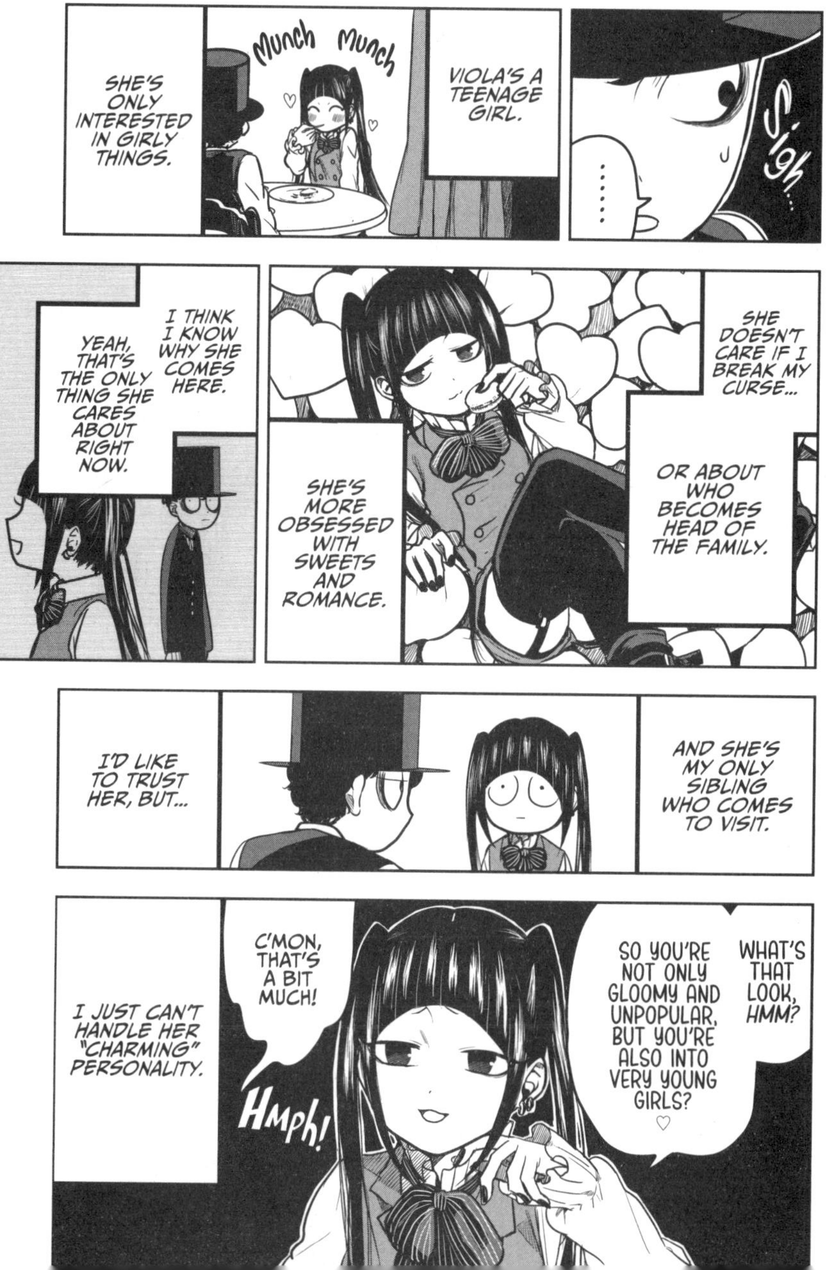

Sigh...
......
VIOLA'S A TEENAGE GIRL.
Munch Munch
SHE'S ONLY INTERESTED IN GIRLY THINGS.
SHE DOESN'T CARE IF I BREAK MY CURSE...
OR ABOUT WHO BECOMES HEAD OF THE FAMILY.
SHE'S MORE OBSESSED WITH SWEETS AND ROMANCE.
I THINK I KNOW WHY SHE COMES HERE.
YEAH, THAT'S THE ONLY THING SHE CARES ABOUT RIGHT NOW.
AND SHE'S MY ONLY SIBLING WHO COMES TO VISIT.
I'D LIKE TO TRUST HER, BUT...
WHAT'S THAT LOOK, HMM?
SO YOU'RE NOT ONLY GLOOMY AND UNPOPULAR, BUT YOU'RE ALSO INTO VERY YOUNG GIRLS? ♡
C'MON, THAT'S A BIT MUCH!
Hmph!
I JUST CAN'T HANDLE HER "CHARMING" PERSONALITY.

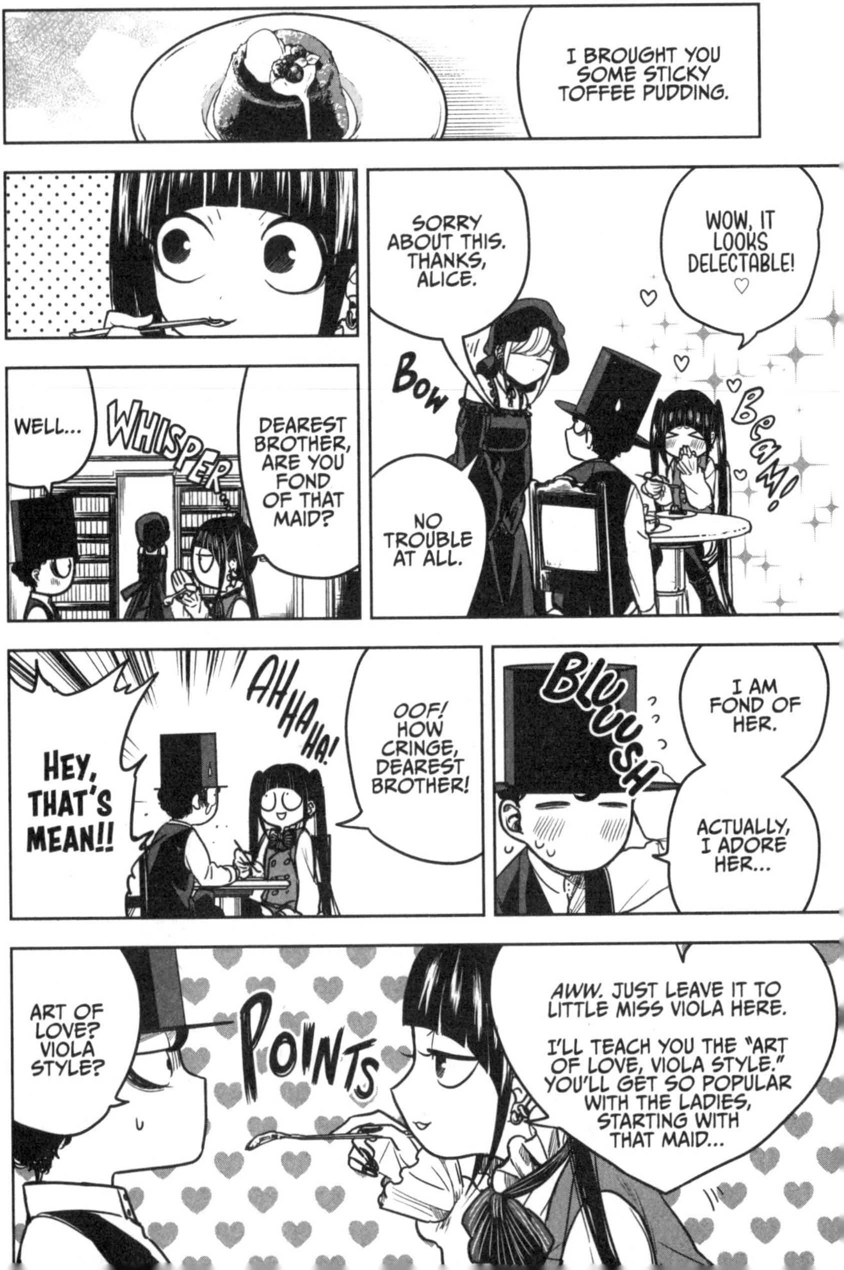
I BROUGHT YOU SOME STICKY TOFFEE PUDDING.
WOW, IT LOOKS DELECTABLE! ♡
SORRY ABOUT THIS. THANKS, ALICE.
BEAM!
BOW
NO TROUBLE AT ALL.
DEAREST BROTHER, ARE YOU FOND OF THAT MAID?
WHISPER
WELL...
BLUUSH
I AM FOND OF HER.
ACTUALLY, I ADORE HER...
OOF! HOW CRINGE, DEAREST BROTHER!
AHHAHAHA!
HEY, THAT'S MEAN!!
AWW. JUST LEAVE IT TO LITTLE MISS VIOLA HERE.
I'LL TEACH YOU THE "ART OF LOVE, VIOLA STYLE." YOU'LL GET SO POPULAR WITH THE LADIES, STARTING WITH THAT MAID...
POINTS
ART OF LOVE? VIOLA STYLE?

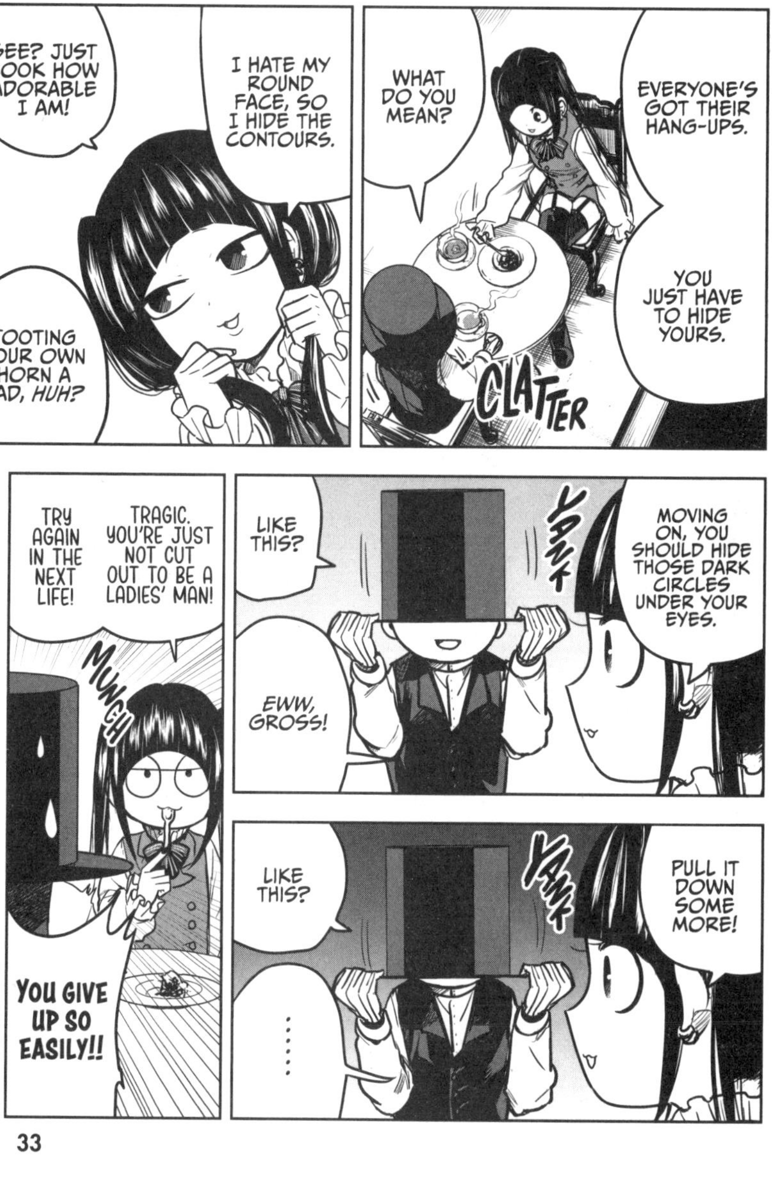
EVERYONE'S GOT THEIR HANG-UPS.
WHAT DO YOU MEAN?
YOU JUST HAVE TO HIDE YOURS.
CLATTER
I HATE MY ROUND FACE, SO I HIDE THE CONTOURS.
SEE? JUST LOOK HOW ADORABLE I AM!
TOOTING YOUR OWN HORN A TAD, *HUH?*
MOVING ON, YOU SHOULD HIDE THOSE DARK CIRCLES UNDER YOUR EYES.
YANK
LIKE THIS?
EWW, GROSS!
PULL IT DOWN SOME MORE!
YANK
LIKE THIS?
......
TRAGIC. YOU'RE JUST NOT CUT OUT TO BE A LADIES' MAN!
TRY AGAIN IN THE NEXT LIFE!
MUNCH
YOU GIVE UP SO EASILY!!

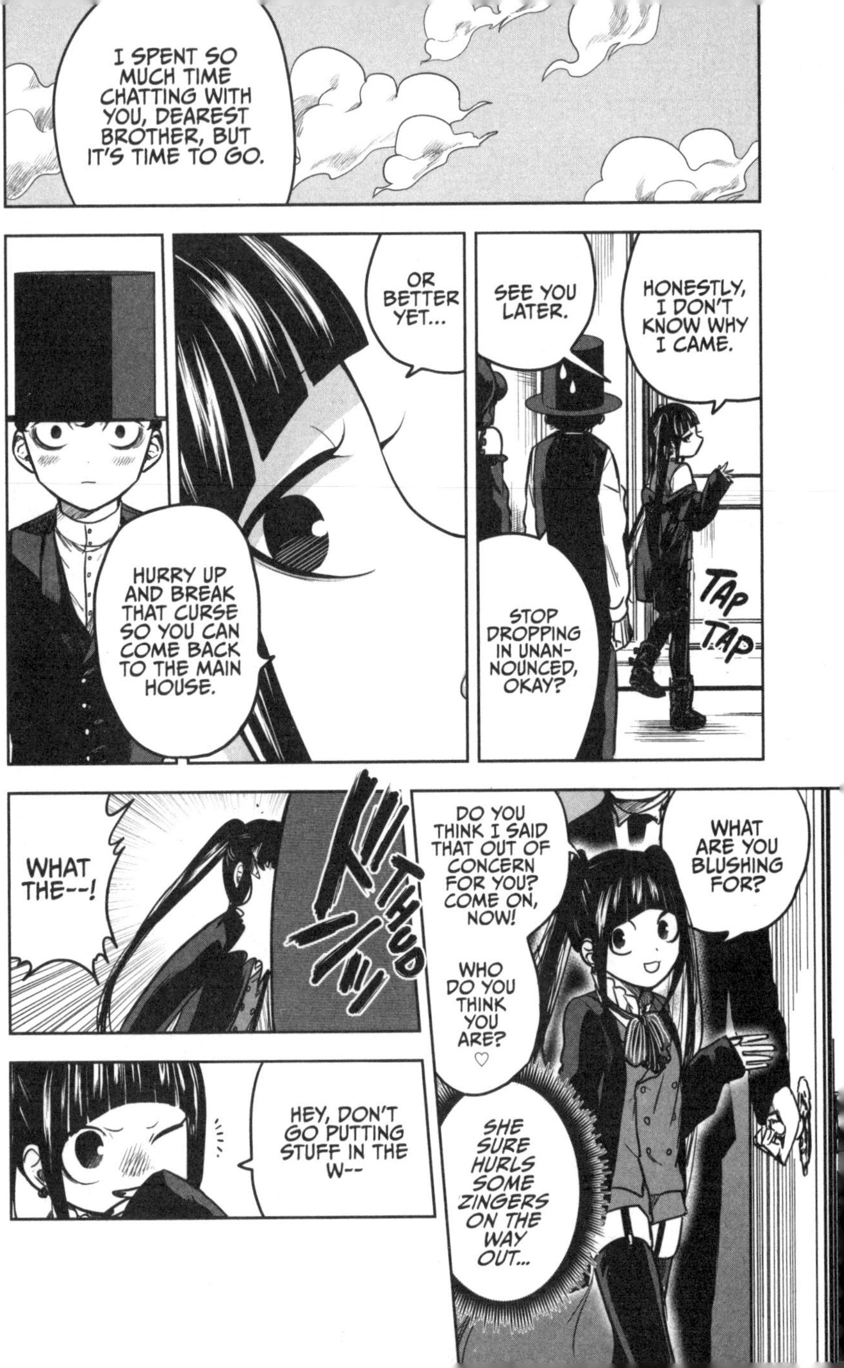
I SPENT SO MUCH TIME CHATTING WITH YOU, DEAREST BROTHER, BUT IT'S TIME TO GO.
HONESTLY, I DON'T KNOW WHY I CAME.
SEE YOU LATER.
STOP DROPPING IN UNAN-NOUNCED, OKAY?
TAP TAP
OR BETTER YET...
HURRY UP AND BREAK THAT CURSE SO YOU CAN COME BACK TO THE MAIN HOUSE.
WHAT ARE YOU BLUSHING FOR?
DO YOU THINK I SAID THAT OUT OF CONCERN FOR YOU? COME ON, NOW!
WHO DO YOU THINK YOU ARE? ♡
SHE SURE HURLS SOME ZINGERS ON THE WAY OUT...
THUD
WHAT THE--!
HEY, DON'T GO PUTTING STUFF IN THE W--

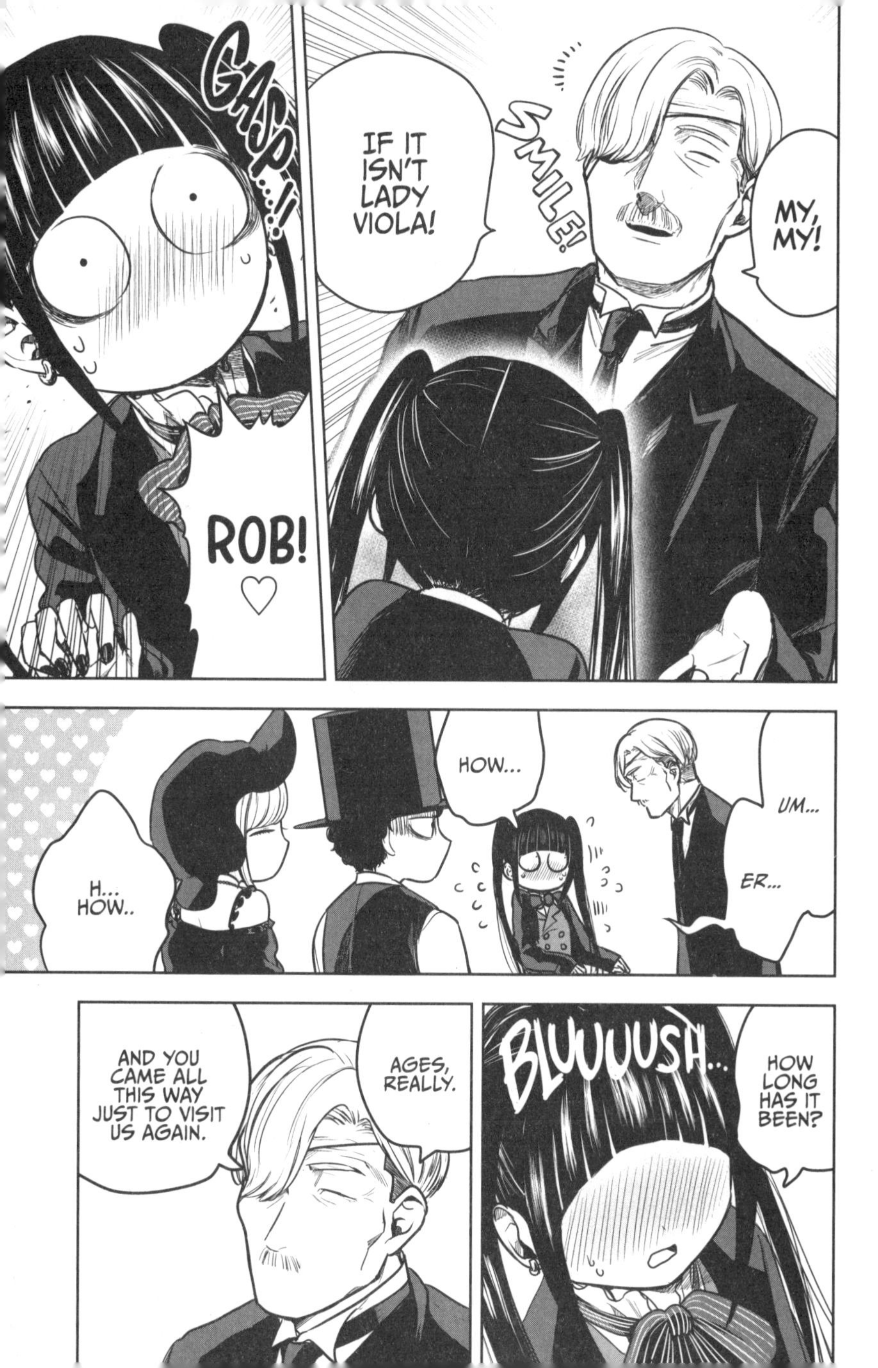
MY, MY!
IF IT ISN'T LADY VIOLA!
SMILE!
GASP...!!
ROB! ♡
UM...
ER...
HOW...
H... HOW..
HOW LONG HAS IT BEEN?
BLUUUUSH...
AGES, REALLY.
AND YOU CAME ALL THIS WAY JUST TO VISIT US AGAIN.

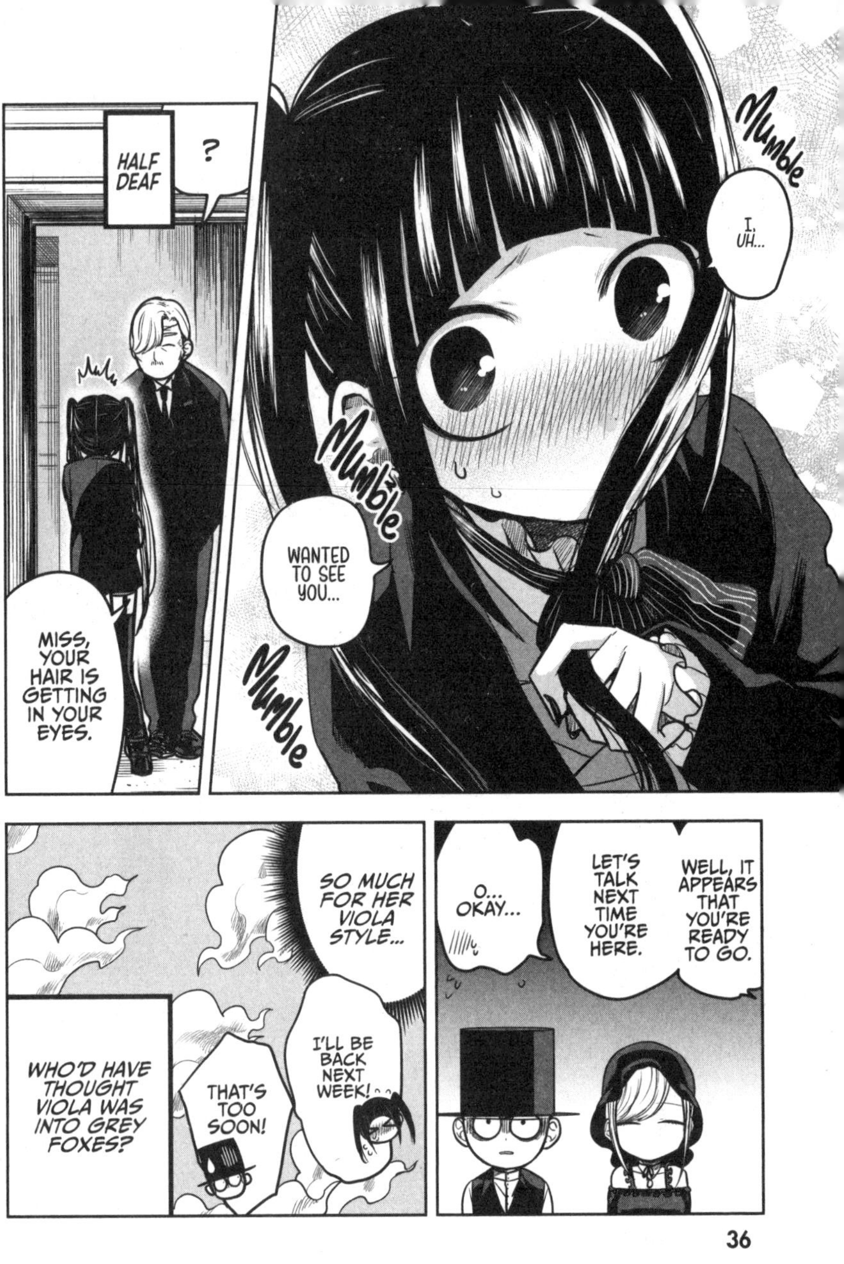
Mumble
I, UH...
Mumble
WANTED TO SEE YOU...
Mumble
?
HALF DEAF
MISS, YOUR HAIR IS GETTING IN YOUR EYES.
WELL, IT APPEARS THAT YOU'RE READY TO GO.
LET'S TALK NEXT TIME YOU'RE HERE.
O... OKAY...
SO MUCH FOR HER VIOLA STYLE...
I'LL BE BACK NEXT WEEK!
THAT'S TOO SOON!
WHO'D HAVE THOUGHT VIOLA WAS INTO GREY FOXES?

Chapter 18: Lightning

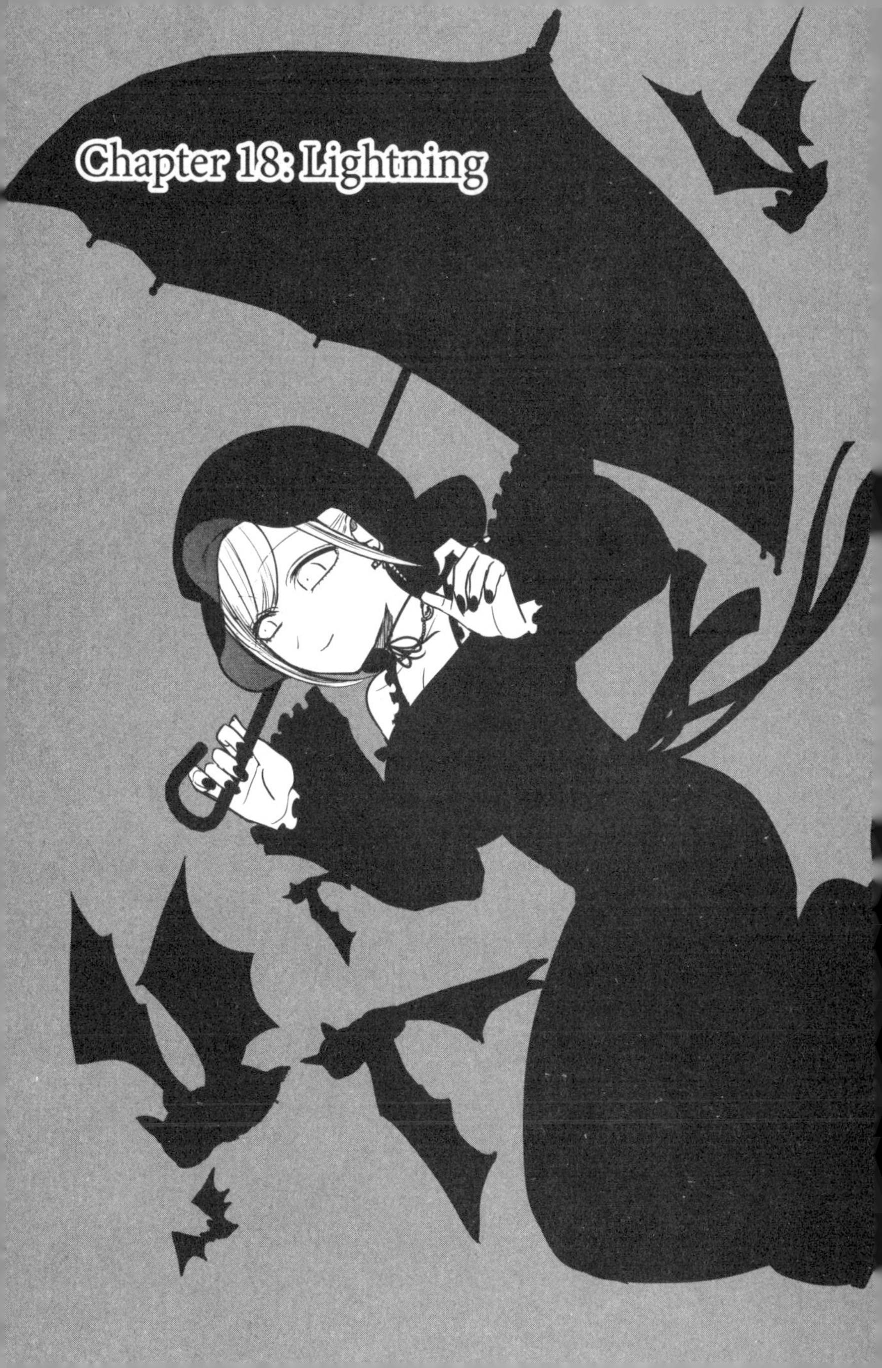

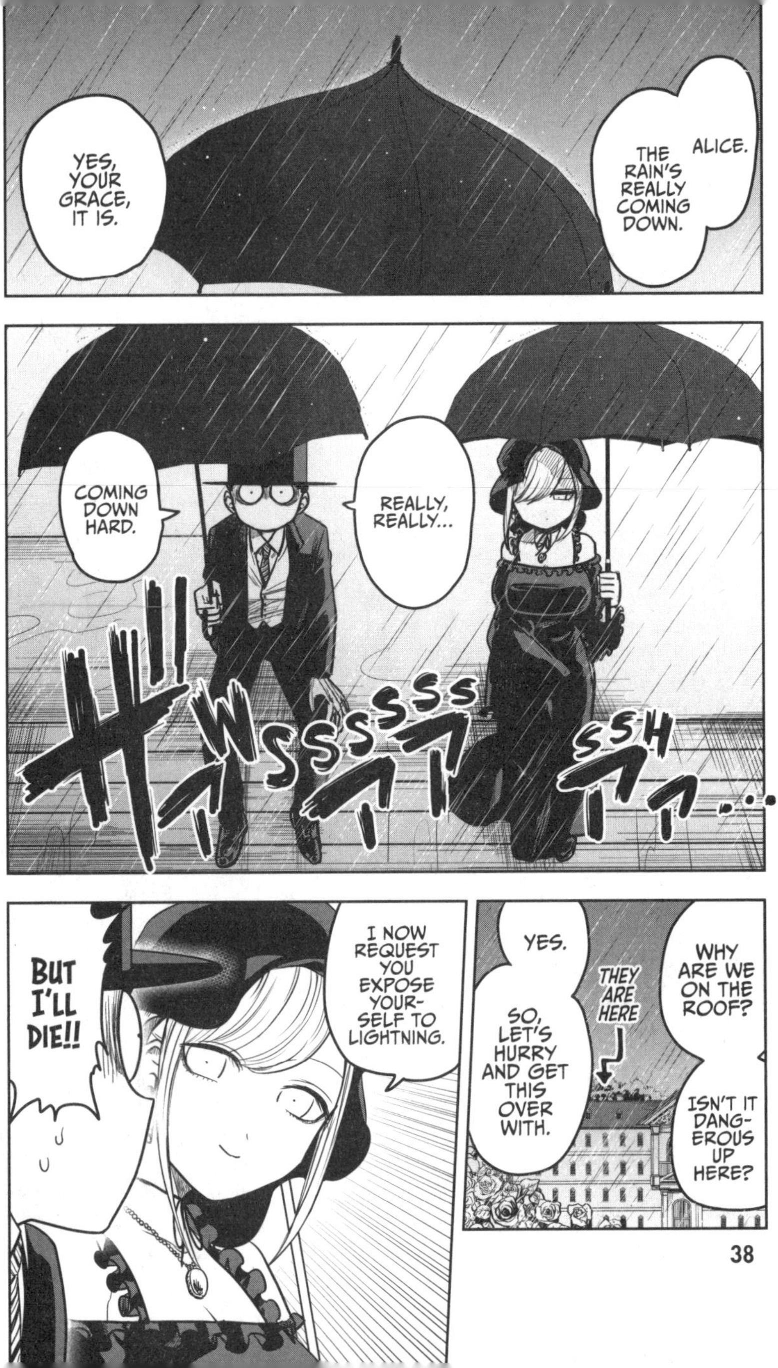
ALICE.
THE RAIN'S REALLY COMING DOWN.
YES, YOUR GRACE, IT IS.
REALLY, REALLY...
COMING DOWN HARD.
SHWSSSSSSSSSH...
WHY ARE WE ON THE ROOF?
ISN'T IT DANGEROUS UP HERE?
YES.
THEY ARE HERE
SO, LET'S HURRY AND GET THIS OVER WITH.
I NOW REQUEST YOU EXPOSE YOURSELF TO LIGHTNING.
BUT I'LL DIE!!

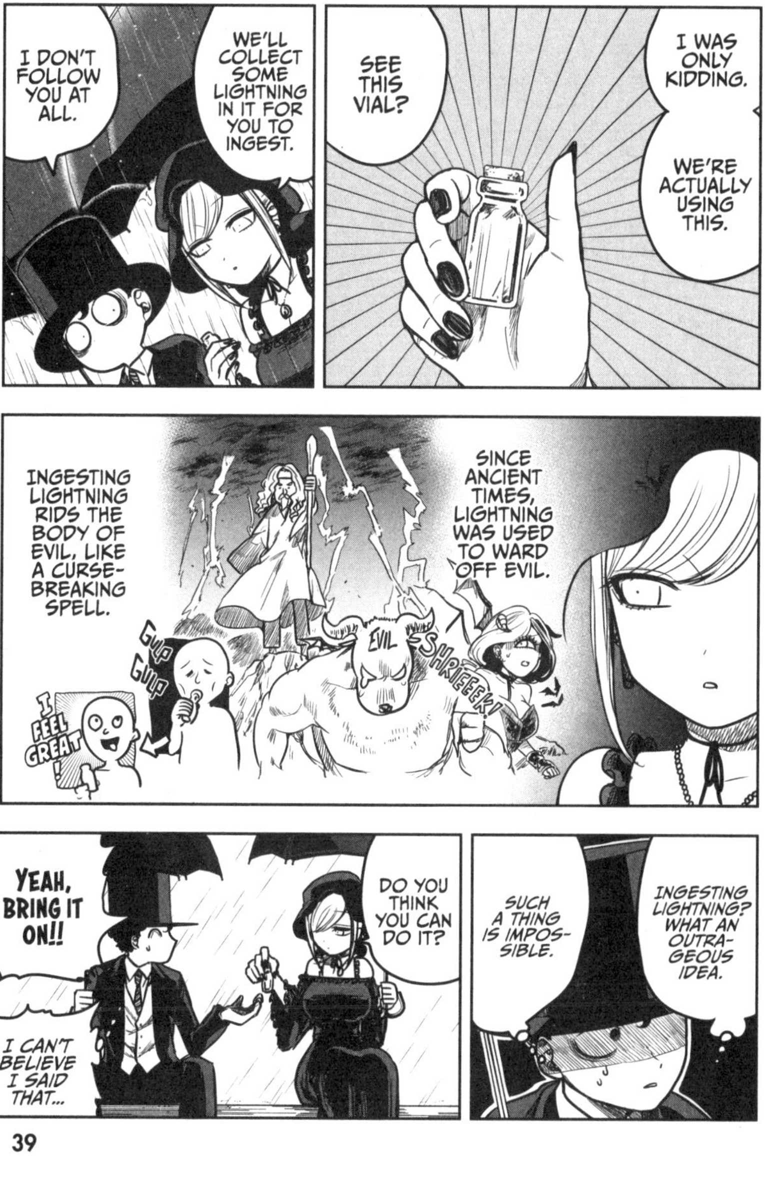
I WAS ONLY KIDDING.
WE'RE ACTUALLY USING THIS.
SEE THIS VIAL?
WE'LL COLLECT SOME LIGHTNING IN IT FOR YOU TO INGEST.
I DON'T FOLLOW YOU AT ALL.
SINCE ANCIENT TIMES, LIGHTNING WAS USED TO WARD OFF EVIL.
INGESTING LIGHTNING RIDS THE BODY OF EVIL, LIKE A CURSE-BREAKING SPELL.
EVIL
SHRIEEEK!
GULP GULP
I FEEL GREAT!
INGESTING LIGHTNING? WHAT AN OUTRAGEOUS IDEA.
SUCH A THING IS IMPOSSIBLE.
DO YOU THINK YOU CAN DO IT?
YEAH, BRING IT ON!!
I CAN'T BELIEVE I SAID THAT...

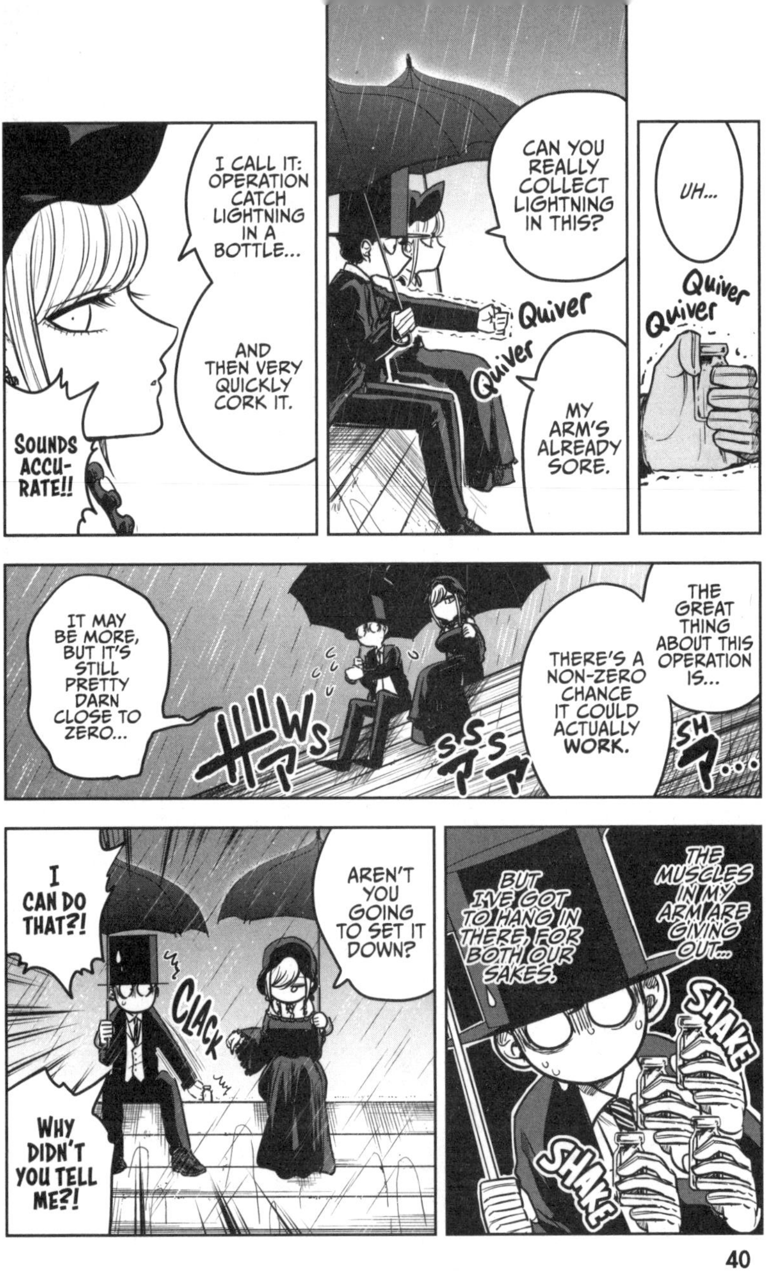
UH...
Quiver
Quiver
CAN YOU REALLY COLLECT LIGHTNING IN THIS?
Quiver
Quiver
MY ARM'S ALREADY SORE.
I CALL IT: OPERATION CATCH LIGHTNING IN A BOTTLE...
AND THEN VERY QUICKLY CORK IT.
SOUNDS ACCU-RATE!!
THE GREAT THING ABOUT THIS OPERATION IS...
SH
THERE'S A NON-ZERO CHANCE IT COULD ACTUALLY WORK.
SSS
IT MAY BE MORE, BUT IT'S STILL PRETTY DARN CLOSE TO ZERO...
WS
THE MUSCLES IN MY ARM ARE GIVING OUT...
BUT I'VE GOT TO HANG IN THERE, FOR BOTH OUR SAKES.
SHAKE
SHAKE
SHAKE
AREN'T YOU GOING TO SET IT DOWN?
CLACK
I CAN DO THAT?!
WHY DIDN'T YOU TELL ME?!

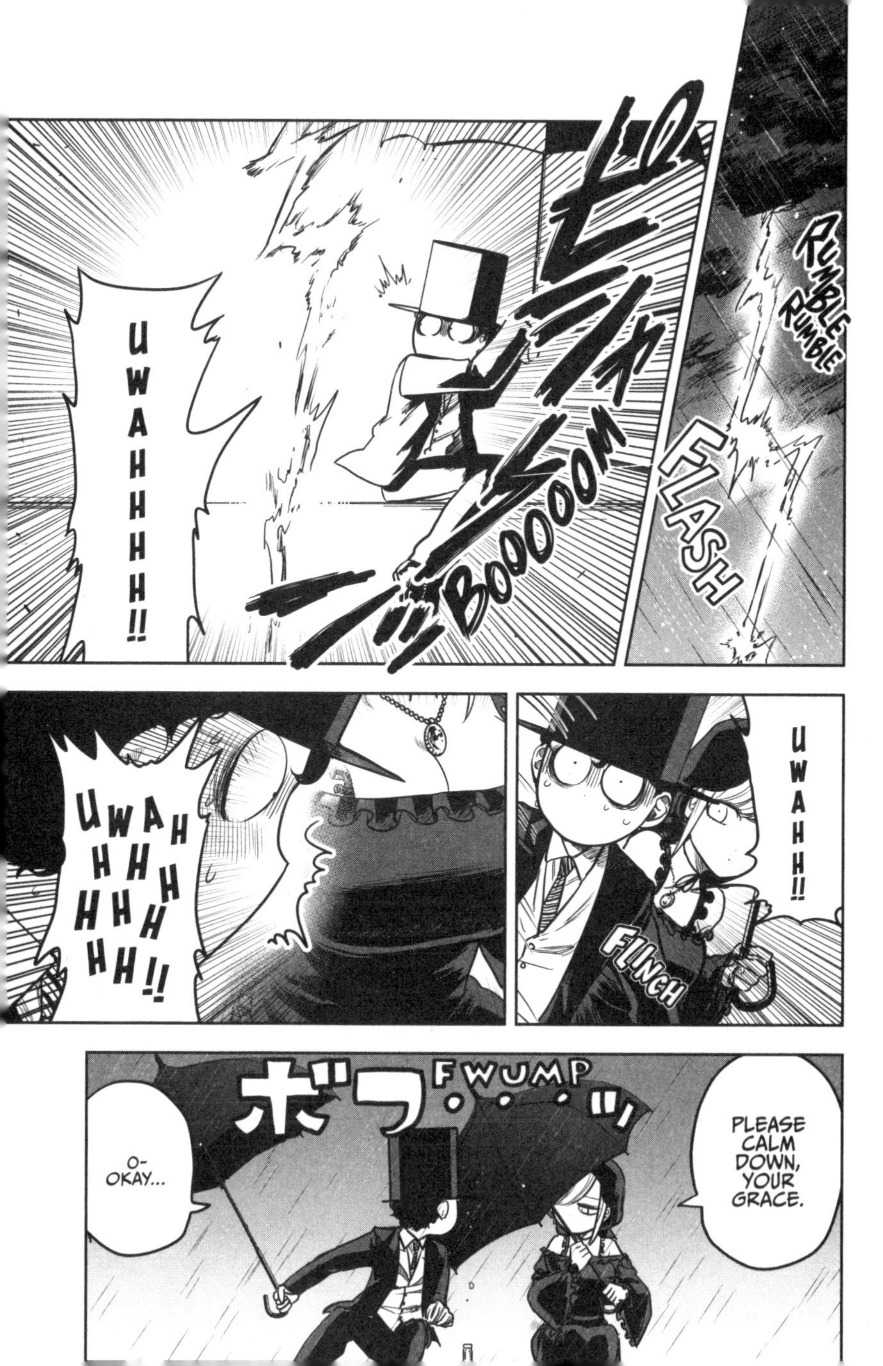
RUMBLE RUMBLE
FLASH
BOOOOOM
UWAHHHHHHH!!
UWAHH!!
FLINCH
UWAHHHHHHHHHHHHH!!
PLEASE CALM DOWN, YOUR GRACE.
ボフ
FWUMP
O-OKAY...

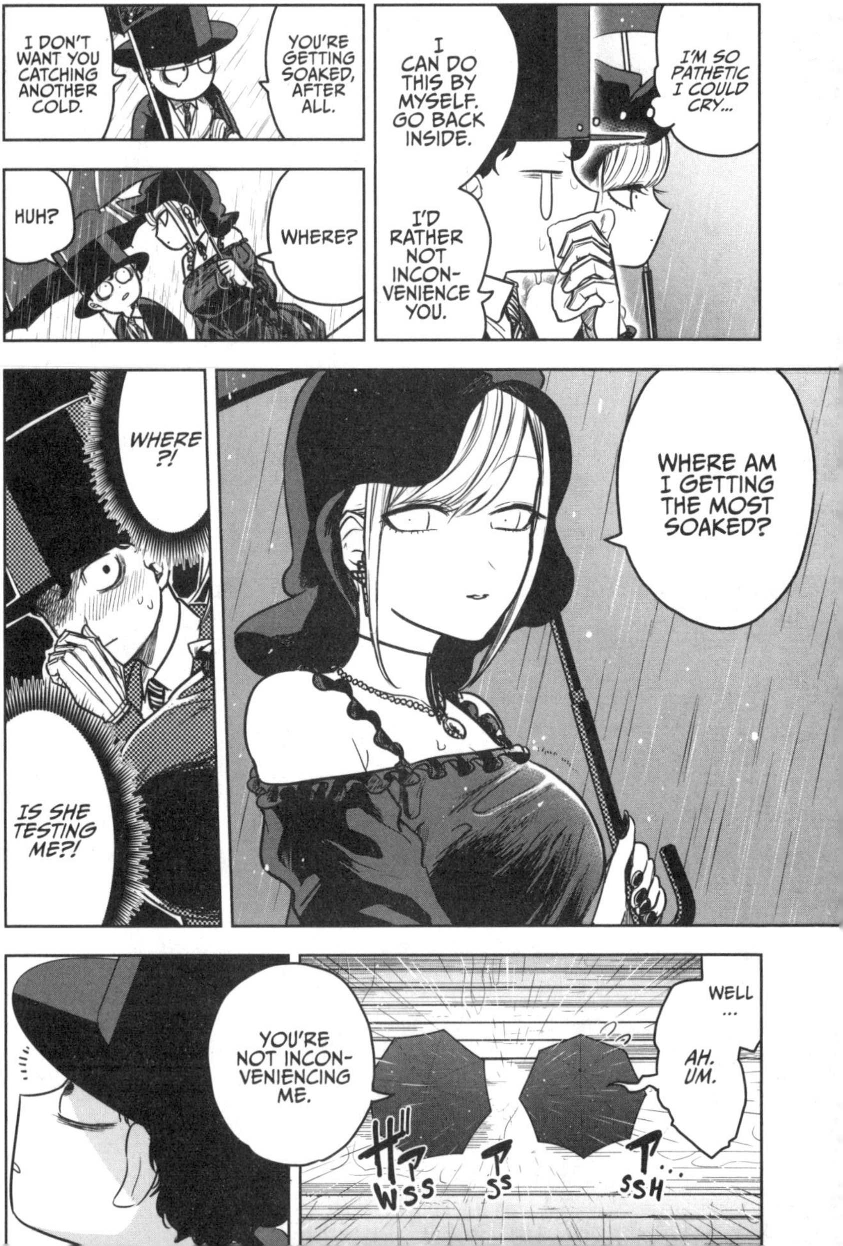
I'M SO PATHETIC I COULD CRY...
I CAN DO THIS BY MYSELF. GO BACK INSIDE.
I'D RATHER NOT INCON-VENIENCE YOU.
YOU'RE GETTING SOAKED, AFTER ALL.
I DON'T WANT YOU CATCHING ANOTHER COLD.
WHERE?
HUH?
WHERE AM I GETTING THE MOST SOAKED?
WHERE?!
IS SHE TESTING ME?!
WELL ...
AH. UM.
SSH
SS
WSS
YOU'RE NOT INCON-VENIENCING ME.

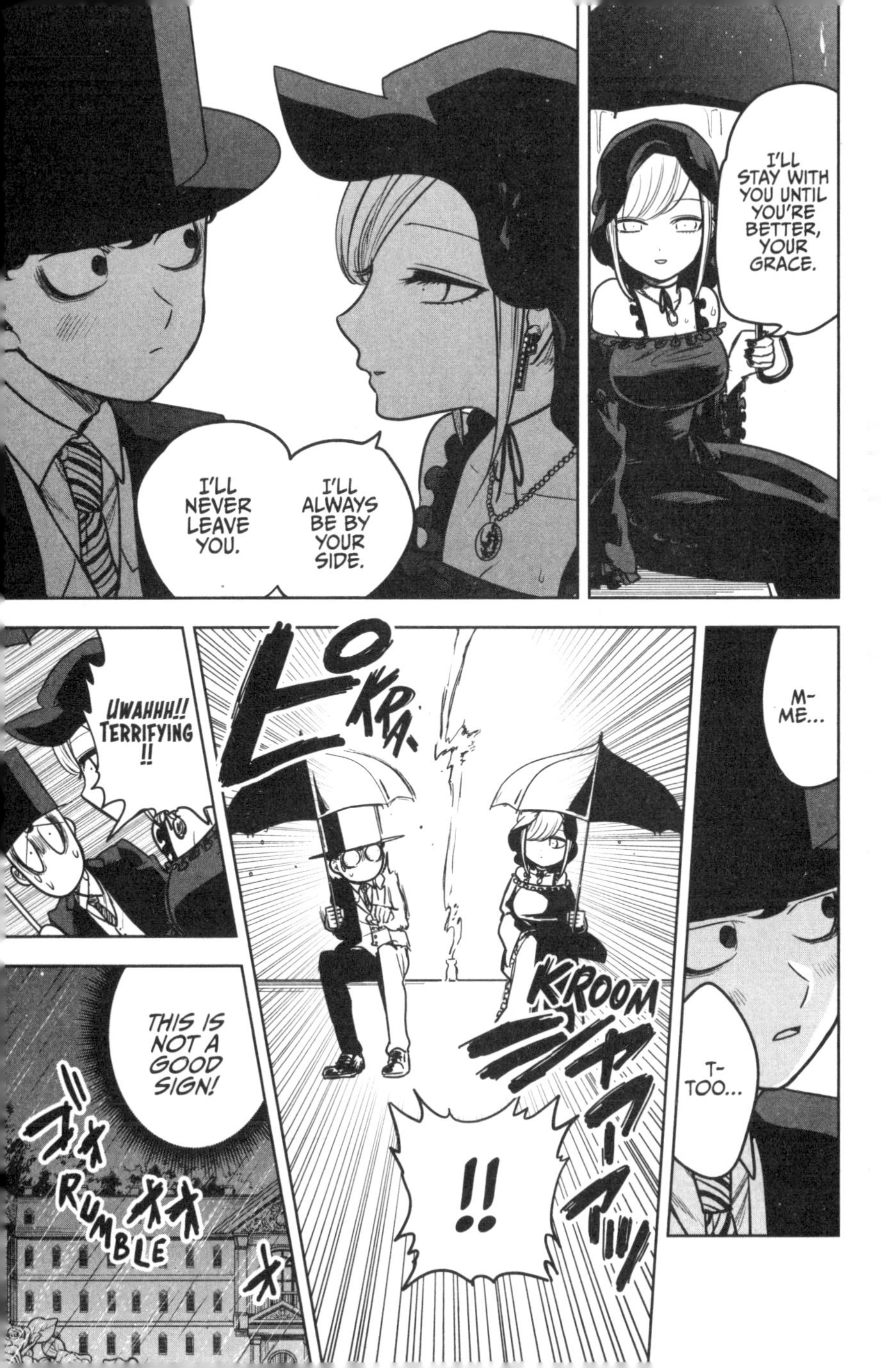
I'LL STAY WITH YOU UNTIL YOU'RE BETTER, YOUR GRACE.
I'LL ALWAYS BE BY YOUR SIDE.
I'LL NEVER LEAVE YOU.
M- ME...
T- TOO...
OKRA-
KROOM
!!
UWAHHH!! TERRIFYING!!
THIS IS NOT A GOOD SIGN!
RUMBLE

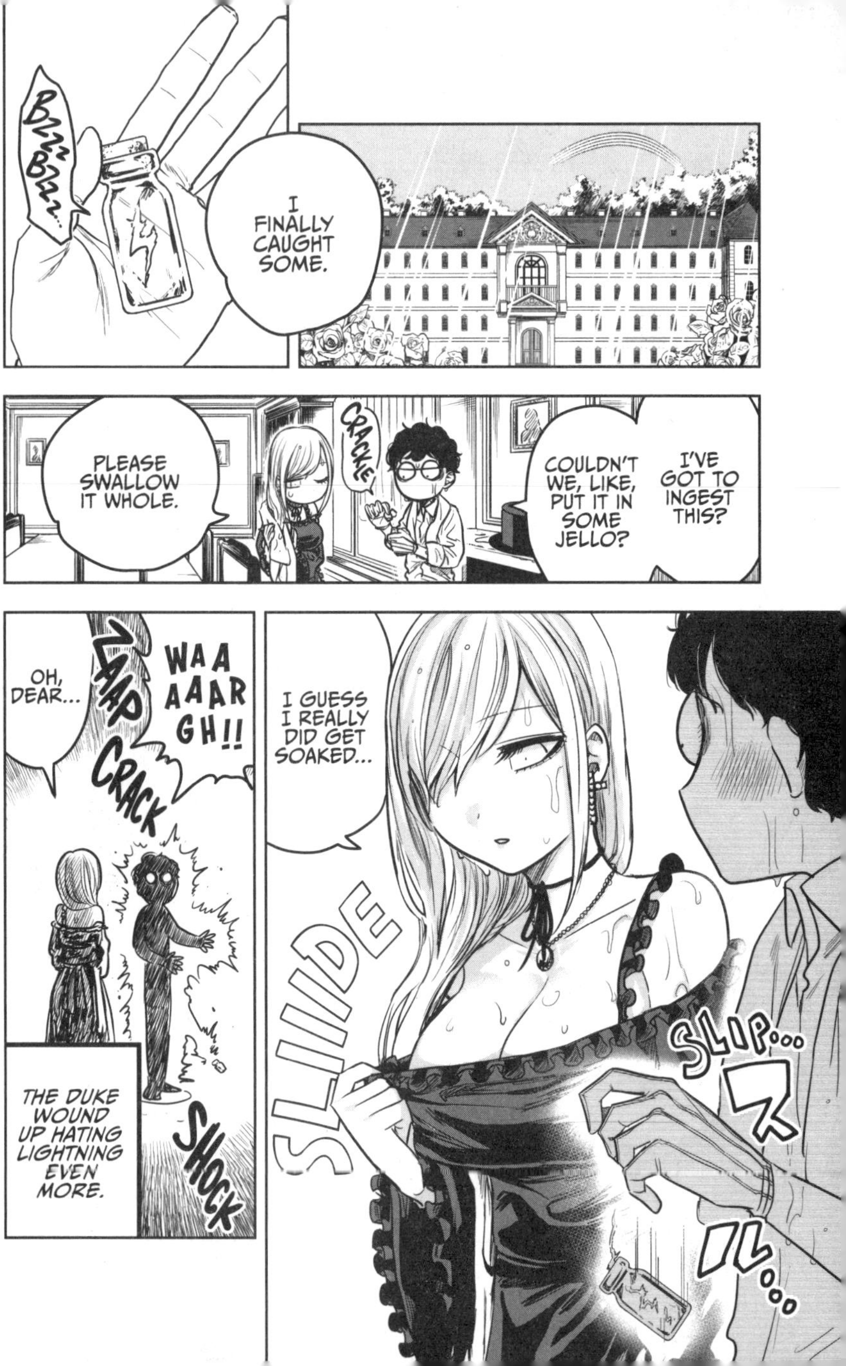
I FINALLY CAUGHT SOME.
BZZZ BZZZ...
I'VE GOT TO INGEST THIS?
COULDN'T WE, LIKE, PUT IT IN SOME JELLO?
CRACKLE
PLEASE SWALLOW IT WHOLE.
I GUESS I REALLY DID GET SOAKED...
SLIP...
スル...
SLIIIDE
WAAAAARGH!!
ZAAAP
CRACK
OH, DEAR...
SHOCK
THE DUKE WOUND UP HATING LIGHTNING EVEN MORE.

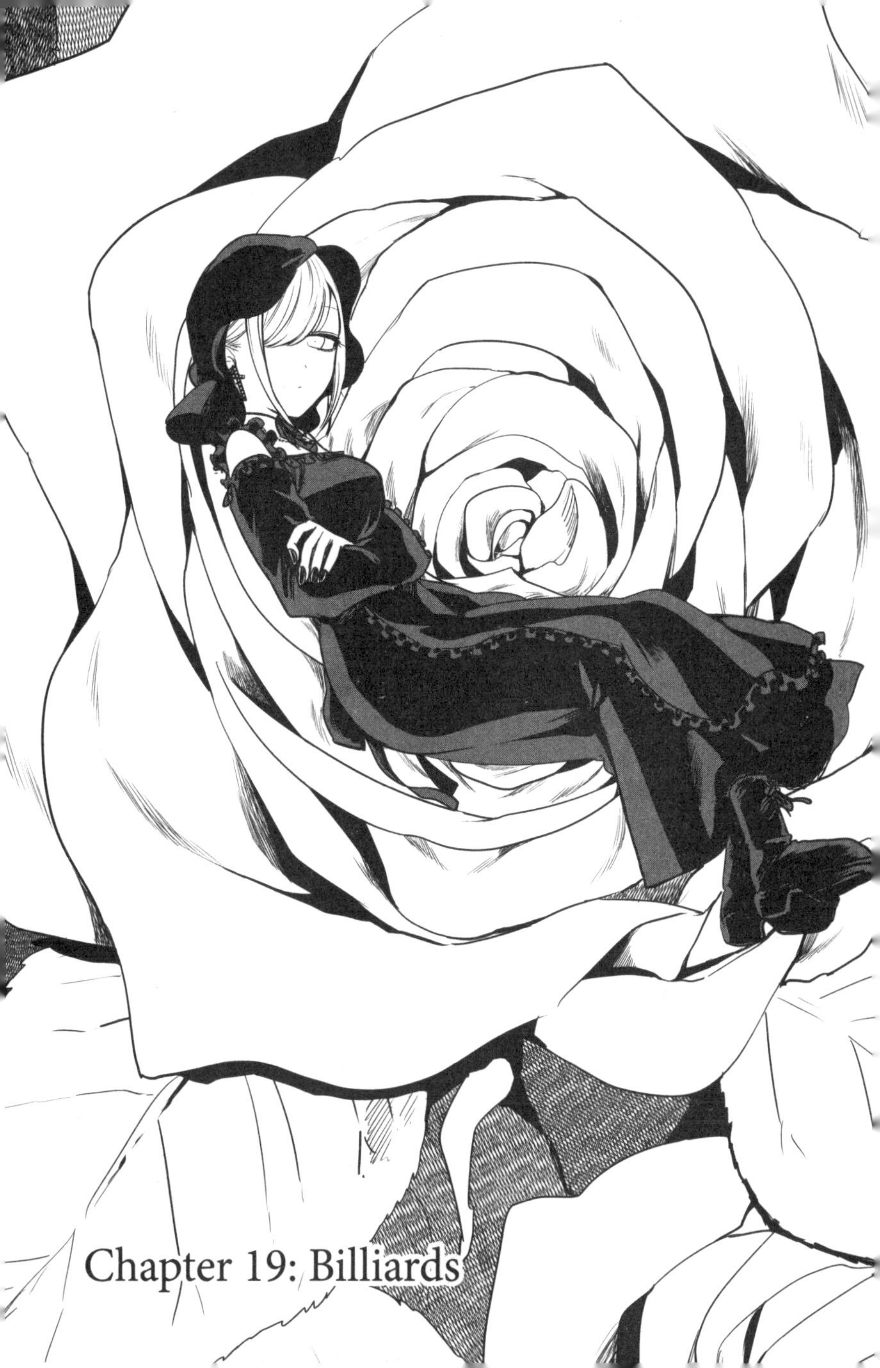
Chapter 19: Billiards

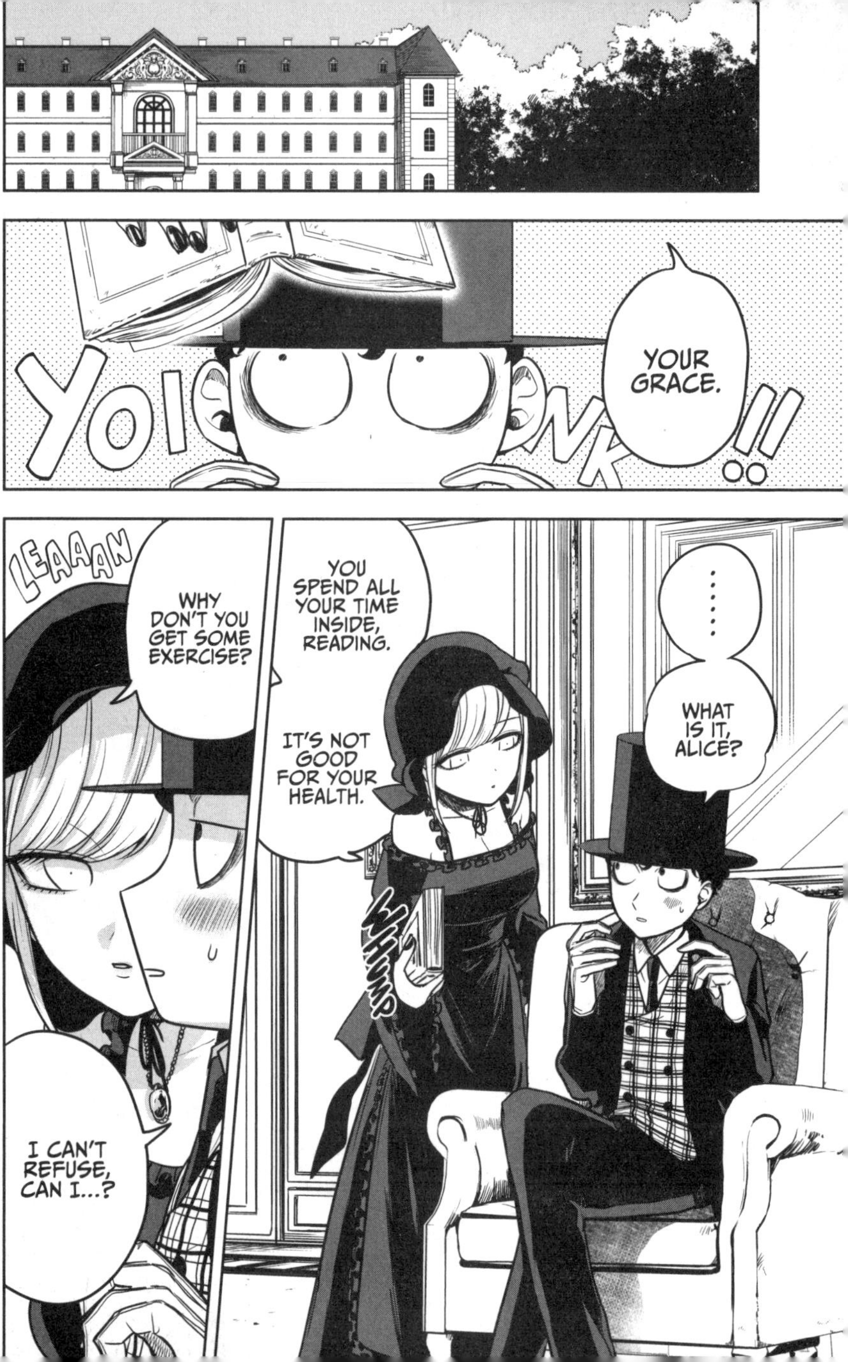
YOI NK!!
YOUR GRACE.
......
WHAT IS IT, ALICE?
YOU SPEND ALL YOUR TIME INSIDE, READING.
IT'S NOT GOOD FOR YOUR HEALTH.
WHUMP
LEAAAN
WHY DON'T YOU GET SOME EXERCISE?
I CAN'T REFUSE, CAN I...?

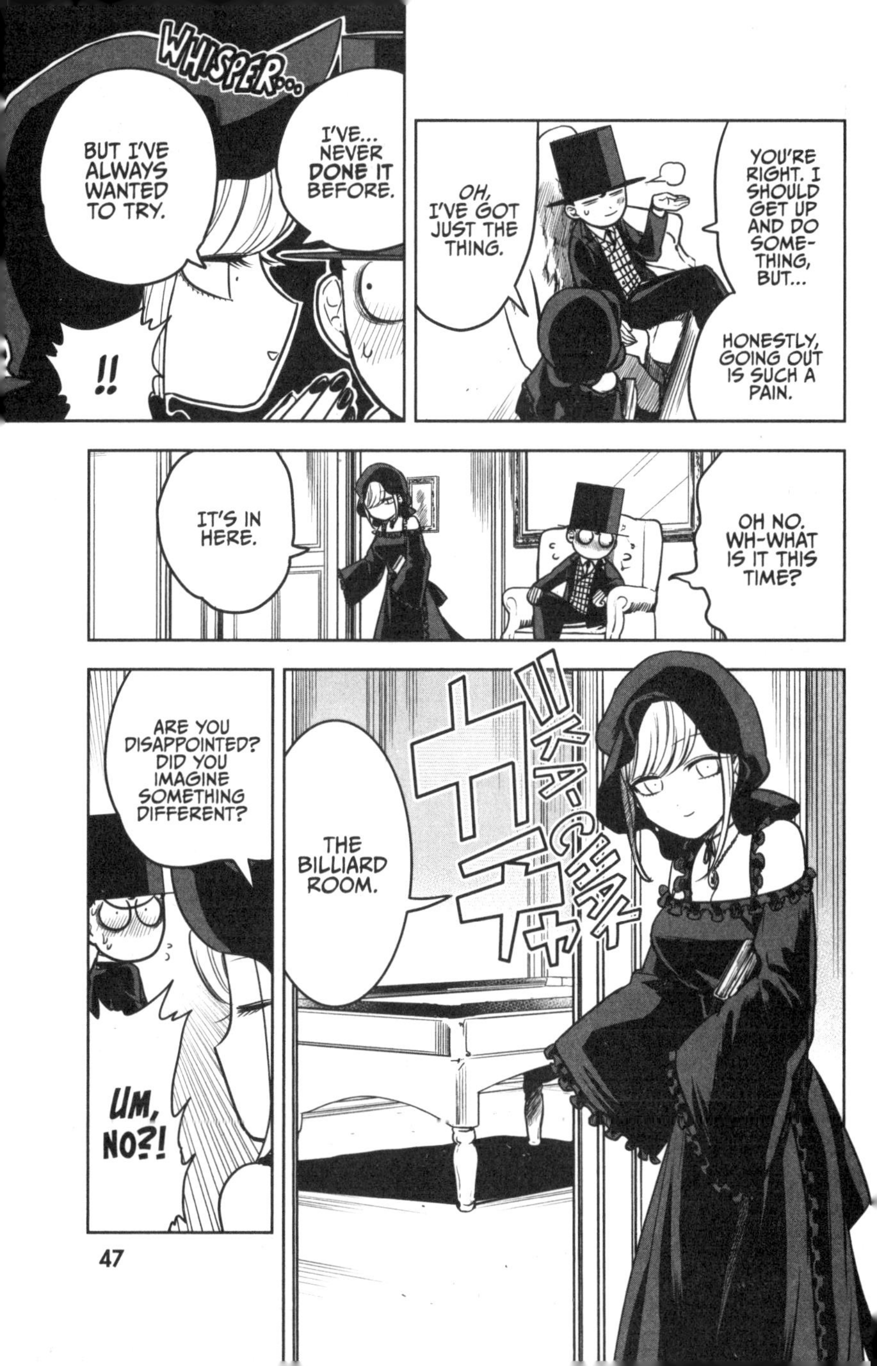
YOU'RE RIGHT. I SHOULD GET UP AND DO SOME-THING, BUT...
HONESTLY, GOING OUT IS SUCH A PAIN.
OH, I'VE GOT JUST THE THING.
WHISPER...
I'VE... NEVER DONE IT BEFORE.
BUT I'VE ALWAYS WANTED TO TRY.
!!
OH NO. WH-WHAT IS IT THIS TIME?
IT'S IN HERE.
KA-CHAK
THE BILLIARD ROOM.
ARE YOU DISAPPOINTED? DID YOU IMAGINE SOMETHING DIFFERENT?
UM, NO?!

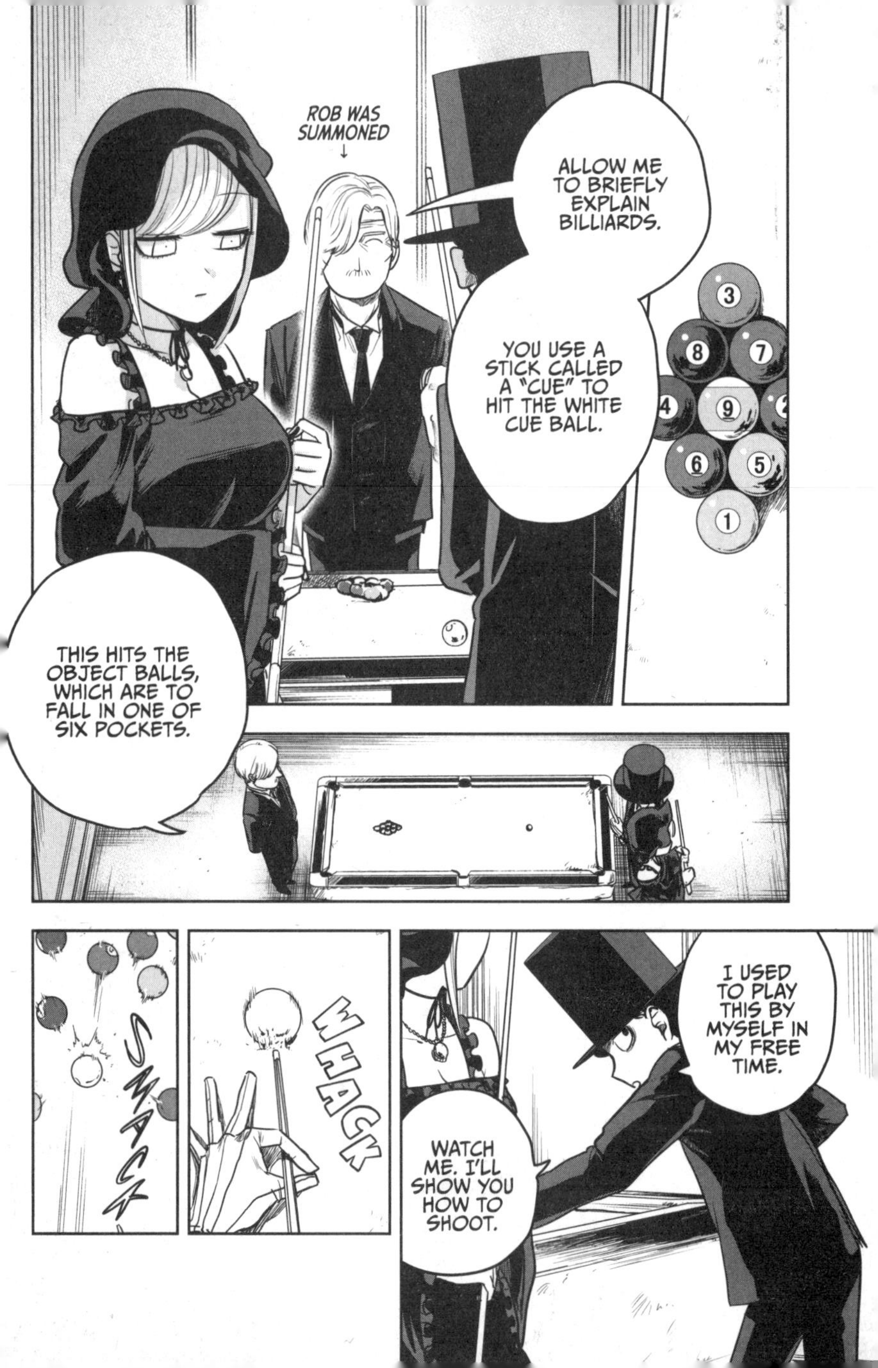
ALLOW ME TO BRIEFLY EXPLAIN BILLIARDS.
ROB WAS SUMMONED
YOU USE A STICK CALLED A "CUE" TO HIT THE WHITE CUE BALL.
THIS HITS THE OBJECT BALLS, WHICH ARE TO FALL IN ONE OF SIX POCKETS.
I USED TO PLAY THIS BY MYSELF IN MY FREE TIME.
WATCH ME. I'LL SHOW YOU HOW TO SHOOT.
WHACK
SMACK

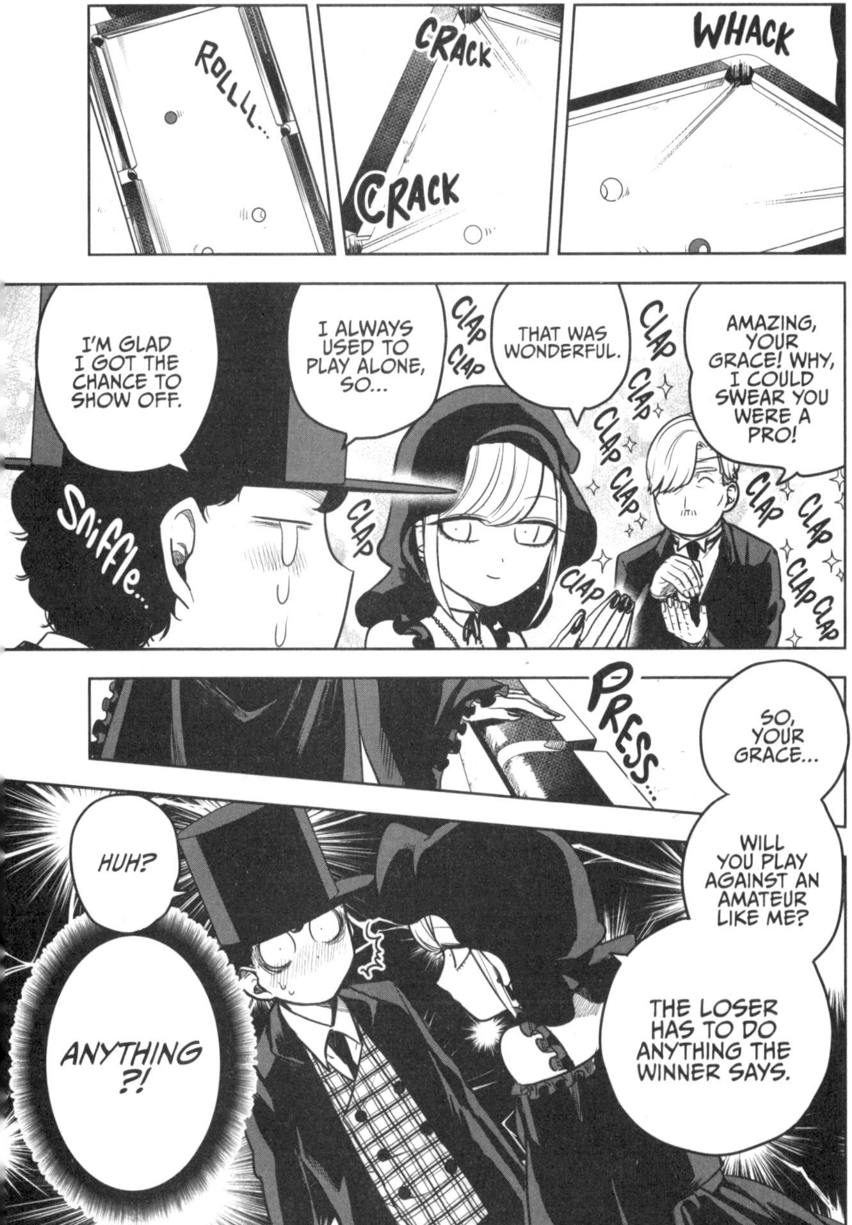
WHACK
CRACK
CRACK
ROLLLL...
AMAZING, YOUR GRACE! WHY, I COULD SWEAR YOU WERE A PRO!
CLAP CLAP CLAP CLAP
CLAP CLAP CLAP CLAP CLAP
THAT WAS WONDERFUL.
CLAP CLAP
I ALWAYS USED TO PLAY ALONE, SO...
I'M GLAD I GOT THE CHANCE TO SHOW OFF.
CLAP CLAP
SNIFFLE...
SO, YOUR GRACE...
PRESS...
WILL YOU PLAY AGAINST AN AMATEUR LIKE ME?
HUH?
THE LOSER HAS TO DO ANYTHING THE WINNER SAYS.
ANYTHING ?!

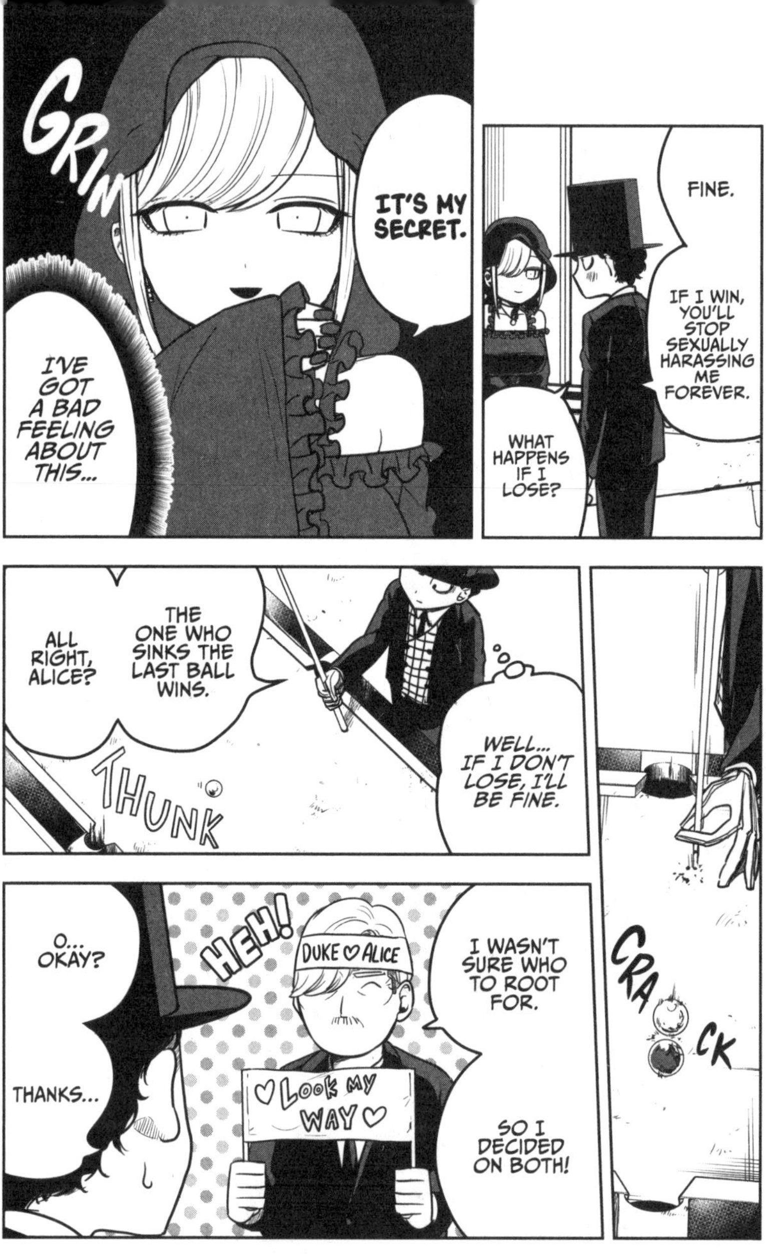
FINE.
IF I WIN, YOU'LL STOP SEXUALLY HARASSING ME FOREVER.
WHAT HAPPENS IF I LOSE?
IT'S MY SECRET.
GRIN
I'VE GOT A BAD FEELING ABOUT THIS...
CRACK
THE ONE WHO SINKS THE LAST BALL WINS.
ALL RIGHT, ALICE?
THUNK
WELL... IF I DON'T LOSE, I'LL BE FINE.
I WASN'T SURE WHO TO ROOT FOR.
SO I DECIDED ON BOTH!
HEH!
DUKE ♡ ALICE
♡ Look my WAY ♡
O... OKAY?
THANKS...

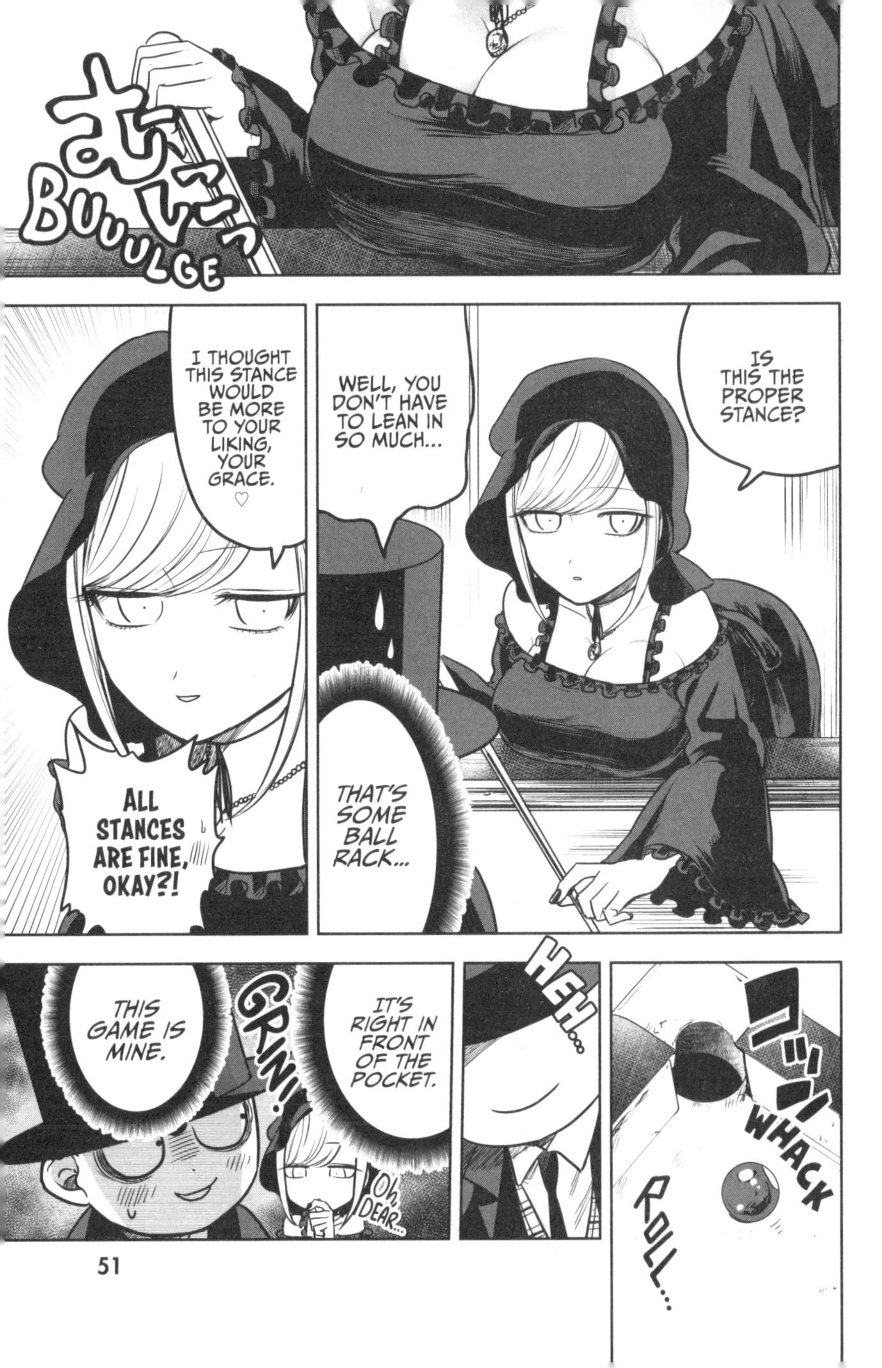
BUUULGE
IS THIS THE PROPER STANCE?
WELL, YOU DON'T HAVE TO LEAN IN SO MUCH...
THAT'S SOME BALL RACK...
I THOUGHT THIS STANCE WOULD BE MORE TO YOUR LIKING, YOUR GRACE. ♡
ALL STANCES ARE FINE, OKAY?!
WHACK
ROLL...
HEH...
IT'S RIGHT IN FRONT OF THE POCKET.
GRIN!!
THIS GAME IS MINE.
OH, DEAR...

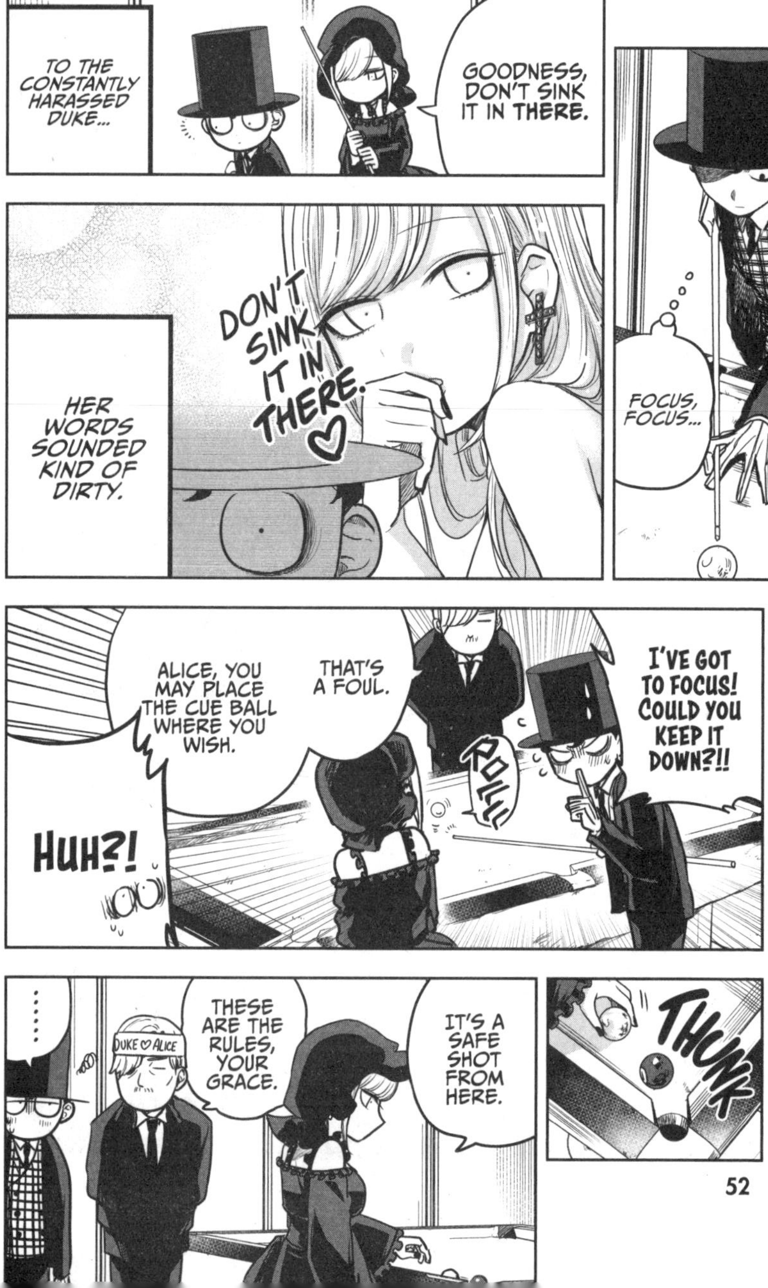
FOCUS, FOCUS...
GOODNESS, DON'T SINK IT IN THERE.
TO THE CONSTANTLY HARASSED DUKE...
DON'T SINK IT IN THERE. ♥
HER WORDS SOUNDED KIND OF DIRTY.
I'VE GOT TO FOCUS! COULD YOU KEEP IT DOWN?!!
ROLL
THAT'S A FOUL.
ALICE, YOU MAY PLACE THE CUE BALL WHERE YOU WISH.
HUH?!
THUNK
IT'S A SAFE SHOT FROM HERE.
THESE ARE THE RULES, YOUR GRACE.
DUKE ♡ ALICE
......

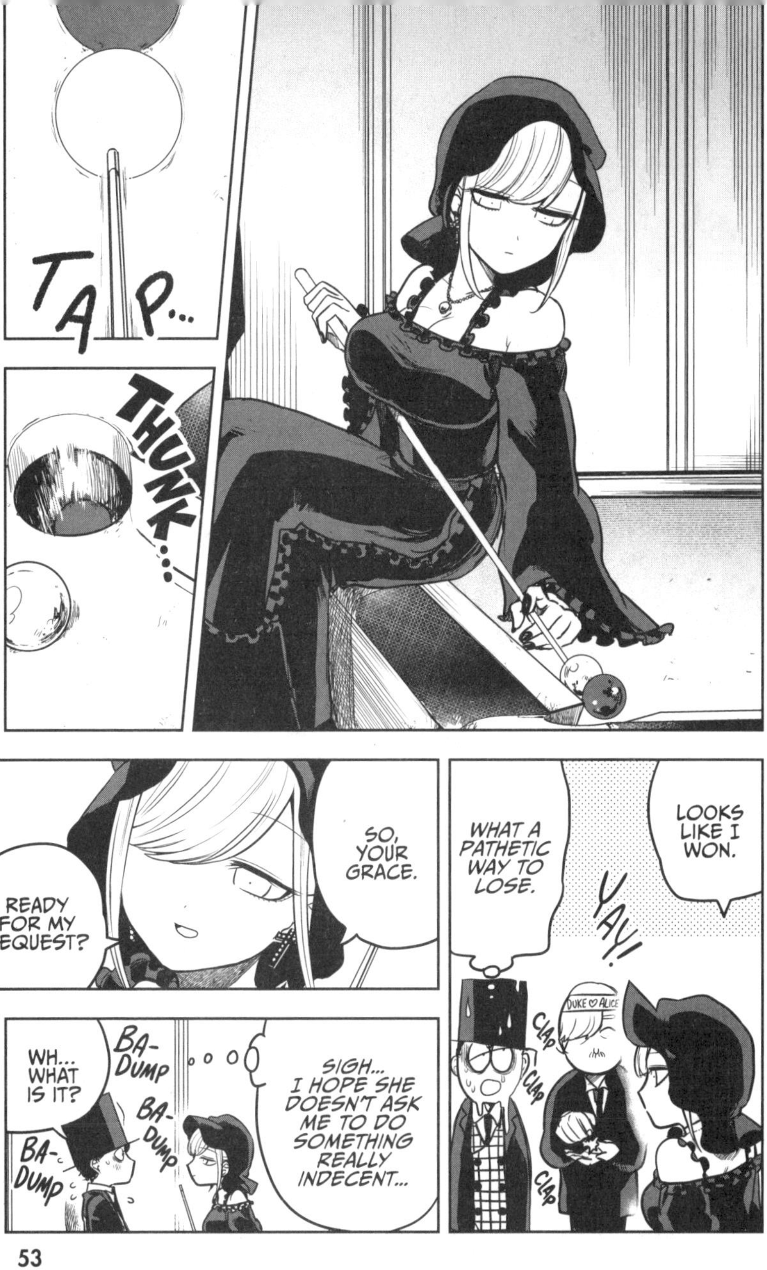
TAP...
THUNK...
LOOKS LIKE I WON.
YAY!
WHAT A PATHETIC WAY TO LOSE.
DUKE ♡ ALICE
CLAP
CLAP
CLAP
SO, YOUR GRACE.
READY FOR MY REQUEST?
SIGH... I HOPE SHE DOESN'T ASK ME TO DO SOMETHING REALLY INDECENT...
BA-DUMP
BA-DUMP
WH... WHAT IS IT?
BA-DUMP

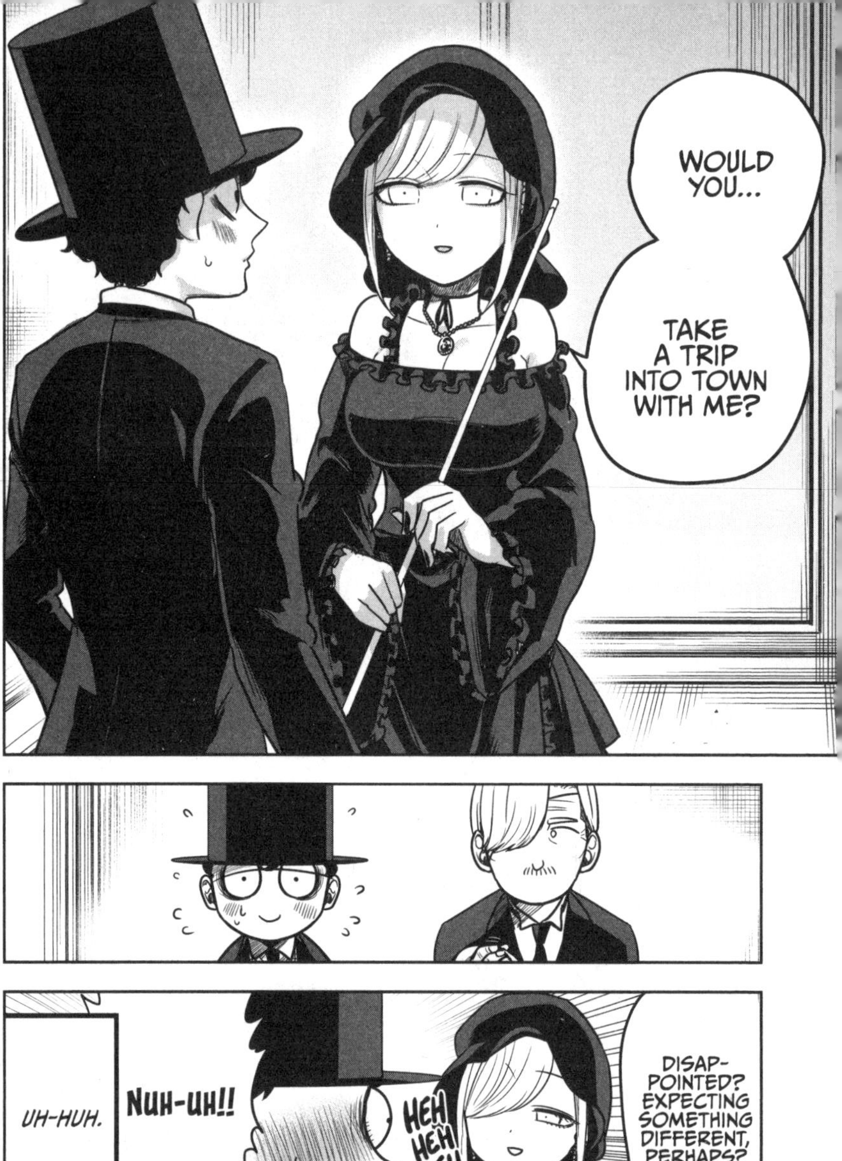
WOULD YOU...
TAKE A TRIP INTO TOWN WITH ME?
DISAP-POINTED? EXPECTING SOMETHING DIFFERENT, PERHAPS?
HEH HEH HEH ♡
NUH-UH!!
UH-HUH.

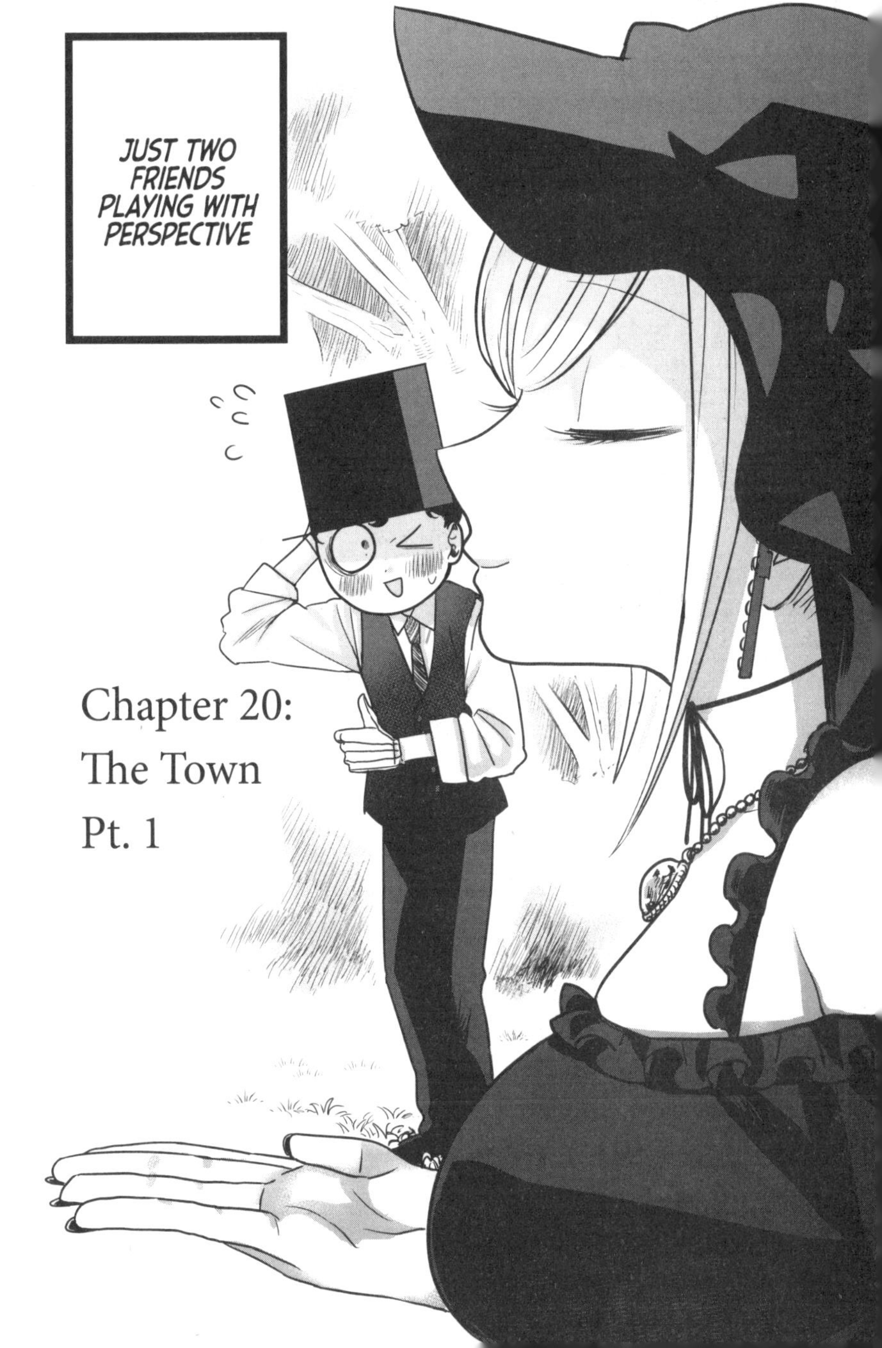
JUST TWO FRIENDS PLAYING WITH PERSPECTIVE

Chapter 20: The Town Pt. 1

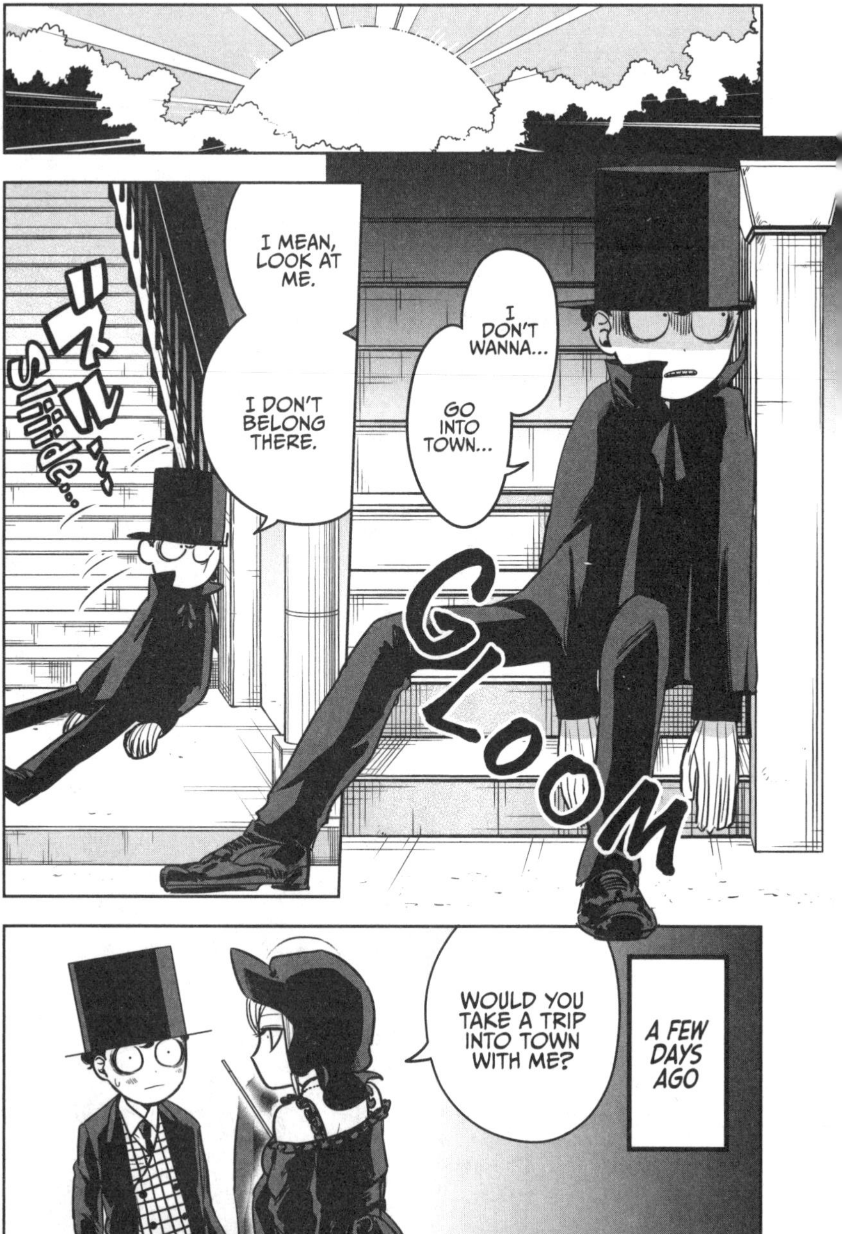
I DON'T WANNA... GO INTO TOWN...
GLOOM
I MEAN, LOOK AT ME. I DON'T BELONG THERE.
ズル... sliiide...
A FEW DAYS AGO
WOULD YOU TAKE A TRIP INTO TOWN WITH ME?

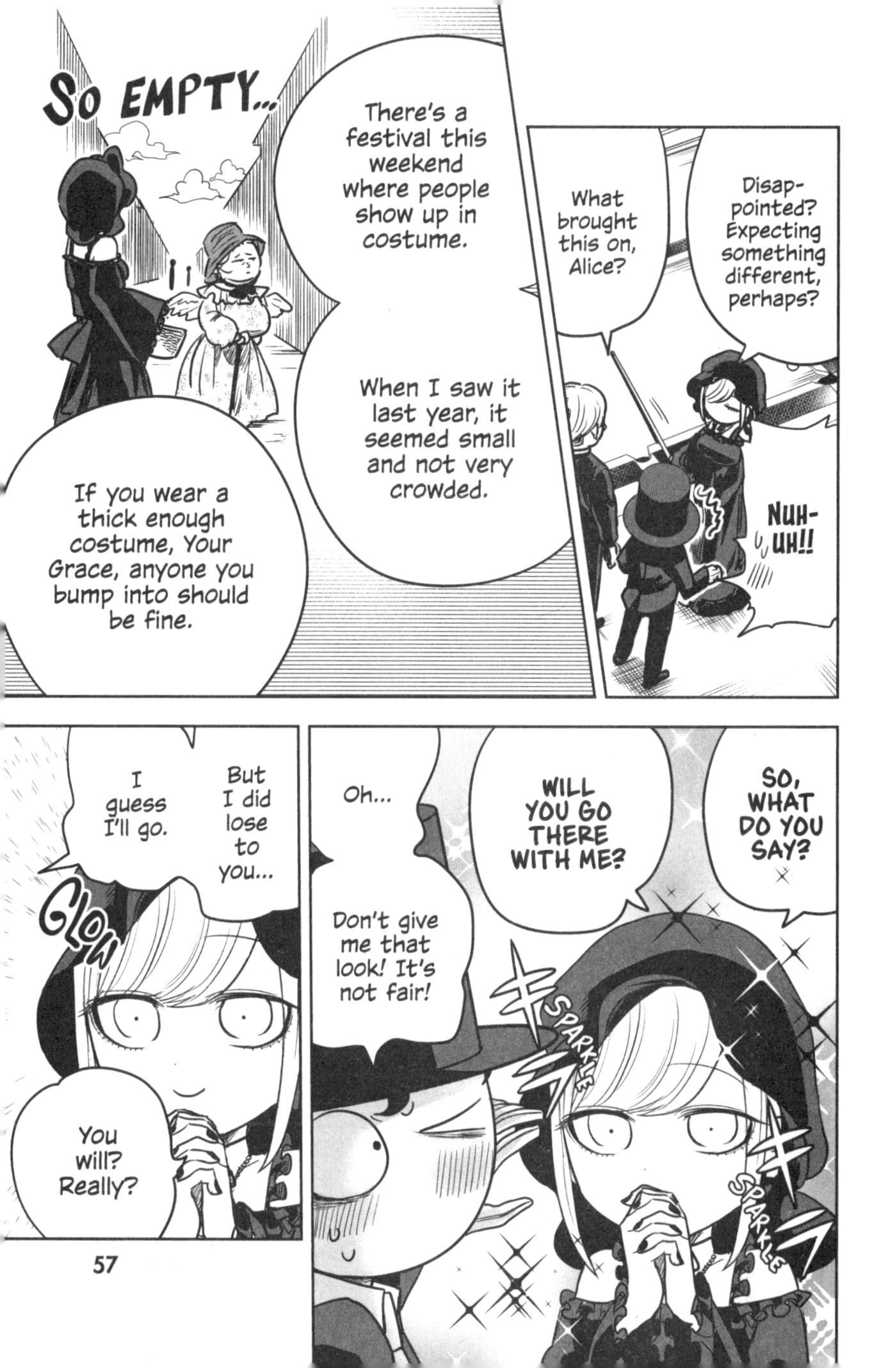
Disap-pointed? Expecting something different, perhaps?
What brought this on, Alice?
NUH-UH!!
There's a festival this weekend where people show up in costume.
SO EMPTY...
When I saw it last year, it seemed small and not very crowded.
If you wear a thick enough costume, Your Grace, anyone you bump into should be fine.
SO, WHAT DO YOU SAY?
WILL YOU GO THERE WITH ME?
Oh...
Don't give me that look! It's not fair!
SPARKLE
SPARKLE
But I did lose to you...
I guess I'll go.
GLOW
You will? Really?

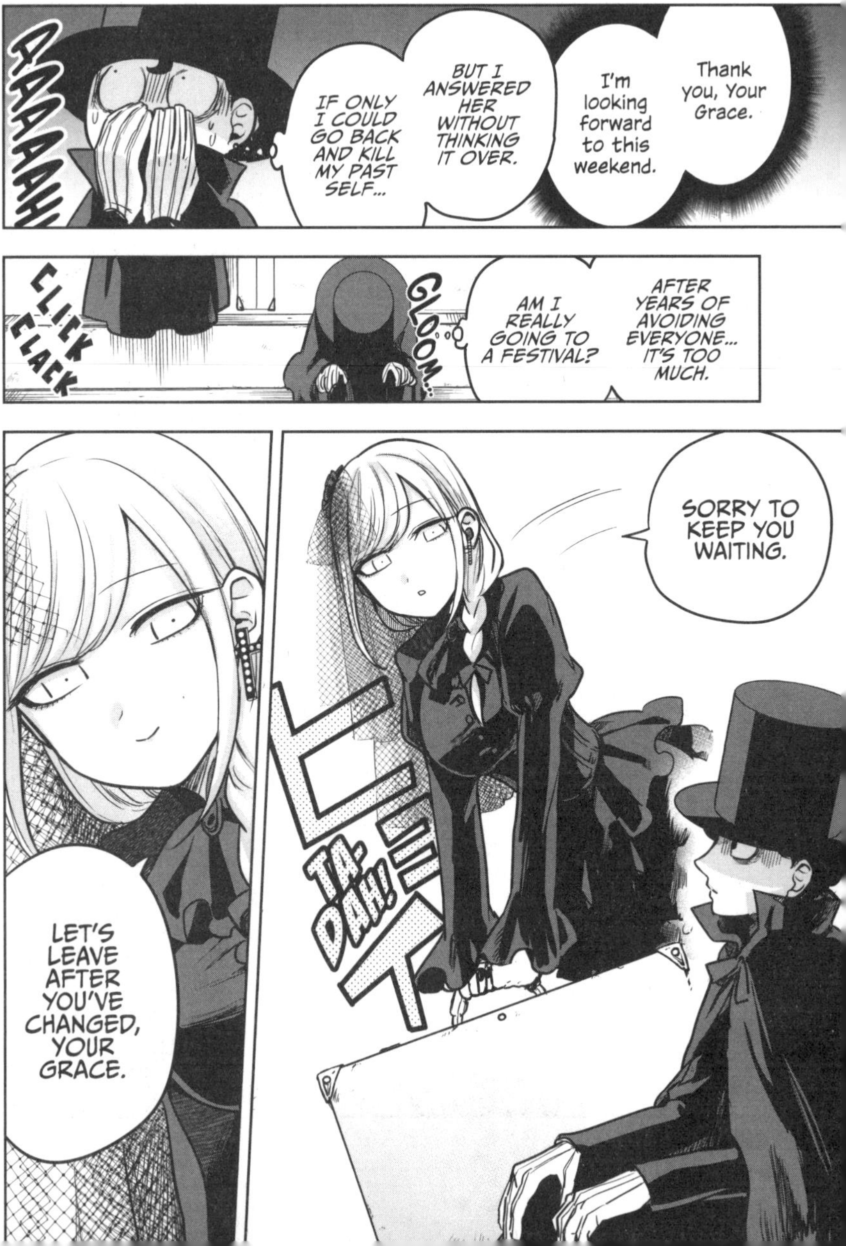
Thank you, Your Grace.
I'm looking forward to this weekend.
BUT I ANSWERED HER WITHOUT THINKING IT OVER.
IF ONLY I COULD GO BACK AND KILL MY PAST SELF...
AAAAAAH
AFTER YEARS OF AVOIDING EVERYONE... IT'S TOO MUCH.
AM I REALLY GOING TO A FESTIVAL?
GLOOM...
CLICK CLACK
SORRY TO KEEP YOU WAITING.
TA-DAH!
LET'S LEAVE AFTER YOU'VE CHANGED, YOUR GRACE.

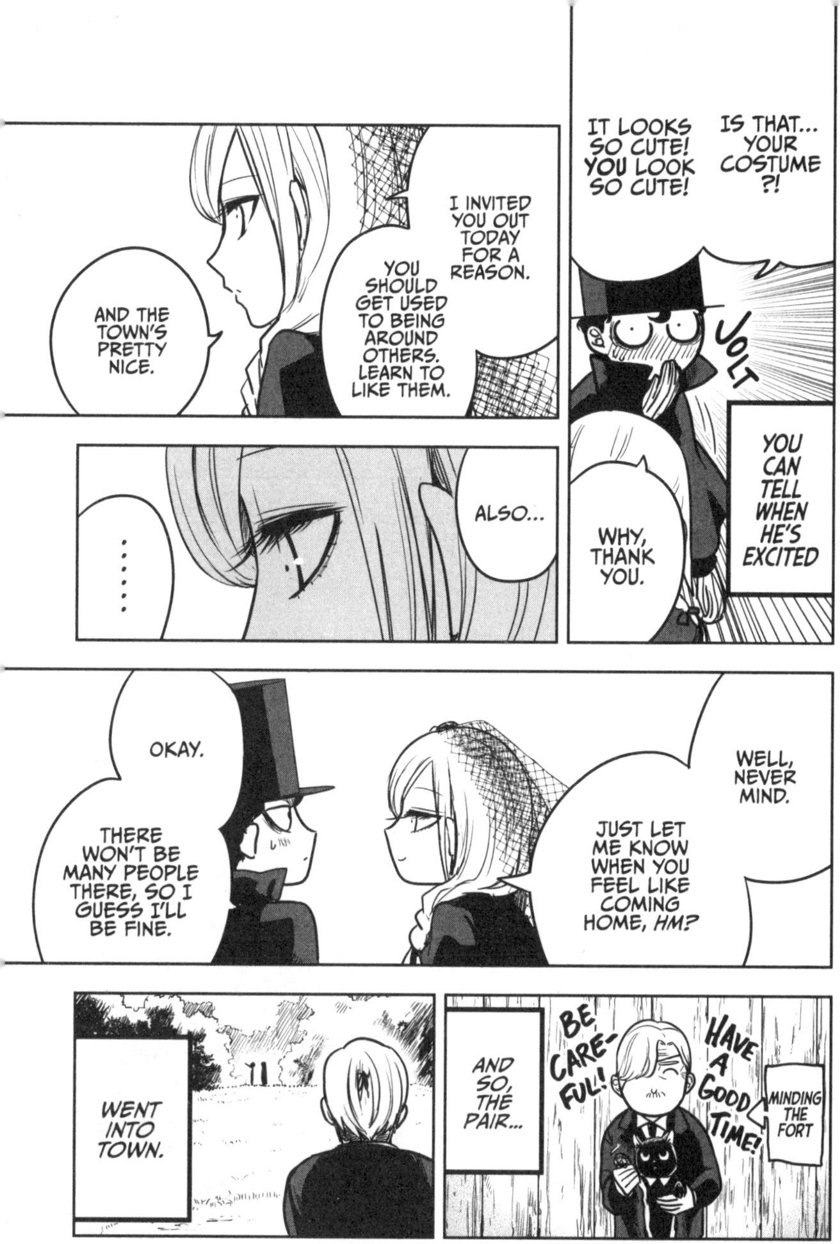
IS THAT... YOUR COSTUME?!
IT LOOKS SO CUTE! YOU LOOK SO CUTE!
JOLT
YOU CAN TELL WHEN HE'S EXCITED
WHY, THANK YOU.
I INVITED YOU OUT TODAY FOR A REASON.
YOU SHOULD GET USED TO BEING AROUND OTHERS. LEARN TO LIKE THEM.
AND THE TOWN'S PRETTY NICE.
ALSO...
......
WELL, NEVER MIND.
JUST LET ME KNOW WHEN YOU FEEL LIKE COMING HOME, HM?
OKAY.
THERE WON'T BE MANY PEOPLE THERE, SO I GUESS I'LL BE FINE.
MINDING THE FORT
HAVE A GOOD TIME!
BE CAREFUL!
AND SO, THE PAIR...
WENT INTO TOWN.

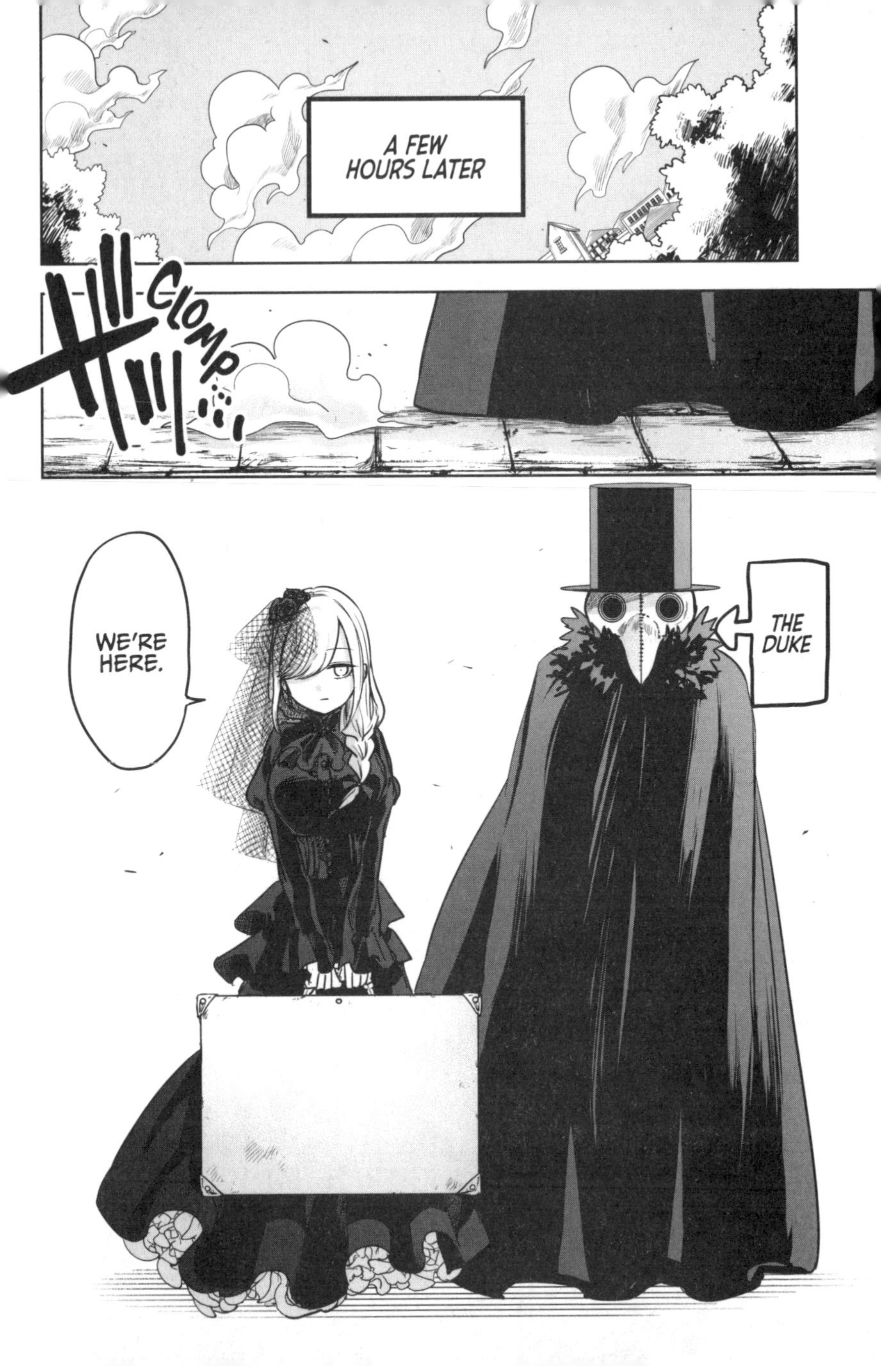
A FEW HOURS LATER
CLOMP
THE DUKE
WE'RE HERE.

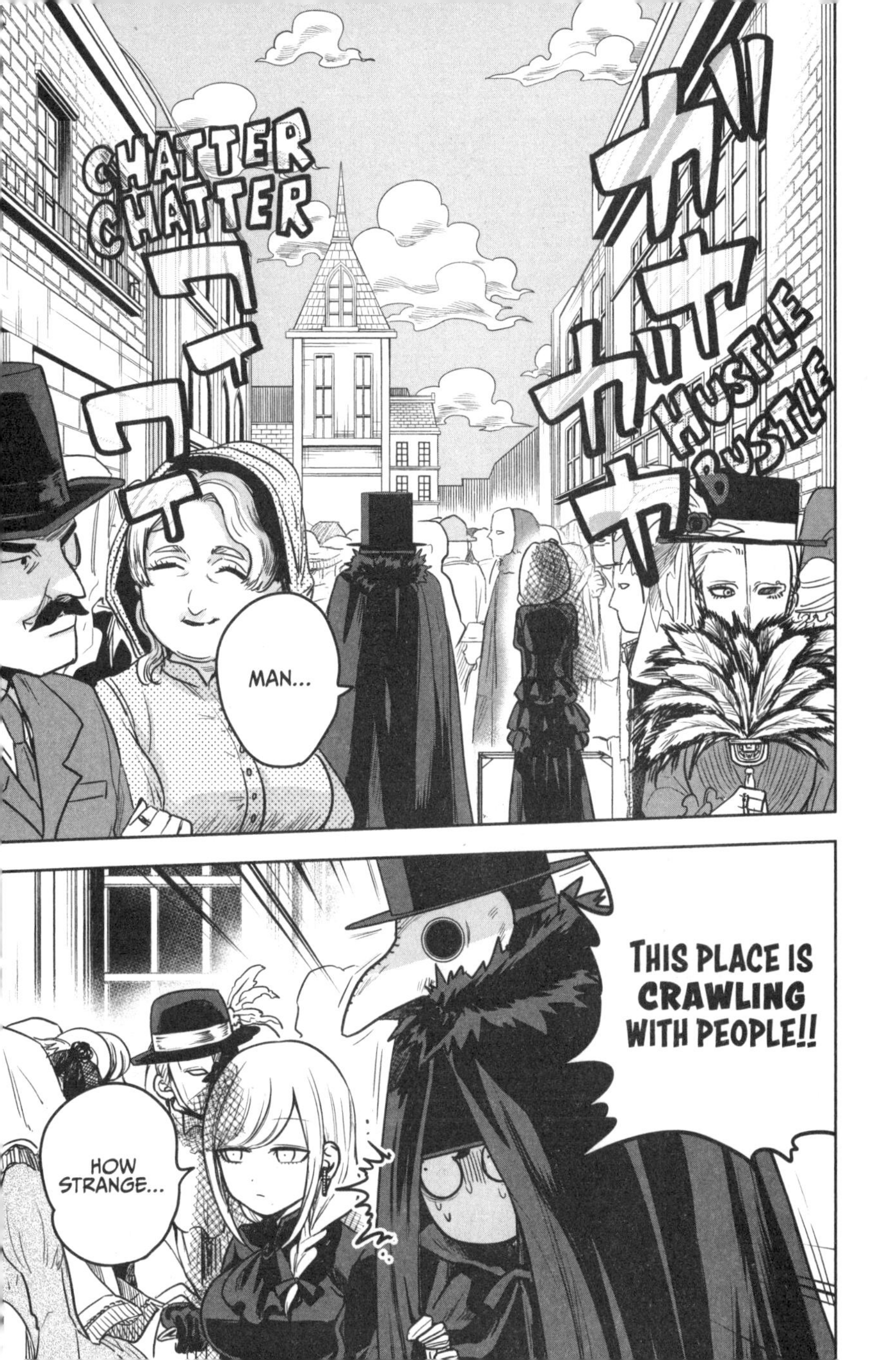
HUSTLE BUSTLE
CHATTER CHATTER
MAN...
THIS PLACE IS CRAWLING WITH PEOPLE!!
HOW STRANGE...

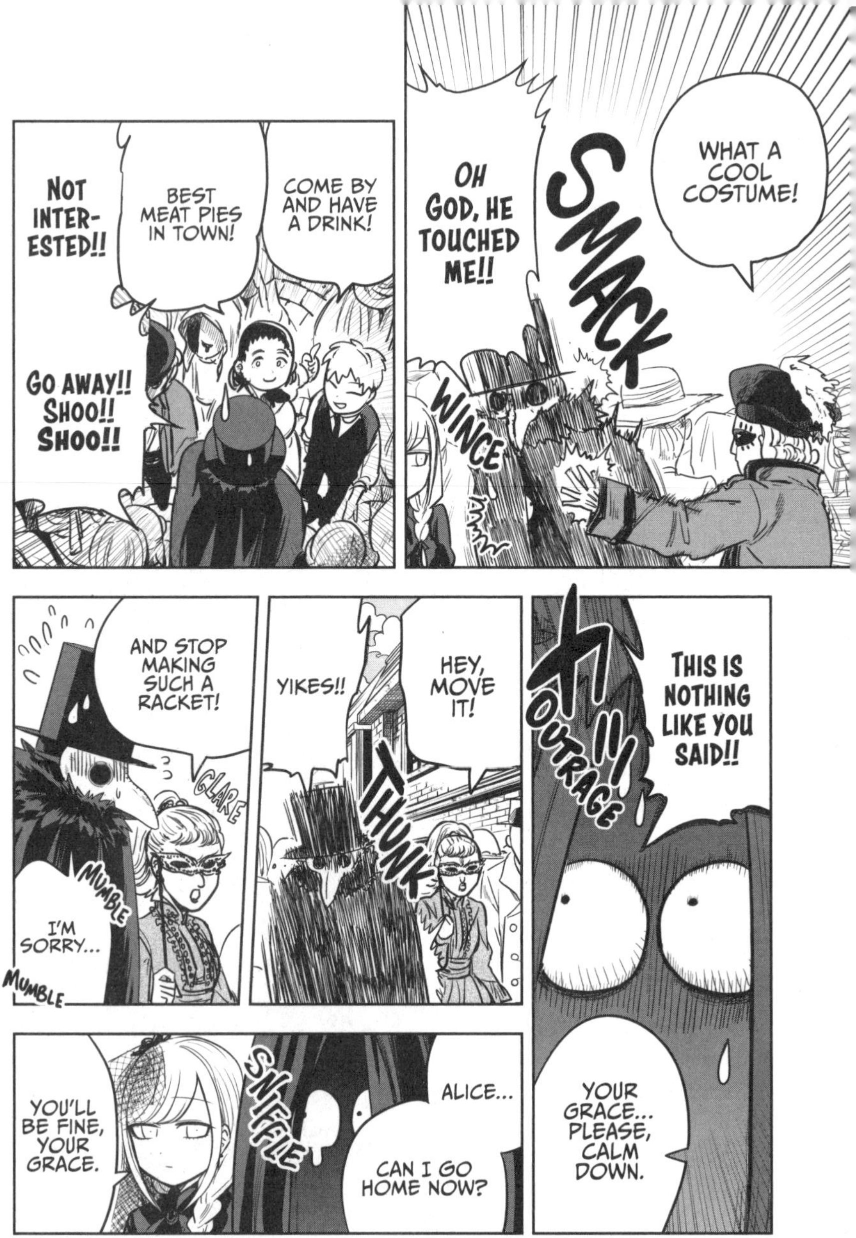
WHAT A COOL COSTUME!
SMACK
OH GOD, HE TOUCHED ME!!
WINCE
COME BY AND HAVE A DRINK!
BEST MEAT PIES IN TOWN!
NOT INTER-ESTED!!
GO AWAY!! SHOO!! SHOO!!
THIS IS NOTHING LIKE YOU SAID!!
OUTRAGE
YOUR GRACE... PLEASE, CALM DOWN.
HEY, MOVE IT!
YIKES!!
THUNK
AND STOP MAKING SUCH A RACKET!
GLARE
MUMBLE
I'M SORRY...
MUMBLE
ALICE...
CAN I GO HOME NOW?
SNIFFLE
YOU'LL BE FINE, YOUR GRACE.

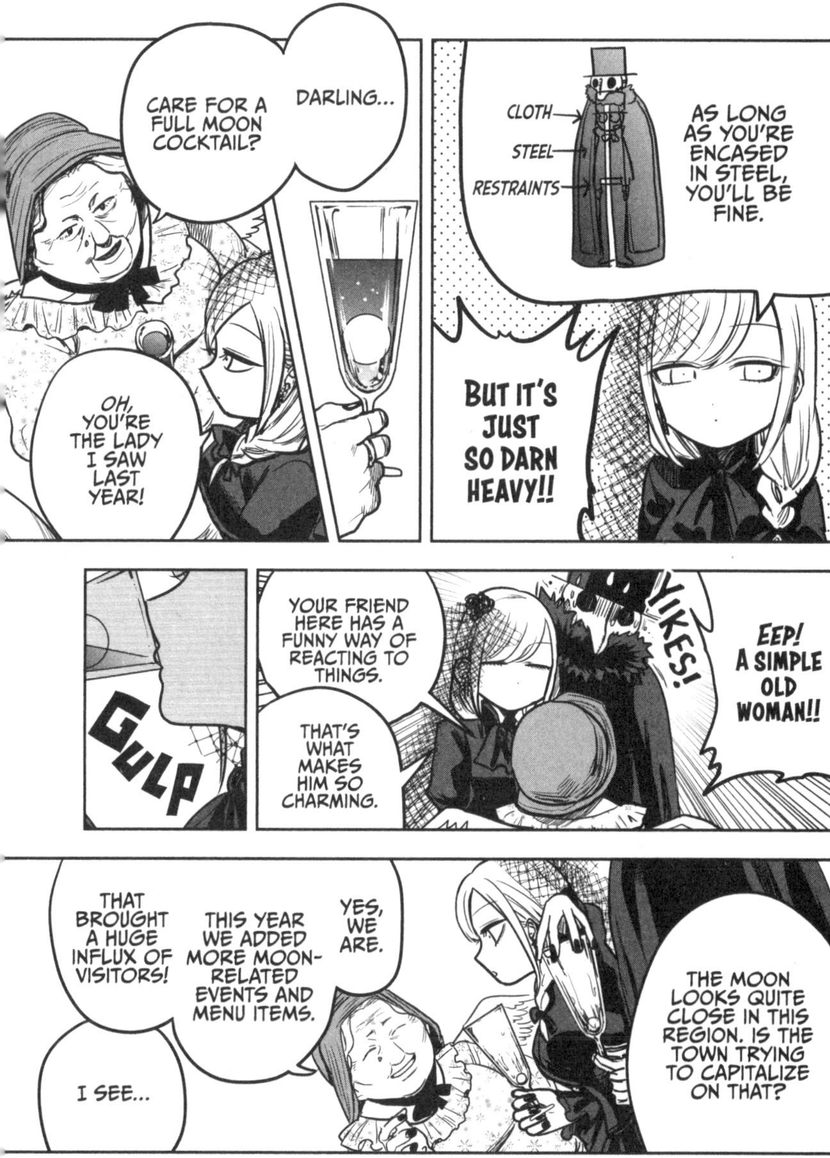
AS LONG AS YOU'RE ENCASED IN STEEL, YOU'LL BE FINE.
CLOTH
STEEL
RESTRAINTS
BUT IT'S JUST SO DARN HEAVY!!
DARLING...
CARE FOR A FULL MOON COCKTAIL?
OH, YOU'RE THE LADY I SAW LAST YEAR!
EEP! A SIMPLE OLD WOMAN!!
YIKES!
YOUR FRIEND HERE HAS A FUNNY WAY OF REACTING TO THINGS.
THAT'S WHAT MAKES HIM SO CHARMING.
GULP
THE MOON LOOKS QUITE CLOSE IN THIS REGION. IS THE TOWN TRYING TO CAPITALIZE ON THAT?
YES, WE ARE.
THIS YEAR WE ADDED MORE MOON-RELATED EVENTS AND MENU ITEMS.
THAT BROUGHT A HUGE INFLUX OF VISITORS!
I SEE...

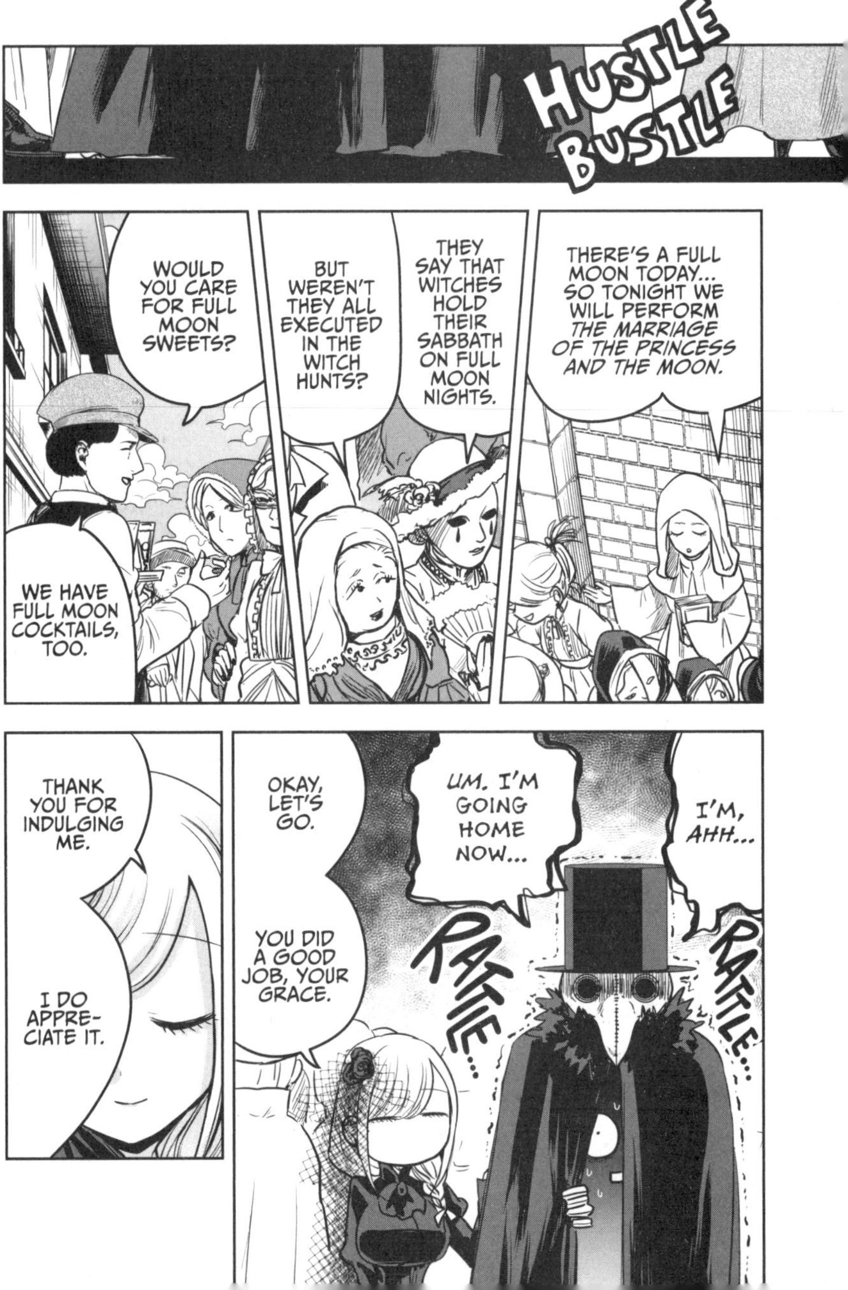
HUSTLE BUSTLE
THERE'S A FULL MOON TODAY... SO TONIGHT WE WILL PERFORM *THE MARRIAGE OF THE PRINCESS AND THE MOON.*
THEY SAY THAT WITCHES HOLD THEIR SABBATH ON FULL MOON NIGHTS.
BUT WEREN'T THEY ALL EXECUTED IN THE WITCH HUNTS?
WOULD YOU CARE FOR FULL MOON SWEETS?
WE HAVE FULL MOON COCKTAILS, TOO.
I'M, AHH...
UM. I'M GOING HOME NOW...
RATTLE...
RATTLE...
OKAY, LET'S GO.
YOU DID A GOOD JOB, YOUR GRACE.
THANK YOU FOR INDULGING ME.
I DO APPRECIATE IT.

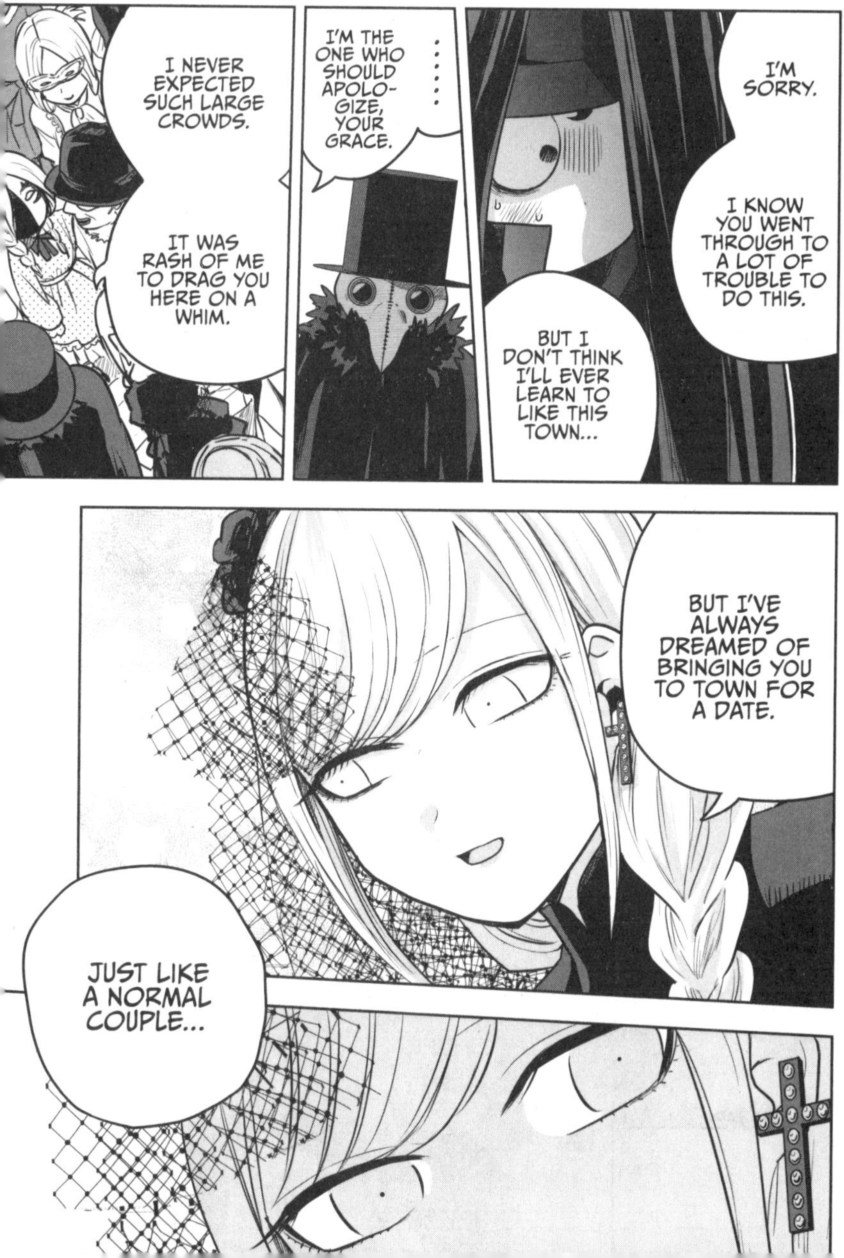
I'M SORRY.
I KNOW YOU WENT THROUGH TO A LOT OF TROUBLE TO DO THIS.
BUT I DON'T THINK I'LL EVER LEARN TO LIKE THIS TOWN...
......
I'M THE ONE WHO SHOULD APOLOGIZE, YOUR GRACE.
I NEVER EXPECTED SUCH LARGE CROWDS.
IT WAS RASH OF ME TO DRAG YOU HERE ON A WHIM.
BUT I'VE ALWAYS DREAMED OF BRINGING YOU TO TOWN FOR A DATE.
JUST LIKE A NORMAL COUPLE...

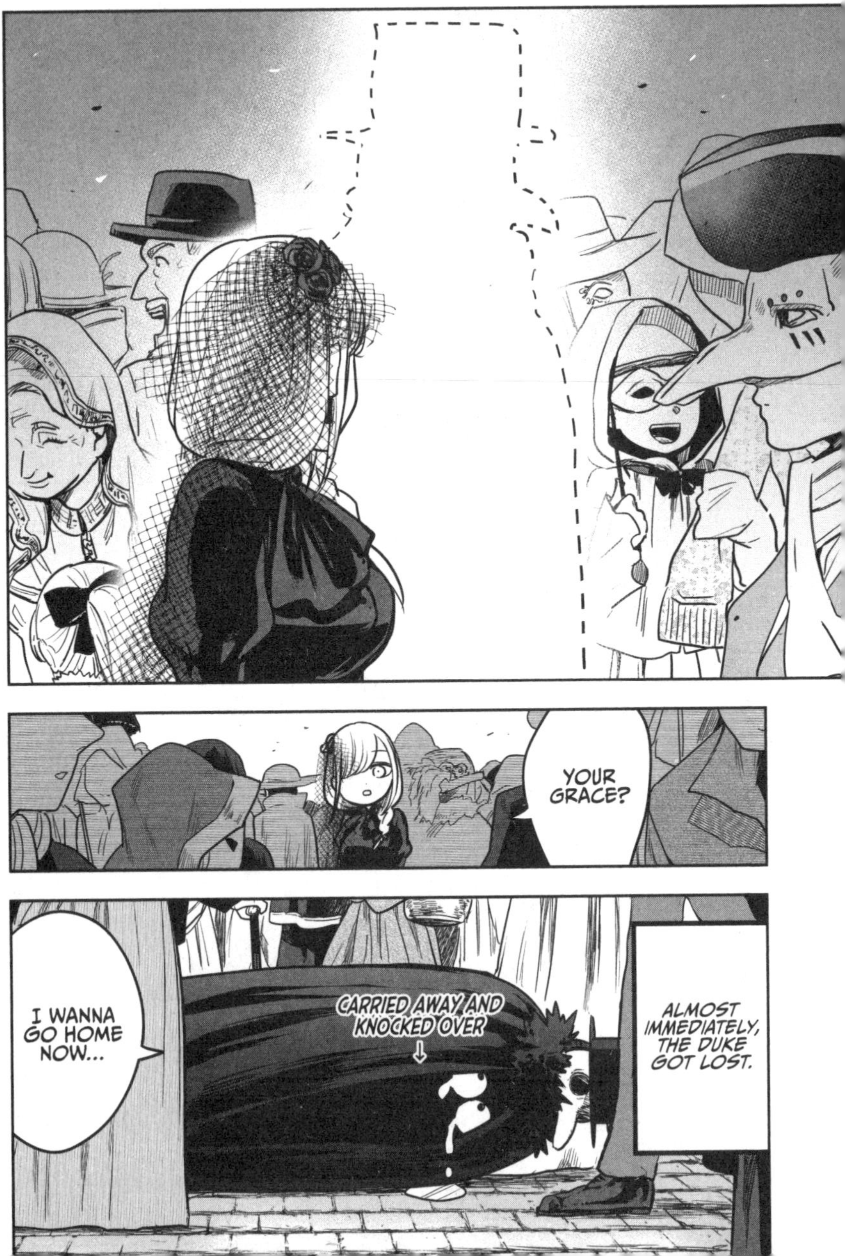
YOUR GRACE?
ALMOST IMMEDIATELY, THE DUKE GOT LOST.
CARRIED AWAY AND KNOCKED OVER
I WANNA GO HOME NOW...

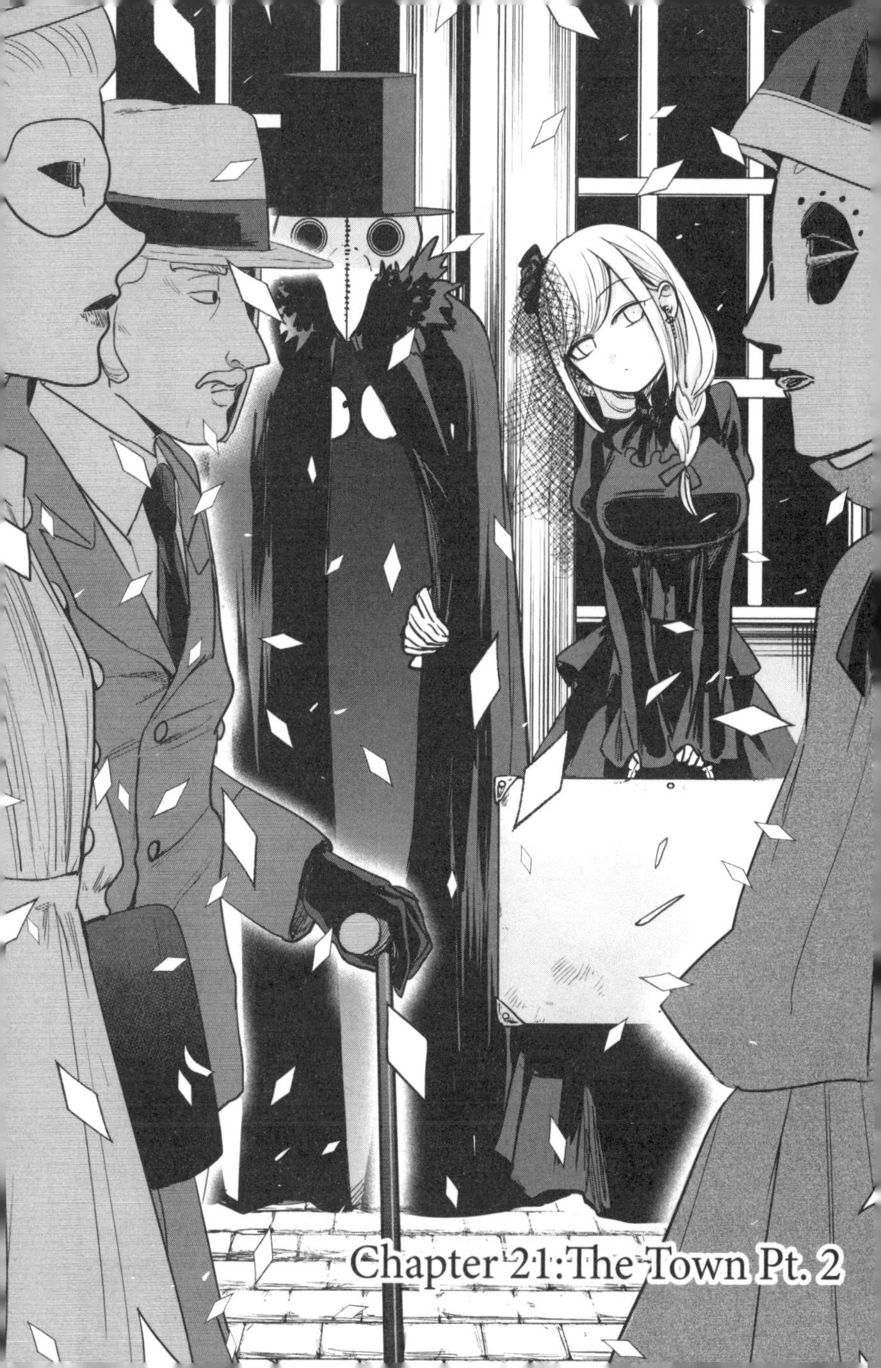
Chapter 21: The Town Pt. 2

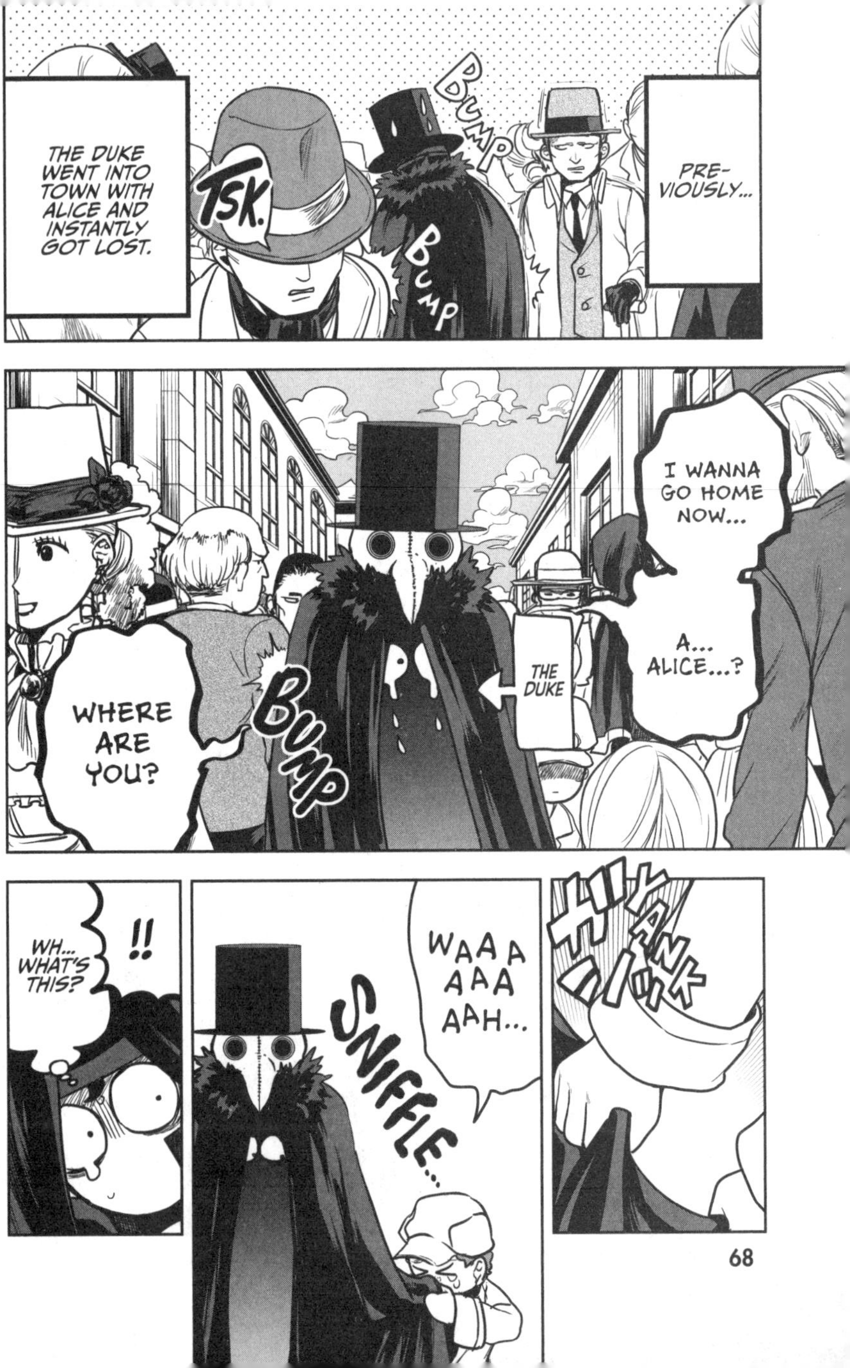

PRE-VIOUSLY...
BUMP
BUMP
TSK.
THE DUKE WENT INTO TOWN WITH ALICE AND INSTANTLY GOT LOST.
I WANNA GO HOME NOW...
A... ALICE...?
THE DUKE
BUMP
WHERE ARE YOU?
YANK
WAAA AAA AAH...
SNIFFLE...
!!
WH... WHAT'S THIS?

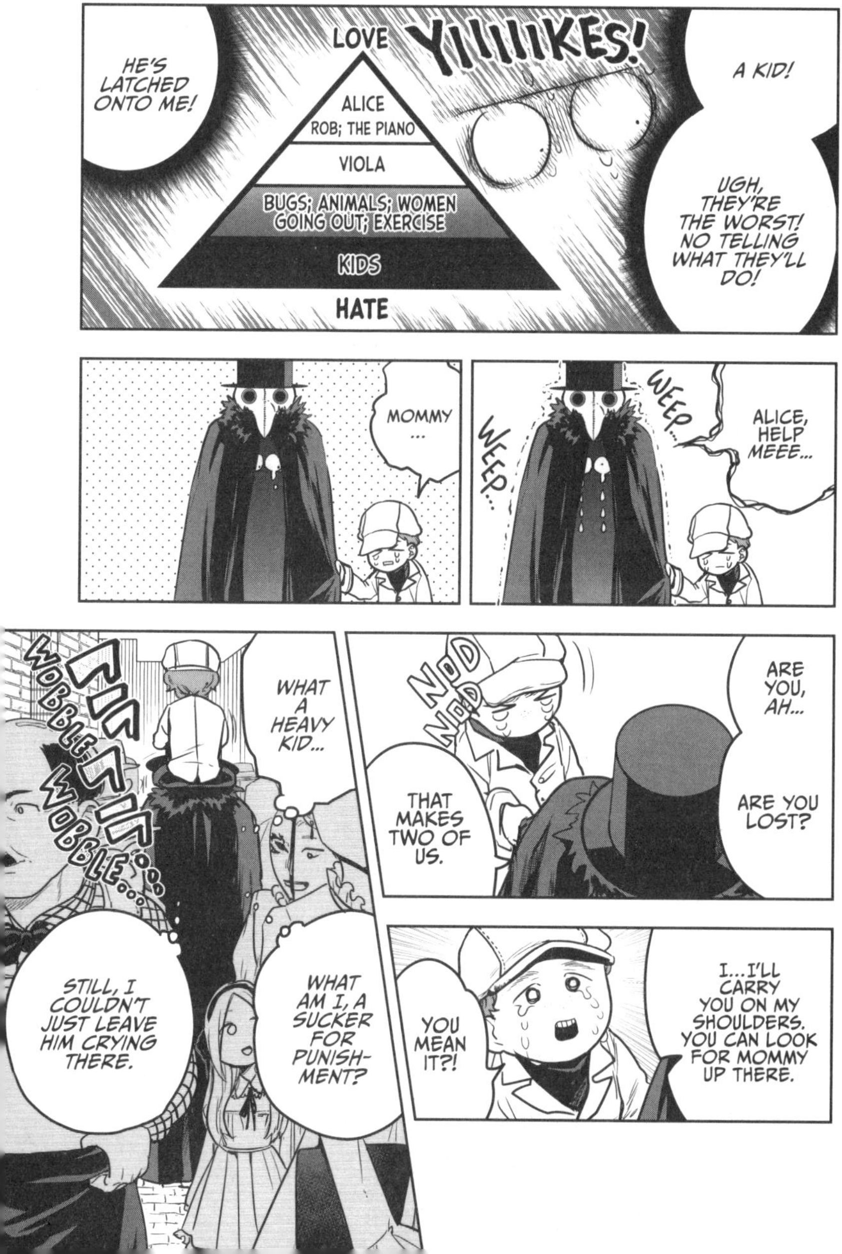
A KID!
UGH, THEY'RE THE WORST! NO TELLING WHAT THEY'LL DO!
YIIIIIKES!
LOVE
ALICE
ROB; THE PIANO
VIOLA
BUGS; ANIMALS; WOMEN GOING OUT; EXERCISE
KIDS
HATE
HE'S LATCHED ONTO ME!
ALICE, HELP MEEE...
WEEP...
WEEP...
MOMMY ...
ARE YOU, AH...
ARE YOU LOST?
NOD NOD
THAT MAKES TWO OF US.
I...I'LL CARRY YOU ON MY SHOULDERS. YOU CAN LOOK FOR MOMMY UP THERE.
YOU MEAN IT?!
WHAT A HEAVY KID...
WOBBLE WOBBLE...
WHAT AM I, A SUCKER FOR PUNISH-MENT?
STILL, I COULDN'T JUST LEAVE HIM CRYING THERE.

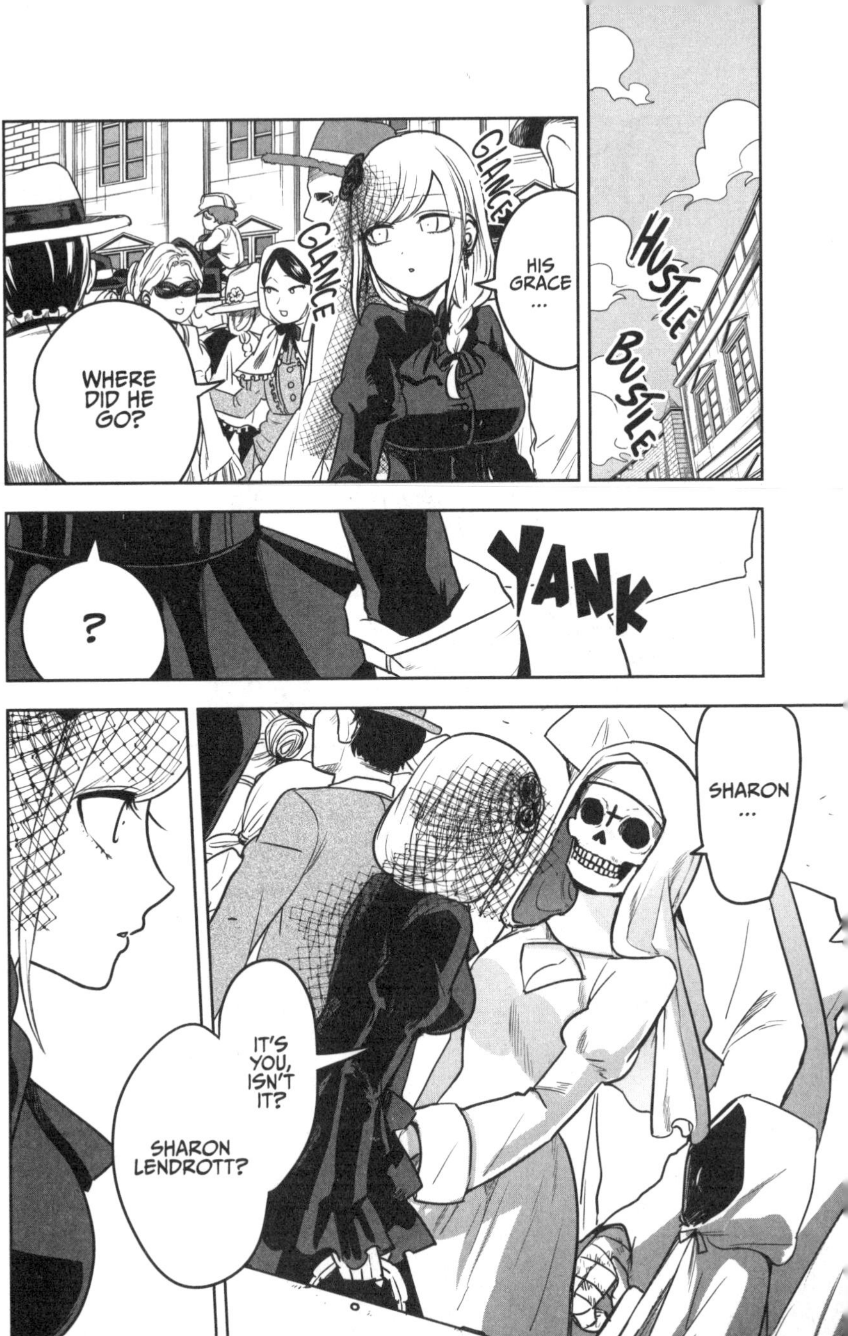
HUSTLE
BUSTLE
GLANCE
GLANCE
HIS GRACE ...
WHERE DID HE GO?
YANK
?
SHARON ...
IT'S YOU, ISN'T IT?
SHARON LENDROTT?

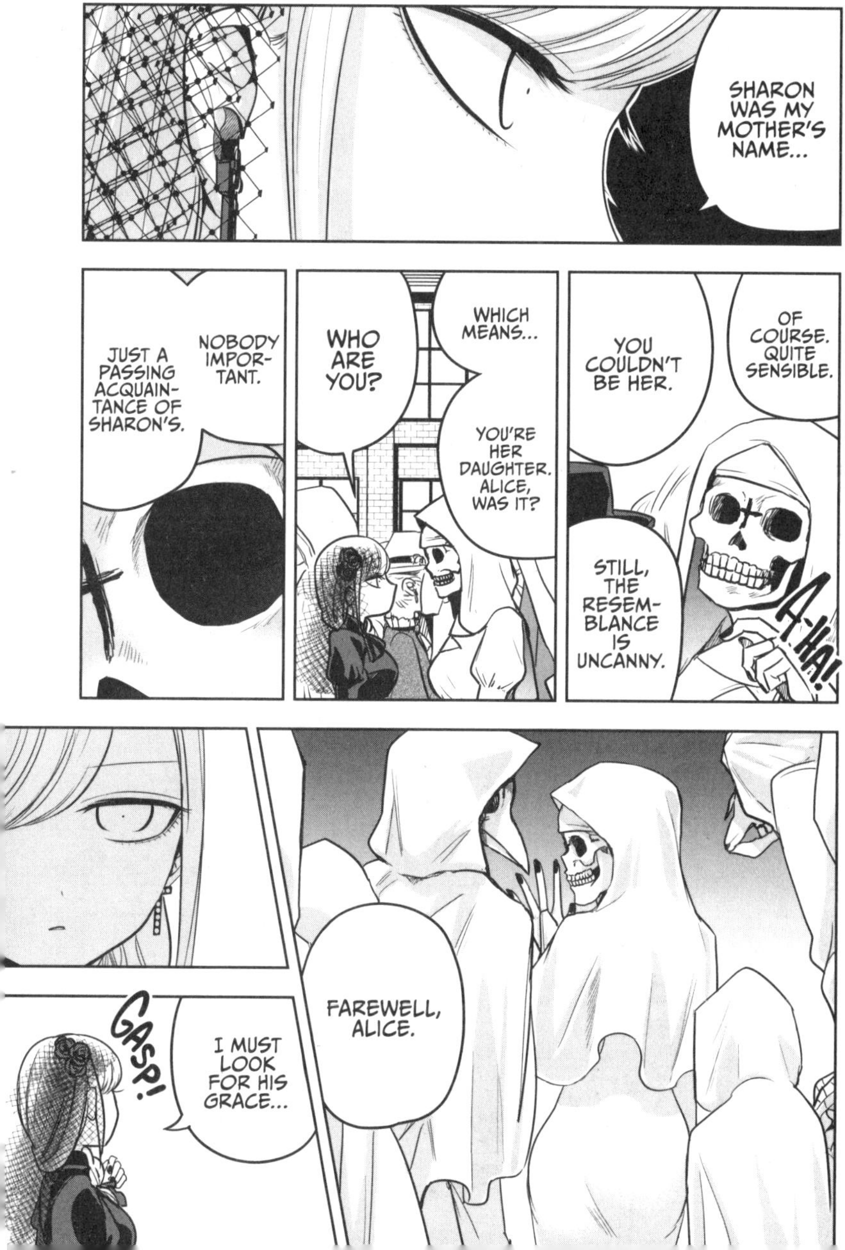
SHARON WAS MY MOTHER'S NAME...
OF COURSE. QUITE SENSIBLE.
YOU COULDN'T BE HER.
STILL, THE RESEMBLANCE IS UNCANNY.
A-HA!
WHICH MEANS...
YOU'RE HER DAUGHTER. ALICE, WAS IT?
WHO ARE YOU?
NOBODY IMPORTANT.
JUST A PASSING ACQUAINTANCE OF SHARON'S.
FAREWELL, ALICE.
I MUST LOOK FOR HIS GRACE...
GASP!

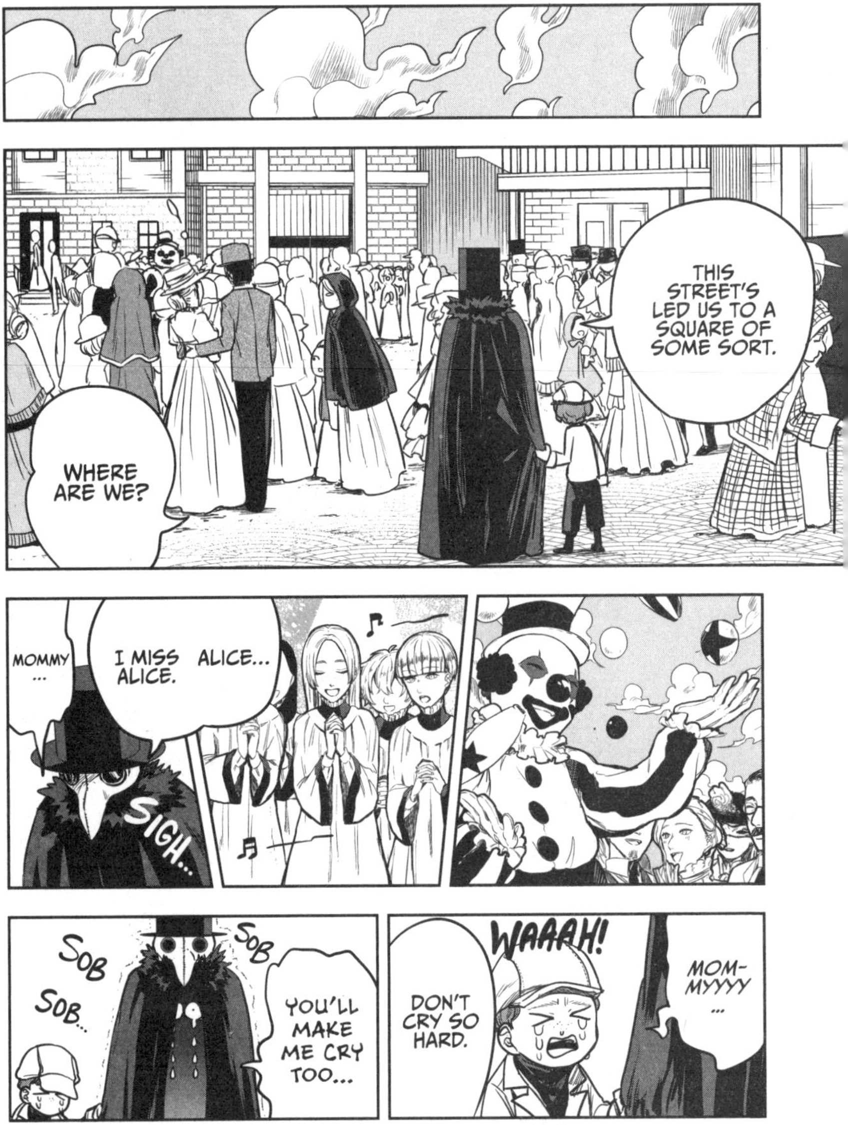
THIS STREET'S LED US TO A SQUARE OF SOME SORT.
WHERE ARE WE?
ALICE...
I MISS ALICE.
MOMMY ...
SIGH...
WAAAH!
MOM-MYYYY ...
DON'T CRY SO HARD.
SOB
YOU'LL MAKE ME CRY TOO...
SOB
SOB...

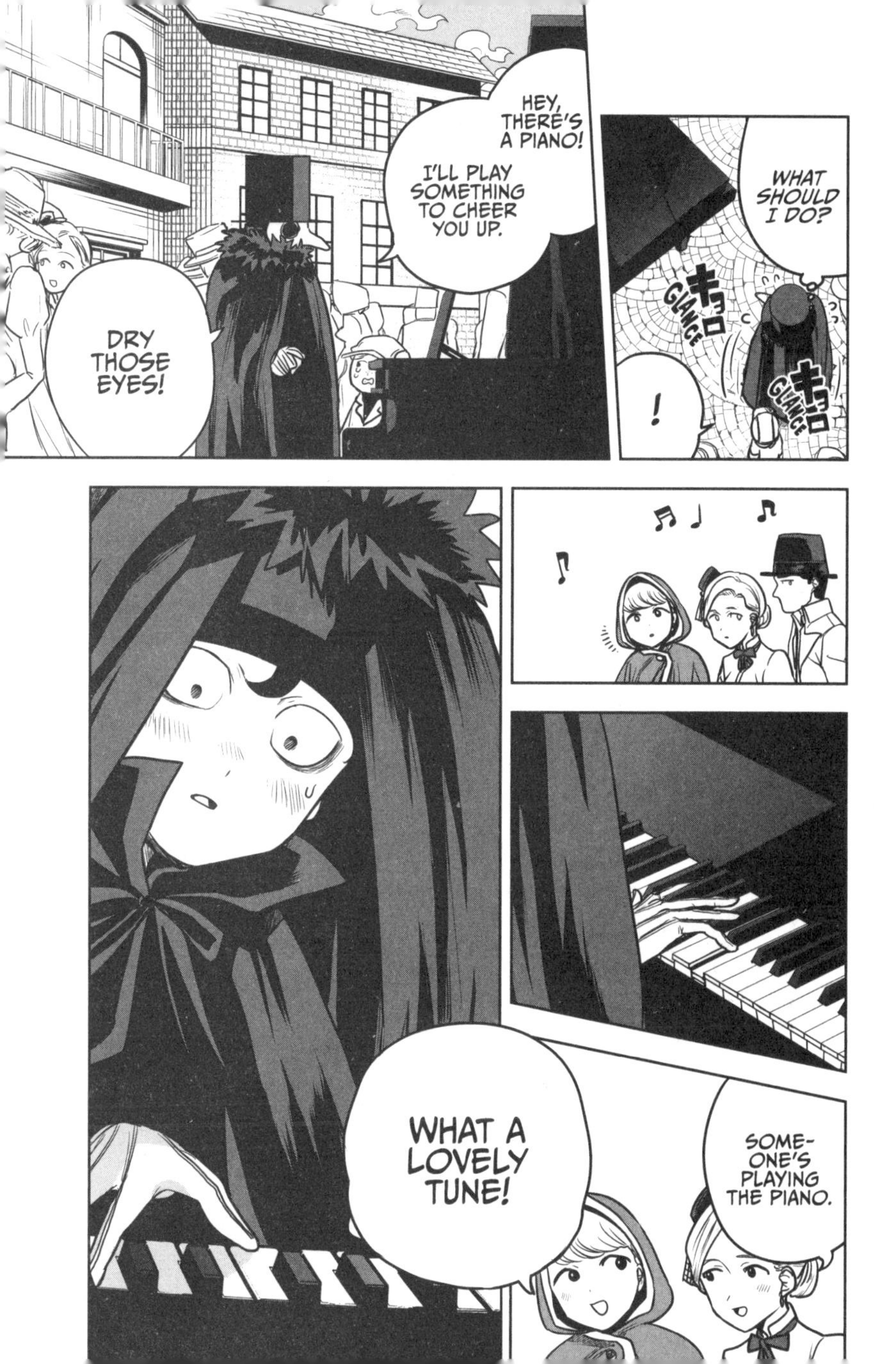
WHAT SHOULD I DO?
キョロ GLANCE
キョロ GLANCE
!
HEY, THERE'S A PIANO!
I'LL PLAY SOMETHING TO CHEER YOU UP.
DRY THOSE EYES!
SOME-ONE'S PLAYING THE PIANO.
WHAT A LOVELY TUNE!

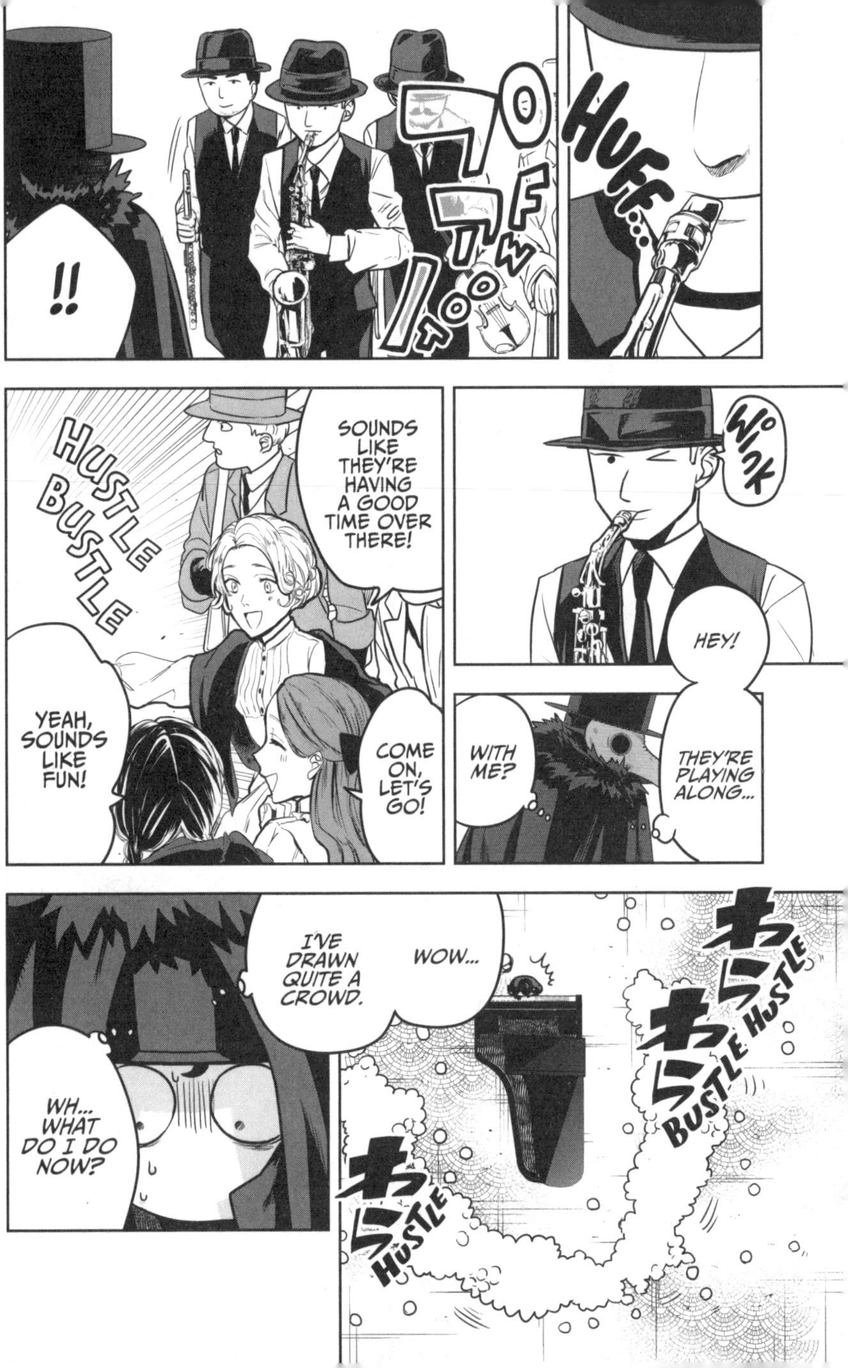
HUFF...
!!
WINK
HEY!
THEY'RE PLAYING ALONG...
WITH ME?
SOUNDS LIKE THEY'RE HAVING A GOOD TIME OVER THERE!
HUSTLE BUSTLE
COME ON, LET'S GO!
YEAH, SOUNDS LIKE FUN!
わら
BUSTLE HUSTLE
WOW...
I'VE DRAWN QUITE A CROWD.
わら
HUSTLE
WH... WHAT DO I DO NOW?

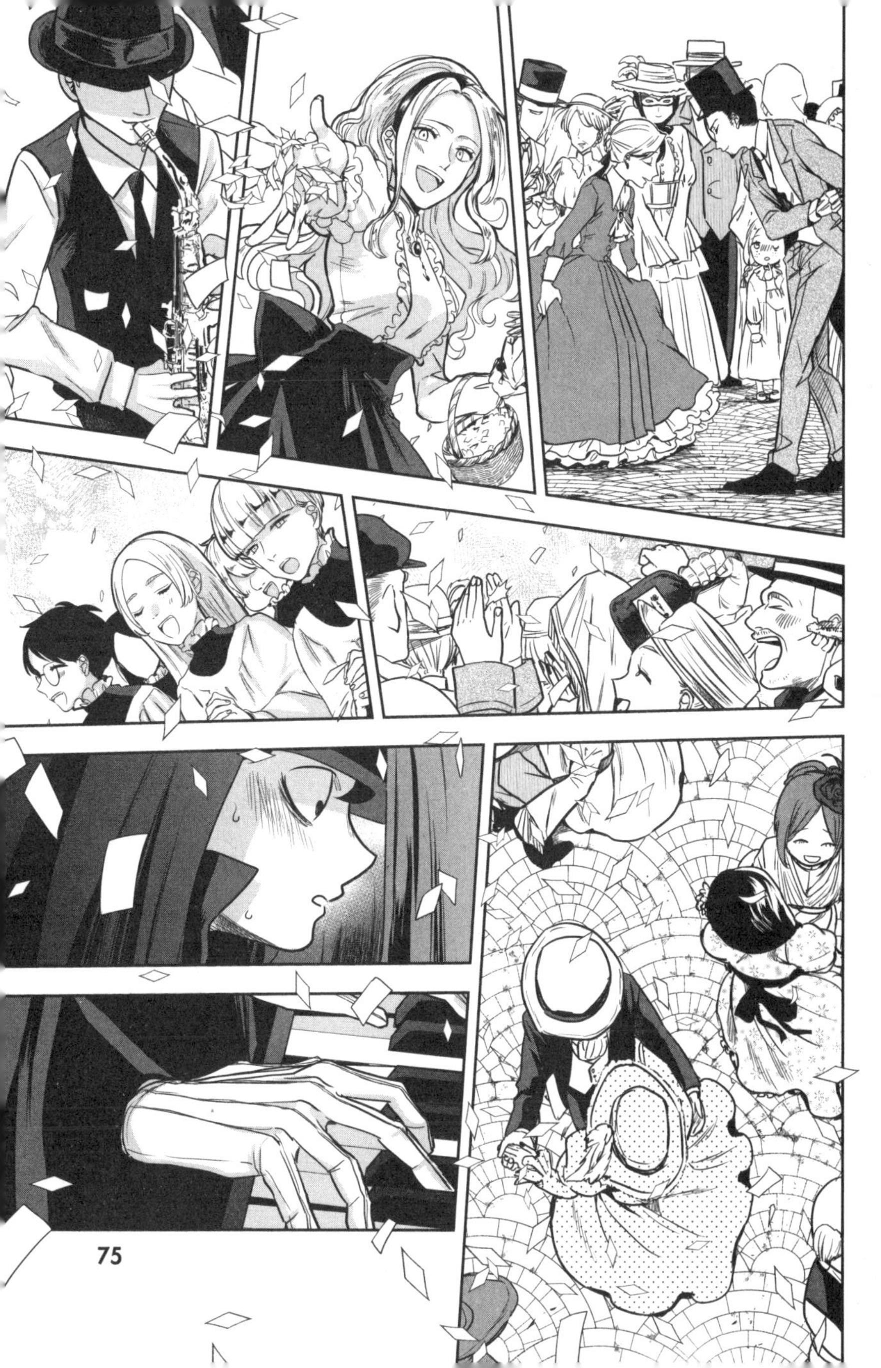

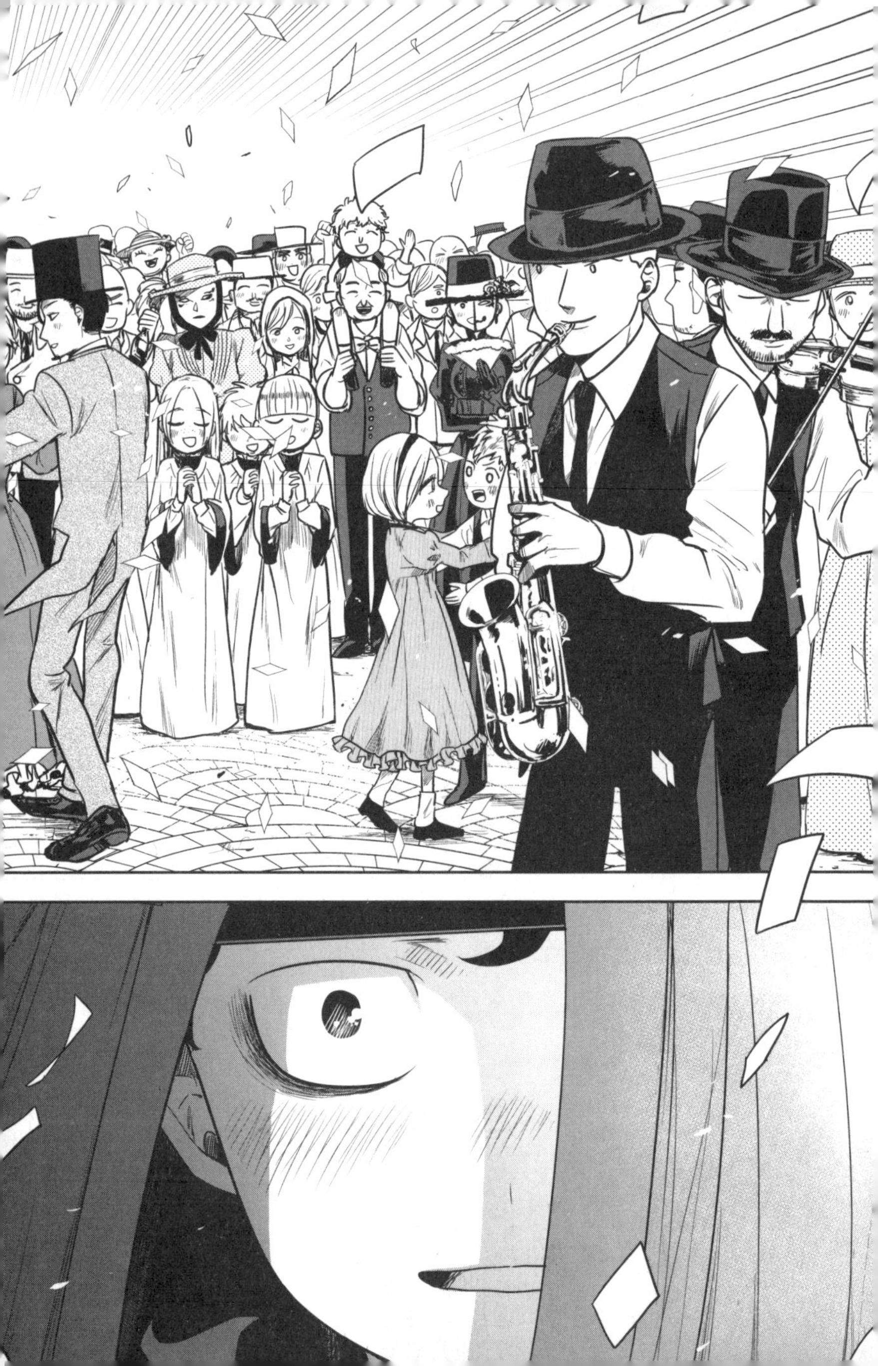

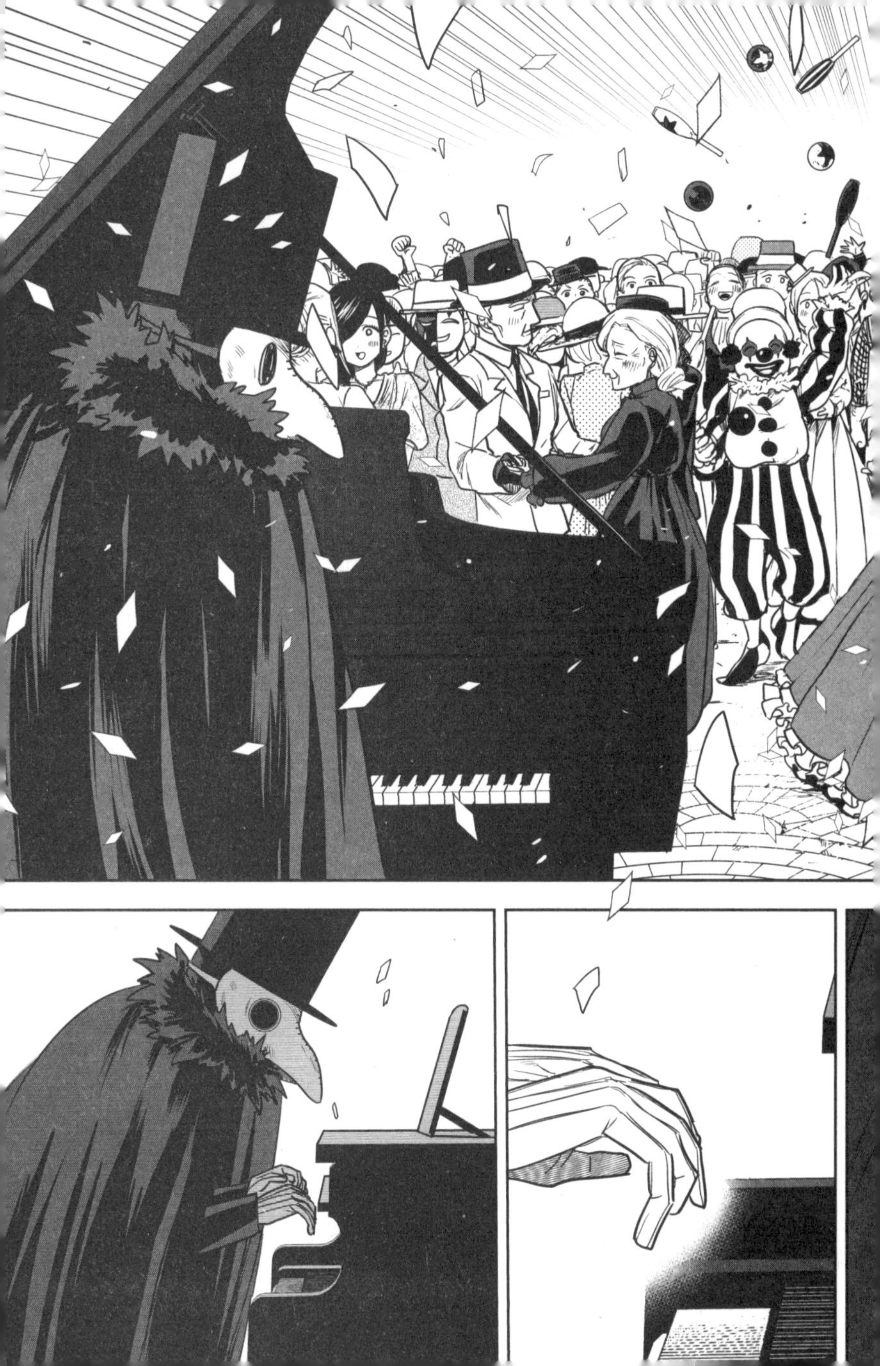

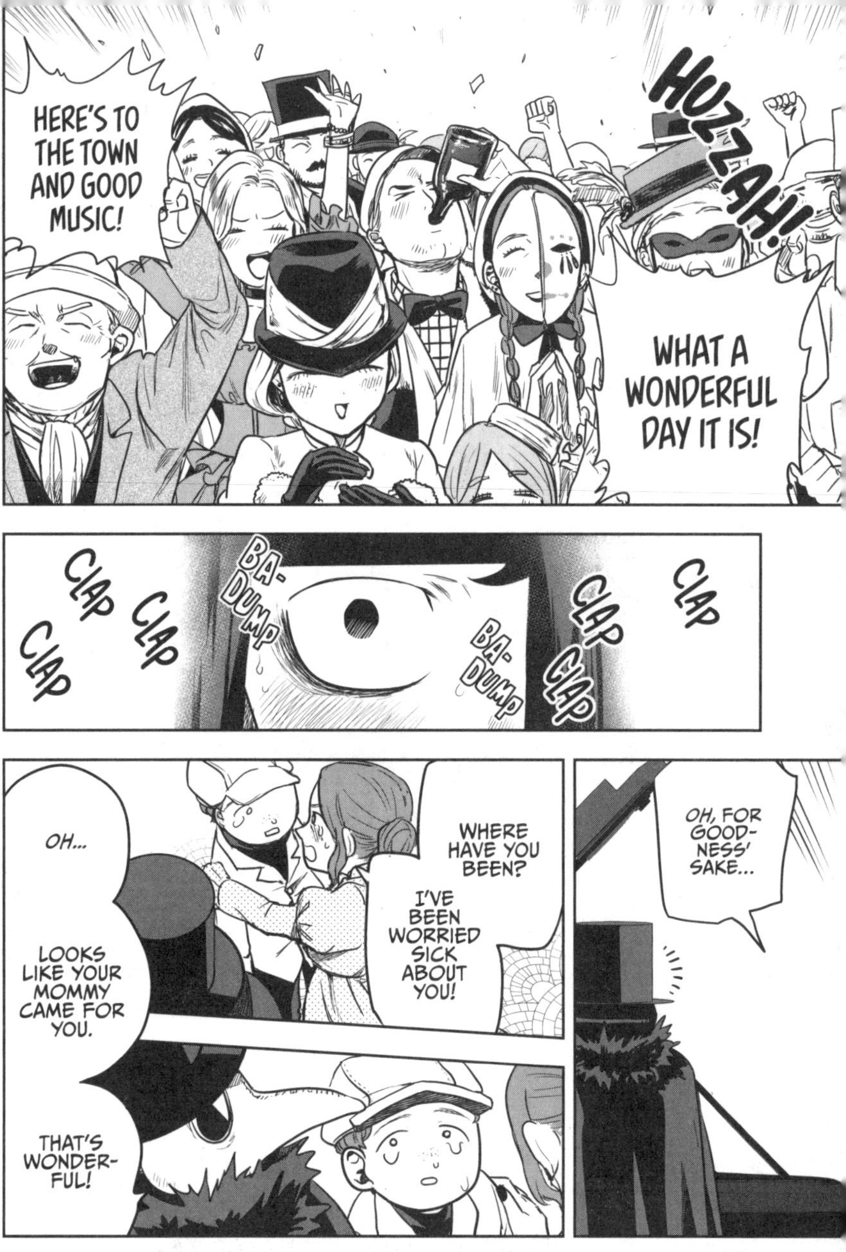
HUZZAH!
WHAT A WONDERFUL DAY IT IS!
HERE'S TO THE TOWN AND GOOD MUSIC!
CLAP CLAP CLAP
BA-DUMP
BA-DUMP
CLAP CLAP CLAP
OH, FOR GOODNESS' SAKE...
WHERE HAVE YOU BEEN?
I'VE BEEN WORRIED SICK ABOUT YOU!
OH...
LOOKS LIKE YOUR MOMMY CAME FOR YOU.
THAT'S WONDERFUL!

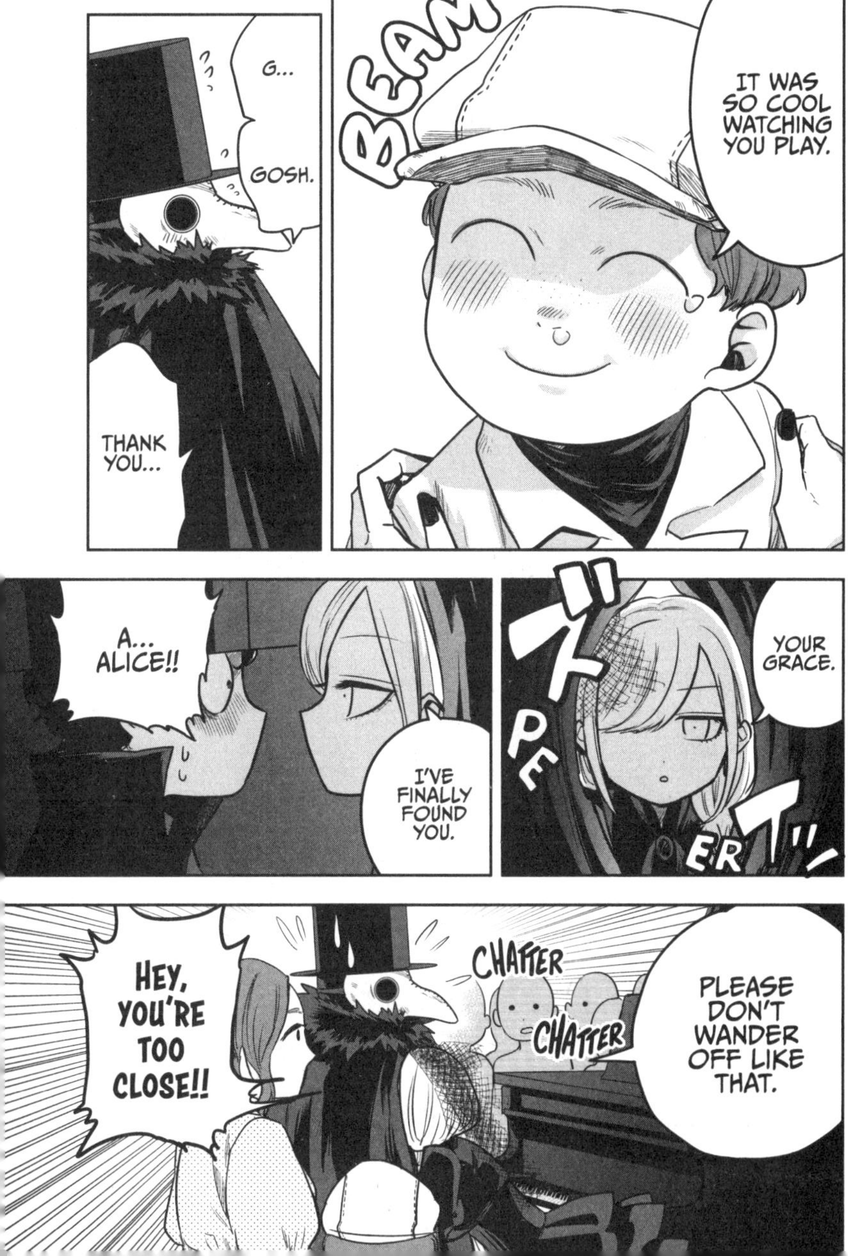
BEAM
IT WAS SO COOL WATCHING YOU PLAY.
G...
GOSH.
THANK YOU...
YOUR GRACE.
PE
ER
A... ALICE!!
I'VE FINALLY FOUND YOU.
PLEASE DON'T WANDER OFF LIKE THAT.
CHATTER
CHATTER
HEY, YOU'RE TOO CLOSE!!

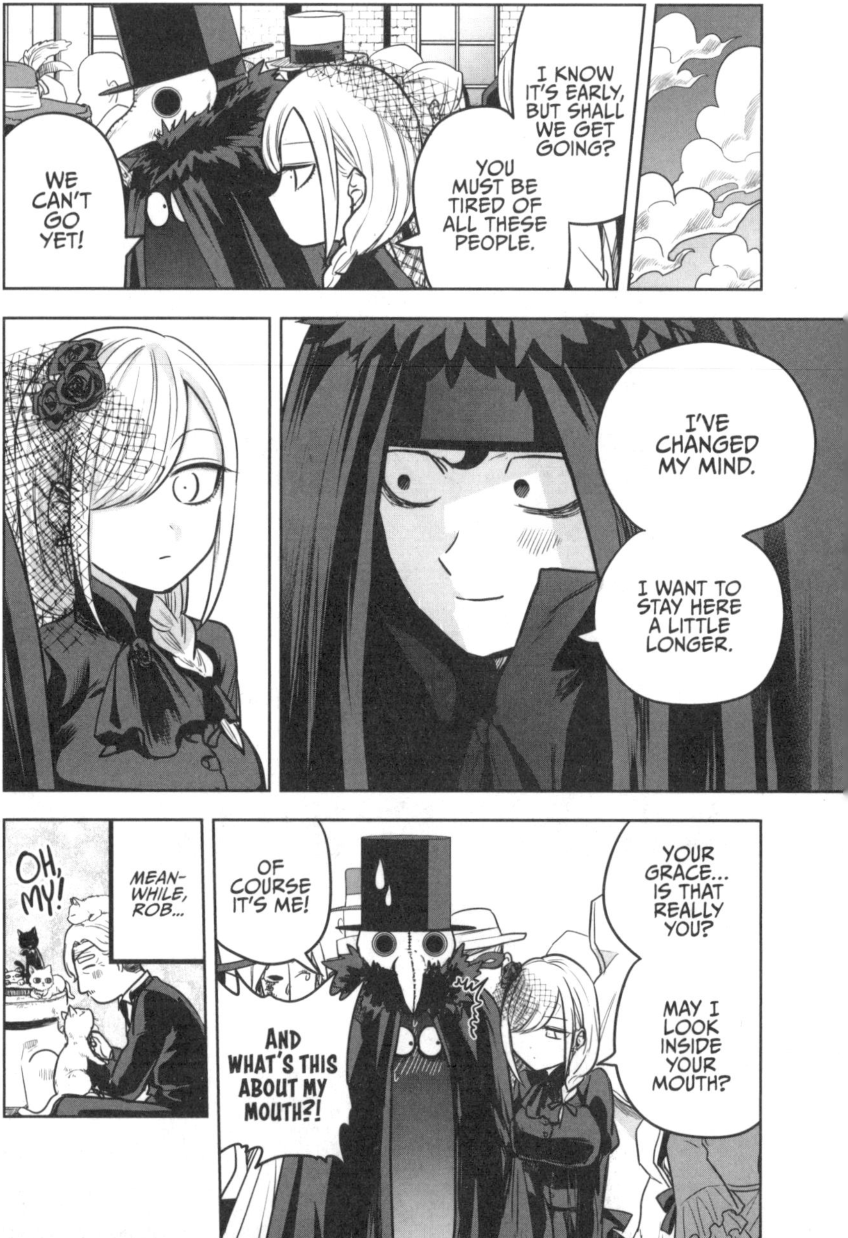
I KNOW IT'S EARLY, BUT SHALL WE GET GOING?
YOU MUST BE TIRED OF ALL THESE PEOPLE.
WE CAN'T GO YET!
I'VE CHANGED MY MIND.
I WANT TO STAY HERE A LITTLE LONGER.
YOUR GRACE... IS THAT REALLY YOU?
MAY I LOOK INSIDE YOUR MOUTH?
OF COURSE IT'S ME!
AND WHAT'S THIS ABOUT MY MOUTH?!
MEAN-WHILE, ROB...
OH, MY!

Chapter 22: The Town Pt. 3

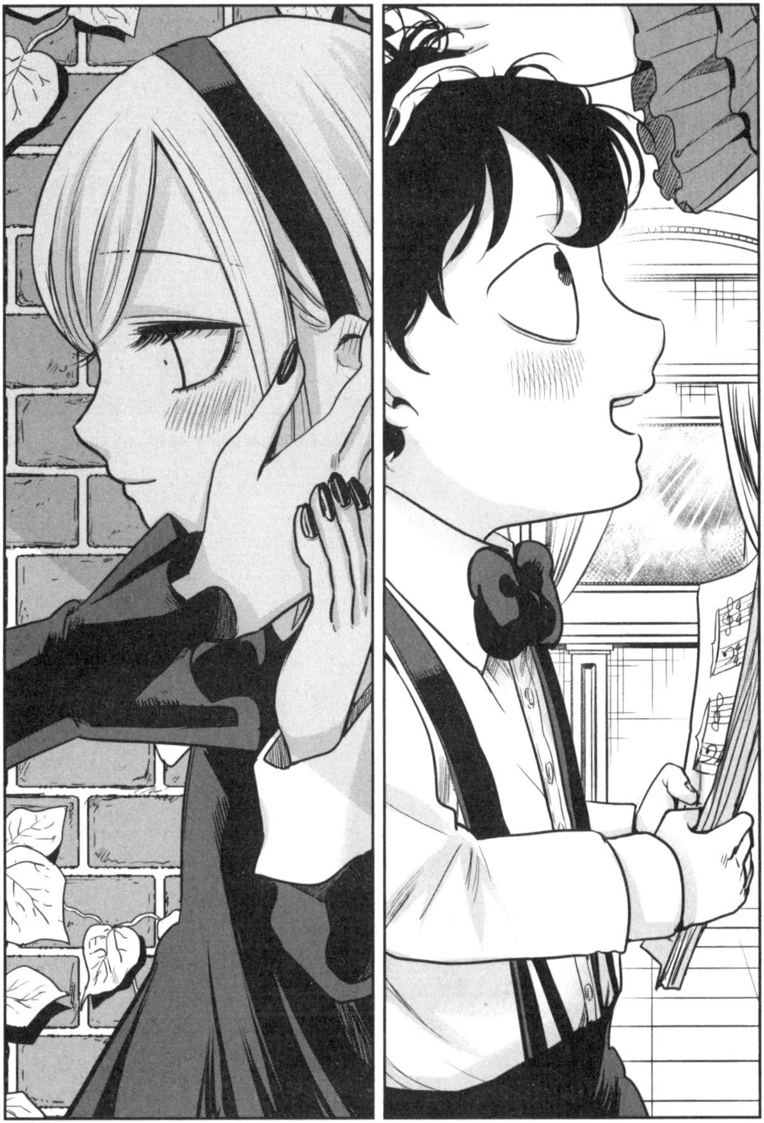

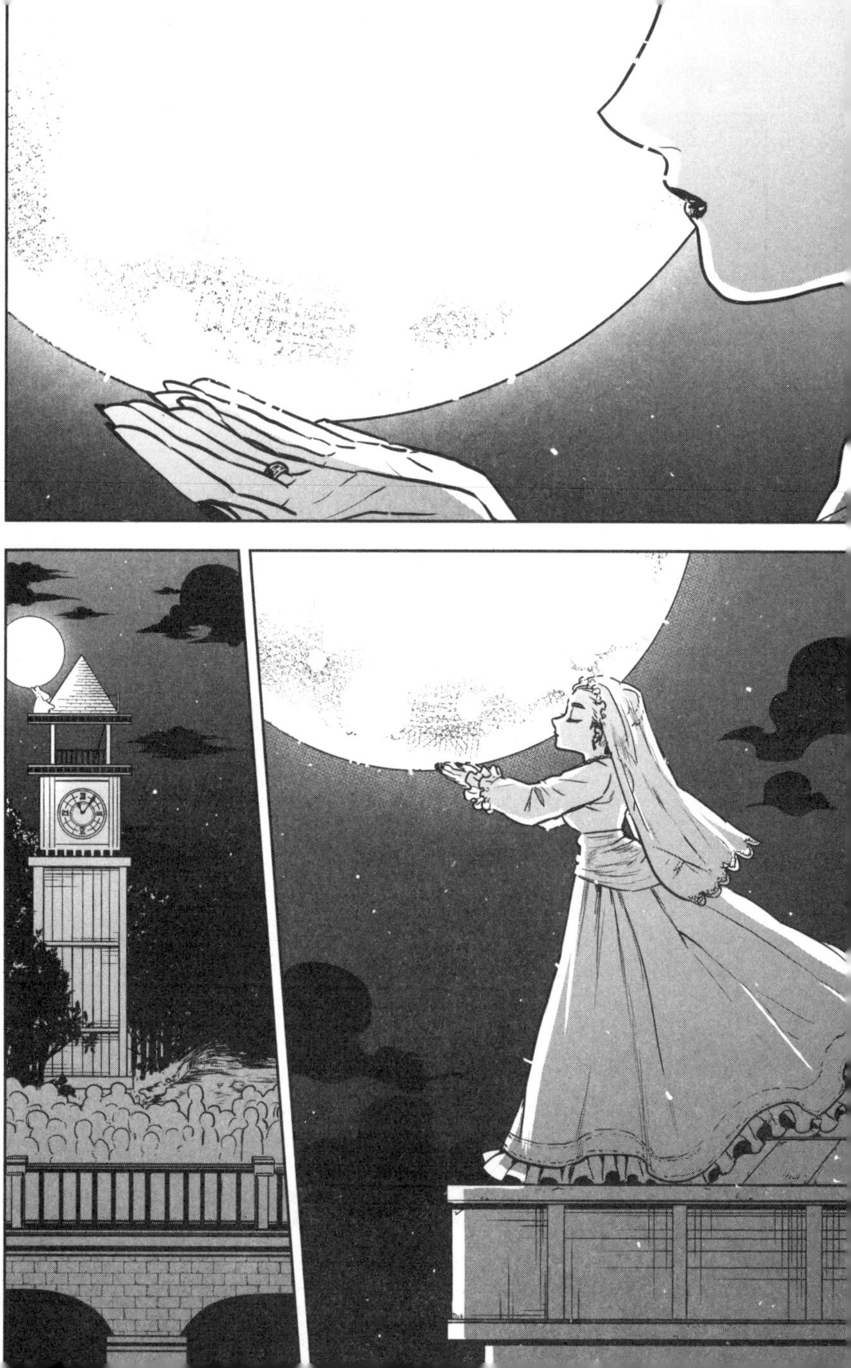

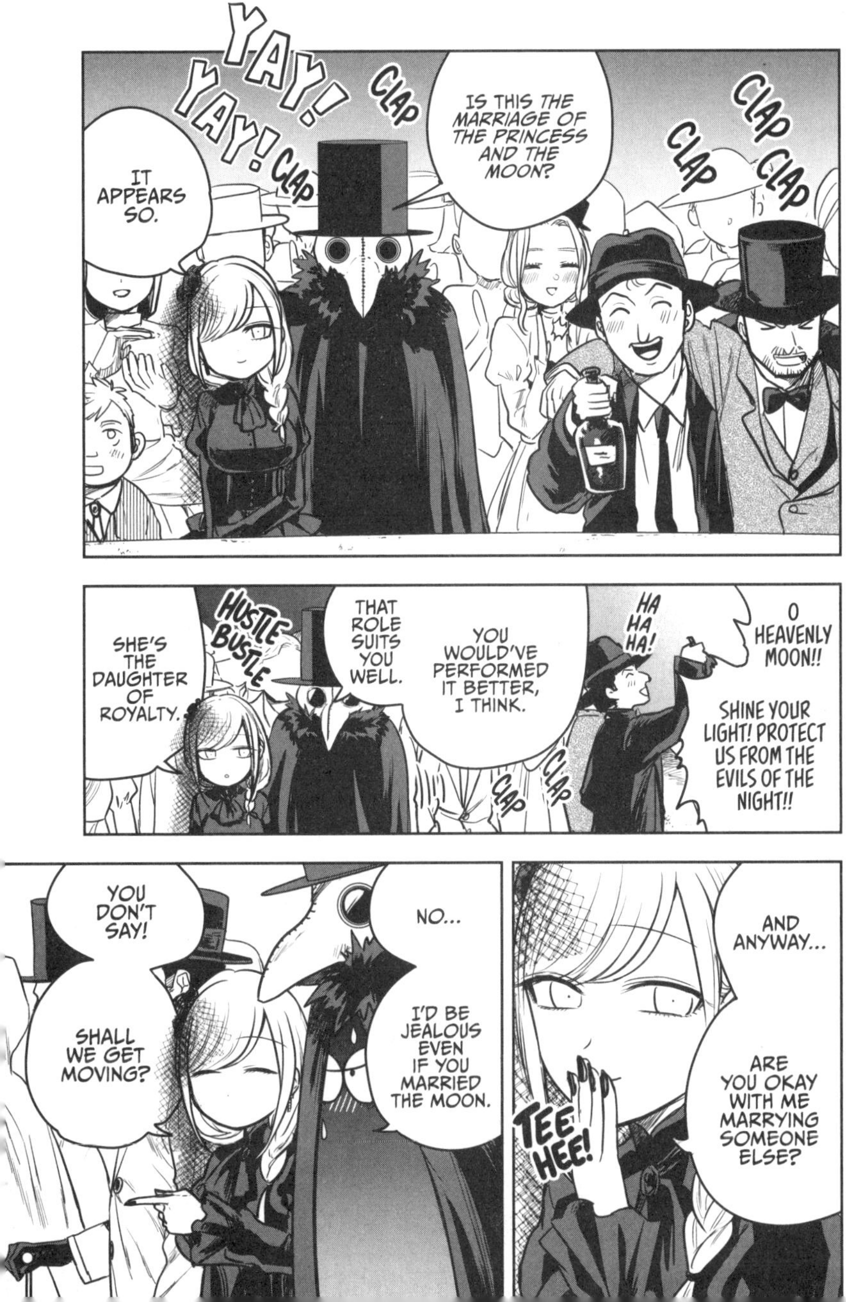
CLAP CLAP
CLAP
IS THIS THE MARRIAGE OF THE PRINCESS AND THE MOON?
CLAP
YAY! YAY!
CLAP
IT APPEARS SO.
O HEAVENLY MOON!!
SHINE YOUR LIGHT! PROTECT US FROM THE EVILS OF THE NIGHT!!
HA HA HA!
CLAP CLAP
THAT ROLE SUITS YOU WELL.
YOU WOULD'VE PERFORMED IT BETTER, I THINK.
HUSTLE BUSTLE
SHE'S THE DAUGHTER OF ROYALTY.
AND ANYWAY...
ARE YOU OKAY WITH ME MARRYING SOMEONE ELSE?
TEE HEE!
NO...
I'D BE JEALOUS EVEN IF YOU MARRIED THE MOON.
YOU DON'T SAY!
SHALL WE GET MOVING?

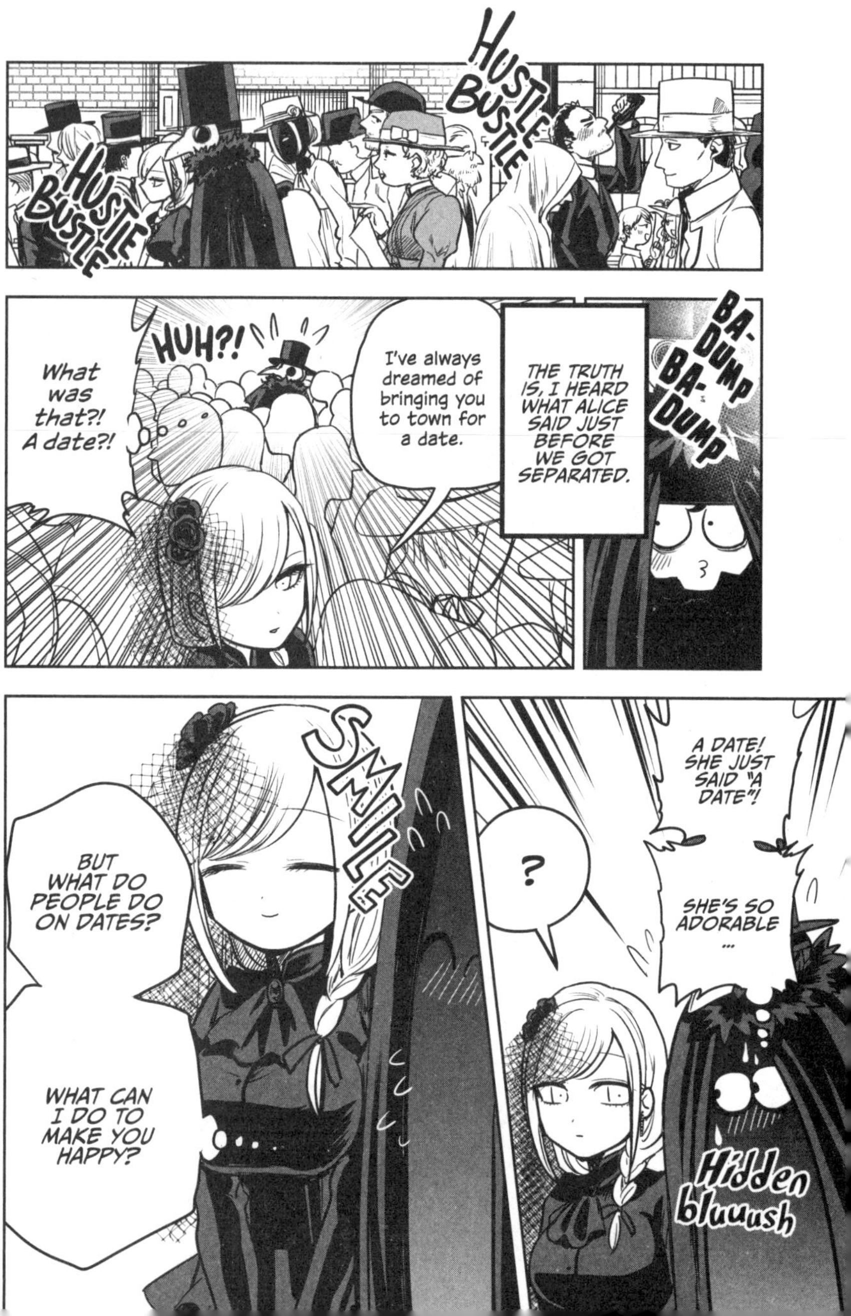
HUSTLE BUSTLE
HUSTLE BUSTLE
BA-DUMP BA-DUMP
THE TRUTH IS, I HEARD WHAT ALICE SAID JUST BEFORE WE GOT SEPARATED.
I've always dreamed of bringing you to town for a date.
HUH?!
What was that?! A date?!
A DATE! SHE JUST SAID "A DATE"!
SHE'S SO ADORABLE ...
?
Hidden bluuush
SMILE
BUT WHAT DO PEOPLE DO ON DATES?
WHAT CAN I DO TO MAKE YOU HAPPY?

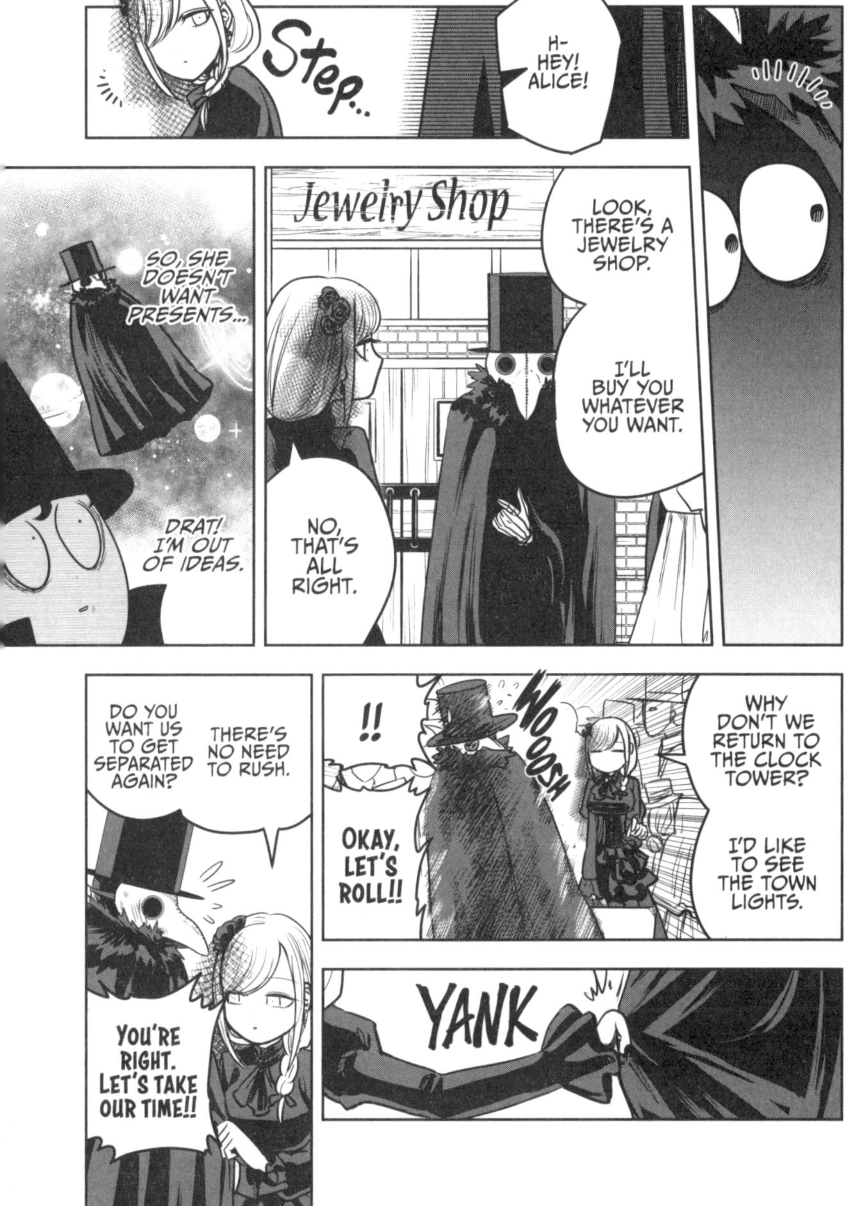
H-HEY! ALICE!
Step...
LOOK, THERE'S A JEWELRY SHOP.
Jewelry Shop
I'LL BUY YOU WHATEVER YOU WANT.
NO, THAT'S ALL RIGHT.
SO, SHE DOESN'T WANT PRESENTS...
DRAT! I'M OUT OF IDEAS.
WHY DON'T WE RETURN TO THE CLOCK TOWER?
I'D LIKE TO SEE THE TOWN LIGHTS.
WOOOSH
!!
OKAY, LET'S ROLL!!
YANK
THERE'S NO NEED TO RUSH.
DO YOU WANT US TO GET SEPARATED AGAIN?
YOU'RE RIGHT. LET'S TAKE OUR TIME!!

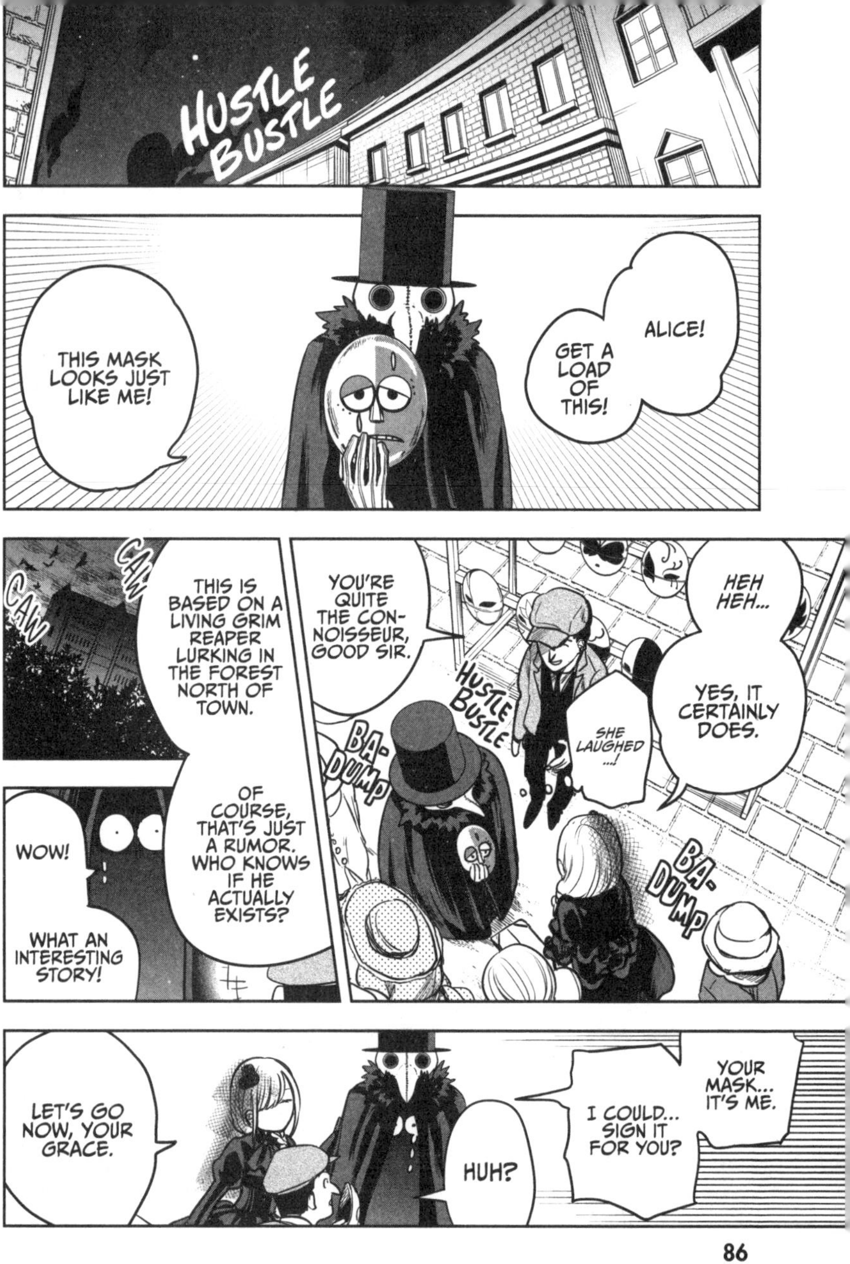
HUSTLE BUSTLE
ALICE!
GET A LOAD OF THIS!
THIS MASK LOOKS JUST LIKE ME!
HEH HEH...
YES, IT CERTAINLY DOES.
SHE LAUGHED...!
BA-DUMP
BA-DUMP
HUSTLE BUSTLE
YOU'RE QUITE THE CON-NOISSEUR, GOOD SIR.
CAW
CAW
THIS IS BASED ON A LIVING GRIM REAPER LURKING IN THE FOREST NORTH OF TOWN.
OF COURSE, THAT'S JUST A RUMOR. WHO KNOWS IF HE ACTUALLY EXISTS?
WOW!
WHAT AN INTERESTING STORY!
YOUR MASK... IT'S ME.
I COULD... SIGN IT FOR YOU?
HUH?
LET'S GO NOW, YOUR GRACE.

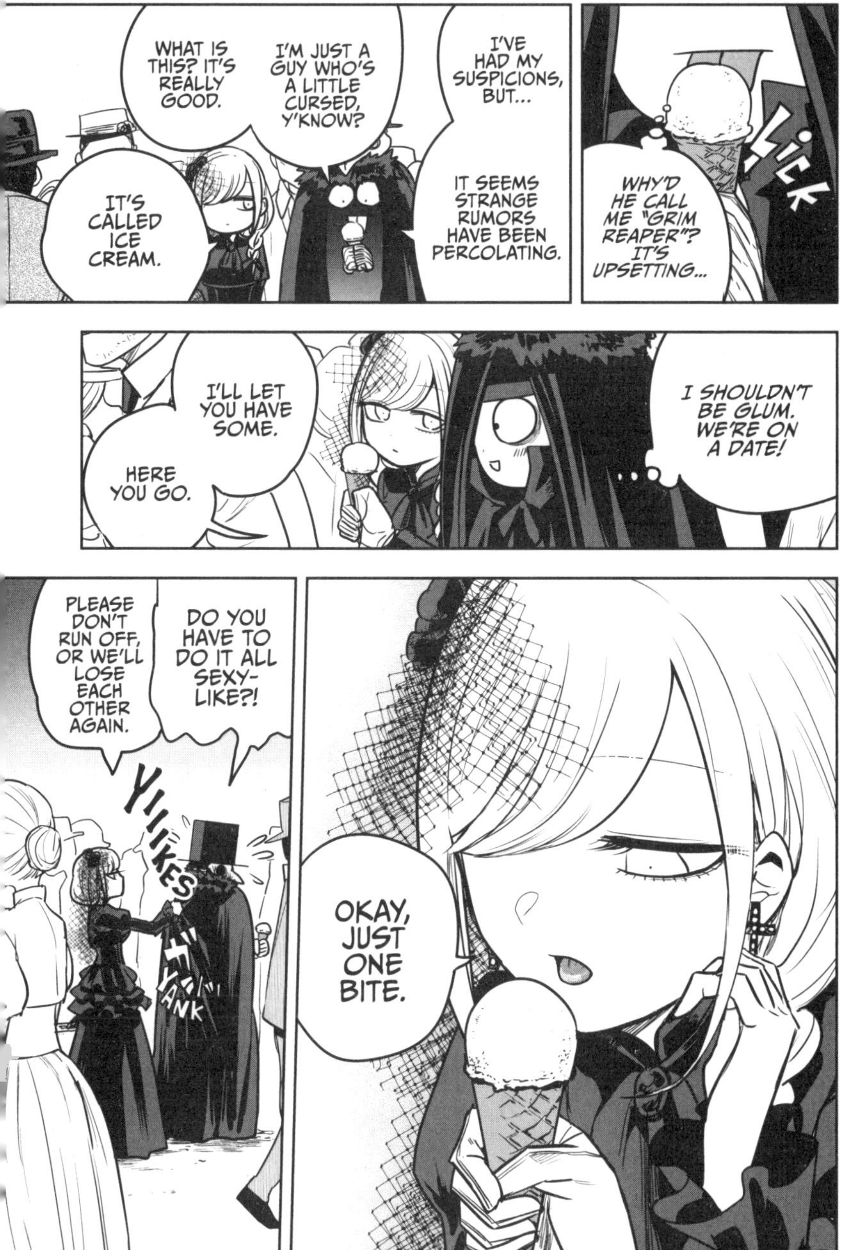
LICK
WHY'D HE CALL ME "GRIM REAPER"? IT'S UPSETTING...
I'VE HAD MY SUSPICIONS, BUT...
IT SEEMS STRANGE RUMORS HAVE BEEN PERCOLATING.
I'M JUST A GUY WHO'S A LITTLE CURSED, Y'KNOW?
WHAT IS THIS? IT'S REALLY GOOD.
IT'S CALLED ICE CREAM.
I SHOULDN'T BE GLUM. WE'RE ON A DATE!
I'LL LET YOU HAVE SOME.
HERE YOU GO.
OKAY, JUST ONE BITE.
DO YOU HAVE TO DO IT ALL SEXY-LIKE?!
PLEASE DON'T RUN OFF, OR WE'LL LOSE EACH OTHER AGAIN.
YIIIKES
YANK

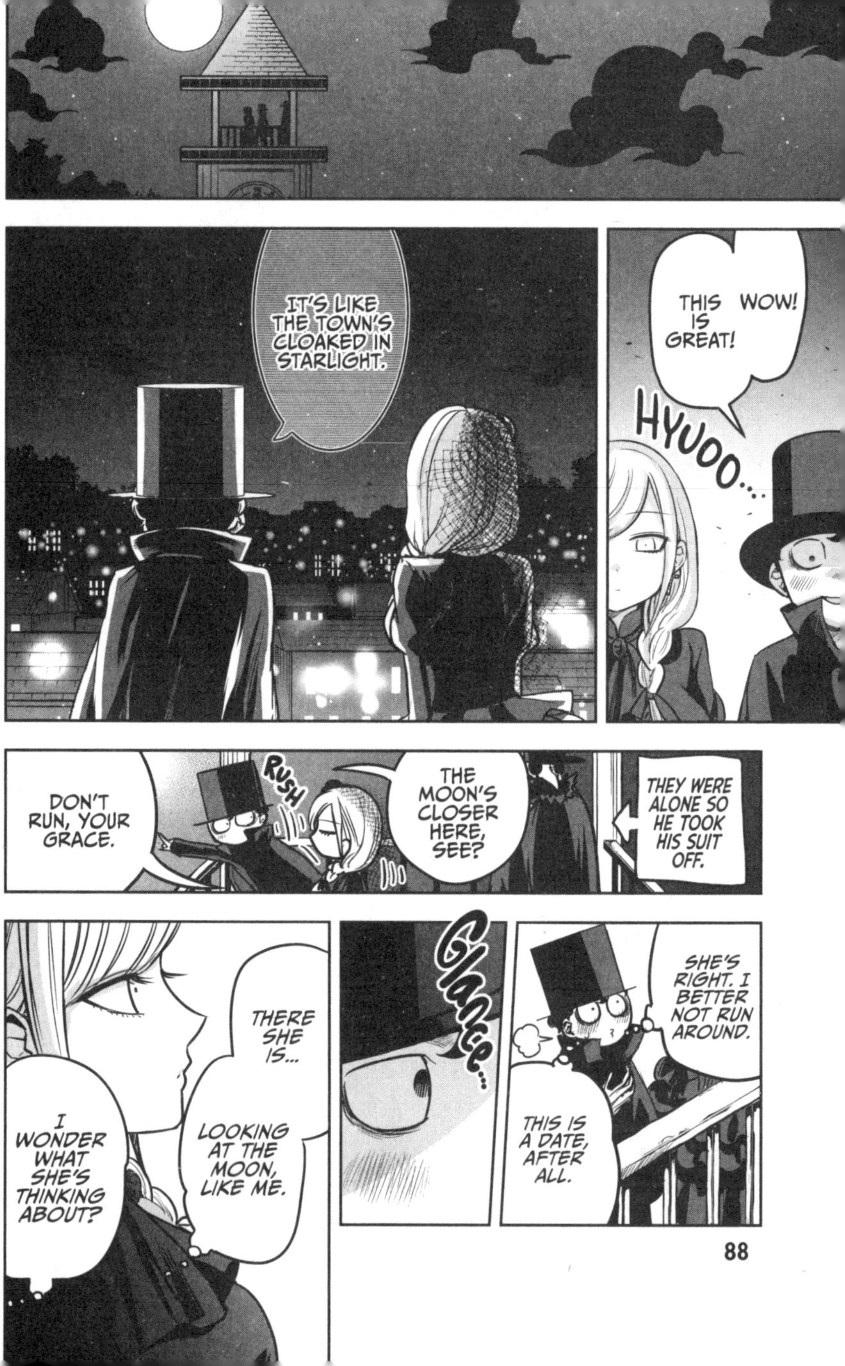
WOW!
THIS IS GREAT!
HYUOO...
IT'S LIKE THE TOWN'S CLOAKED IN STARLIGHT.
THEY WERE ALONE SO HE TOOK HIS SUIT OFF.
THE MOON'S CLOSER HERE, SEE?
RUSH
DON'T RUN, YOUR GRACE.
SHE'S RIGHT. I BETTER NOT RUN AROUND.
THIS IS A DATE, AFTER ALL.
Glance...
THERE SHE IS...
LOOKING AT THE MOON, LIKE ME.
I WONDER WHAT SHE'S THINKING ABOUT?

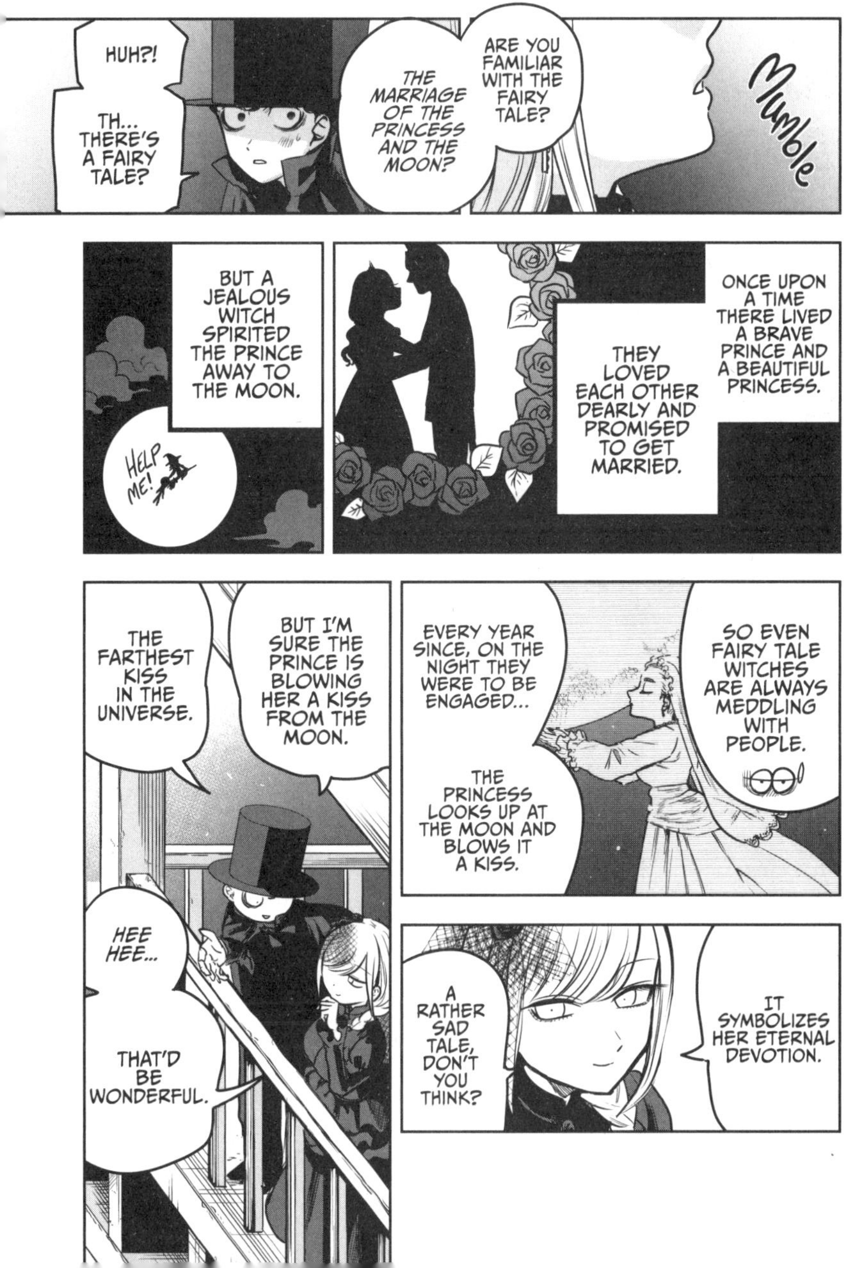
Mumble
ARE YOU FAMILIAR WITH THE FAIRY TALE?
THE MARRIAGE OF THE PRINCESS AND THE MOON?
HUH?!
TH... THERE'S A FAIRY TALE?
ONCE UPON A TIME THERE LIVED A BRAVE PRINCE AND A BEAUTIFUL PRINCESS.
THEY LOVED EACH OTHER DEARLY AND PROMISED TO GET MARRIED.
BUT A JEALOUS WITCH SPIRITED THE PRINCE AWAY TO THE MOON.
HELP ME!
SO EVEN FAIRY TALE WITCHES ARE ALWAYS MEDDLING WITH PEOPLE.
EVERY YEAR SINCE, ON THE NIGHT THEY WERE TO BE ENGAGED...
THE PRINCESS LOOKS UP AT THE MOON AND BLOWS IT A KISS.
IT SYMBOLIZES HER ETERNAL DEVOTION.
A RATHER SAD TALE, DON'T YOU THINK?
BUT I'M SURE THE PRINCE IS BLOWING HER A KISS FROM THE MOON.
THE FARTHEST KISS IN THE UNIVERSE.
HEE HEE...
THAT'D BE WONDERFUL.

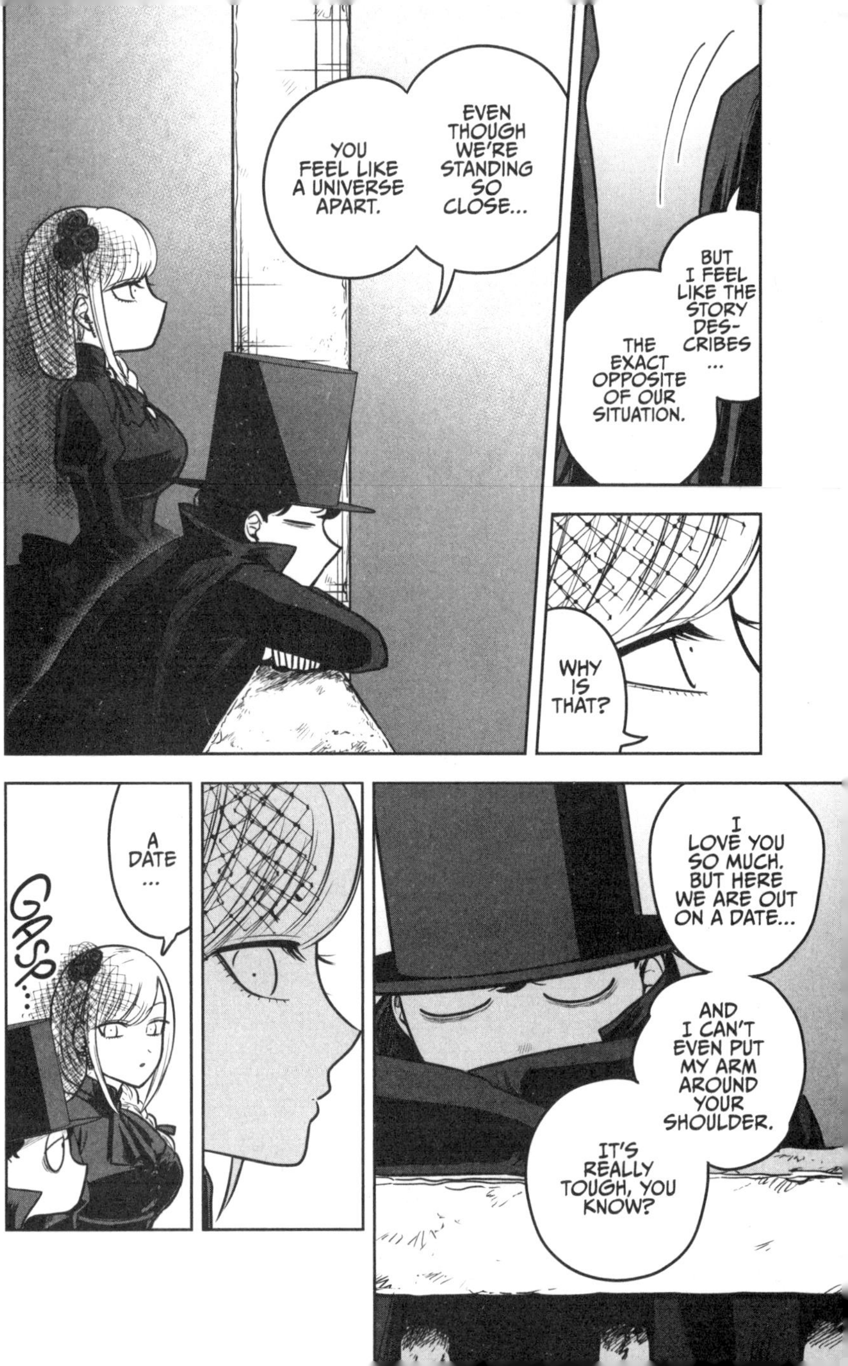

BUT I FEEL LIKE THE STORY DES-CRIBES...
THE EXACT OPPOSITE OF OUR SITUATION.
WHY IS THAT?
EVEN THOUGH WE'RE STANDING SO CLOSE...
YOU FEEL LIKE A UNIVERSE APART.
I LOVE YOU SO MUCH. BUT HERE WE ARE OUT ON A DATE...
AND I CAN'T EVEN PUT MY ARM AROUND YOUR SHOULDER.
IT'S REALLY TOUGH, YOU KNOW?
A DATE...
GASP...

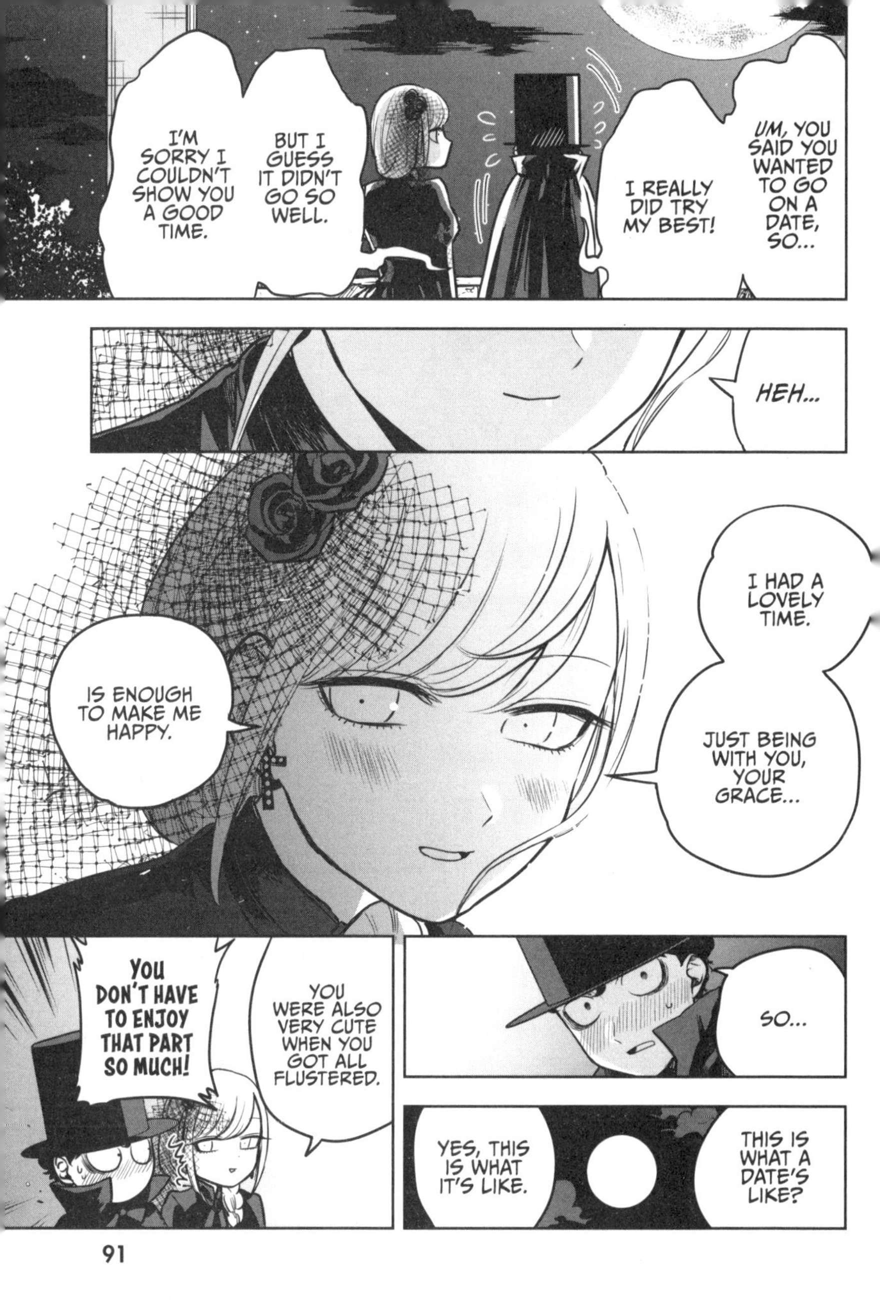
UM, YOU SAID YOU WANTED TO GO ON A DATE, SO...
I REALLY DID TRY MY BEST!
BUT I GUESS IT DIDN'T GO SO WELL.
I'M SORRY I COULDN'T SHOW YOU A GOOD TIME.
HEH...
I HAD A LOVELY TIME.
JUST BEING WITH YOU, YOUR GRACE...
IS ENOUGH TO MAKE ME HAPPY.
SO...
THIS IS WHAT A DATE'S LIKE?
YES, THIS IS WHAT IT'S LIKE.
YOU WERE ALSO VERY CUTE WHEN YOU GOT ALL FLUSTERED.
YOU DON'T HAVE TO ENJOY THAT PART SO MUCH!

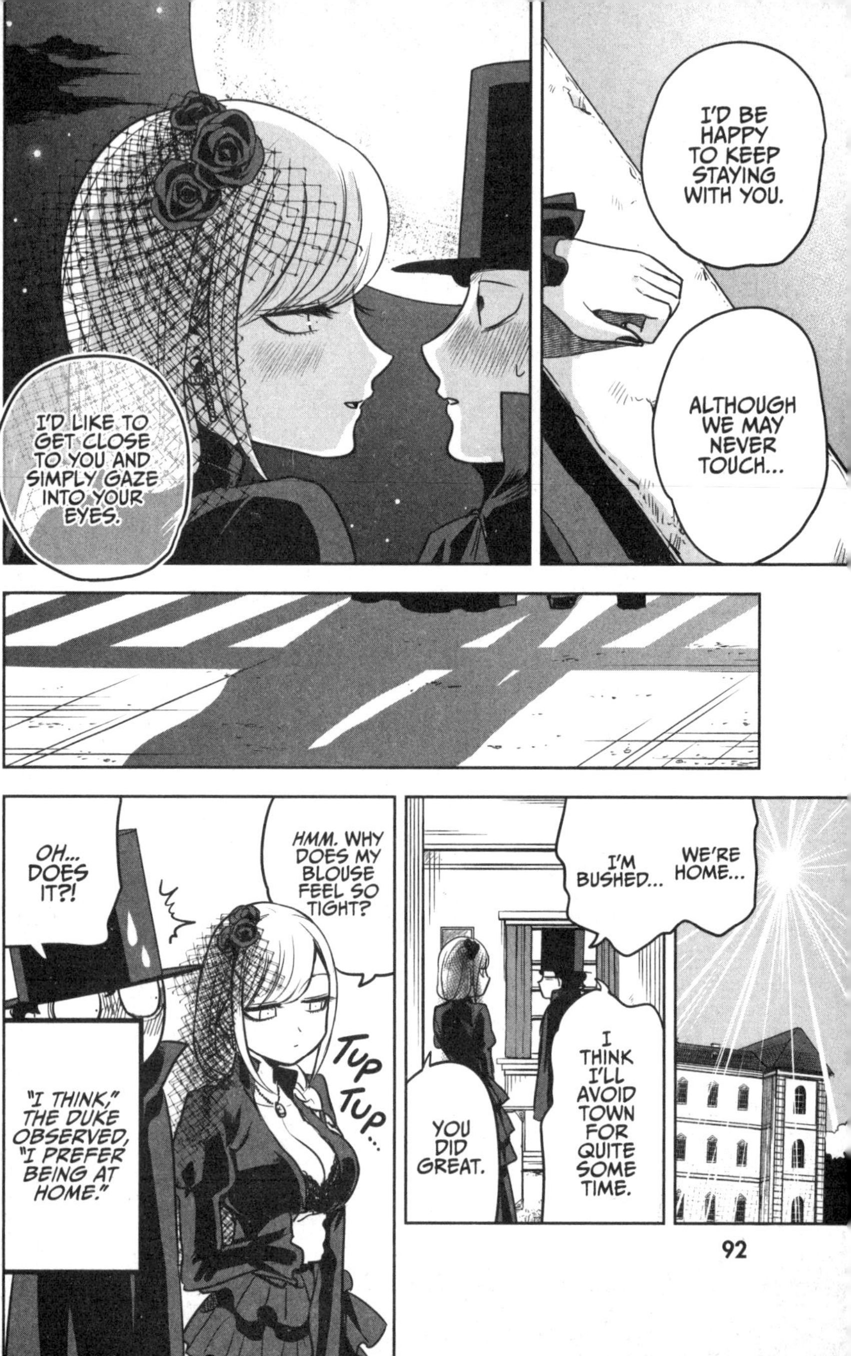
I'D BE HAPPY TO KEEP STAYING WITH YOU.
ALTHOUGH WE MAY NEVER TOUCH...
I'D LIKE TO GET CLOSE TO YOU AND SIMPLY GAZE INTO YOUR EYES.
WE'RE HOME...
I'M BUSHED...
I THINK I'LL AVOID TOWN FOR QUITE SOME TIME.
YOU DID GREAT.
HMM. WHY DOES MY BLOUSE FEEL SO TIGHT?
OH... DOES IT?!
TUP TUP...
"I THINK," THE DUKE OBSERVED, "I PREFER BEING AT HOME."

Chapter 23: McFarlane's Score

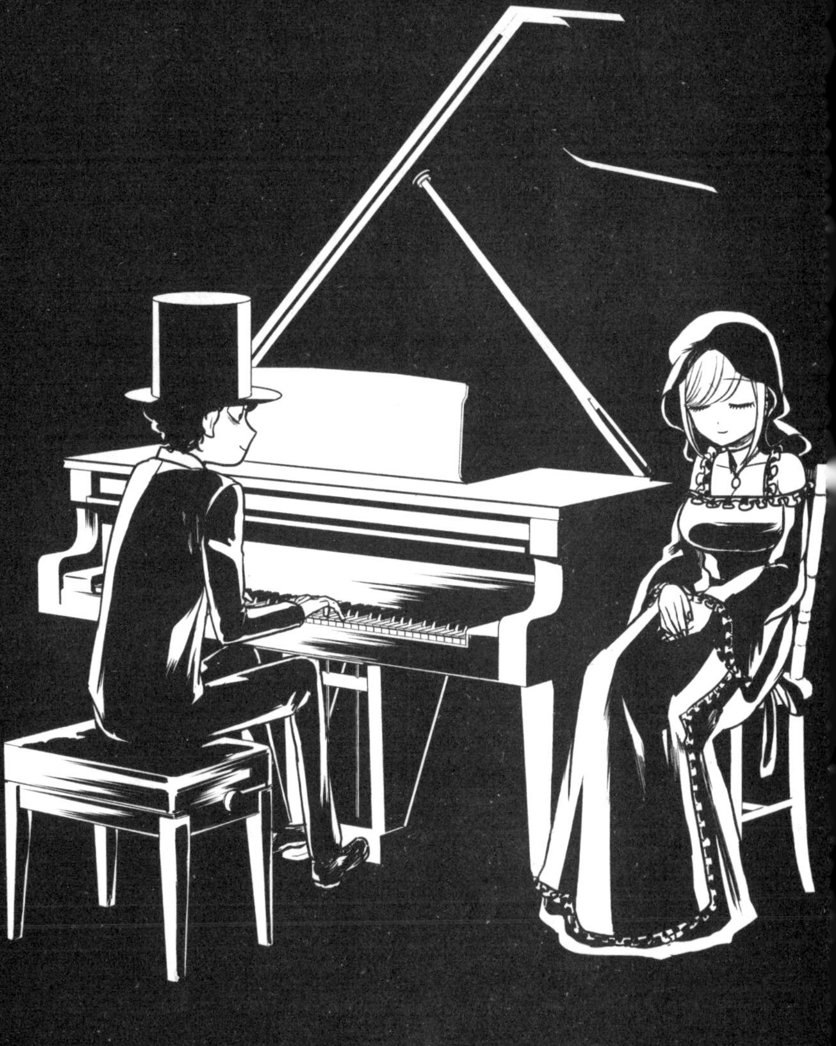

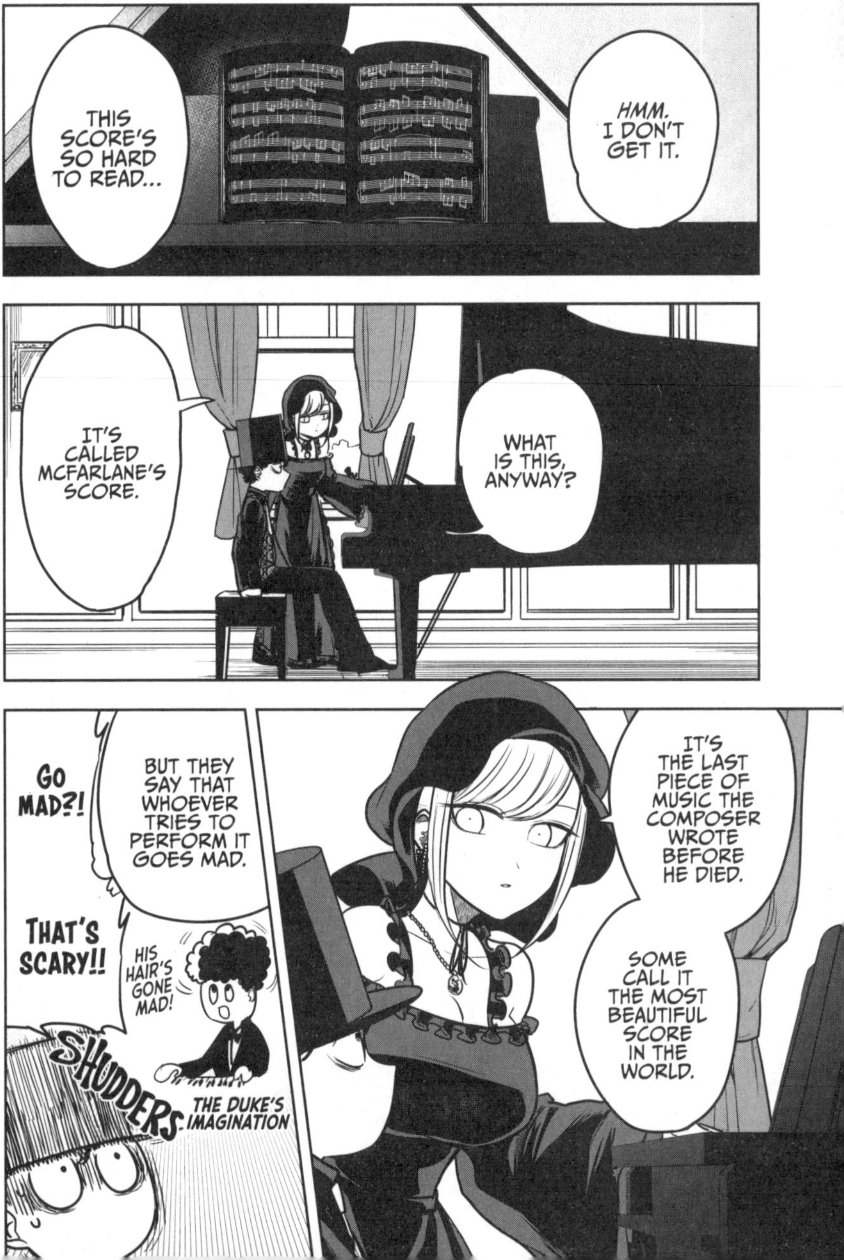
HMM. I DON'T GET IT.
THIS SCORE'S SO HARD TO READ...
WHAT IS THIS, ANYWAY?
IT'S CALLED MCFARLANE'S SCORE.
IT'S THE LAST PIECE OF MUSIC THE COMPOSER WROTE BEFORE HE DIED.
SOME CALL IT THE MOST BEAUTIFUL SCORE IN THE WORLD.
BUT THEY SAY THAT WHOEVER TRIES TO PERFORM IT GOES MAD.
GO MAD?!
THAT'S SCARY!!
HIS HAIR'S GONE MAD!
SHUDDERS
THE DUKE'S IMAGINATION

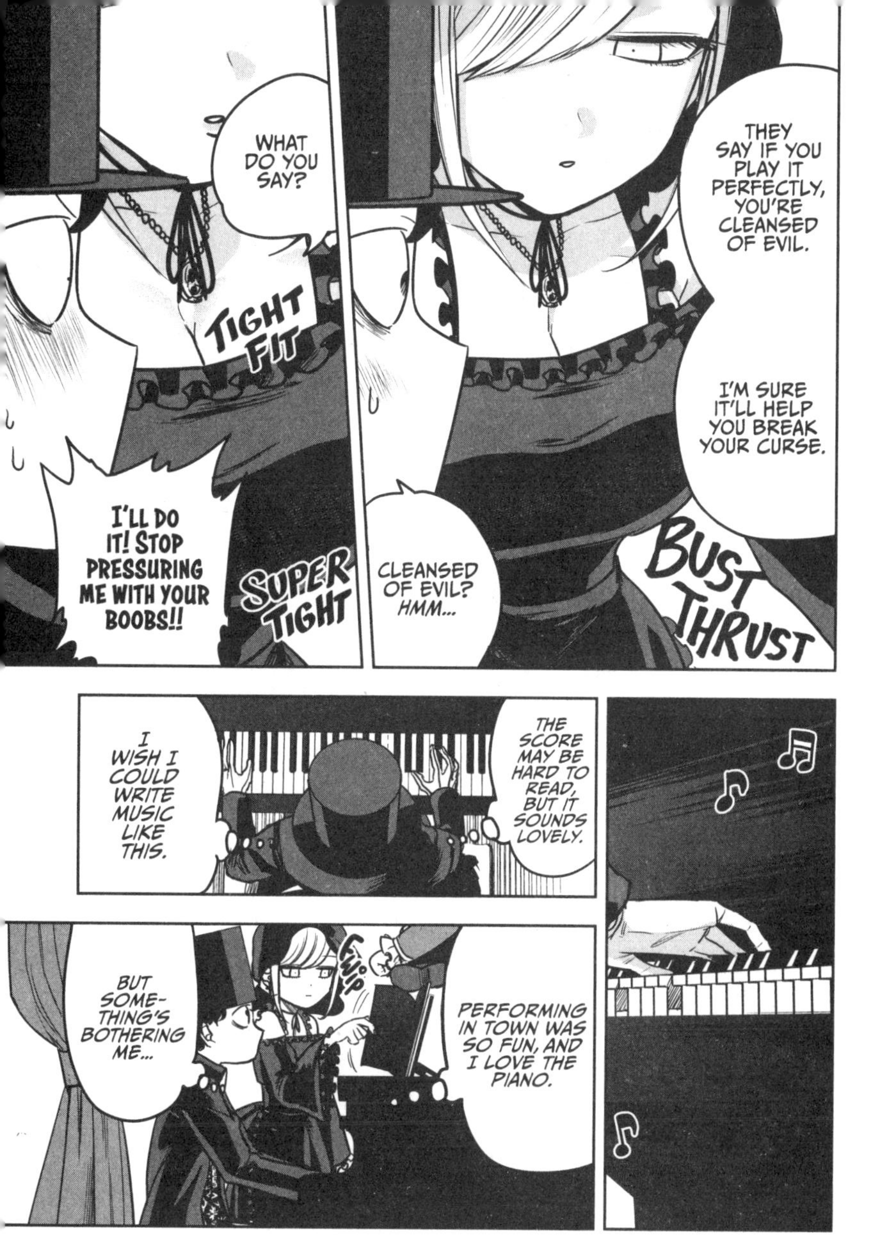
THEY SAY IF YOU PLAY IT PERFECTLY, YOU'RE CLEANSED OF EVIL.
I'M SURE IT'LL HELP YOU BREAK YOUR CURSE.
BUST THRUST
CLEANSED OF EVIL? HMM...
WHAT DO YOU SAY?
TIGHT FIT
I'LL DO IT! STOP PRESSURING ME WITH YOUR BOOBS!!
SUPER TIGHT
THE SCORE MAY BE HARD TO READ, BUT IT SOUNDS LOVELY.
I WISH I COULD WRITE MUSIC LIKE THIS.
PERFORMING IN TOWN WAS SO FUN, AND I LOVE THE PIANO.
FWIP
BUT SOMETHING'S BOTHERING ME...

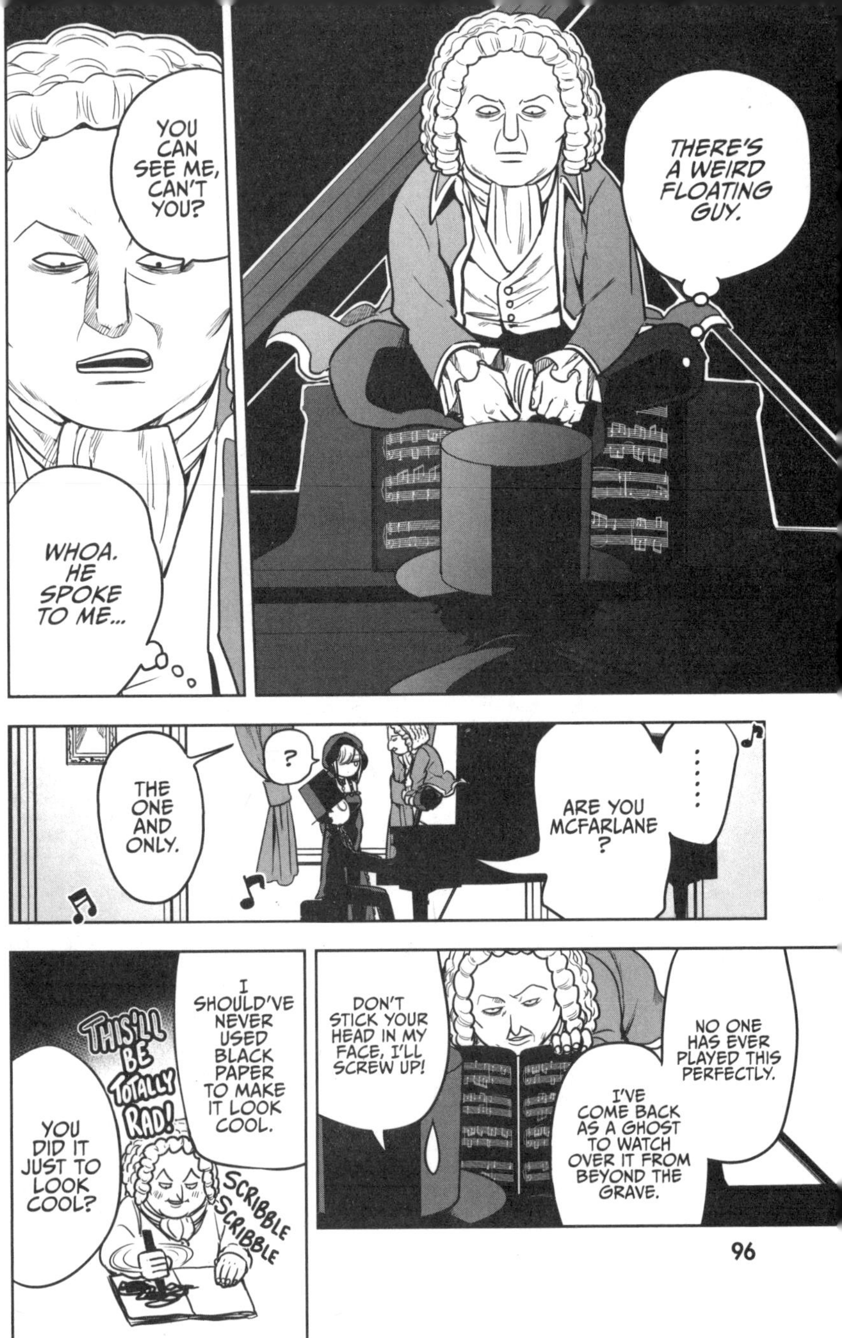
THERE'S A WEIRD FLOATING GUY.
YOU CAN SEE ME, CAN'T YOU?
WHOA. HE SPOKE TO ME...
......
ARE YOU MCFARLANE?
?
THE ONE AND ONLY.
NO ONE HAS EVER PLAYED THIS PERFECTLY.
I'VE COME BACK AS A GHOST TO WATCH OVER IT FROM BEYOND THE GRAVE.
DON'T STICK YOUR HEAD IN MY FACE, I'LL SCREW UP!
I SHOULD'VE NEVER USED BLACK PAPER TO MAKE IT LOOK COOL.
THIS'LL BE TOTALLY RAD!
YOU DID IT JUST TO LOOK COOL?
SCRIBBLE SCRIBBLE

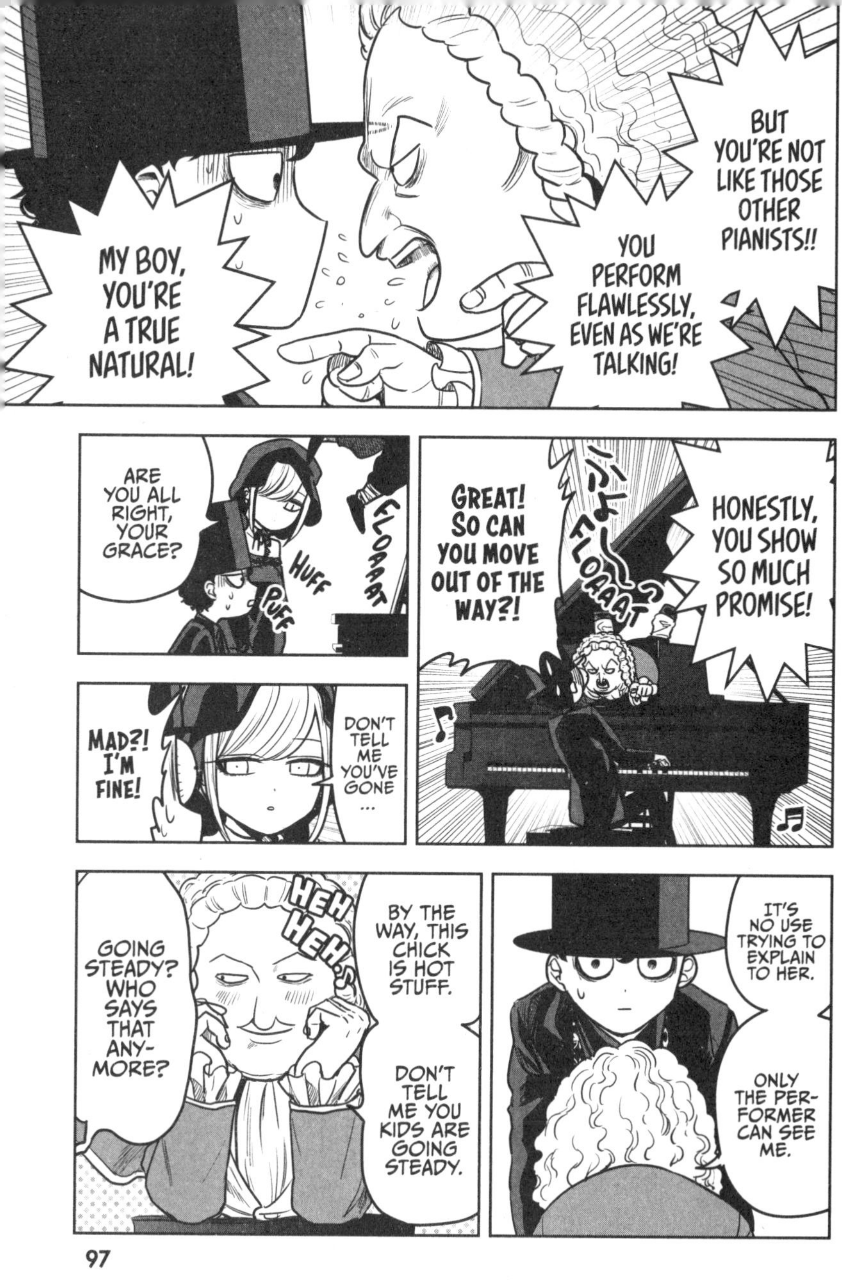
BUT YOU'RE NOT LIKE THOSE OTHER PIANISTS!!
YOU PERFORM FLAWLESSLY, EVEN AS WE'RE TALKING!
MY BOY, YOU'RE A TRUE NATURAL!
HONESTLY, YOU SHOW SO MUCH PROMISE!
FLOAAAT
GREAT! SO CAN YOU MOVE OUT OF THE WAY?!
FLOAAAT
HUFF
PUFF
ARE YOU ALL RIGHT, YOUR GRACE?
DON'T TELL ME YOU'VE GONE ...
MAD?! I'M FINE!
IT'S NO USE TRYING TO EXPLAIN TO HER.
ONLY THE PERFORMER CAN SEE ME.
HEH HEH
BY THE WAY, THIS CHICK IS HOT STUFF.
DON'T TELL ME YOU KIDS ARE GOING STEADY.
GOING STEADY? WHO SAYS THAT ANYMORE?

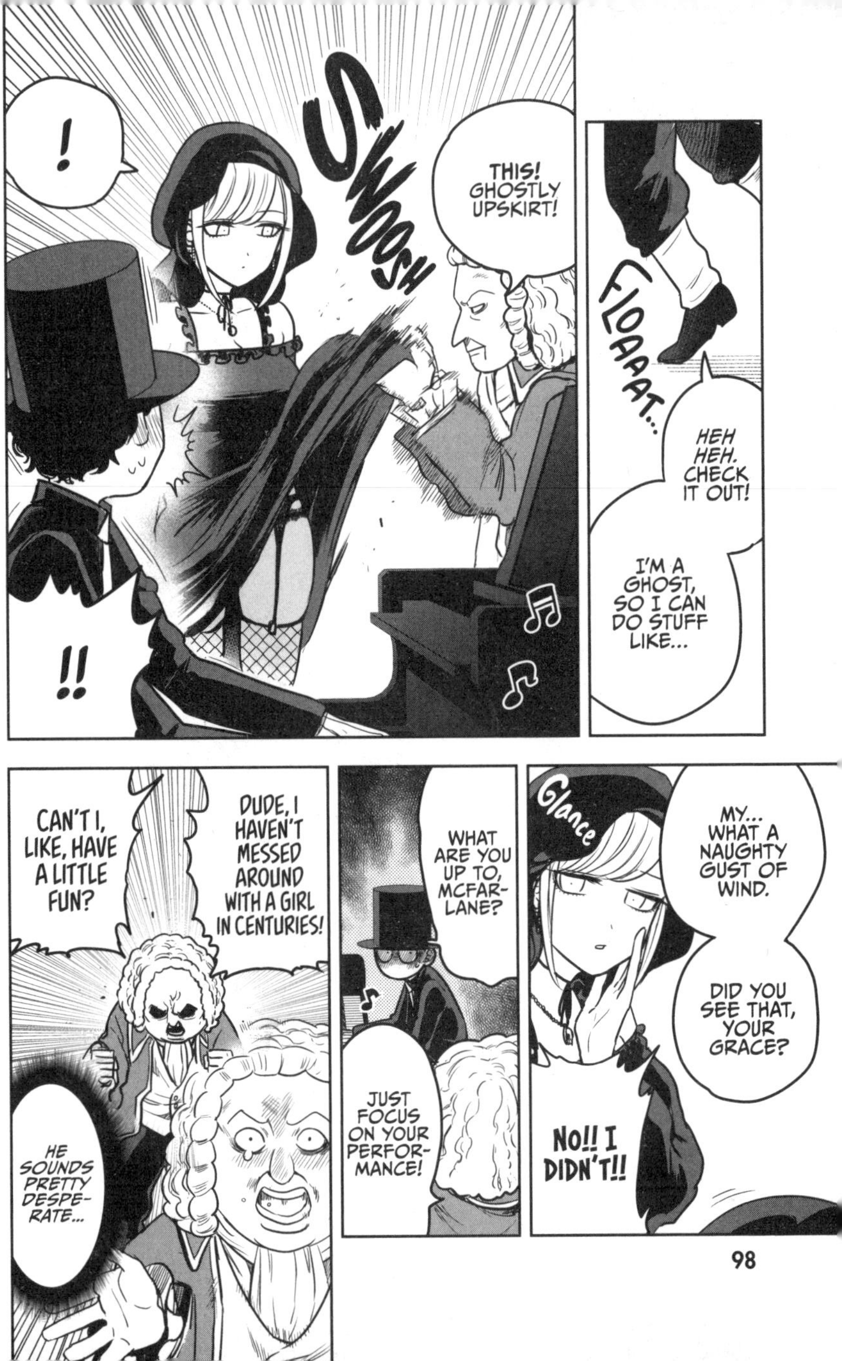
FLOAAAT...
HEH HEH. CHECK IT OUT!
I'M A GHOST, SO I CAN DO STUFF LIKE...
THIS! GHOSTLY UPSKIRT!
SWOOSH
!
!!
Glance
MY... WHAT A NAUGHTY GUST OF WIND.
DID YOU SEE THAT, YOUR GRACE?
NO!! I DIDN'T!!
WHAT ARE YOU UP TO, MCFARLANE?
JUST FOCUS ON YOUR PERFORMANCE!
DUDE, I HAVEN'T MESSED AROUND WITH A GIRL IN CENTURIES!
CAN'T I, LIKE, HAVE A LITTLE FUN?
HE SOUNDS PRETTY DESPERATE...

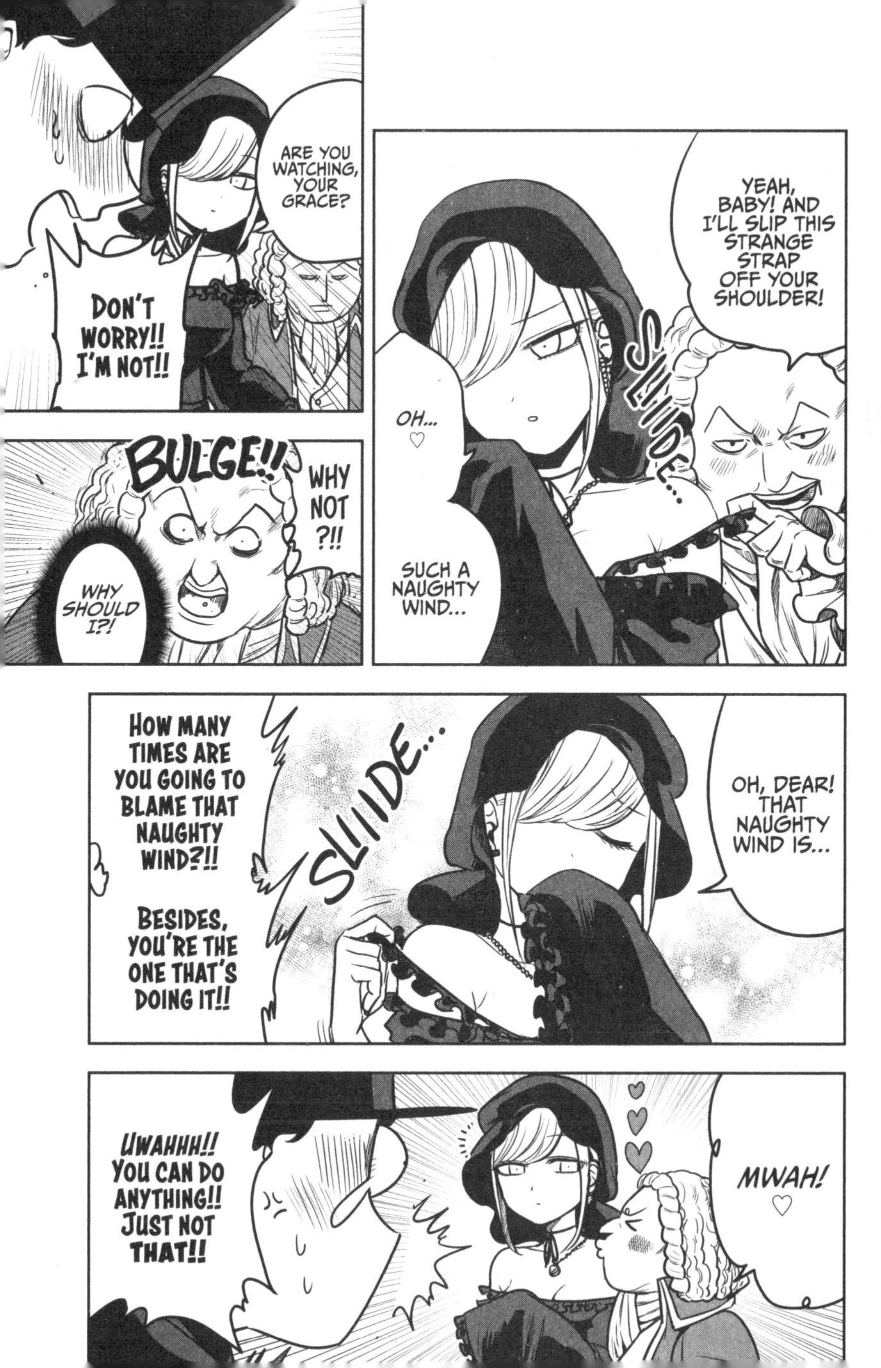
YEAH, BABY! AND I'LL SLIP THIS STRANGE STRAP OFF YOUR SHOULDER!
SLIIIDE...
OH... ♡
SUCH A NAUGHTY WIND...
ARE YOU WATCHING, YOUR GRACE?
DON'T WORRY!! I'M NOT!!
WHY NOT ?!!
BULGE!!
WHY SHOULD I?!
OH, DEAR! THAT NAUGHTY WIND IS...
SLIIIDE...
HOW MANY TIMES ARE YOU GOING TO BLAME THAT NAUGHTY WIND?!!
BESIDES, YOU'RE THE ONE THAT'S DOING IT!!
MWAH! ♡
UWAHHH!! YOU CAN DO ANYTHING!! JUST NOT THAT!!

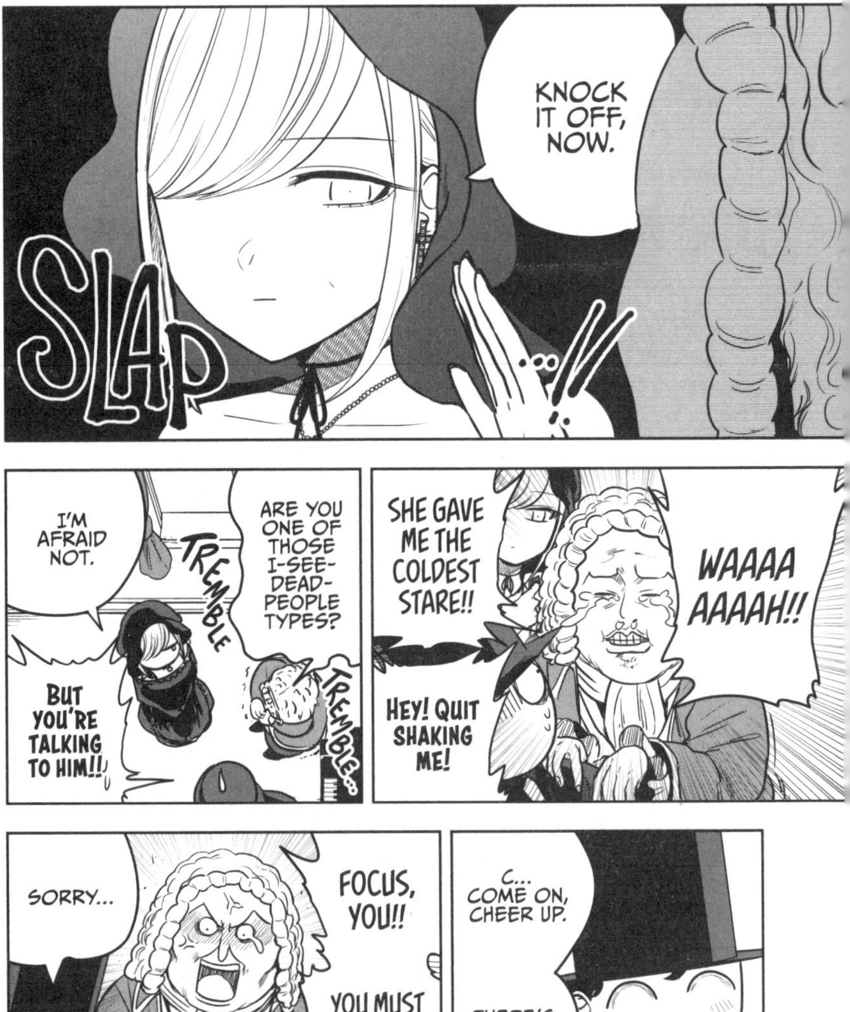
KNOCK IT OFF, NOW.
SLAP
...
WAAAA AAAAH!!
SHE GAVE ME THE COLDEST STARE!!
HEY! QUIT SHAKING ME!
ARE YOU ONE OF THOSE I-SEE-DEAD-PEOPLE TYPES?
TREMBLE
I'M AFRAID NOT.
TREMBLE
TREMBLE...
BUT YOU'RE TALKING TO HIM!!
C... COME ON, CHEER UP.
THERE'S NOTHING TO CRY ABOUT...
FOCUS, YOU!!
YOU MUST PLAY IT PERFECTLY !!
SORRY...

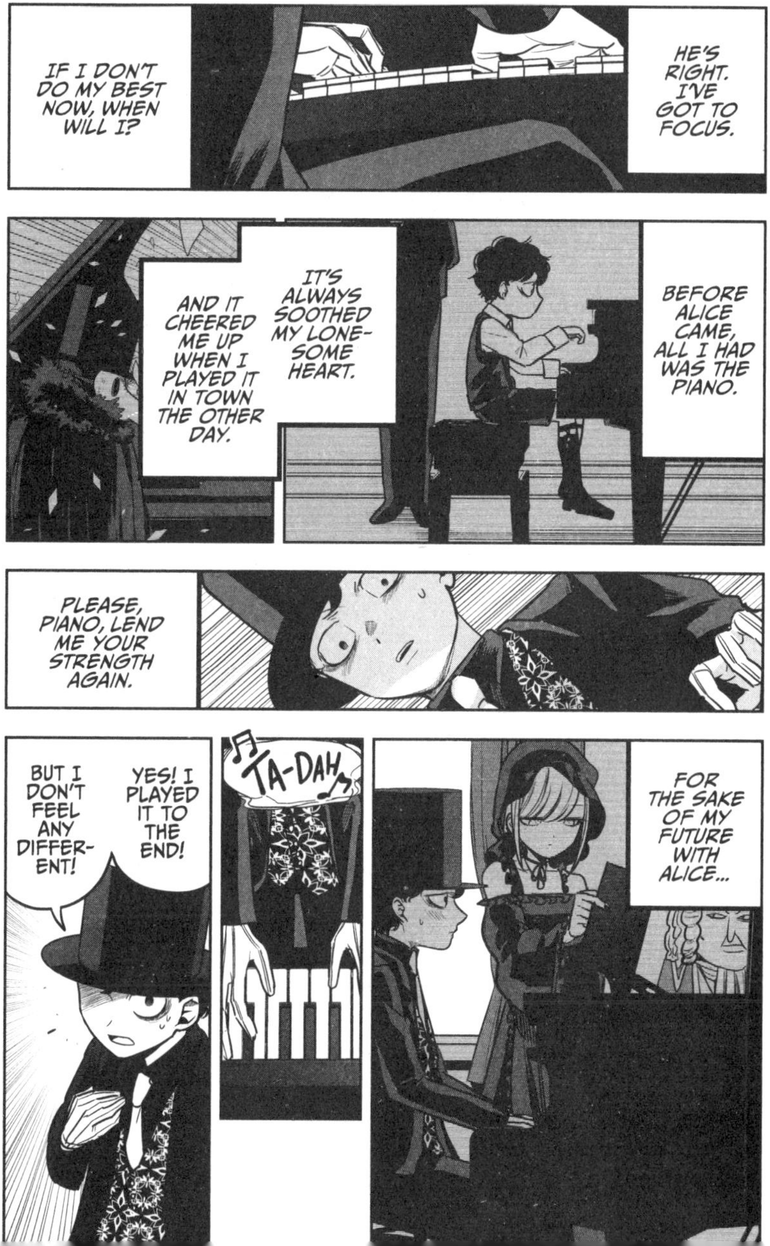
HE'S RIGHT. I'VE GOT TO FOCUS.
IF I DON'T DO MY BEST NOW, WHEN WILL I?
BEFORE ALICE CAME, ALL I HAD WAS THE PIANO.
IT'S ALWAYS SOOTHED MY LONE-SOME HEART.
AND IT CHEERED ME UP WHEN I PLAYED IT IN TOWN THE OTHER DAY.
PLEASE, PIANO, LEND ME YOUR STRENGTH AGAIN.
FOR THE SAKE OF MY FUTURE WITH ALICE...
TA-DAH
YES! I PLAYED IT TO THE END!
BUT I DON'T FEEL ANY DIFFER-ENT!

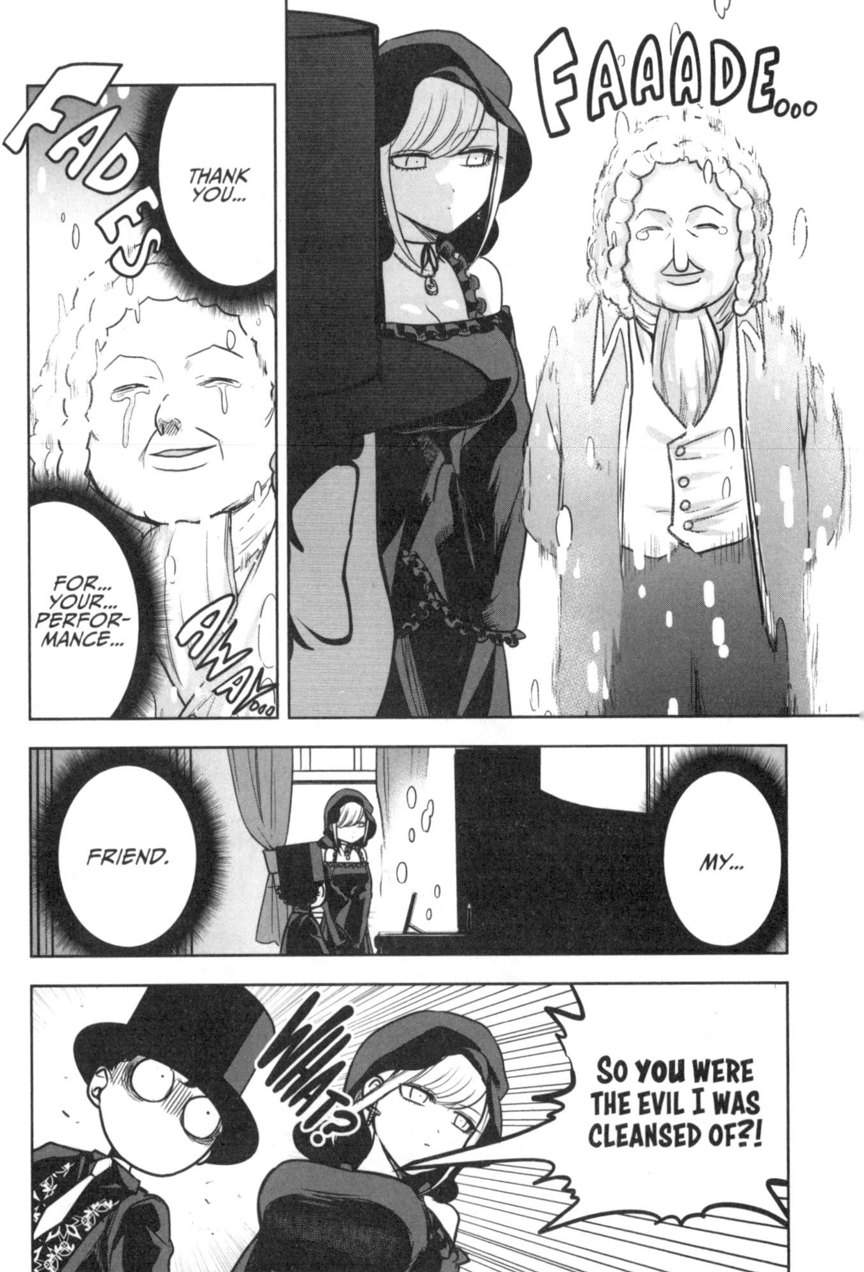
FAAADE...
THANK YOU...
FADES
FOR... YOUR... PERFORMANCE...
AWAY...
MY...
FRIEND.
SO YOU WERE THE EVIL I WAS CLEANSED OF?!
WHAT?!

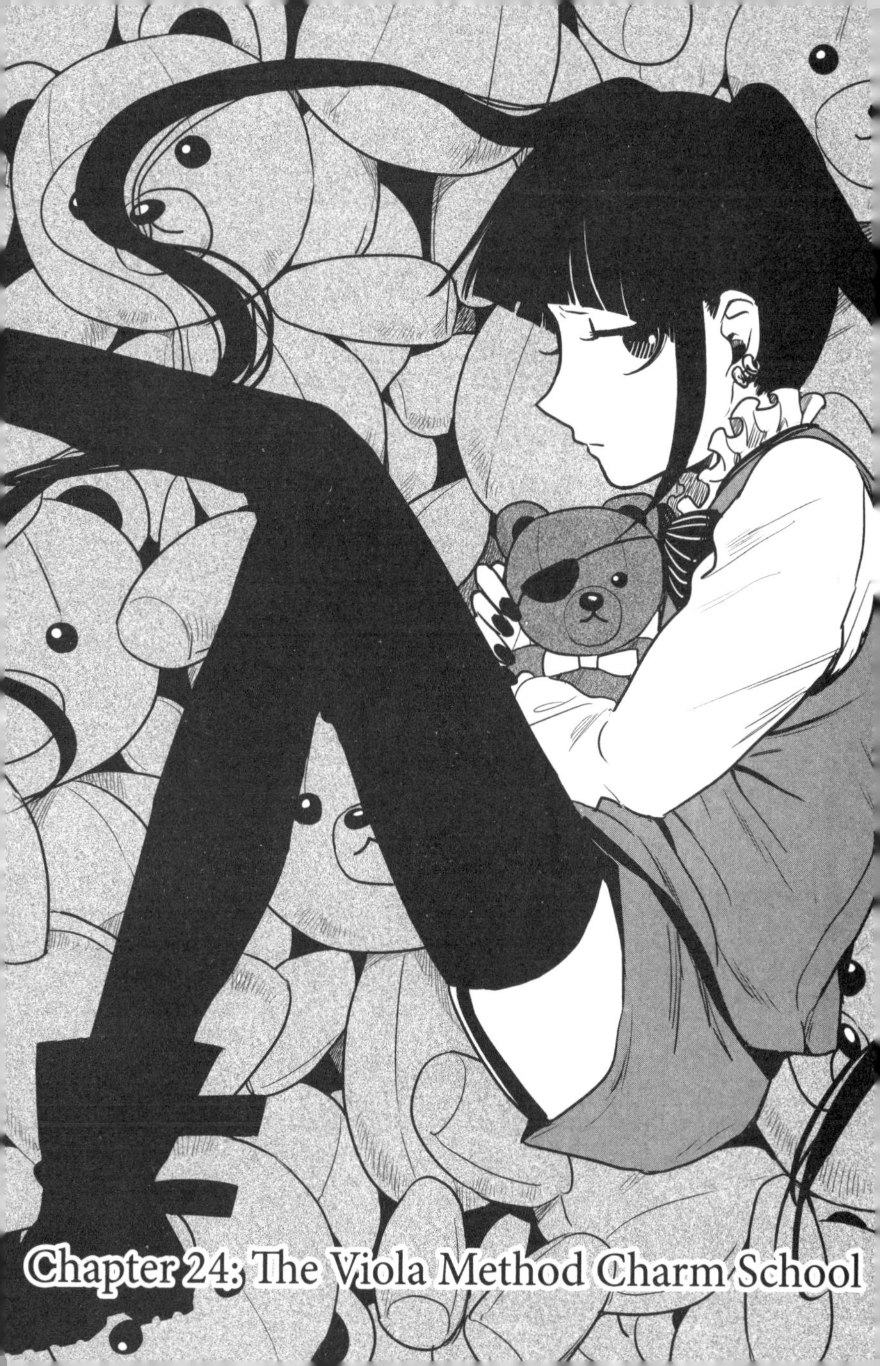

Chapter 24: The Viola Method Charm School

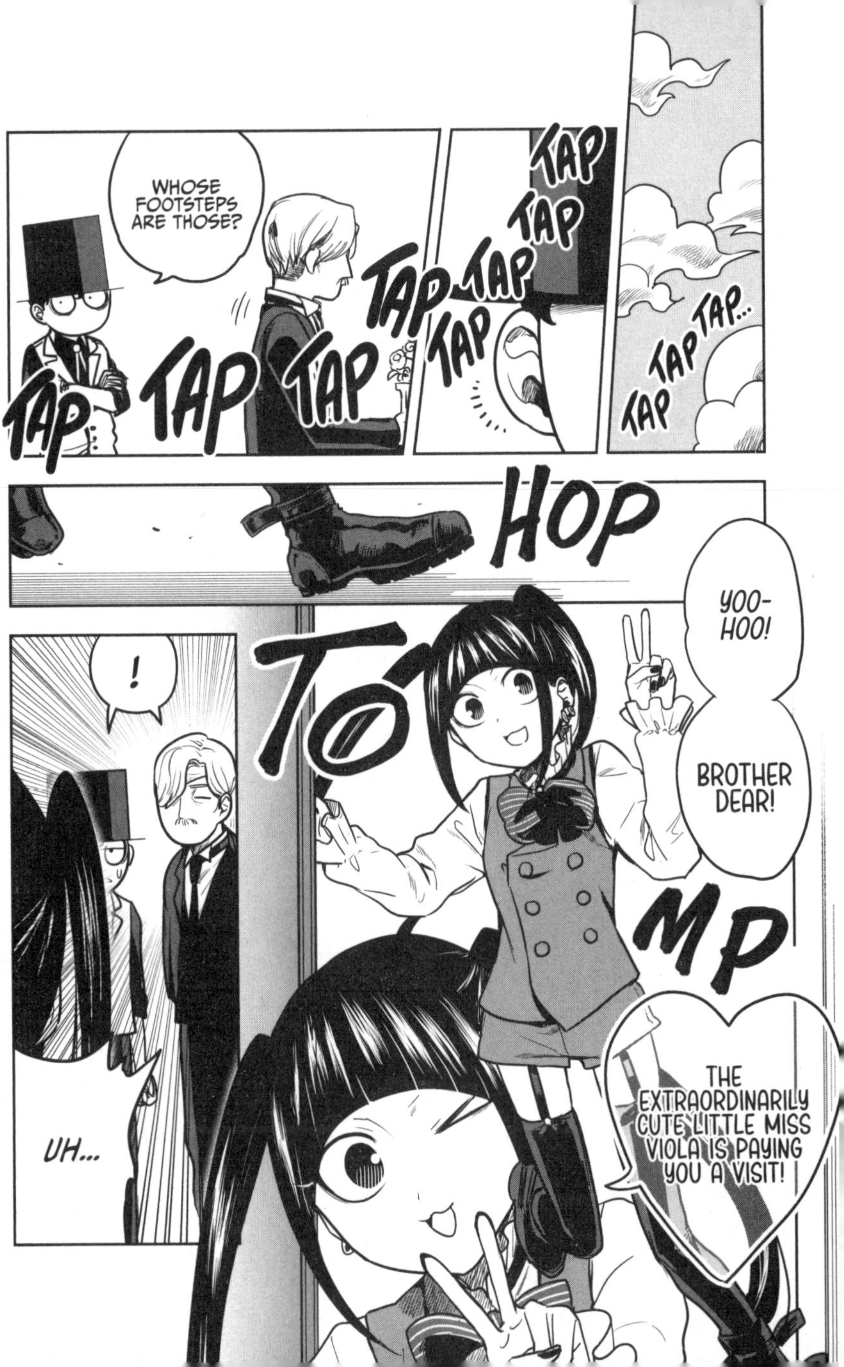
TAP TAP TAP...
TAP TAP TAP TAP
WHOSE FOOTSTEPS ARE THOSE?
TAP TAP TAP TAP
HOP
YOO-HOO!
BROTHER DEAR!
TOMP
THE EXTRAORDINARILY CUTE LITTLE MISS VIOLA IS PAYING YOU A VISIT!
!
UH...

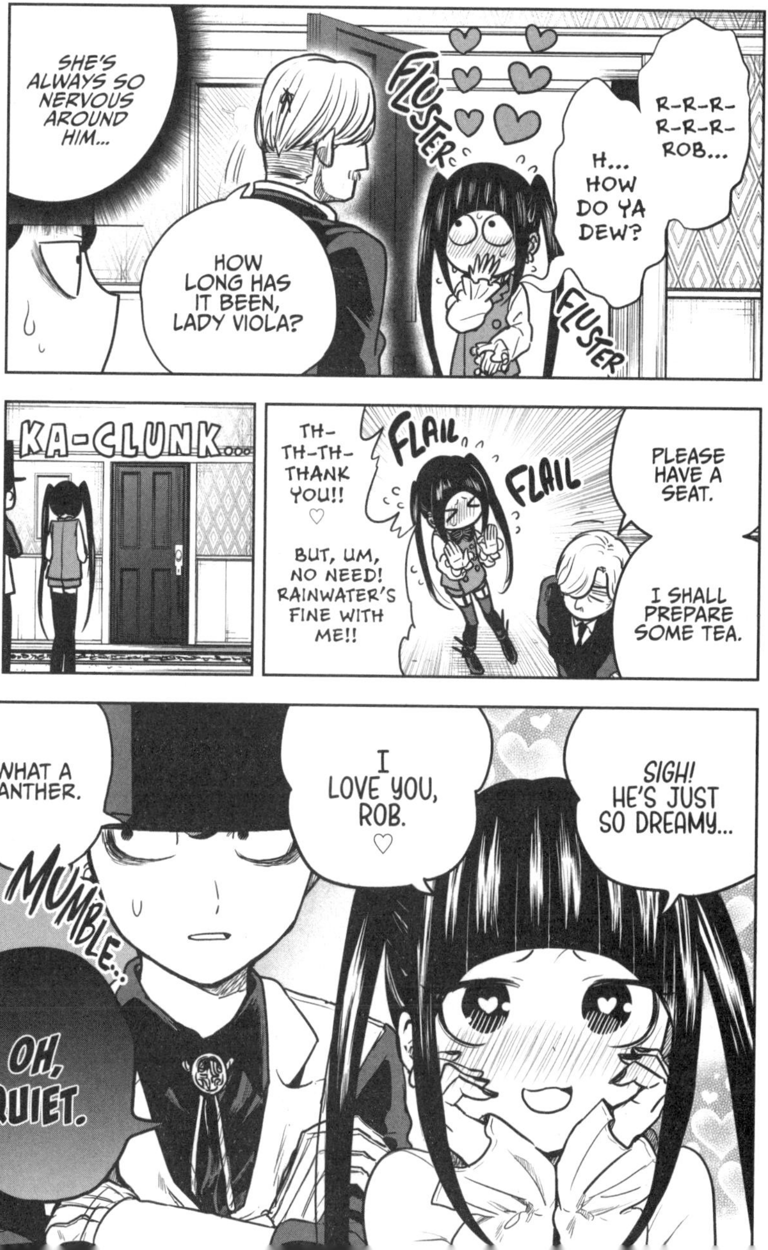
R-R-R-R-R-R-ROB...
H... HOW DO YA DEW?
FLUSTER
FLUSTER
HOW LONG HAS IT BEEN, LADY VIOLA?
SHE'S ALWAYS SO NERVOUS AROUND HIM...
PLEASE HAVE A SEAT.
I SHALL PREPARE SOME TEA.
FLAIL
FLAIL
TH-TH-TH-THANK YOU!! ♡
BUT, UM, NO NEED! RAINWATER'S FINE WITH ME!!
KA-CLUNK...
SIGH! HE'S JUST SO DREAMY...
I LOVE YOU, ROB. ♡
WHAT A PANTHER.
MUMBLE...
OH, QUIET.

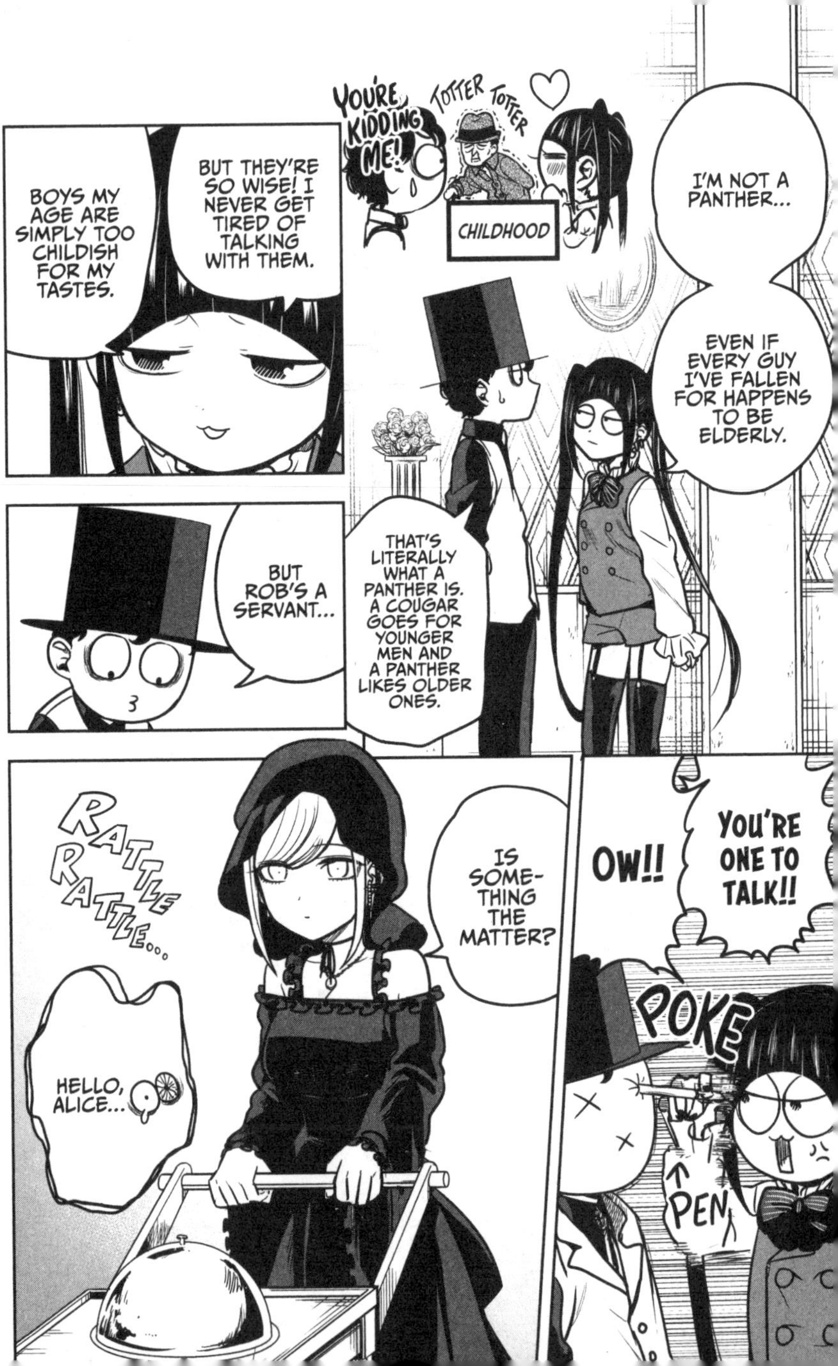

BOYS MY AGE ARE SIMPLY TOO CHILDISH FOR MY TASTES.
BUT THEY'RE SO WISE! I NEVER GET TIRED OF TALKING WITH THEM.
YOU'RE KIDDING ME!
TOTTER TOTTER
CHILDHOOD
BUT ROB'S A SERVANT...
THAT'S LITERALLY WHAT A PANTHER IS. A COUGAR GOES FOR YOUNGER MEN AND A PANTHER LIKES OLDER ONES.
I'M NOT A PANTHER...
EVEN IF EVERY GUY I'VE FALLEN FOR HAPPENS TO BE ELDERLY.
YOU'RE ONE TO TALK!!
OW!!
POKE
PEN
IS SOMETHING THE MATTER?
RATTLE RATTLE...
HELLO, ALICE...

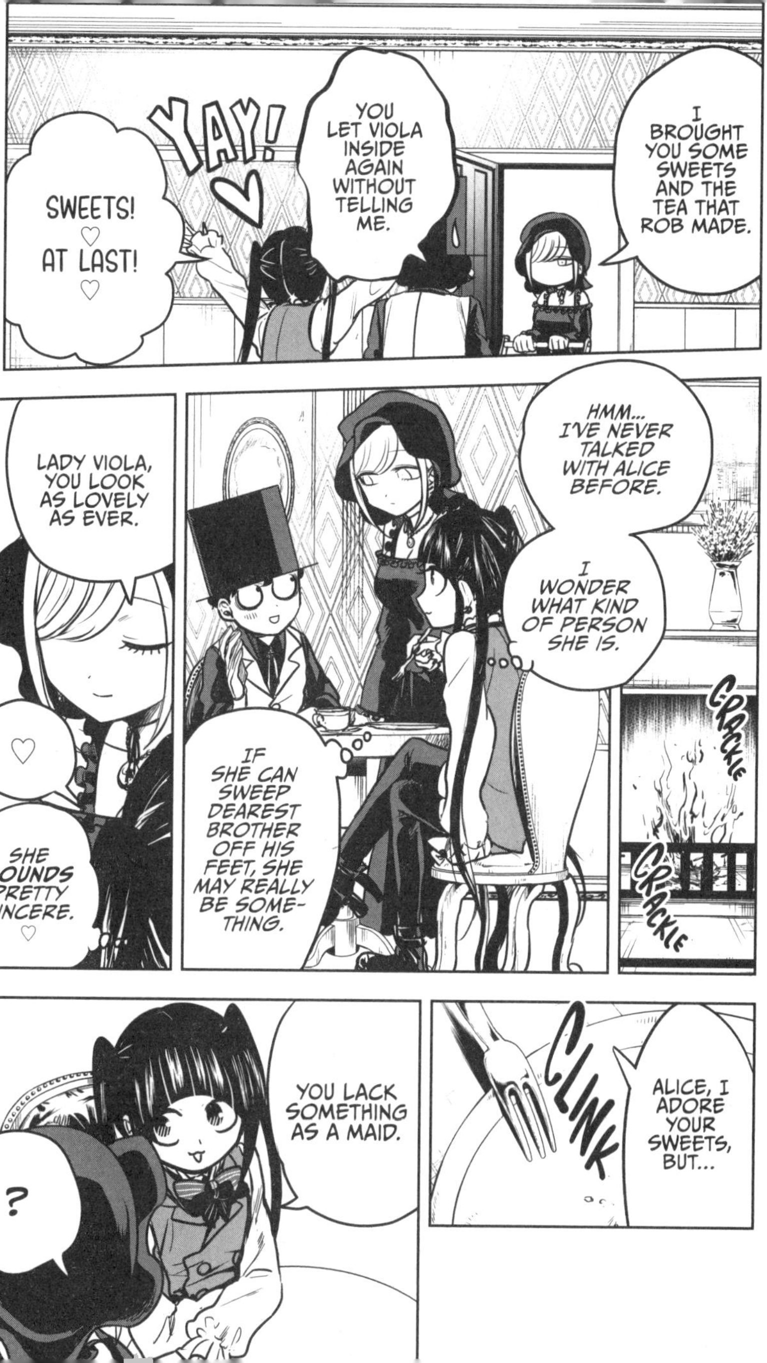
I BROUGHT YOU SOME SWEETS AND THE TEA THAT ROB MADE.
YOU LET VIOLA INSIDE AGAIN WITHOUT TELLING ME.
YAY!
SWEETS! ♡ AT LAST! ♡
HMM... I'VE NEVER TALKED WITH ALICE BEFORE.
I WONDER WHAT KIND OF PERSON SHE IS.
CRACKLE
CRACKLE
IF SHE CAN SWEEP DEAREST BROTHER OFF HIS FEET, SHE MAY REALLY BE SOME-THING.
LADY VIOLA, YOU LOOK AS LOVELY AS EVER.
♡
SHE SOUNDS PRETTY SINCERE. ♡
ALICE, I ADORE YOUR SWEETS, BUT...
CLINK
YOU LACK SOMETHING AS A MAID.
?

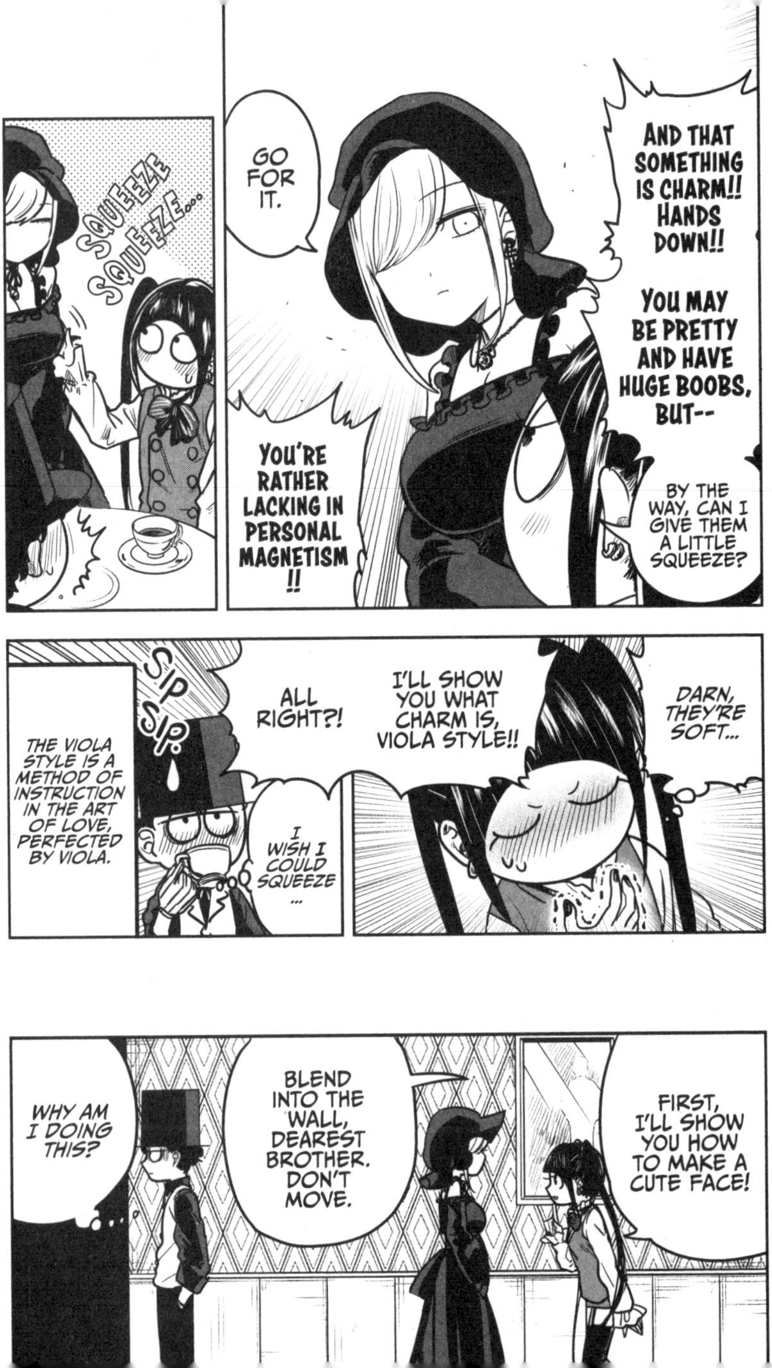
AND THAT SOMETHING IS CHARM!! HANDS DOWN!!
YOU MAY BE PRETTY AND HAVE HUGE BOOBS, BUT--
BY THE WAY, CAN I GIVE THEM A LITTLE SQUEEZE?
GO FOR IT.
YOU'RE RATHER LACKING IN PERSONAL MAGNETISM!!
SQUEEZE SQUEEZE...
DARN, THEY'RE SOFT...
I'LL SHOW YOU WHAT CHARM IS, VIOLA STYLE!!
ALL RIGHT?!
SIP SIP
I WISH I COULD SQUEEZE ...
THE VIOLA STYLE IS A METHOD OF INSTRUCTION IN THE ART OF LOVE, PERFECTED BY VIOLA.
FIRST, I'LL SHOW YOU HOW TO MAKE A CUTE FACE!
BLEND INTO THE WALL, DEAREST BROTHER. DON'T MOVE.
WHY AM I DOING THIS?

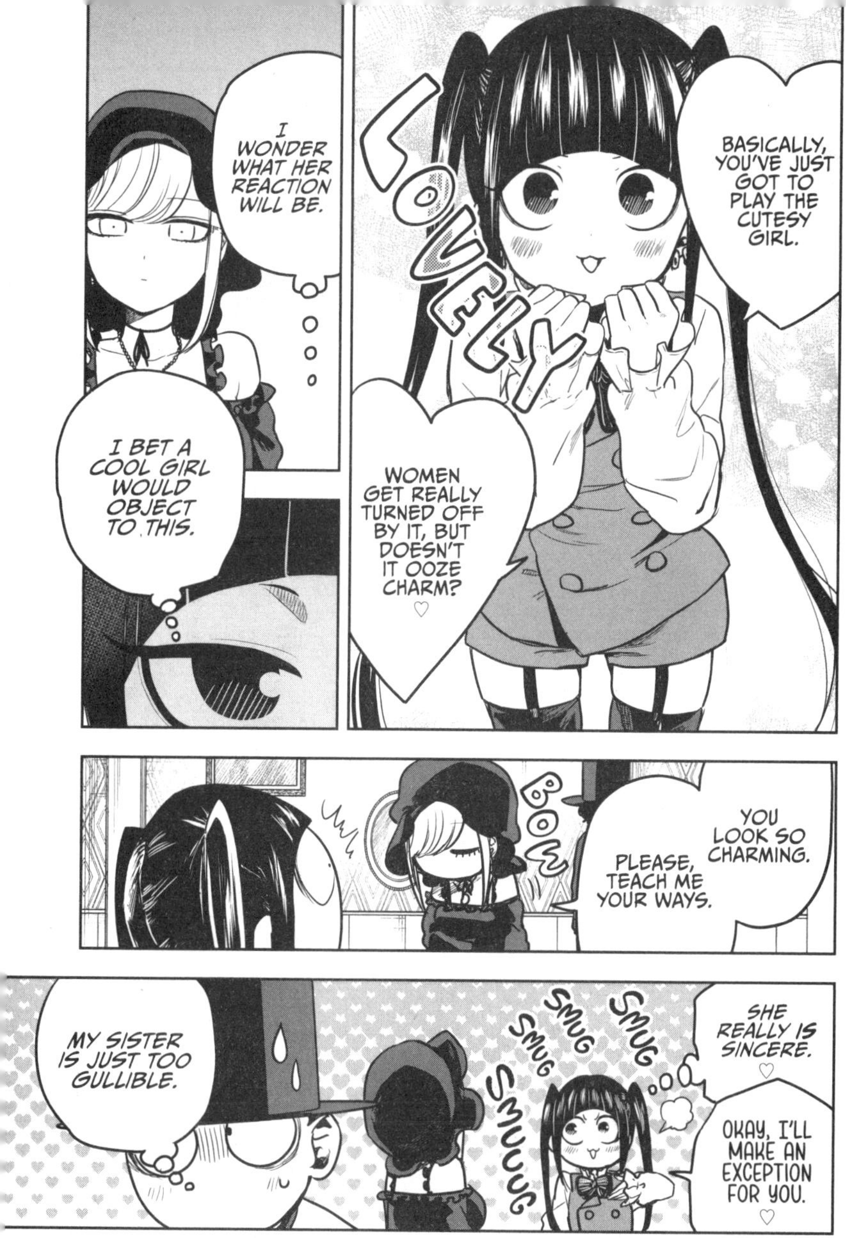
BASICALLY, YOU'VE JUST GOT TO PLAY THE CUTESY GIRL.
LOVELY
WOMEN GET REALLY TURNED OFF BY IT, BUT DOESN'T IT OOZE CHARM? ♡
I WONDER WHAT HER REACTION WILL BE.
I BET A COOL GIRL WOULD OBJECT TO THIS.
YOU LOOK SO CHARMING.
PLEASE, TEACH ME YOUR WAYS.
BOW
SHE REALLY IS SINCERE. ♡
OKAY, I'LL MAKE AN EXCEPTION FOR YOU. ♡
SMUG
SMUG
SMUG
SMUUUG
MY SISTER IS JUST TOO GULLIBLE.

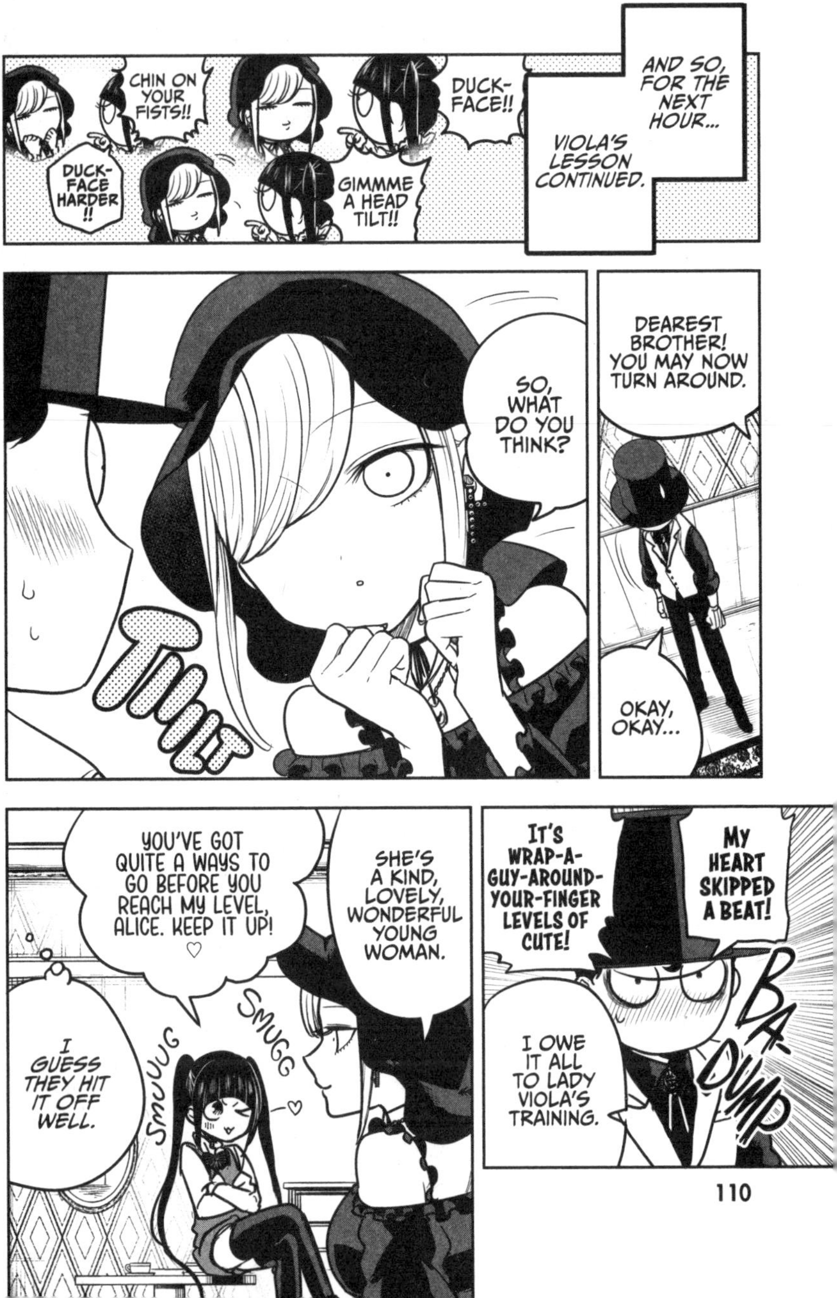
AND SO, FOR THE NEXT HOUR...
VIOLA'S LESSON CONTINUED.
DUCK-FACE!!
CHIN ON YOUR FISTS!!
GIMMME A HEAD TILT!!
DUCK-FACE HARDER!!
DEAREST BROTHER! YOU MAY NOW TURN AROUND.
OKAY, OKAY...
SO, WHAT DO YOU THINK?
TILT
My HEART SKIPPED A BEAT!
IT'S WRAP-A-GUY-AROUND-YOUR-FINGER LEVELS OF CUTE!
BA-DUMP
I OWE IT ALL TO LADY VIOLA'S TRAINING.
SHE'S A KIND, LOVELY, WONDERFUL YOUNG WOMAN.
YOU'VE GOT QUITE A WAYS TO GO BEFORE YOU REACH MY LEVEL, ALICE. KEEP IT UP! ♡
SMUGG
SMUUUG
I GUESS THEY HIT IT OFF WELL.

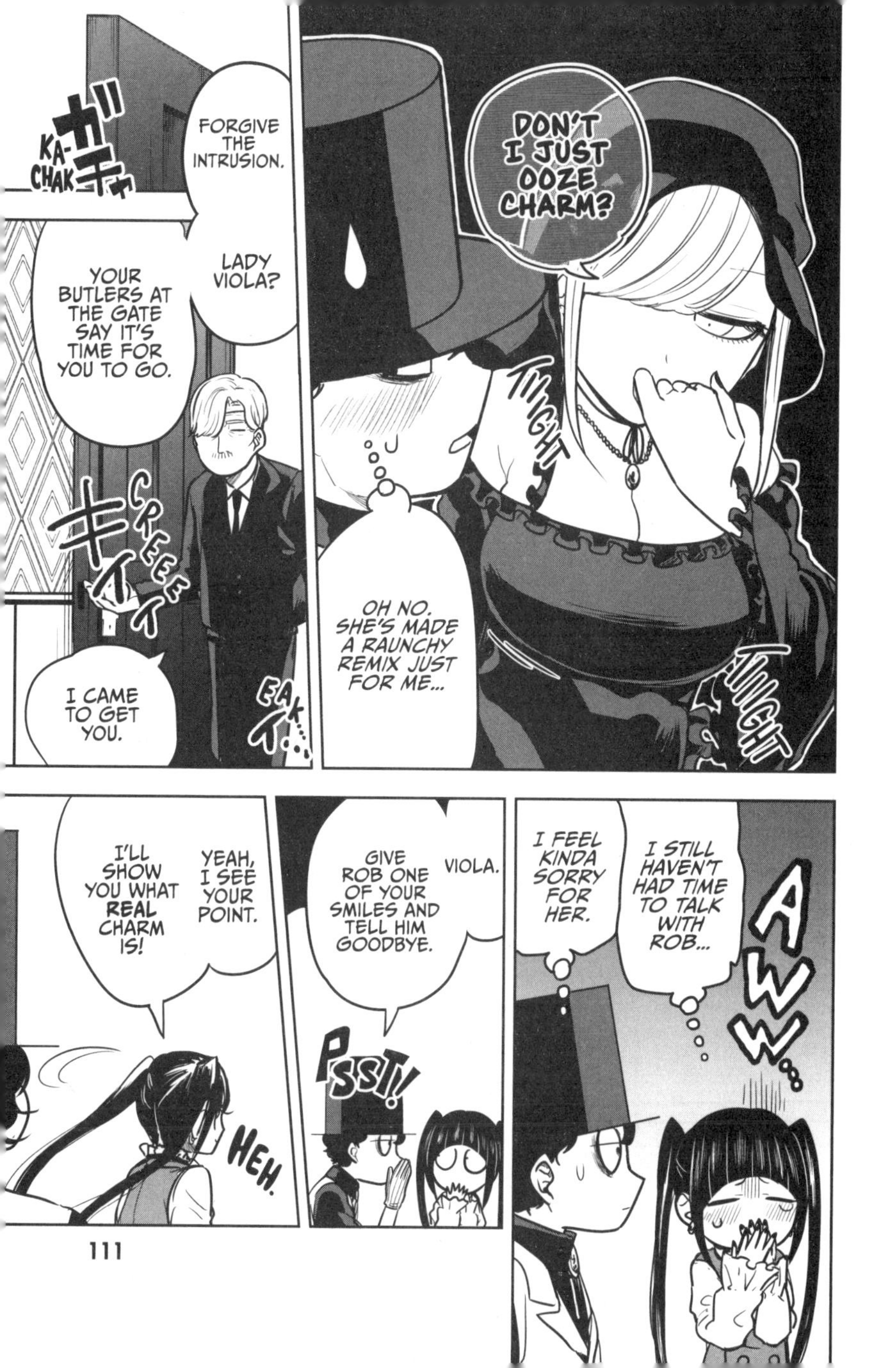
DON'T I JUST OOZE CHARM?
TIIIGHT
OH NO. SHE'S MADE A RAUNCHY REMIX JUST FOR ME...
TIIIGHT
KA-CHAK
FORGIVE THE INTRUSION.
LADY VIOLA?
YOUR BUTLERS AT THE GATE SAY IT'S TIME FOR YOU TO GO.
CREEE
EAK...
I CAME TO GET YOU.
AWWW...
I STILL HAVEN'T HAD TIME TO TALK WITH ROB...
I FEEL KINDA SORRY FOR HER.
VIOLA.
GIVE ROB ONE OF YOUR SMILES AND TELL HIM GOODBYE.
PSST!
YEAH, I SEE YOUR POINT.
I'LL SHOW YOU WHAT **REAL** CHARM IS!
HEH.

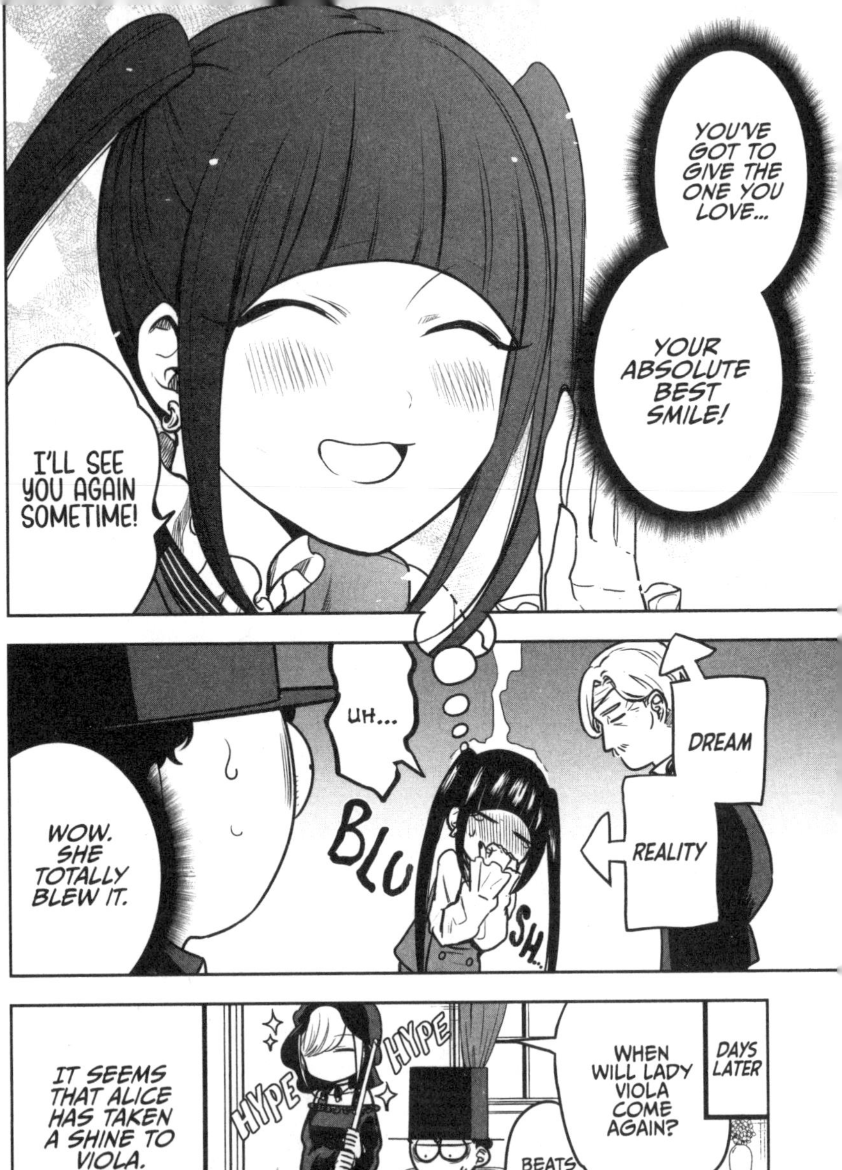

YOU'VE GOT TO GIVE THE ONE YOU LOVE...
YOUR ABSOLUTE BEST SMILE!
I'LL SEE YOU AGAIN SOMETIME!
DREAM
REALITY
UH...
BLUSH..
WOW. SHE TOTALLY BLEW IT.
DAYS LATER
WHEN WILL LADY VIOLA COME AGAIN?
BEATS ME...
HYPE
HYPE
IT SEEMS THAT ALICE HAS TAKEN A SHINE TO VIOLA.

Chapter 25: The Mail Carrier

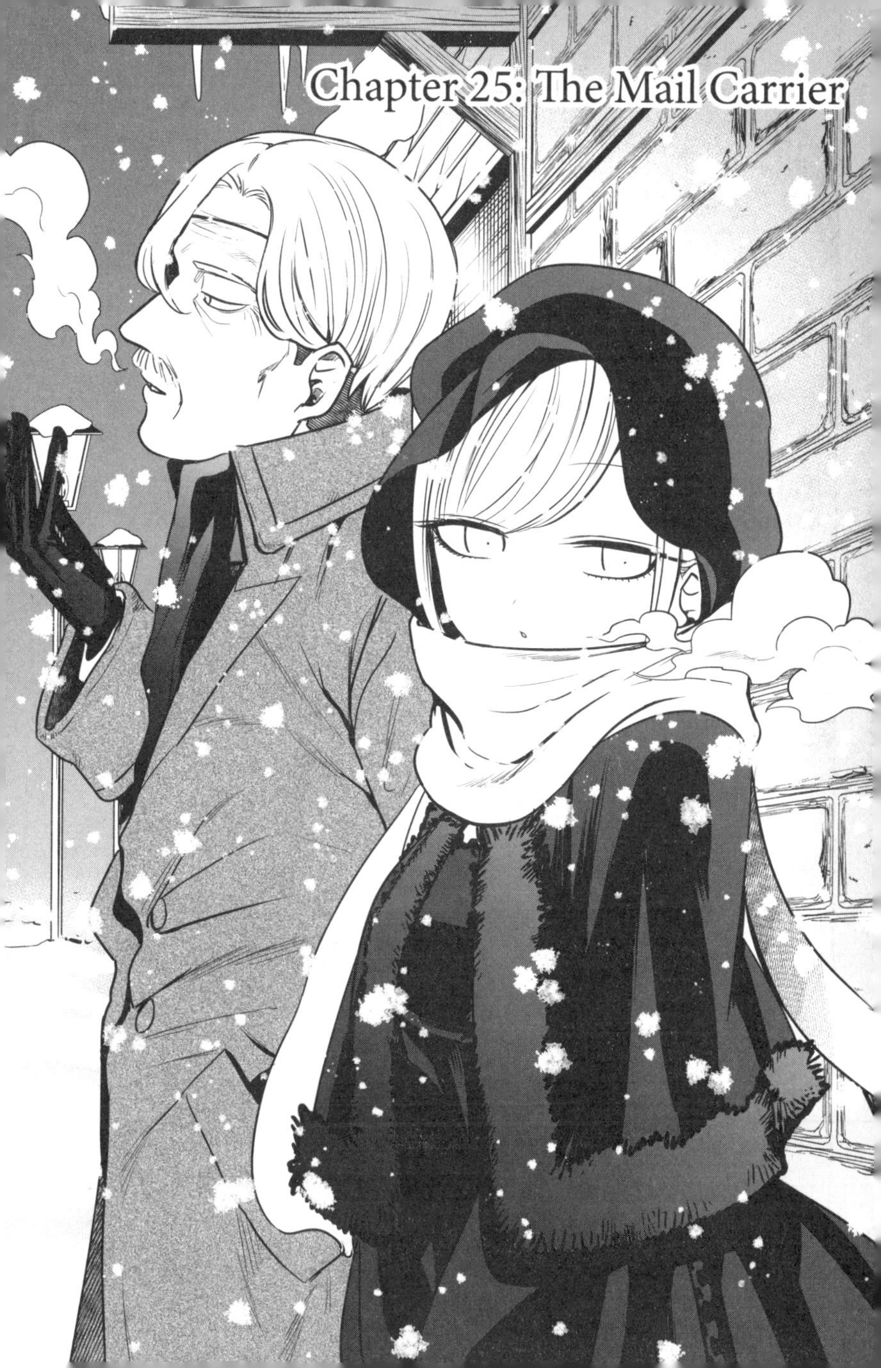

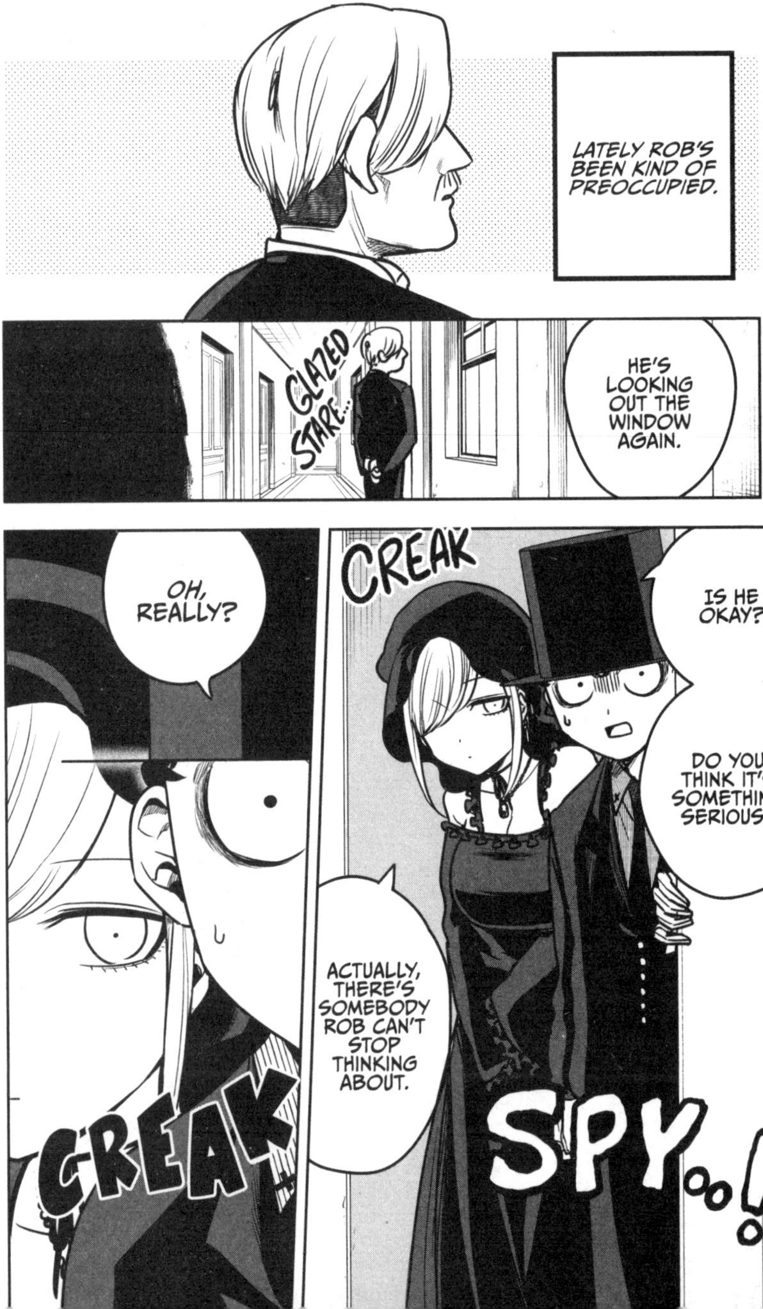

LATELY ROB'S BEEN KIND OF PREOCCUPIED.
HE'S LOOKING OUT THE WINDOW AGAIN.
GLAZED STARE...
CREAK
IS HE OKAY?
DO YOU THINK IT'S SOMETHING SERIOUS?
ACTUALLY, THERE'S SOMEBODY ROB CAN'T STOP THINKING ABOUT.
SPY..!
OH, REALLY?
CREAK

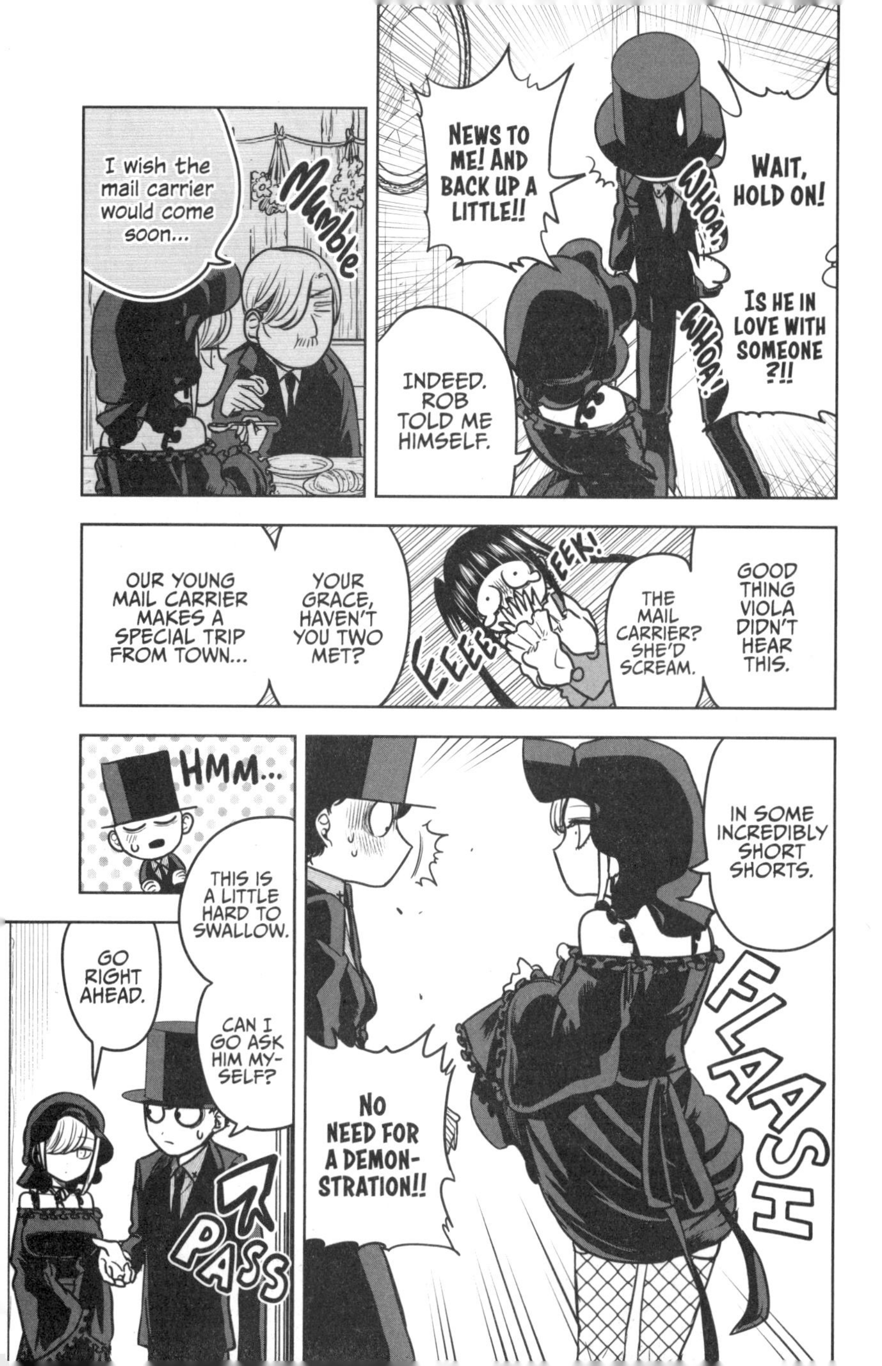
WAIT, HOLD ON!
WHOA!
NEWS TO ME! AND BACK UP A LITTLE!!
IS HE IN LOVE WITH SOMEONE ?!!
WHOA!
INDEED. ROB TOLD ME HIMSELF.
Mumble
I wish the mail carrier would come soon...
GOOD THING VIOLA DIDN'T HEAR THIS.
THE MAIL CARRIER? SHE'D SCREAM.
EEEEEEK!
YOUR GRACE, HAVEN'T YOU TWO MET?
OUR YOUNG MAIL CARRIER MAKES A SPECIAL TRIP FROM TOWN...
IN SOME INCREDIBLY SHORT SHORTS.
FLASH
NO NEED FOR A DEMON-STRATION!!
HMM...
THIS IS A LITTLE HARD TO SWALLOW.
CAN I GO ASK HIM MY-SELF?
GO RIGHT AHEAD.
PASS

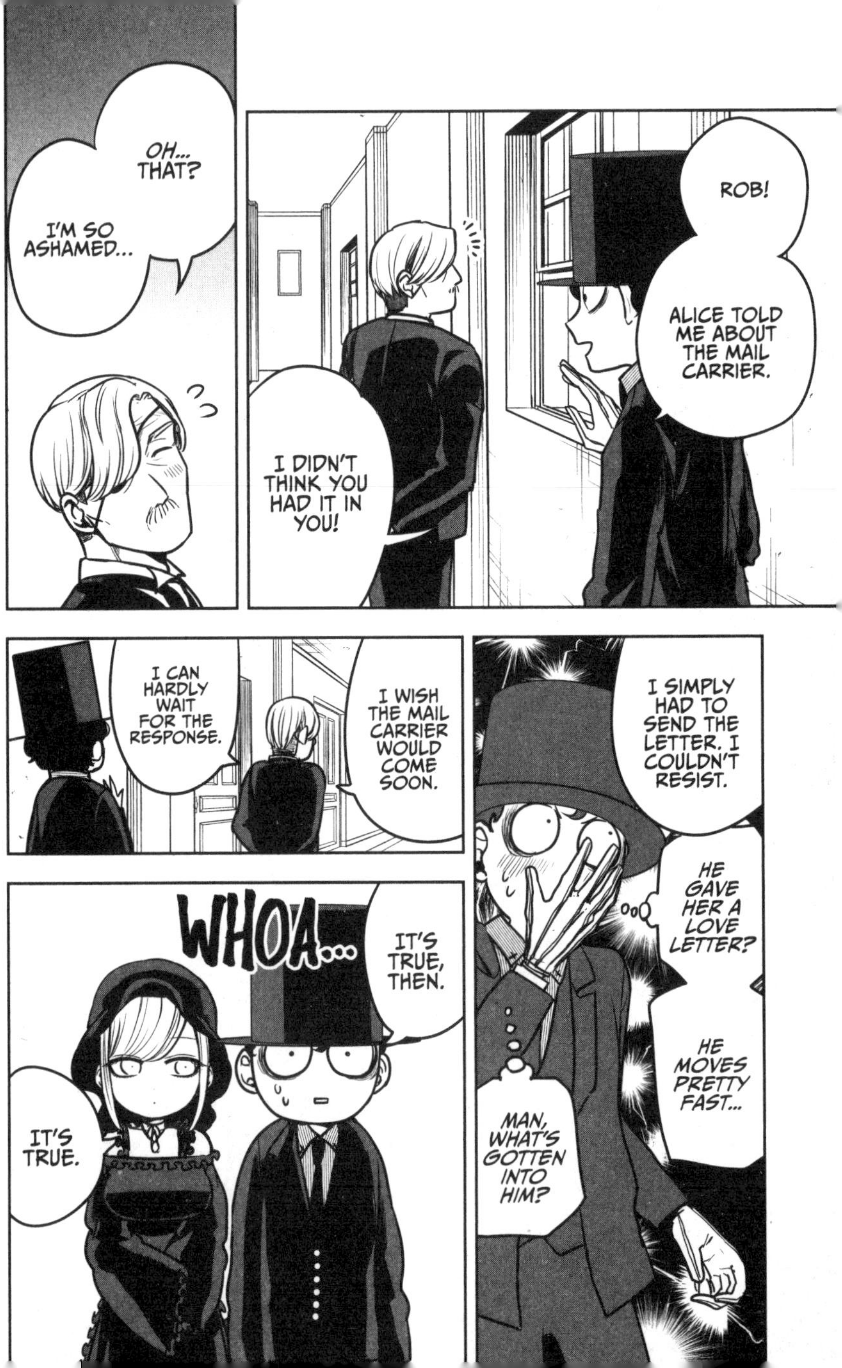
ROB!
ALICE TOLD ME ABOUT THE MAIL CARRIER.
I DIDN'T THINK YOU HAD IT IN YOU!
OH... THAT?
I'M SO ASHAMED...
I SIMPLY HAD TO SEND THE LETTER. I COULDN'T RESIST.
HE GAVE HER A LOVE LETTER?
HE MOVES PRETTY FAST...
MAN, WHAT'S GOTTEN INTO HIM?
I WISH THE MAIL CARRIER WOULD COME SOON.
I CAN HARDLY WAIT FOR THE RESPONSE.
WHOA...
IT'S TRUE, THEN.
IT'S TRUE.

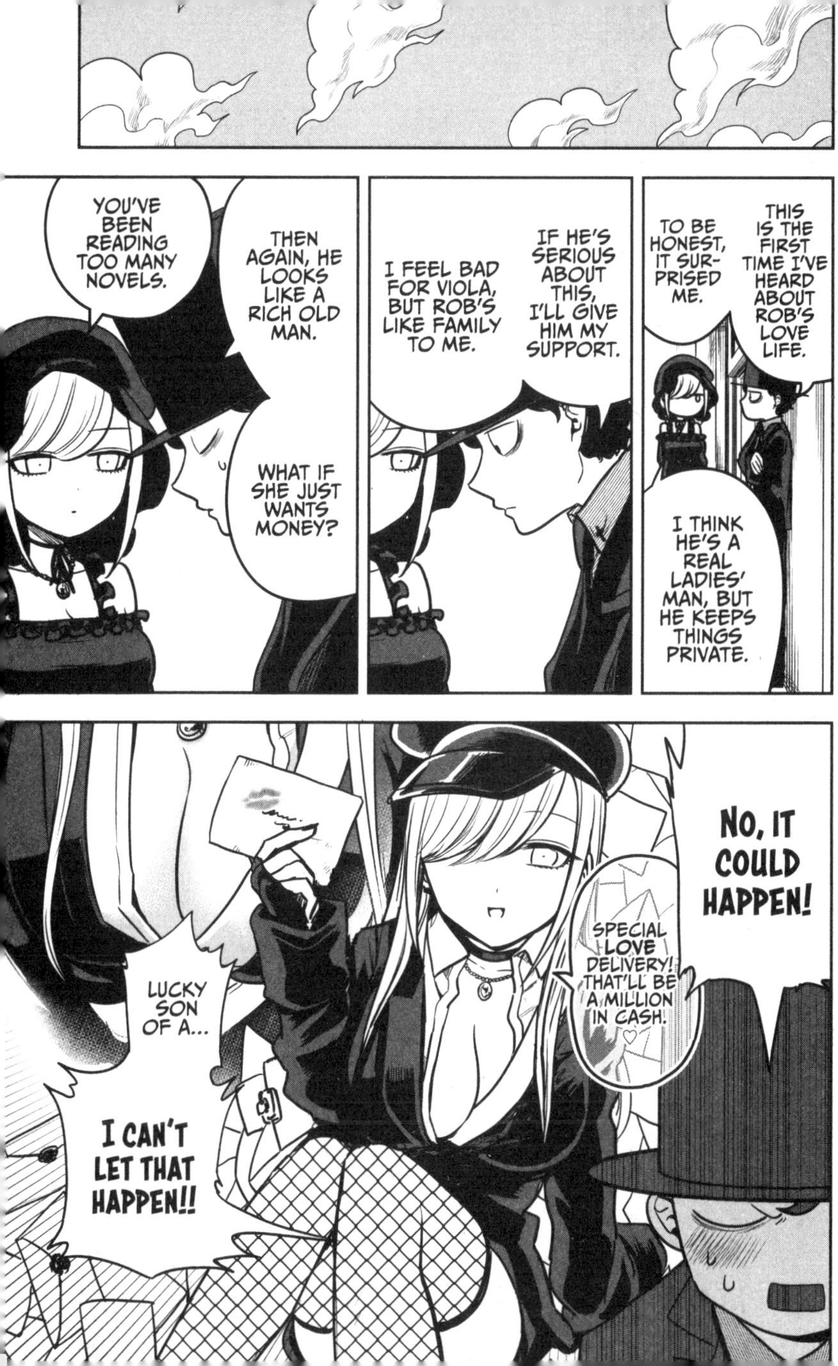
THIS IS THE FIRST TIME I'VE HEARD ABOUT ROB'S LOVE LIFE.
TO BE HONEST, IT SURPRISED ME.
I THINK HE'S A REAL LADIES' MAN, BUT HE KEEPS THINGS PRIVATE.
IF HE'S SERIOUS ABOUT THIS, I'LL GIVE HIM MY SUPPORT.
I FEEL BAD FOR VIOLA, BUT ROB'S LIKE FAMILY TO ME.
THEN AGAIN, HE LOOKS LIKE A RICH OLD MAN.
YOU'VE BEEN READING TOO MANY NOVELS.
WHAT IF SHE JUST WANTS MONEY?
NO, IT COULD HAPPEN!
SPECIAL LOVE DELIVERY! THAT'LL BE A MILLION IN CASH. ♡
LUCKY SON OF A...
I CAN'T LET THAT HAPPEN!!

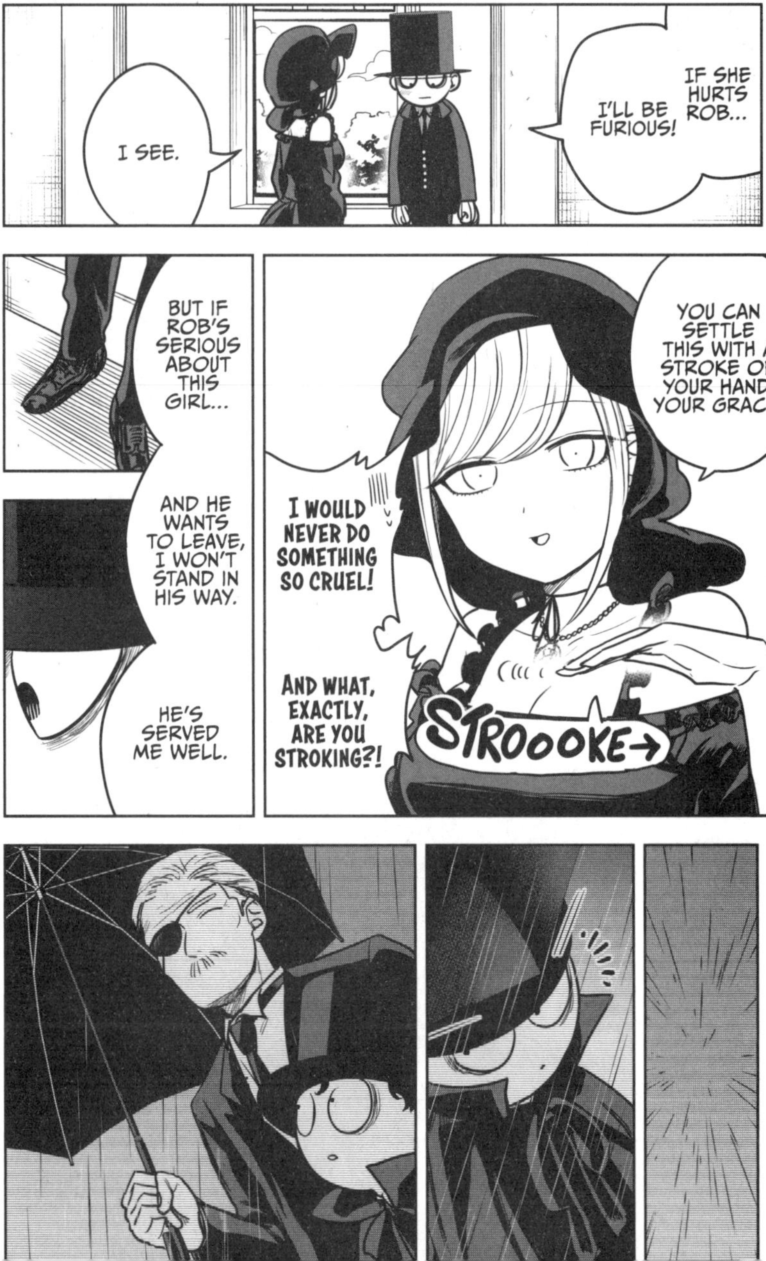
IF SHE HURTS ROB... I'LL BE FURIOUS!
I SEE.
YOU CAN SETTLE THIS WITH A STROKE OF YOUR HAND, YOUR GRACE.
I WOULD NEVER DO SOMETHING SO CRUEL!
STROOOKE→
AND WHAT, EXACTLY, ARE YOU STROKING?!
BUT IF ROB'S SERIOUS ABOUT THIS GIRL...
AND HE WANTS TO LEAVE, I WON'T STAND IN HIS WAY.
HE'S SERVED ME WELL.

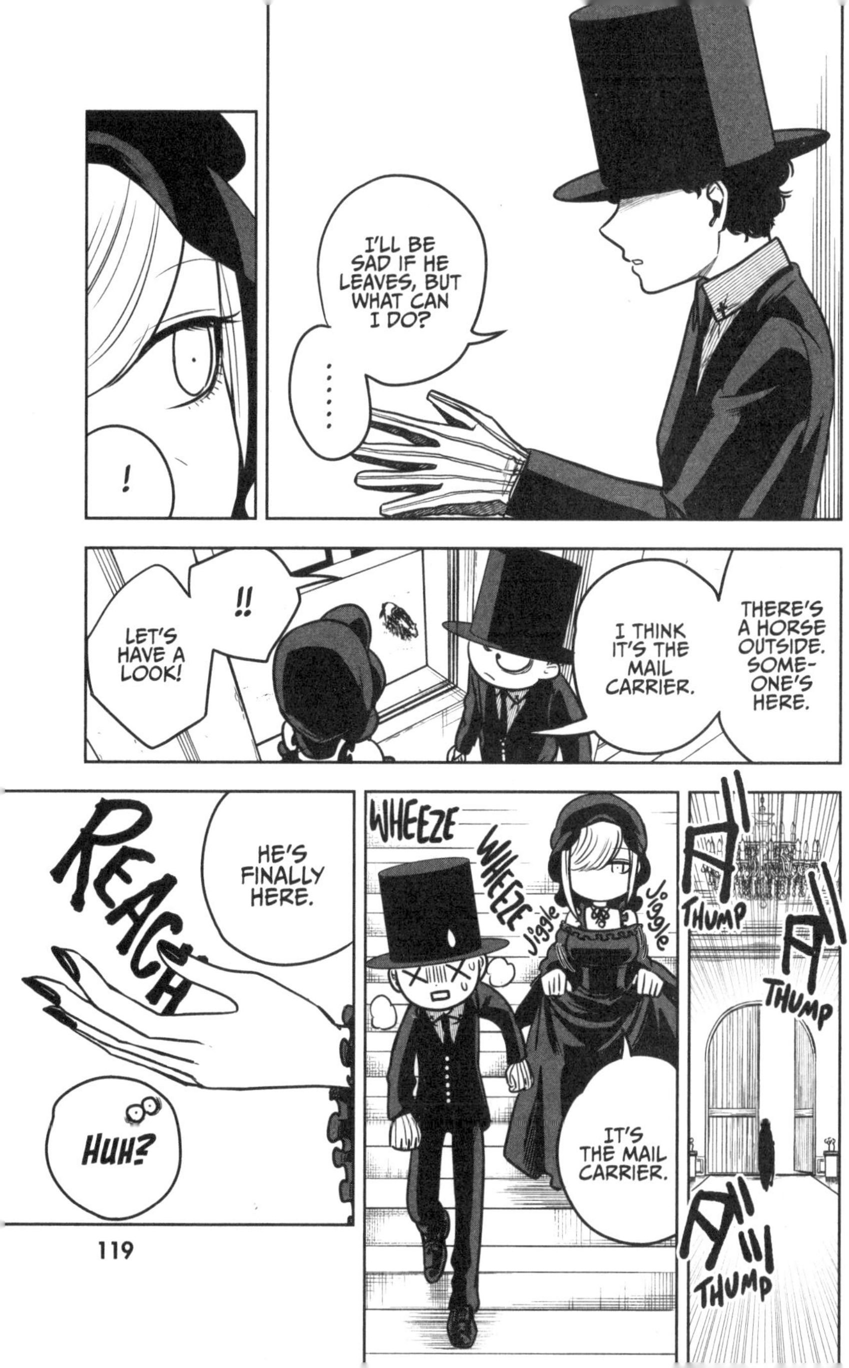
I'LL BE SAD IF HE LEAVES, BUT WHAT CAN I DO?
......
!
THERE'S A HORSE OUTSIDE. SOME-ONE'S HERE.
I THINK IT'S THE MAIL CARRIER.
!!
LET'S HAVE A LOOK!
THUMP
THUMP
THUMP
WHEEZE
WHEEZE
Jiggle
Jiggle
IT'S THE MAIL CARRIER.
HE'S FINALLY HERE.
REACH
HUH?

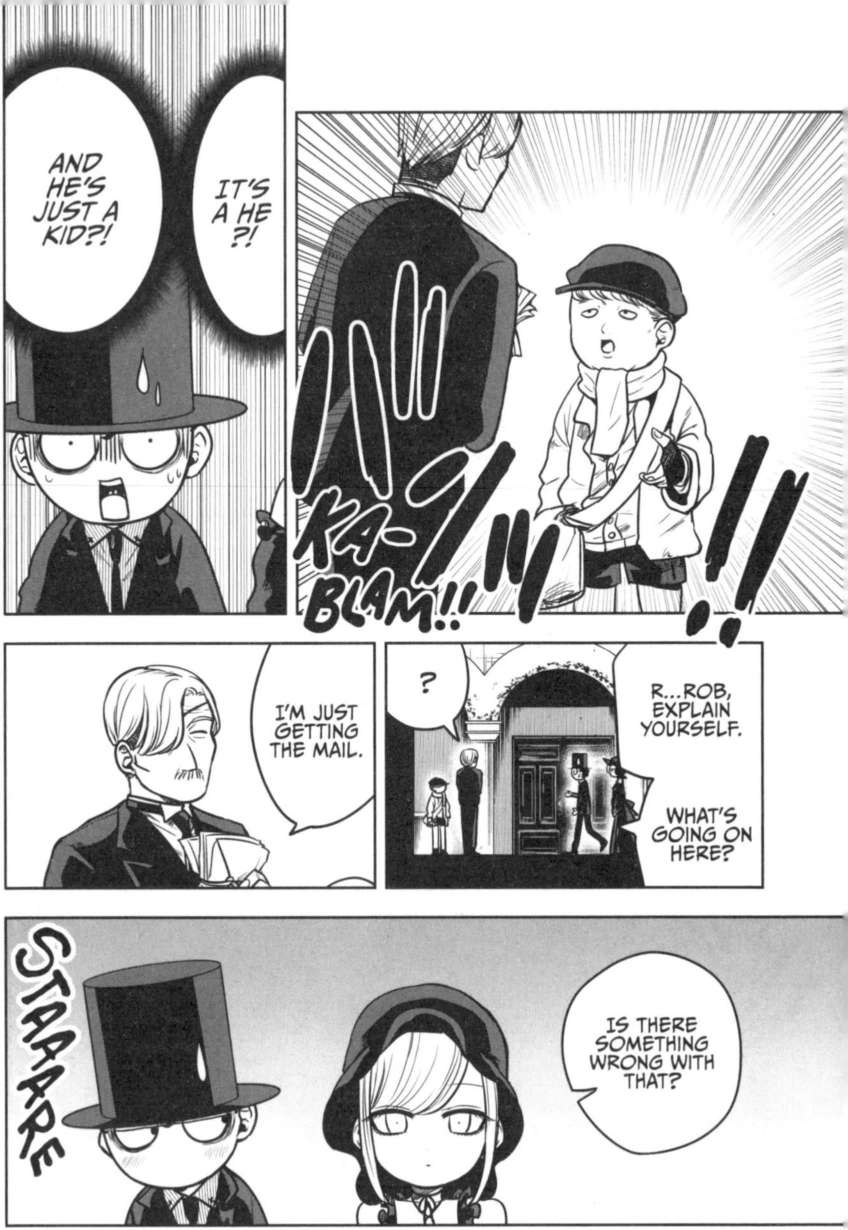
KA-BLAM!!
IT'S A HE ?!
AND HE'S JUST A KID?!
R...ROB, EXPLAIN YOURSELF.
WHAT'S GOING ON HERE?
?
I'M JUST GETTING THE MAIL.
IS THERE SOMETHING WRONG WITH THAT?
STAAAARE

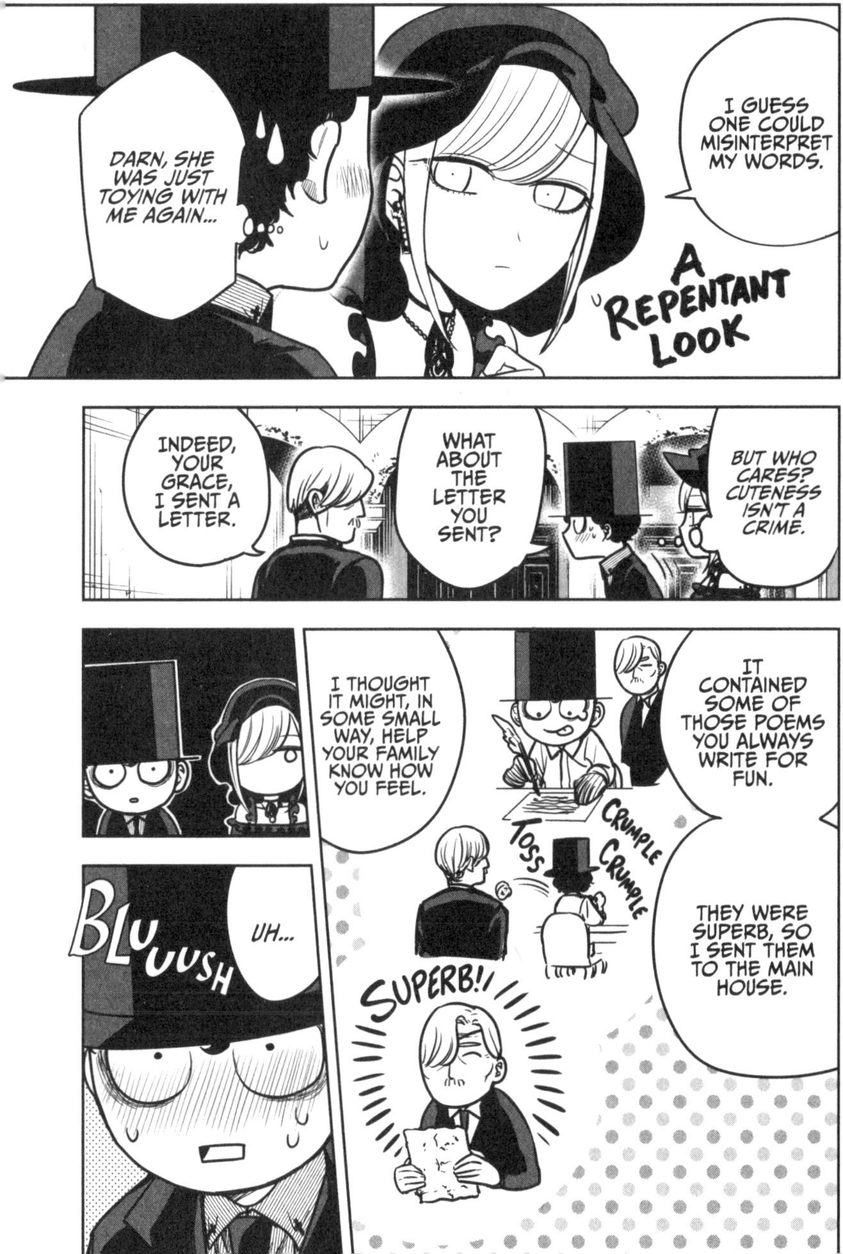
I GUESS ONE COULD MISINTERPRET MY WORDS.
A REPENTANT LOOK
DARN, SHE WAS JUST TOYING WITH ME AGAIN...
BUT WHO CARES? CUTENESS ISN'T A CRIME.
WHAT ABOUT THE LETTER YOU SENT?
INDEED, YOUR GRACE, I SENT A LETTER.
IT CONTAINED SOME OF THOSE POEMS YOU ALWAYS WRITE FOR FUN.
I THOUGHT IT MIGHT, IN SOME SMALL WAY, HELP YOUR FAMILY KNOW HOW YOU FEEL.
CRUMPLE
CRUMPLE
TOSS
THEY WERE SUPERB, SO I SENT THEM TO THE MAIN HOUSE.
SUPERB!!
UH...
BLUUUSH

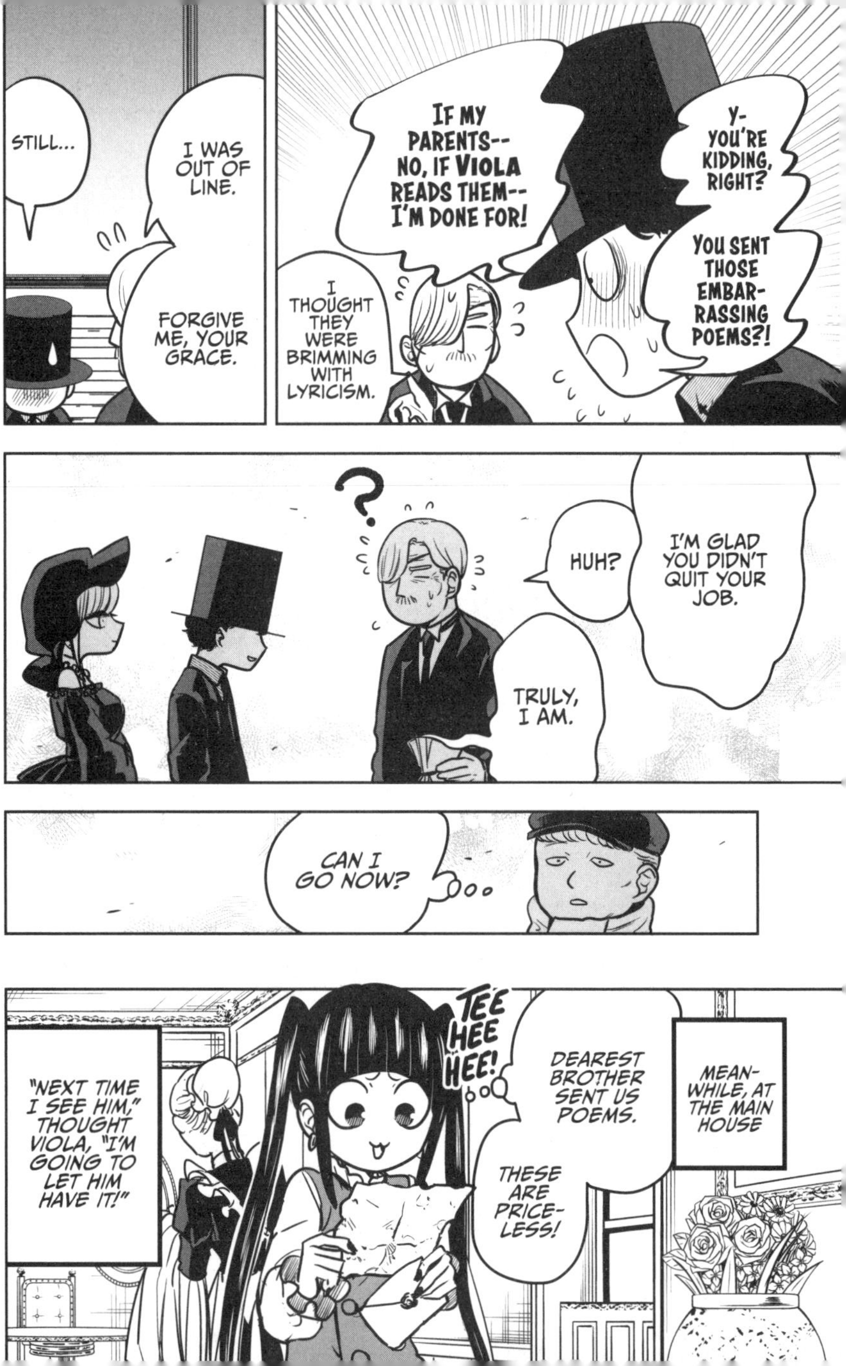
Y-YOU'RE KIDDING, RIGHT?
YOU SENT THOSE EMBARRASSING POEMS?!
IF MY PARENTS--NO, IF VIOLA READS THEM--I'M DONE FOR!
I THOUGHT THEY WERE BRIMMING WITH LYRICISM.
I WAS OUT OF LINE.
FORGIVE ME, YOUR GRACE.
STILL...
I'M GLAD YOU DIDN'T QUIT YOUR JOB.
HUH?
TRULY, I AM.
CAN I GO NOW?
MEANWHILE, AT THE MAIN HOUSE
DEAREST BROTHER SENT US POEMS.
THESE ARE PRICELESS!
TEE HEE HEE!
"NEXT TIME I SEE HIM," THOUGHT VIOLA, "I'M GOING TO LET HIM HAVE IT!"

Chapter 26: The Search for the Black Cat

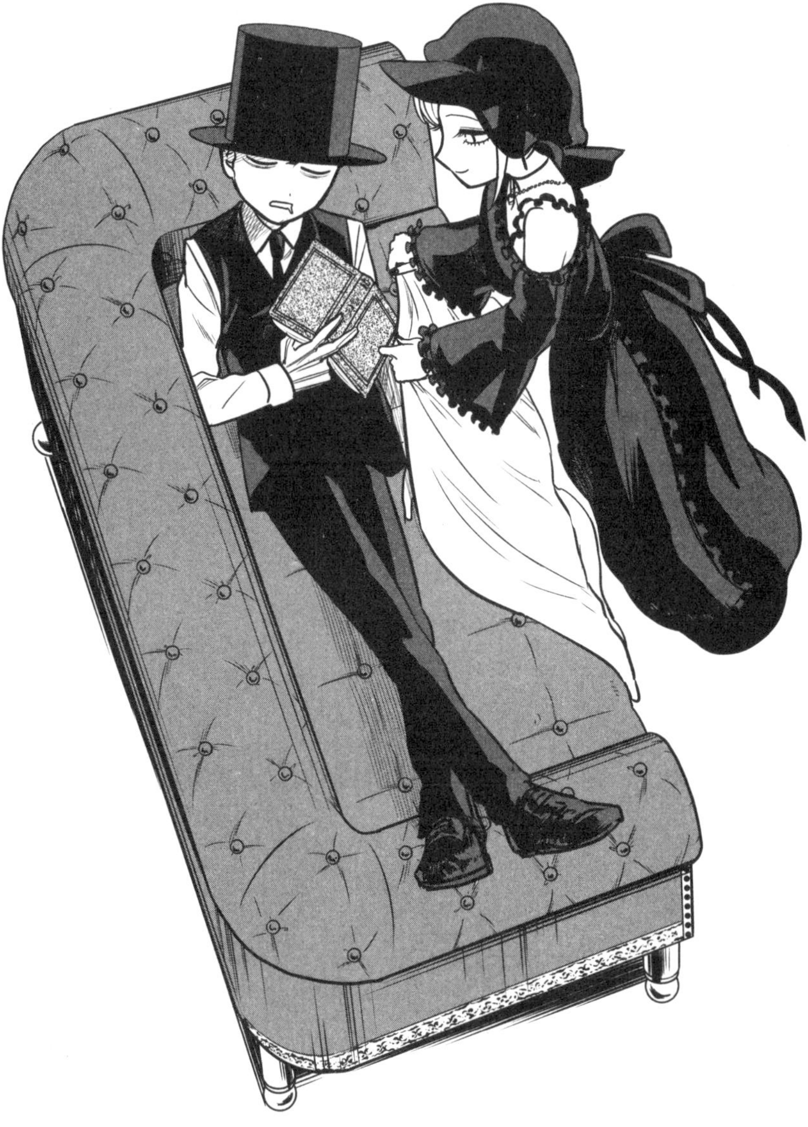

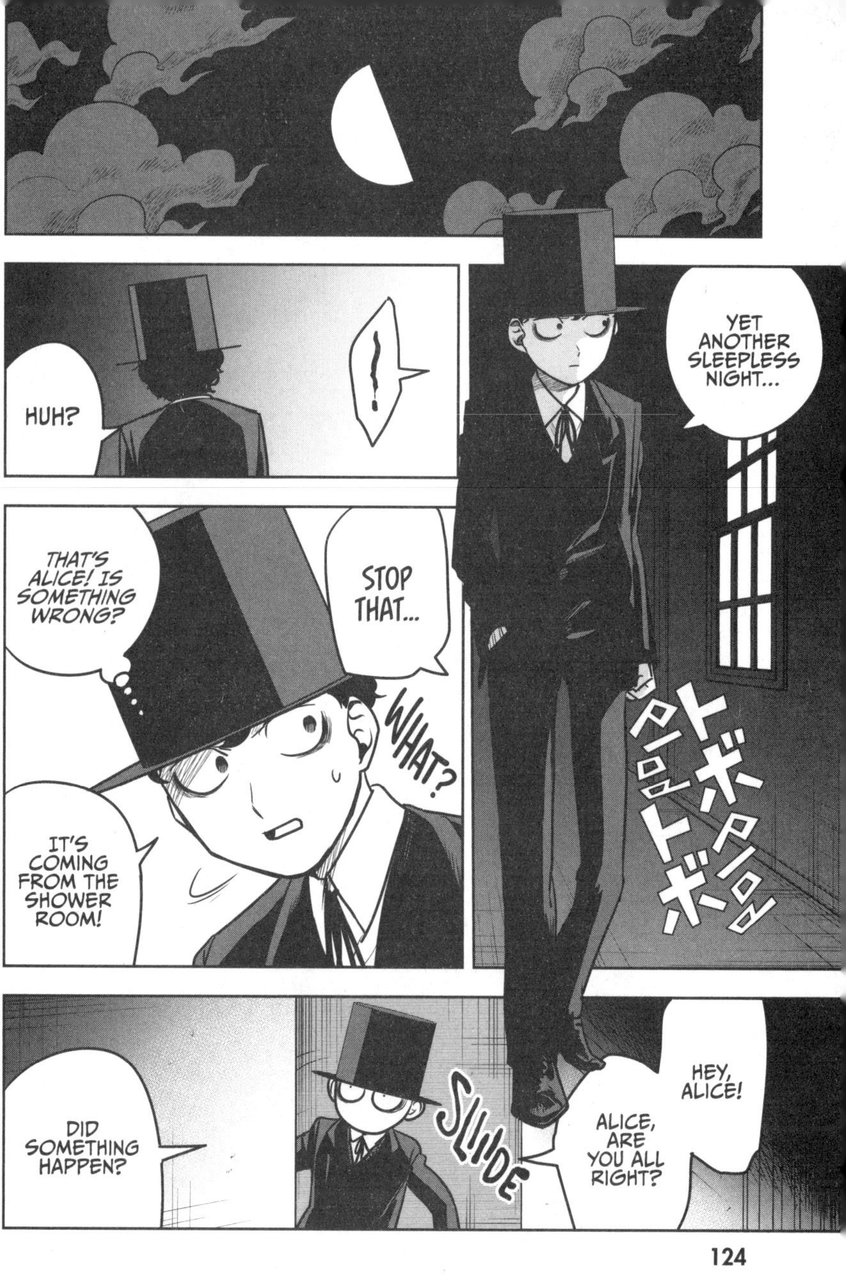
YET ANOTHER SLEEPLESS NIGHT...
トボ トボ
!
HUH?
STOP THAT...
THAT'S ALICE! IS SOMETHING WRONG?
WHAT?
IT'S COMING FROM THE SHOWER ROOM!
HEY, ALICE!
ALICE, ARE YOU ALL RIGHT?
SLIDE
DID SOMETHING HAPPEN?

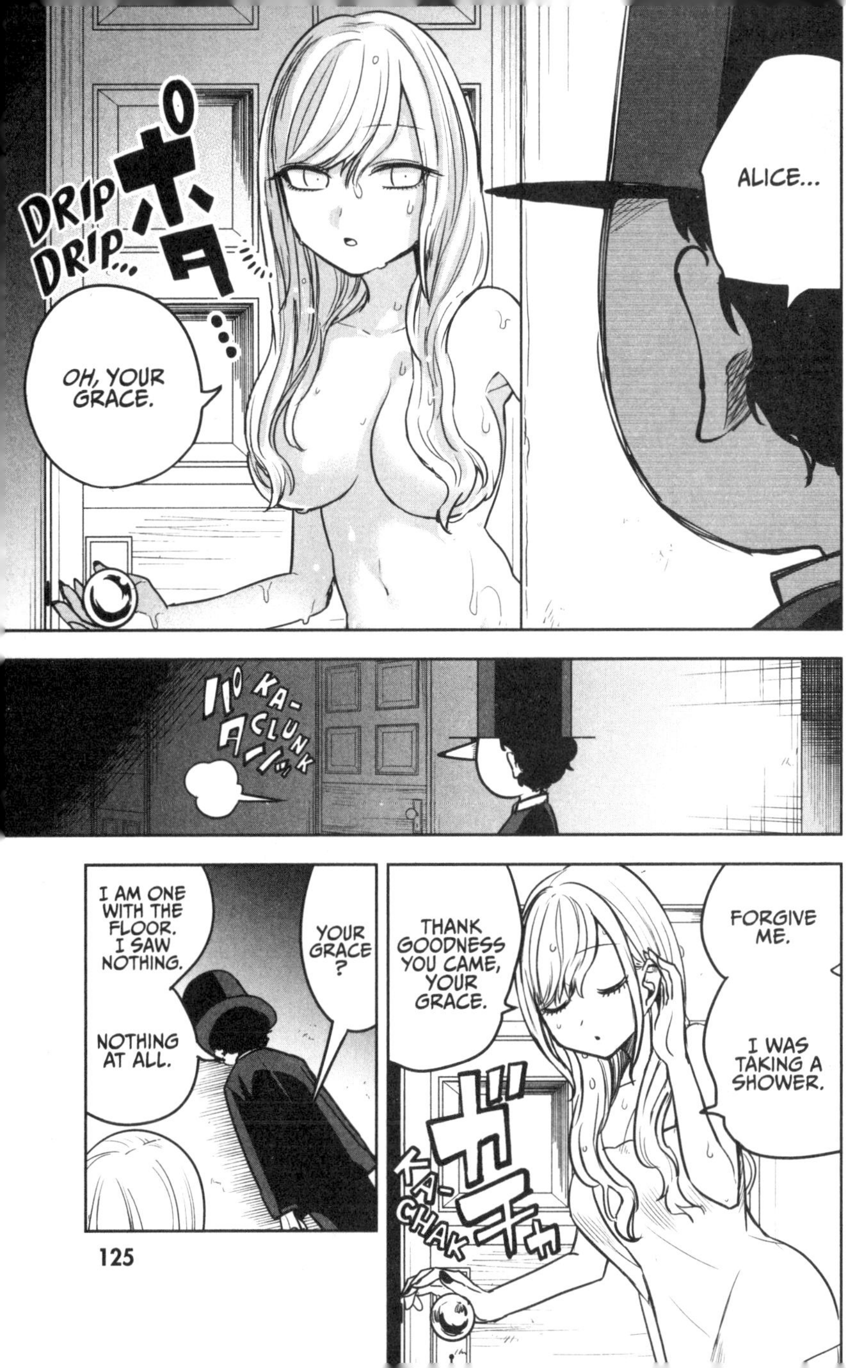
ALICE...
DRIP DRIP...
OH, YOUR GRACE.
KA-CLUNK
FORGIVE ME.
I WAS TAKING A SHOWER.
THANK GOODNESS YOU CAME, YOUR GRACE.
KA-CHAK
YOUR GRACE?
I AM ONE WITH THE FLOOR. I SAW NOTHING.
NOTHING AT ALL.

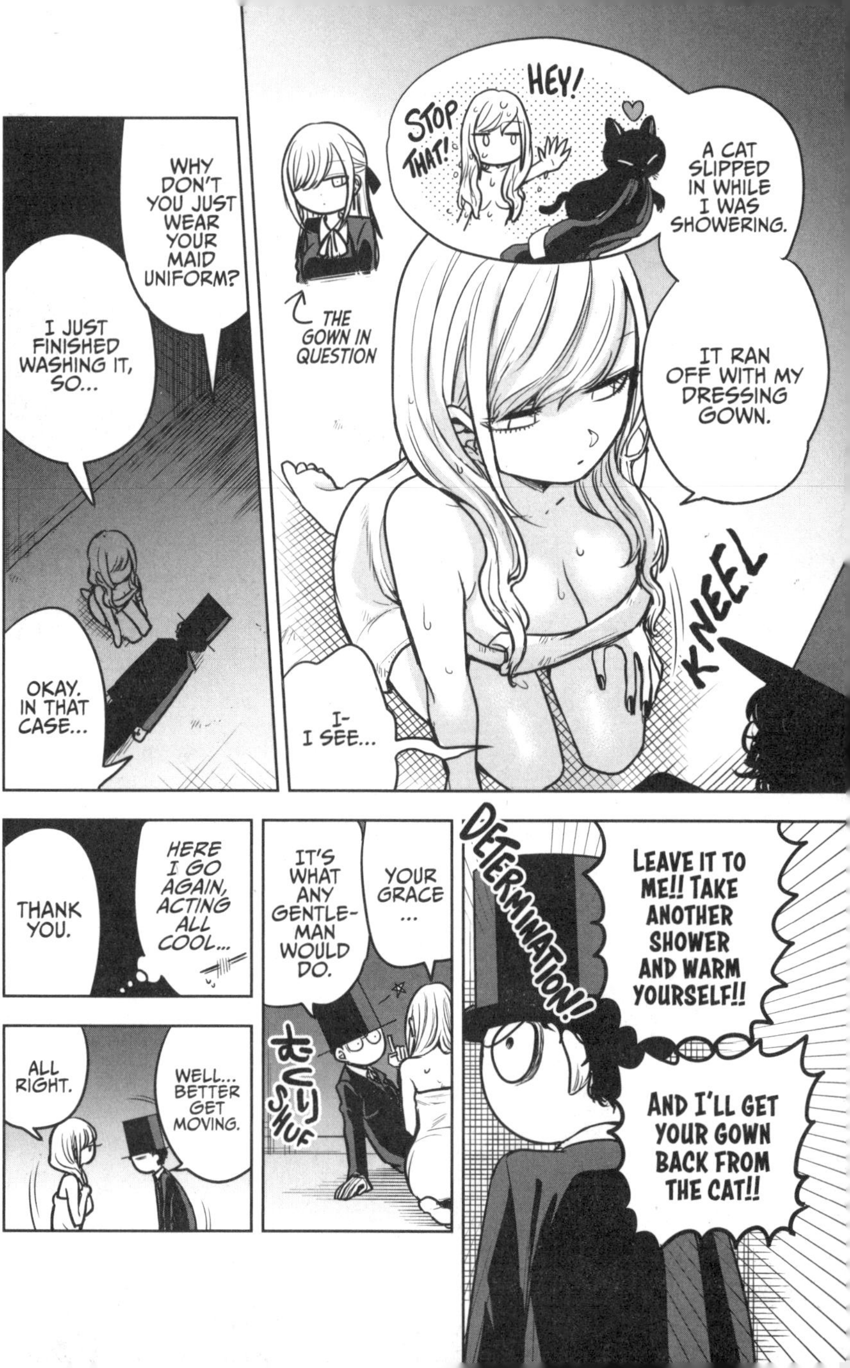
A CAT SLIPPED IN WHILE I WAS SHOWERING.
HEY!
STOP THAT!
THE GOWN IN QUESTION
IT RAN OFF WITH MY DRESSING GOWN.
KNEEL
I- I SEE...
WHY DON'T YOU JUST WEAR YOUR MAID UNIFORM?
I JUST FINISHED WASHING IT, SO...
OKAY. IN THAT CASE...
DETERMINATION!!
LEAVE IT TO ME!! TAKE ANOTHER SHOWER AND WARM YOURSELF!!
AND I'LL GET YOUR GOWN BACK FROM THE CAT!!
YOUR GRACE...
IT'S WHAT ANY GENTLE-MAN WOULD DO.
むくり
SHUF
HERE I GO AGAIN, ACTING ALL COOL...
THANK YOU.
WELL... BETTER GET MOVING.
ALL RIGHT.

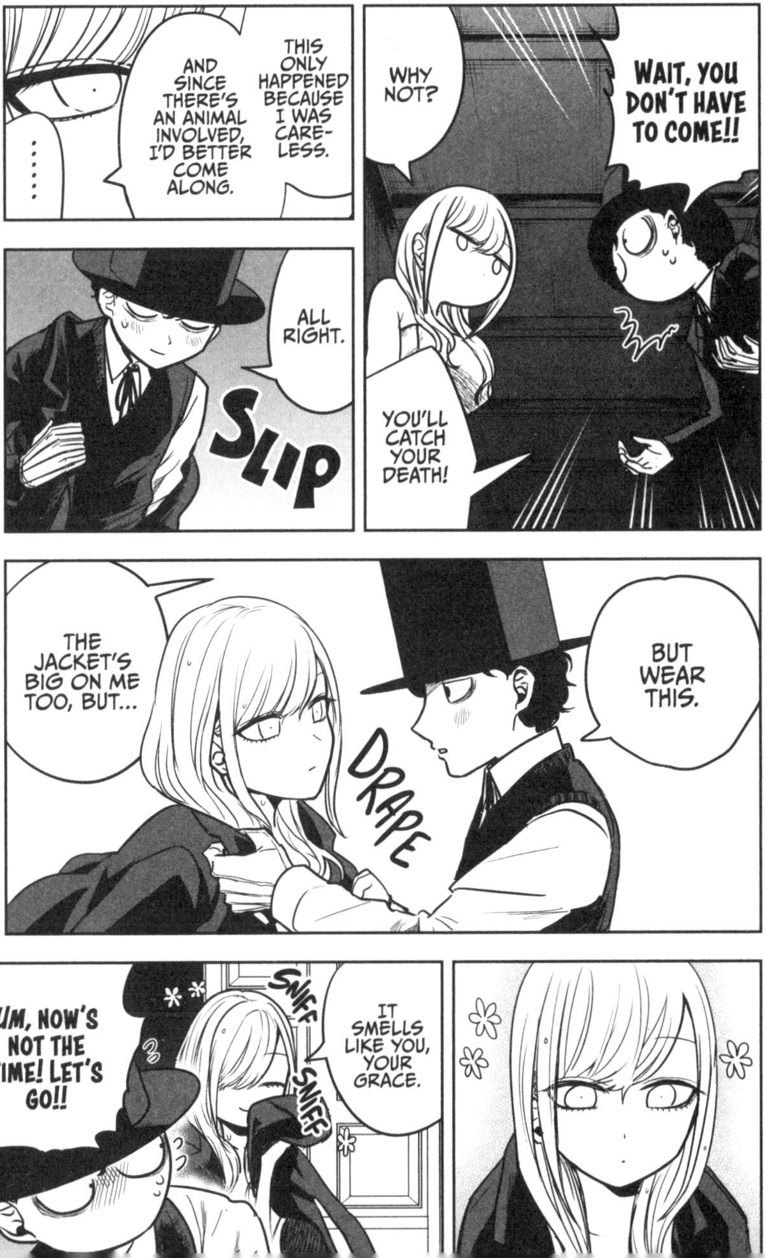
WAIT, YOU DON'T HAVE TO COME!!
WHY NOT?
YOU'LL CATCH YOUR DEATH!
THIS ONLY HAPPENED BECAUSE I WAS CARE-LESS.
AND SINCE THERE'S AN ANIMAL INVOLVED, I'D BETTER COME ALONG.
......
ALL RIGHT.
SLIP
BUT WEAR THIS.
DRAPE
THE JACKET'S BIG ON ME TOO, BUT...
IT SMELLS LIKE YOU, YOUR GRACE.
SNIFF
SNIFF
UM, NOW'S NOT THE TIME! LET'S GO!!

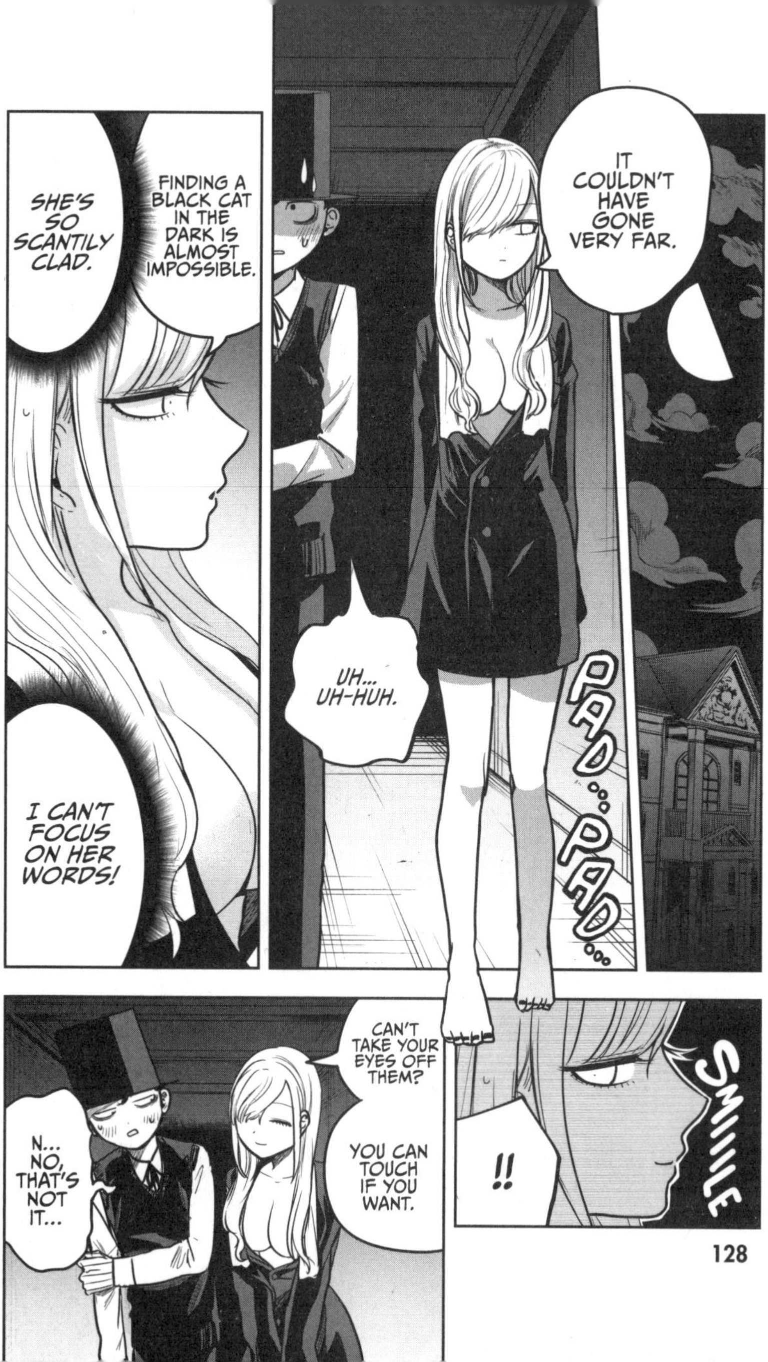
IT COULDN'T HAVE GONE VERY FAR.
PAD... PAD... PAD...
UH... UH-HUH.
FINDING A BLACK CAT IN THE DARK IS ALMOST IMPOSSIBLE.
SHE'S SO SCANTILY CLAD.
I CAN'T FOCUS ON HER WORDS!
SMIIILE
!!
CAN'T TAKE YOUR EYES OFF THEM?
YOU CAN TOUCH IF YOU WANT.
N... NO, THAT'S NOT IT...

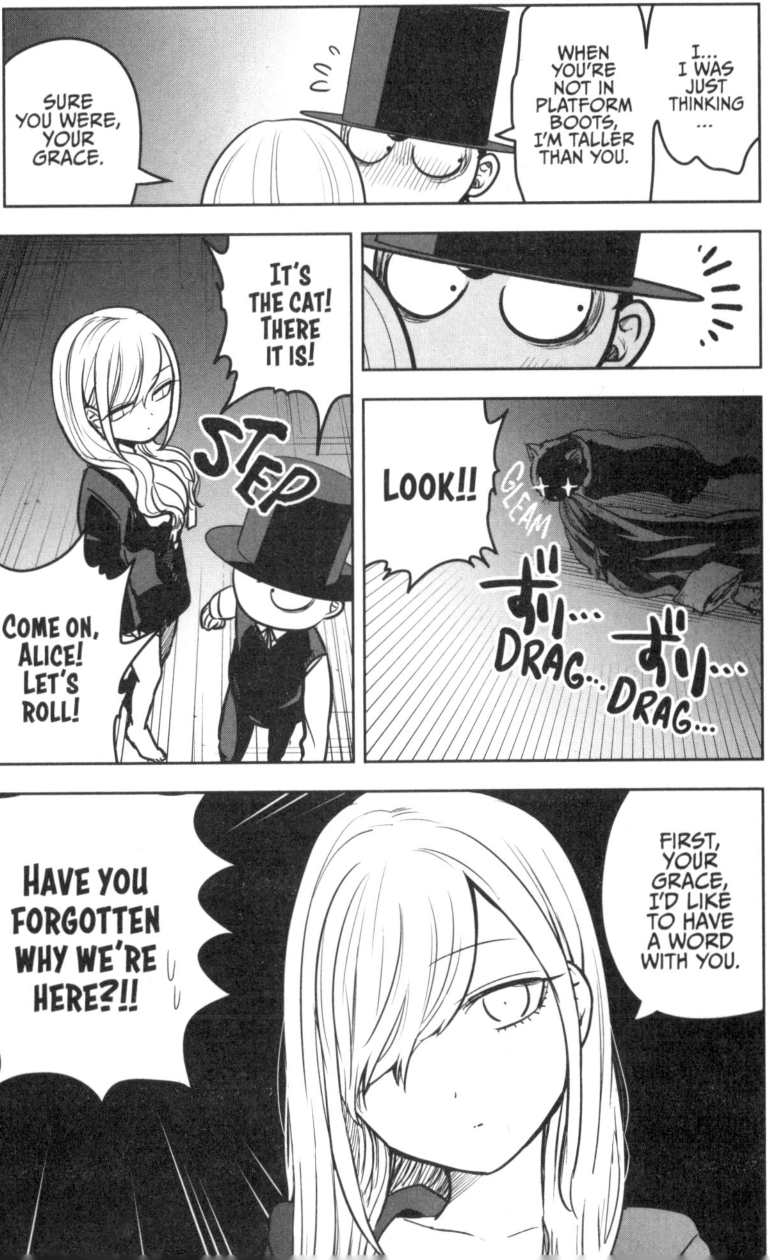
I... I WAS JUST THINKING ...
WHEN YOU'RE NOT IN PLATFORM BOOTS, I'M TALLER THAN YOU.
SURE YOU WERE, YOUR GRACE.
LOOK!!
GLEAM
ずり… DRAG…
ずり… DRAG…
IT'S THE CAT! THERE IT IS!
STEP
COME ON, ALICE! LET'S ROLL!
FIRST, YOUR GRACE, I'D LIKE TO HAVE A WORD WITH YOU.
HAVE YOU FORGOTTEN WHY WE'RE HERE?!!

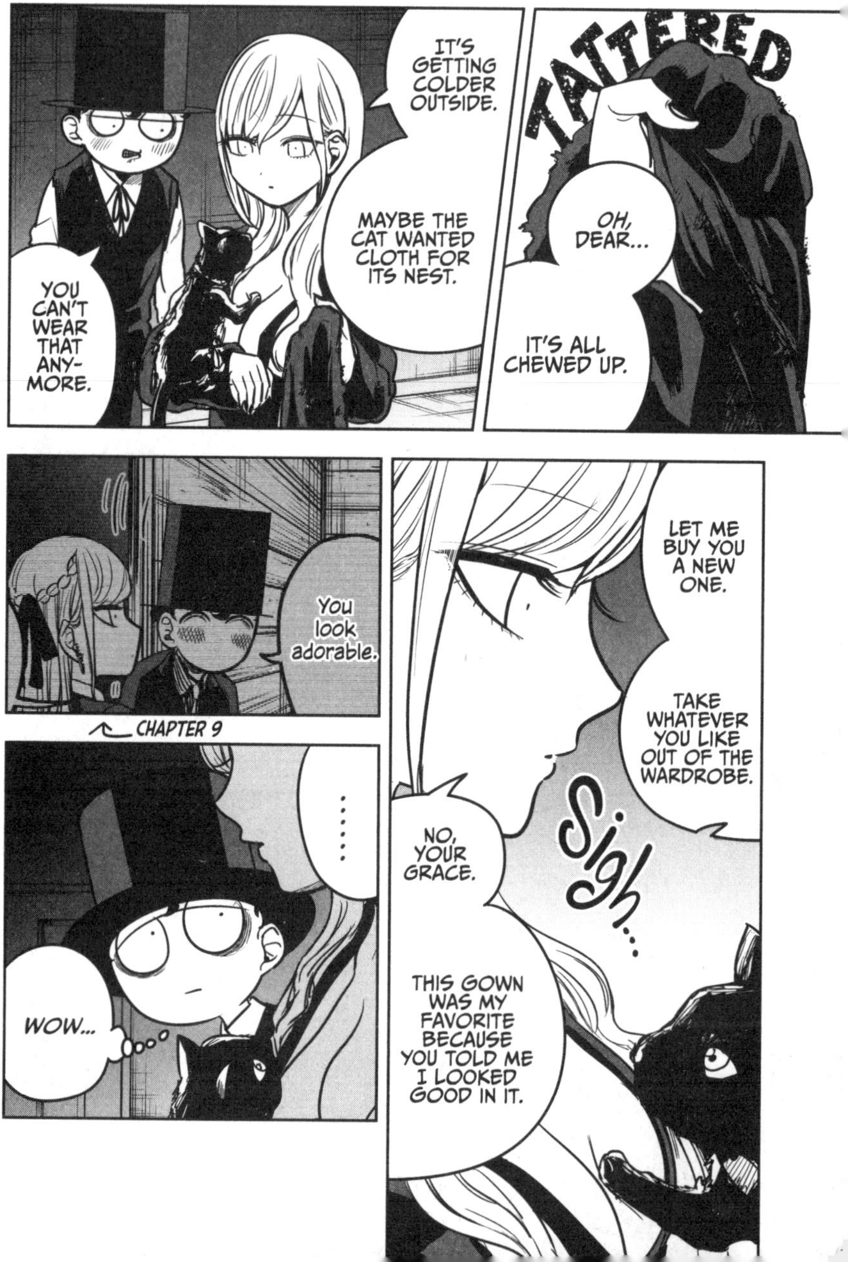
TATTERED
OH, DEAR...
IT'S ALL CHEWED UP.
IT'S GETTING COLDER OUTSIDE.
MAYBE THE CAT WANTED CLOTH FOR ITS NEST.
YOU CAN'T WEAR THAT ANYMORE.
LET ME BUY YOU A NEW ONE.
TAKE WHATEVER YOU LIKE OUT OF THE WARDROBE.
Sigh...
NO, YOUR GRACE.
THIS GOWN WAS MY FAVORITE BECAUSE YOU TOLD ME I LOOKED GOOD IN IT.
You look adorable.
CHAPTER 9
......
WOW...

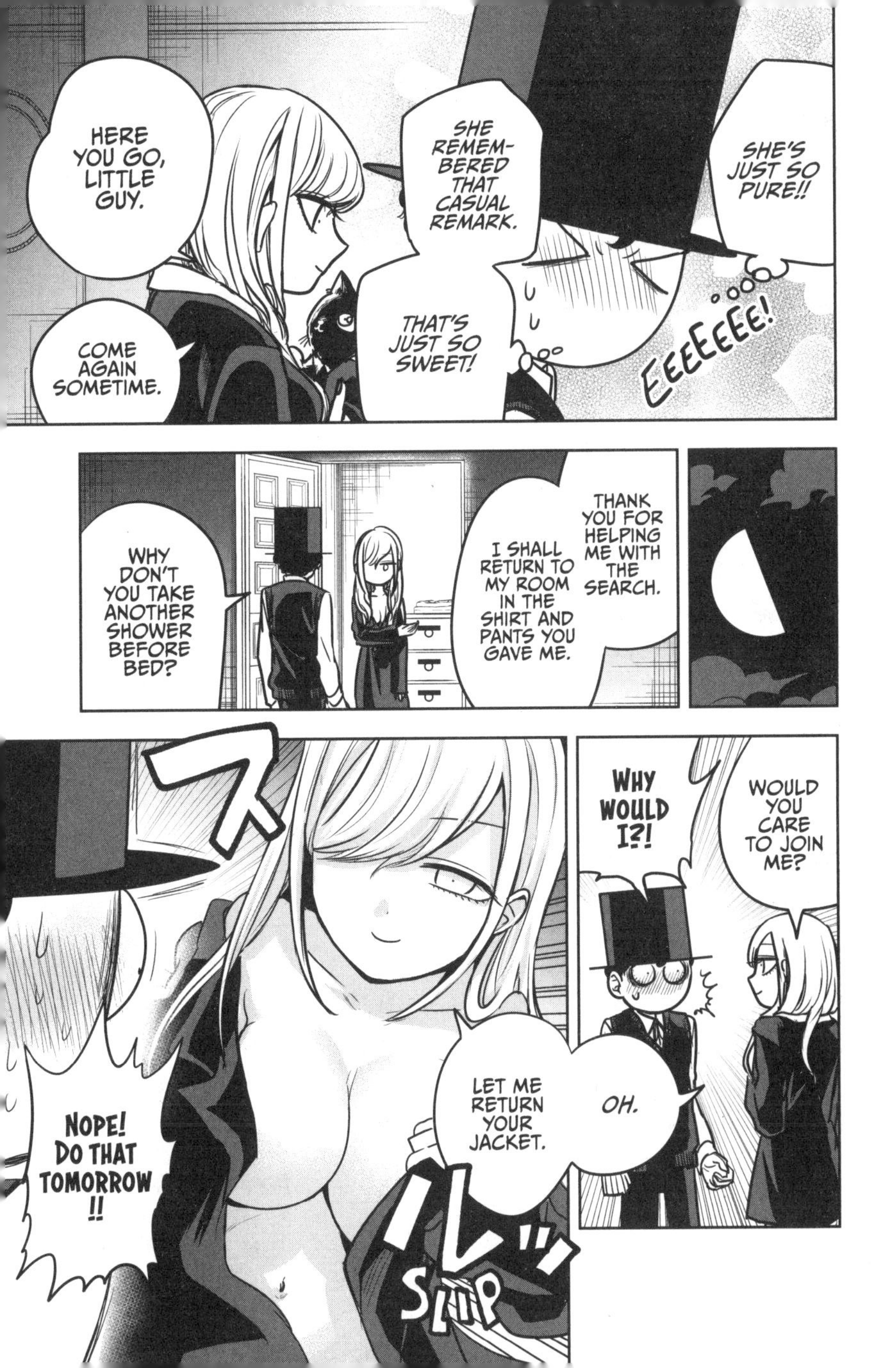
SHE'S JUST SO PURE!!
SHE REMEMBERED THAT CASUAL REMARK.
HERE YOU GO, LITTLE GUY.
EEEEEEE!
THAT'S JUST SO SWEET!
COME AGAIN SOMETIME.
THANK YOU FOR HELPING ME WITH THE SEARCH.
I SHALL RETURN TO MY ROOM IN THE SHIRT AND PANTS YOU GAVE ME.
WHY DON'T YOU TAKE ANOTHER SHOWER BEFORE BED?
WOULD YOU CARE TO JOIN ME?
WHY WOULD I?!
OH.
LET ME RETURN YOUR JACKET.
SLIP
NOPE! DO THAT TOMORROW!!

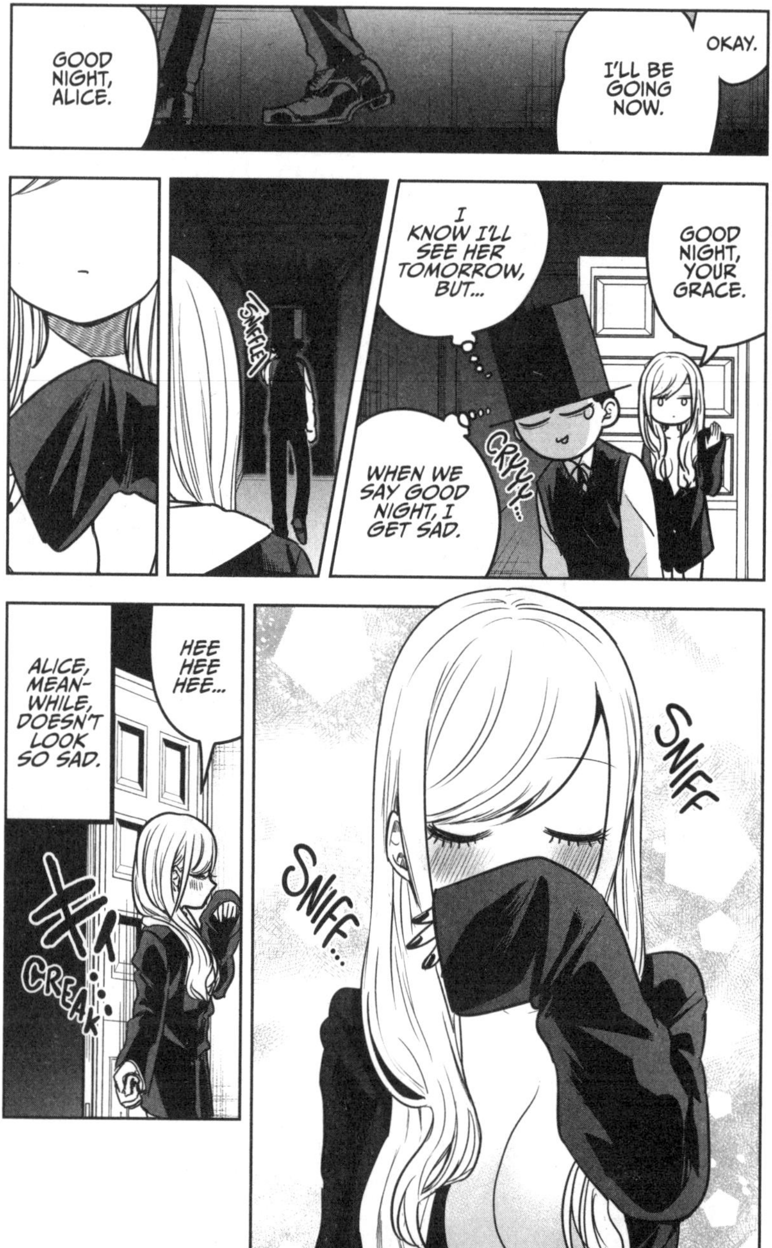

OKAY.
I'LL BE GOING NOW.
GOOD NIGHT, ALICE.
GOOD NIGHT, YOUR GRACE.
I KNOW I'LL SEE HER TOMORROW, BUT...
CRYYY...
WHEN WE SAY GOOD NIGHT, I GET SAD.
SNIFFLE
SNIFF
SNIFF...
HEE HEE HEE...
ALICE, MEAN-WHILE, DOESN'T LOOK SO SAD.
CREAK...

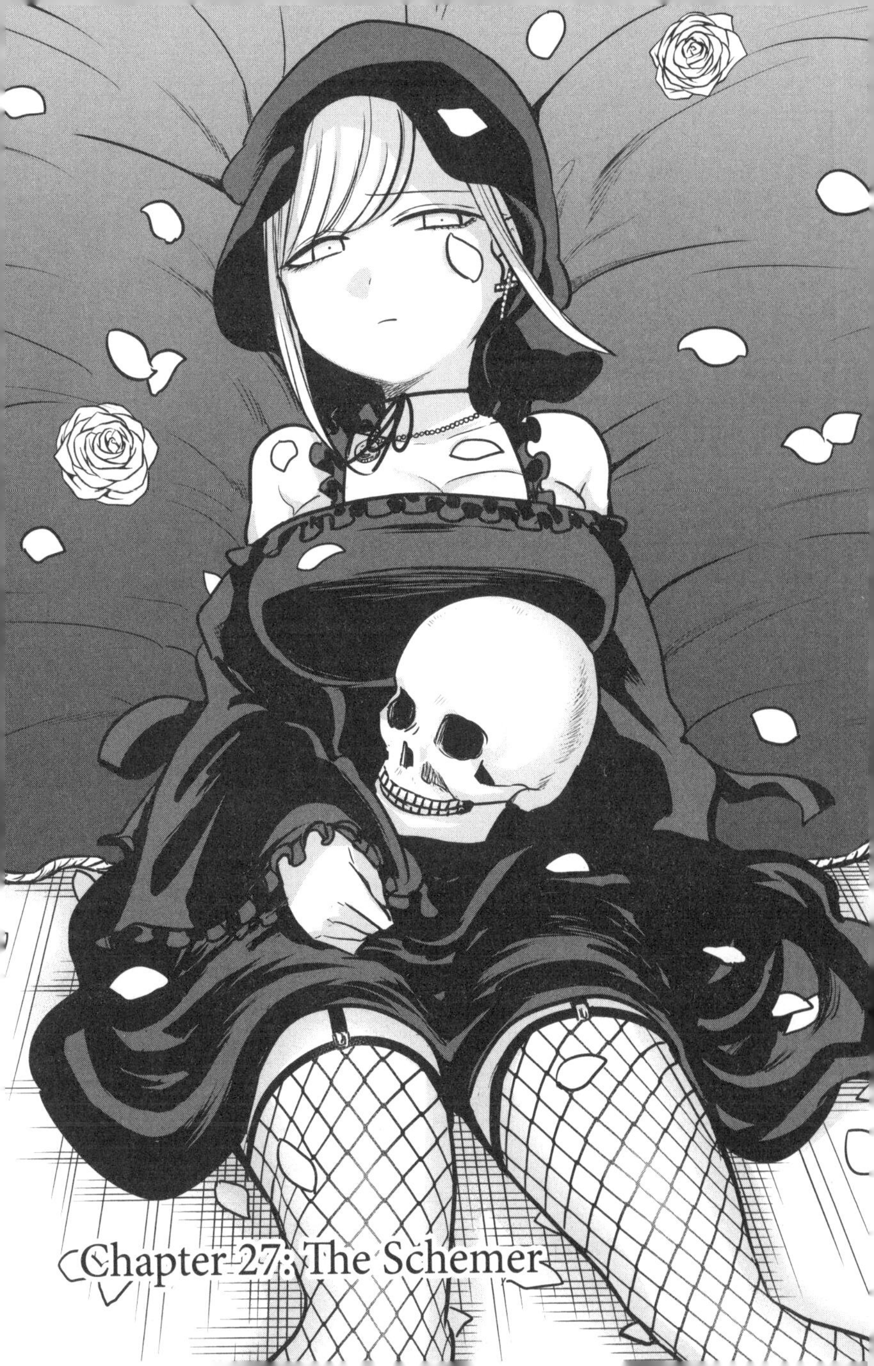
Chapter 27: The Schemer

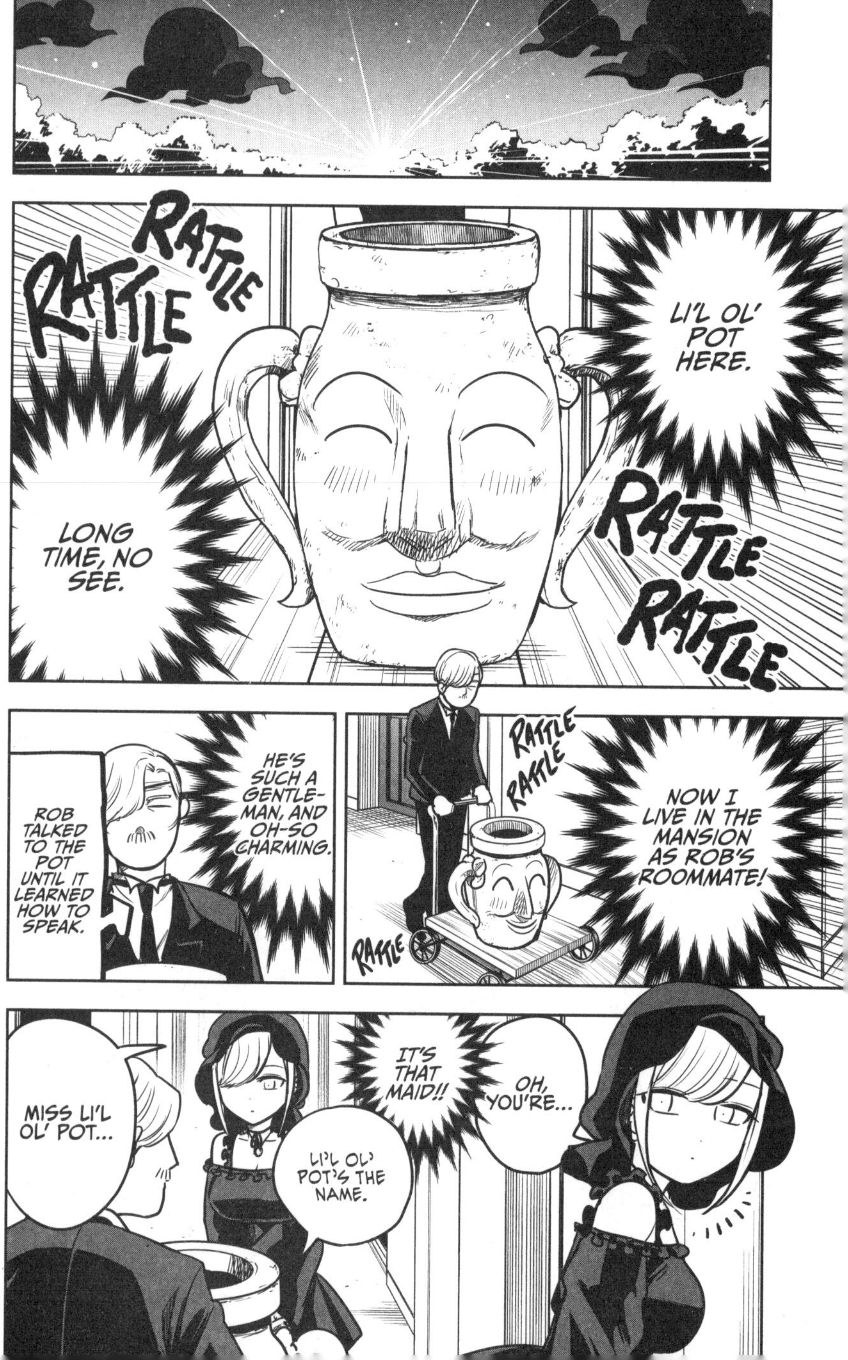
LI'L OL' POT HERE.
RATTLE RATTLE
LONG TIME, NO SEE.
RATTLE RATTLE
NOW I LIVE IN THE MANSION AS ROB'S ROOMMATE!
RATTLE RATTLE
RATTLE
HE'S SUCH A GENTLE-MAN, AND OH-SO CHARMING.
ROB TALKED TO THE POT UNTIL IT LEARNED HOW TO SPEAK.
OH, YOU'RE...
IT'S THAT MAID!!
LI'L OL' POT'S THE NAME.
MISS LI'L OL' POT...

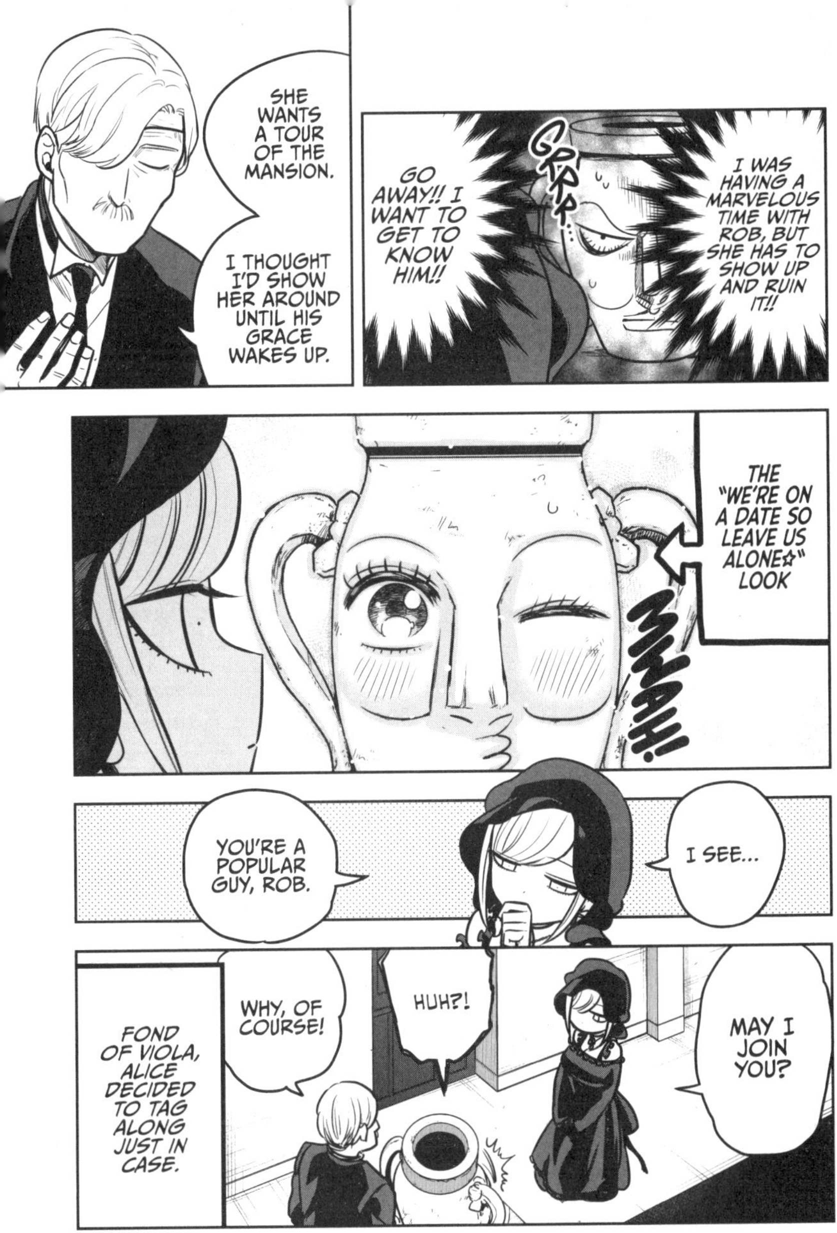
I WAS HAVING A MARVELOUS TIME WITH ROB, BUT SHE HAS TO SHOW UP AND RUIN IT!!
GRRR...
GO AWAY!! I WANT TO GET TO KNOW HIM!!
SHE WANTS A TOUR OF THE MANSION.
I THOUGHT I'D SHOW HER AROUND UNTIL HIS GRACE WAKES UP.
THE "WE'RE ON A DATE SO LEAVE US ALONE✩" LOOK
MWAH!!
I SEE...
YOU'RE A POPULAR GUY, ROB.
MAY I JOIN YOU?
HUH?!
WHY, OF COURSE!
FOND OF VIOLA, ALICE DECIDED TO TAG ALONG JUST IN CASE.

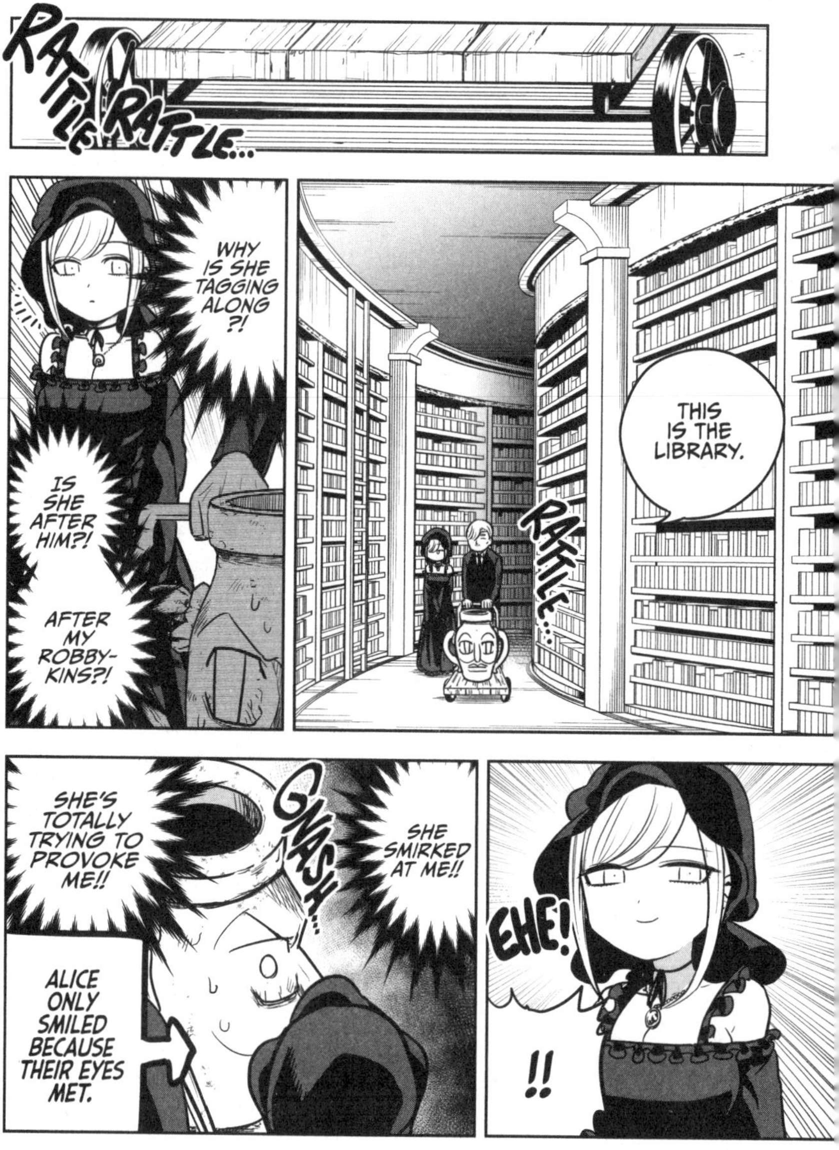
RATTLE RATTLE...
THIS IS THE LIBRARY.
RATTLE...
WHY IS SHE TAGGING ALONG?!
IS SHE AFTER HIM?!
AFTER MY ROBBY-KINS?!
EHE!
!!
SHE SMIRKED AT ME!!
GNASH...
SHE'S TOTALLY TRYING TO PROVOKE ME!!
ALICE ONLY SMILED BECAUSE THEIR EYES MET.

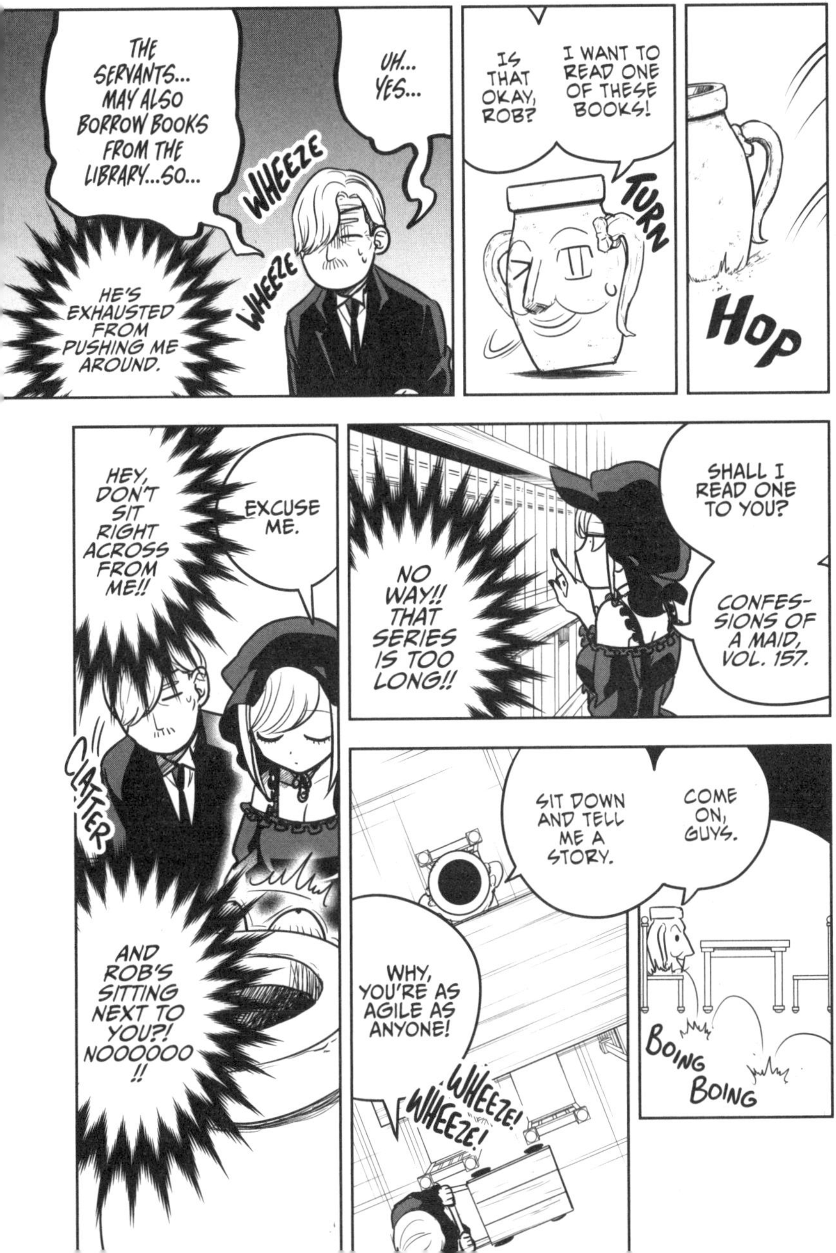
HOP
I WANT TO READ ONE OF THESE BOOKS!
IS THAT OKAY, ROB?
TURN
UH... YES...
THE SERVANTS... MAY ALSO BORROW BOOKS FROM THE LIBRARY...SO...
WHEEZE
WHEEZE
HE'S EXHAUSTED FROM PUSHING ME AROUND.
SHALL I READ ONE TO YOU?
CONFES-SIONS OF A MAID, VOL. 157.
NO WAY!! THAT SERIES IS TOO LONG!!
COME ON, GUYS.
SIT DOWN AND TELL ME A STORY.
BOING
BOING
WHY, YOU'RE AS AGILE AS ANYONE!
WHEEZE!
WHEEZE!
EXCUSE ME.
HEY, DON'T SIT RIGHT ACROSS FROM ME!!
CLATTER
AND ROB'S SITTING NEXT TO YOU?! NOOOOOO!!

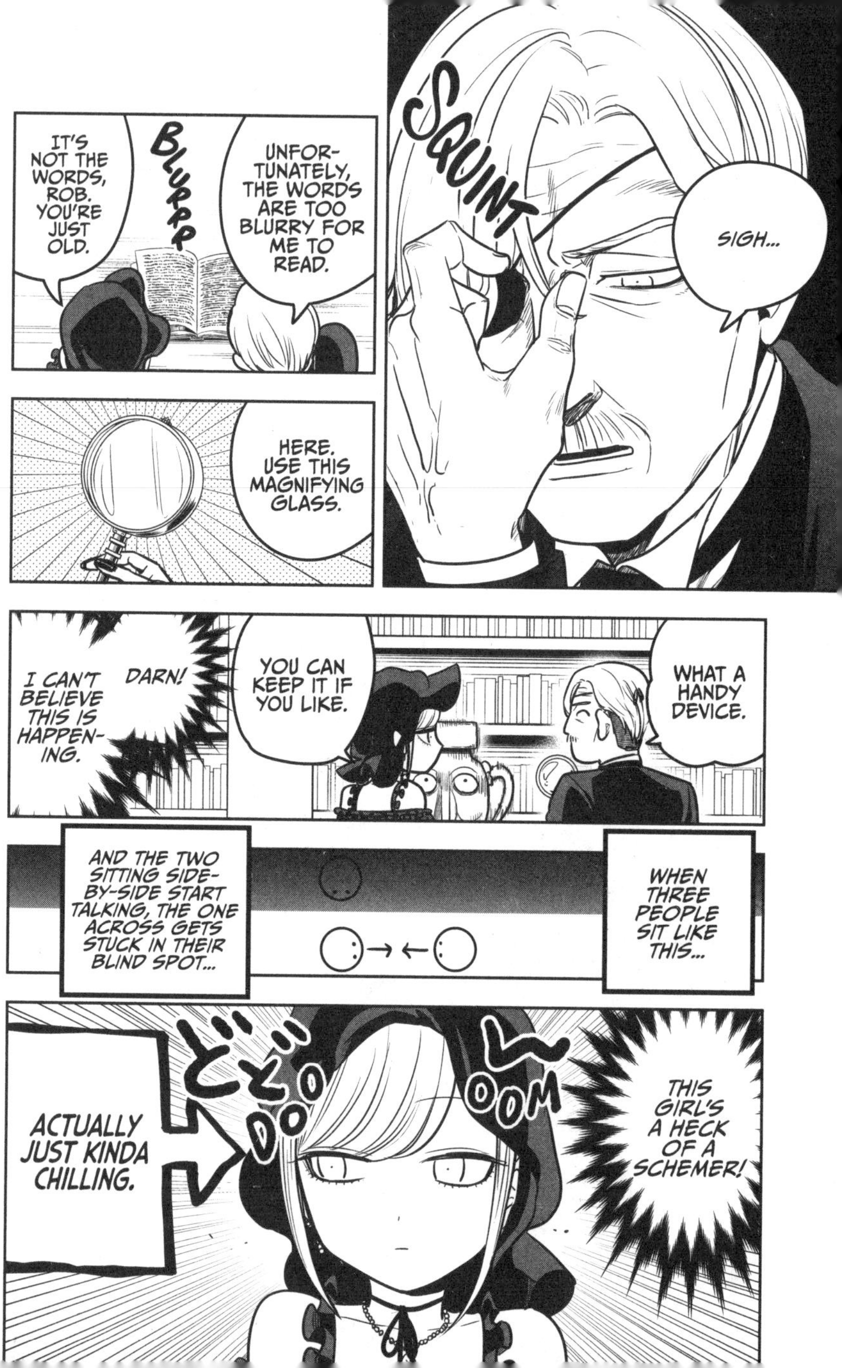
SQUINT
SIGH...
UNFORTUNATELY, THE WORDS ARE TOO BLURRY FOR ME TO READ.
BLURRR
IT'S NOT THE WORDS, ROB. YOU'RE JUST OLD.
HERE. USE THIS MAGNIFYING GLASS.
WHAT A HANDY DEVICE.
YOU CAN KEEP IT IF YOU LIKE.
DARN!
I CAN'T BELIEVE THIS IS HAPPENING.
WHEN THREE PEOPLE SIT LIKE THIS...
AND THE TWO SITTING SIDE-BY-SIDE START TALKING, THE ONE ACROSS GETS STUCK IN THEIR BLIND SPOT...
THIS GIRL'S A HECK OF A SCHEMER!
DOOOOM
ACTUALLY JUST KINDA CHILLING.

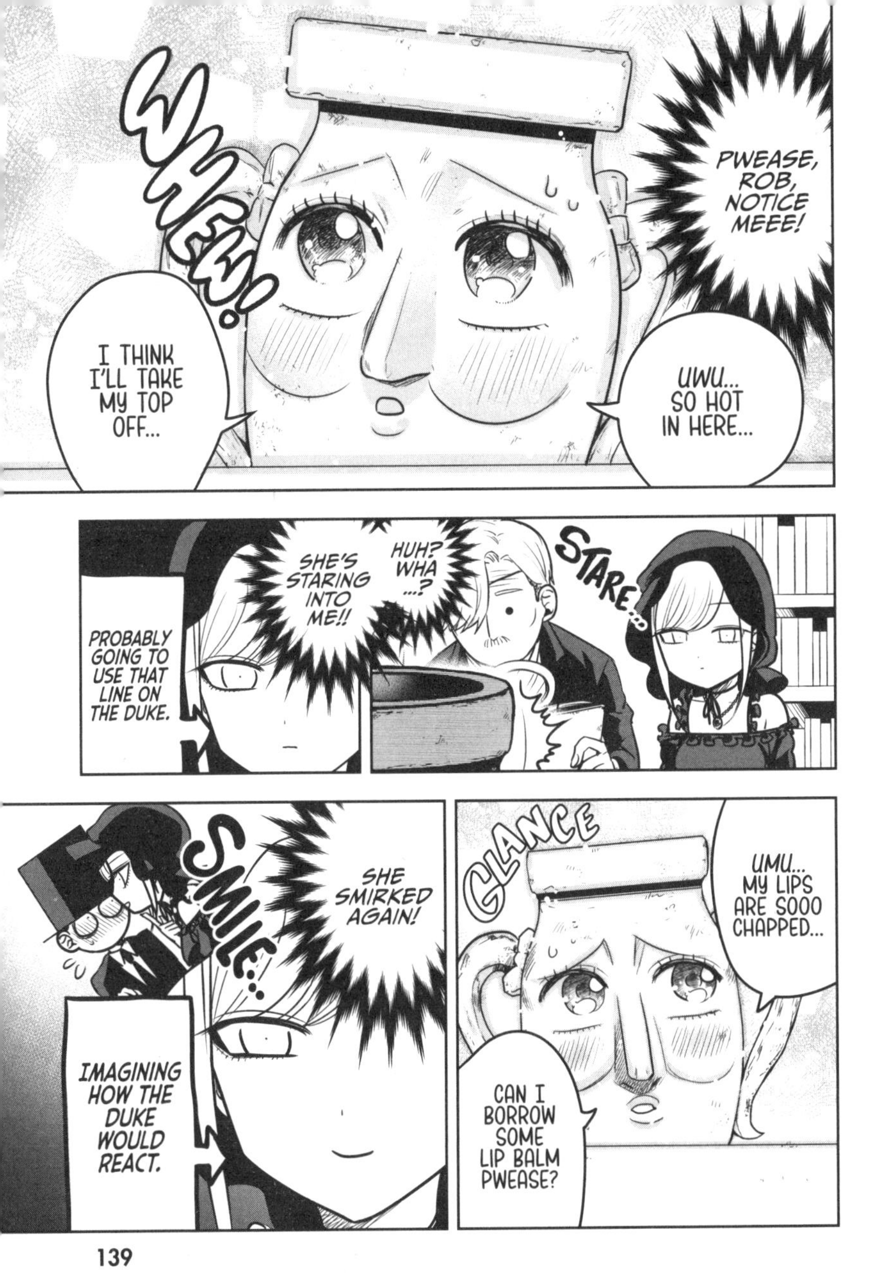
PWEASE, ROB, NOTICE MEEE!
UWU... SO HOT IN HERE...
WHEW!
I THINK I'LL TAKE MY TOP OFF...
STARE...
HUH? WHA...?
SHE'S STARING INTO ME!!
PROBABLY GOING TO USE THAT LINE ON THE DUKE.
UMU... MY LIPS ARE SOOO CHAPPED...
GLANCE
CAN I BORROW SOME LIP BALM PWEASE?
SHE SMIRKED AGAIN!
SMILE...
IMAGINING HOW THE DUKE WOULD REACT.

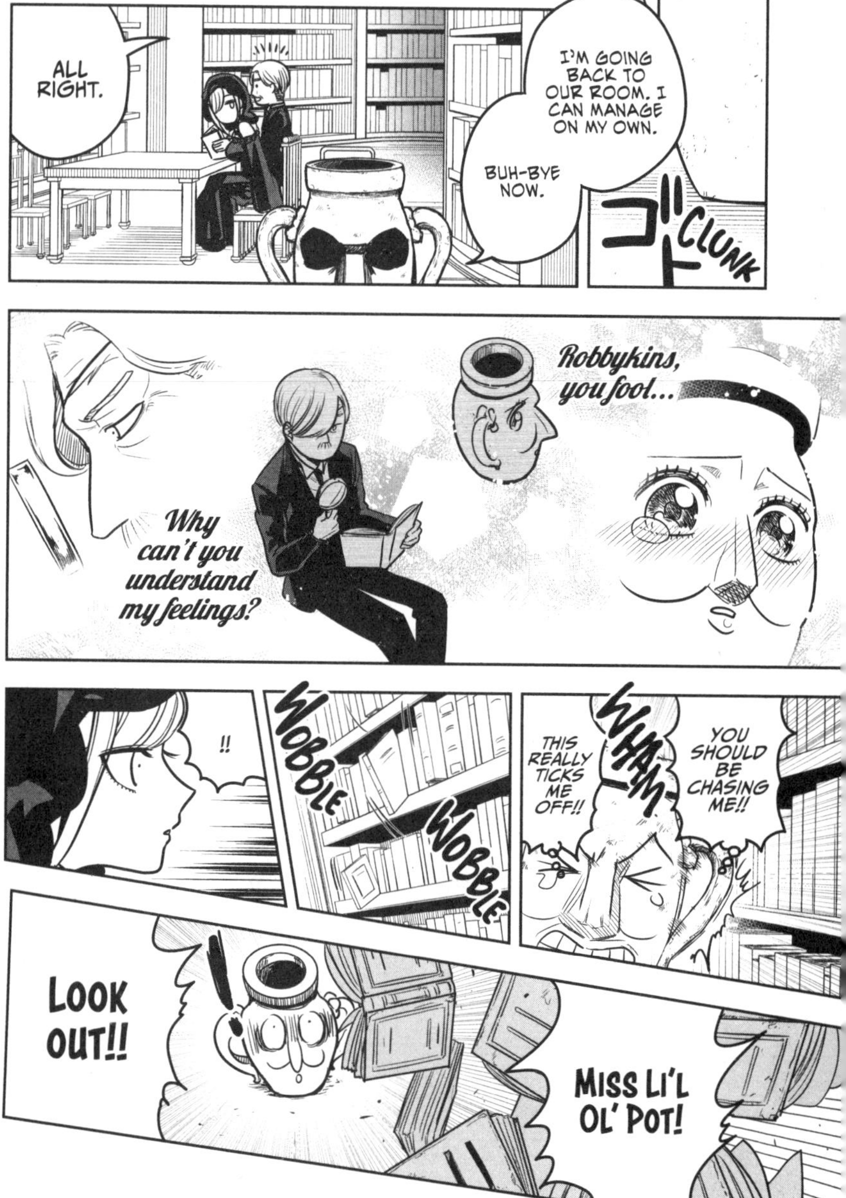
CLUNK
I'M GOING BACK TO OUR ROOM. I CAN MANAGE ON MY OWN.
BUH-BYE NOW.
ALL RIGHT.
Robbykins, you fool...
Why can't you understand my feelings?
YOU SHOULD BE CHASING ME!!
WHAM
THIS REALLY TICKS ME OFF!!
WOBBLE
WOBBLE
!!
MISS LI'L OL' POT!
LOOK OUT!!

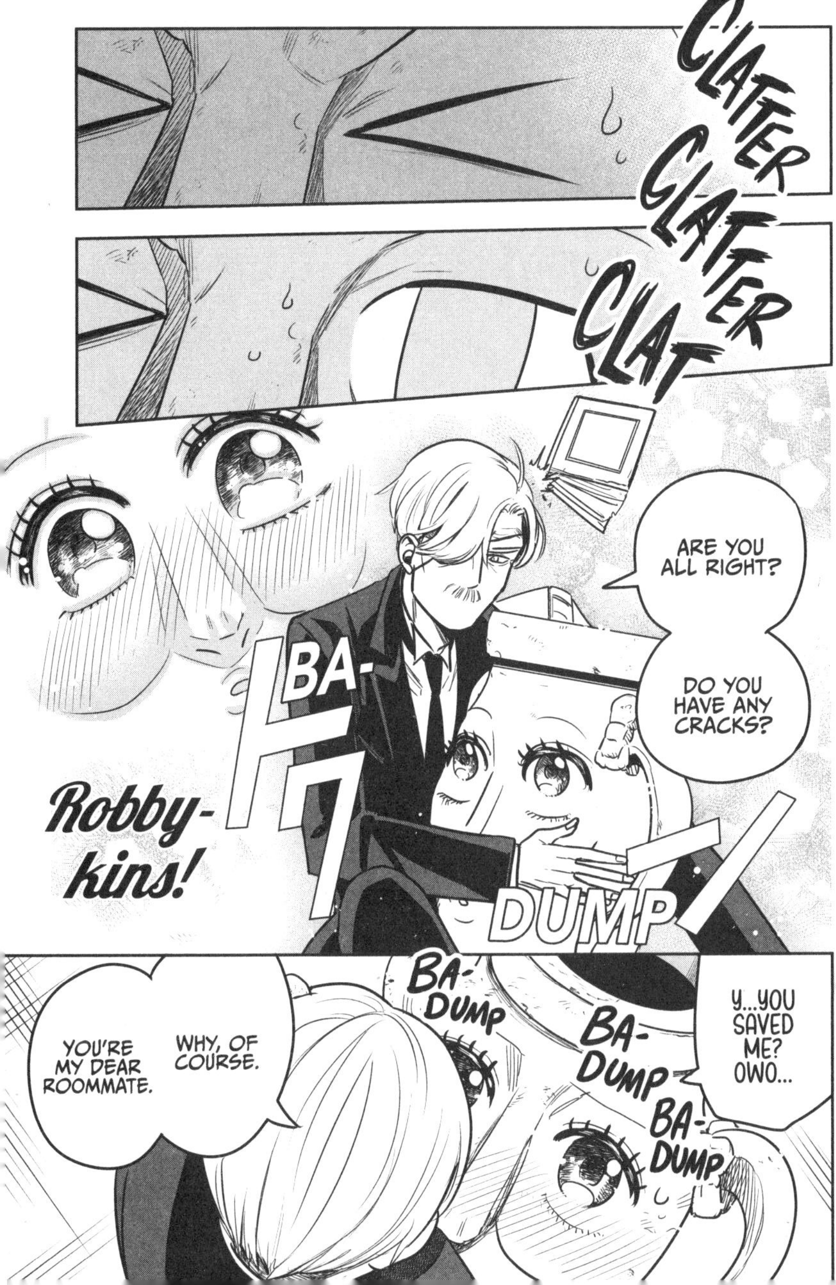
CLATTER
CLATTER
CLAT
ARE YOU ALL RIGHT?
DO YOU HAVE ANY CRACKS?
BA-
DUMP
Robby-kins!
Y...YOU SAVED ME? OWO...
BA-DUMP
BA-DUMP
BA-DUMP
WHY, OF COURSE.
YOU'RE MY DEAR ROOMMATE.

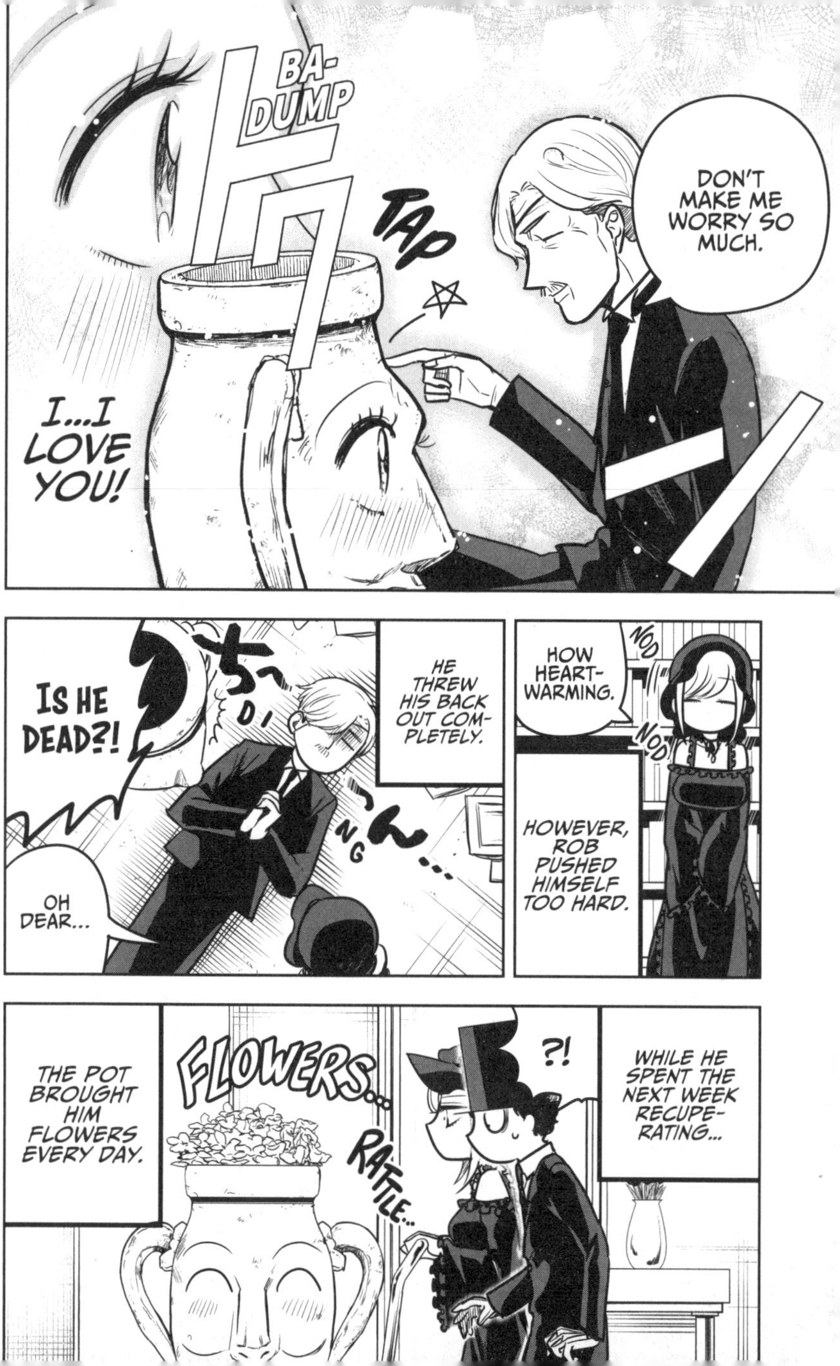
DON'T MAKE ME WORRY SO MUCH.
BA-DUMP
TAP
I...I LOVE YOU!
NOD
HOW HEART-WARMING.
NOD
HOWEVER, ROB PUSHED HIMSELF TOO HARD.
HE THREW HIS BACK OUT COM-PLETELY.
DI
NG
IS HE DEAD?!
OH DEAR...
WHILE HE SPENT THE NEXT WEEK RECUPE-RATING...
?!
FLOWERS...
RATTLE...
THE POT BROUGHT HIM FLOWERS EVERY DAY.

Chapter 28: Preparing for Winter

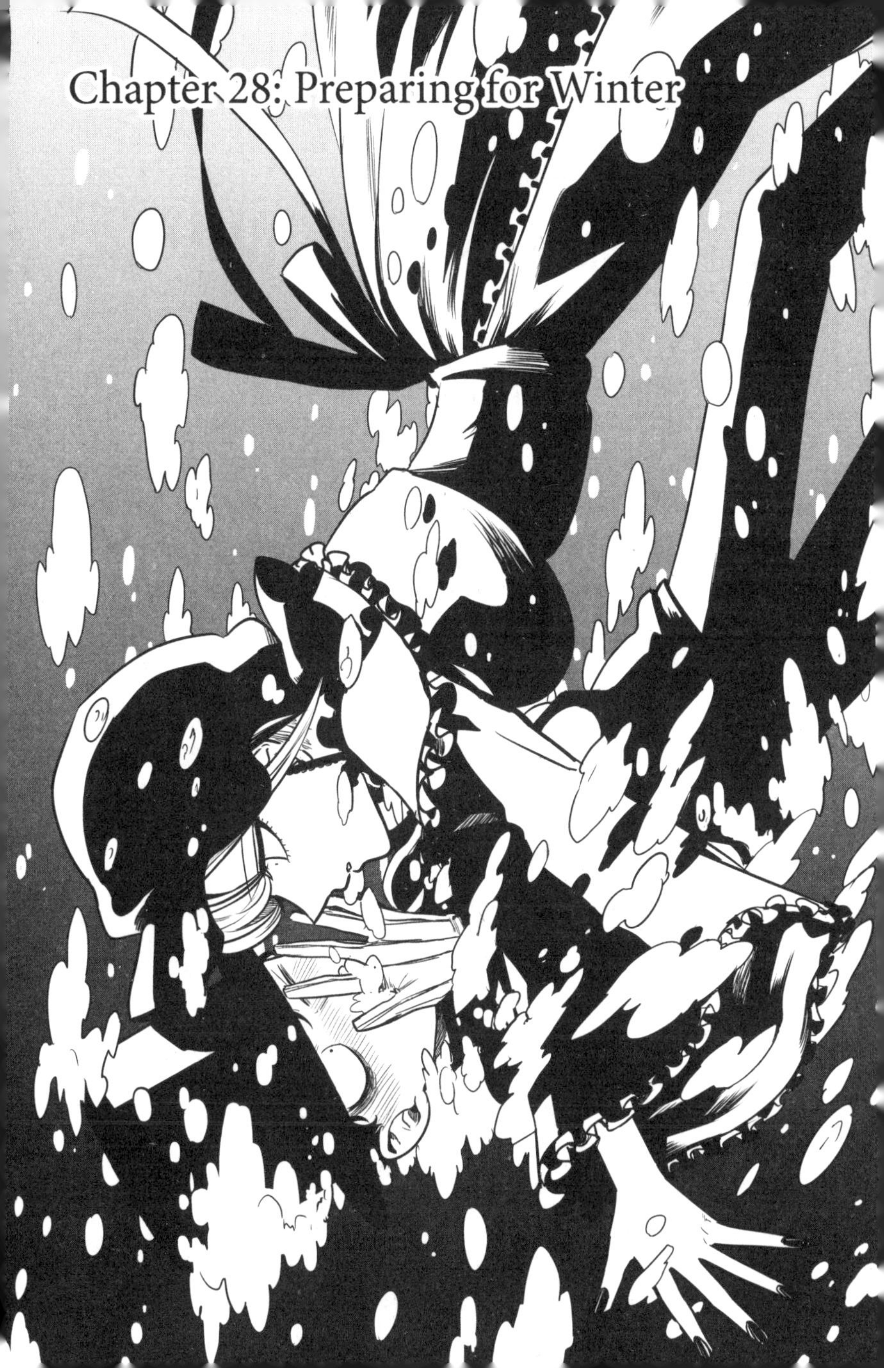

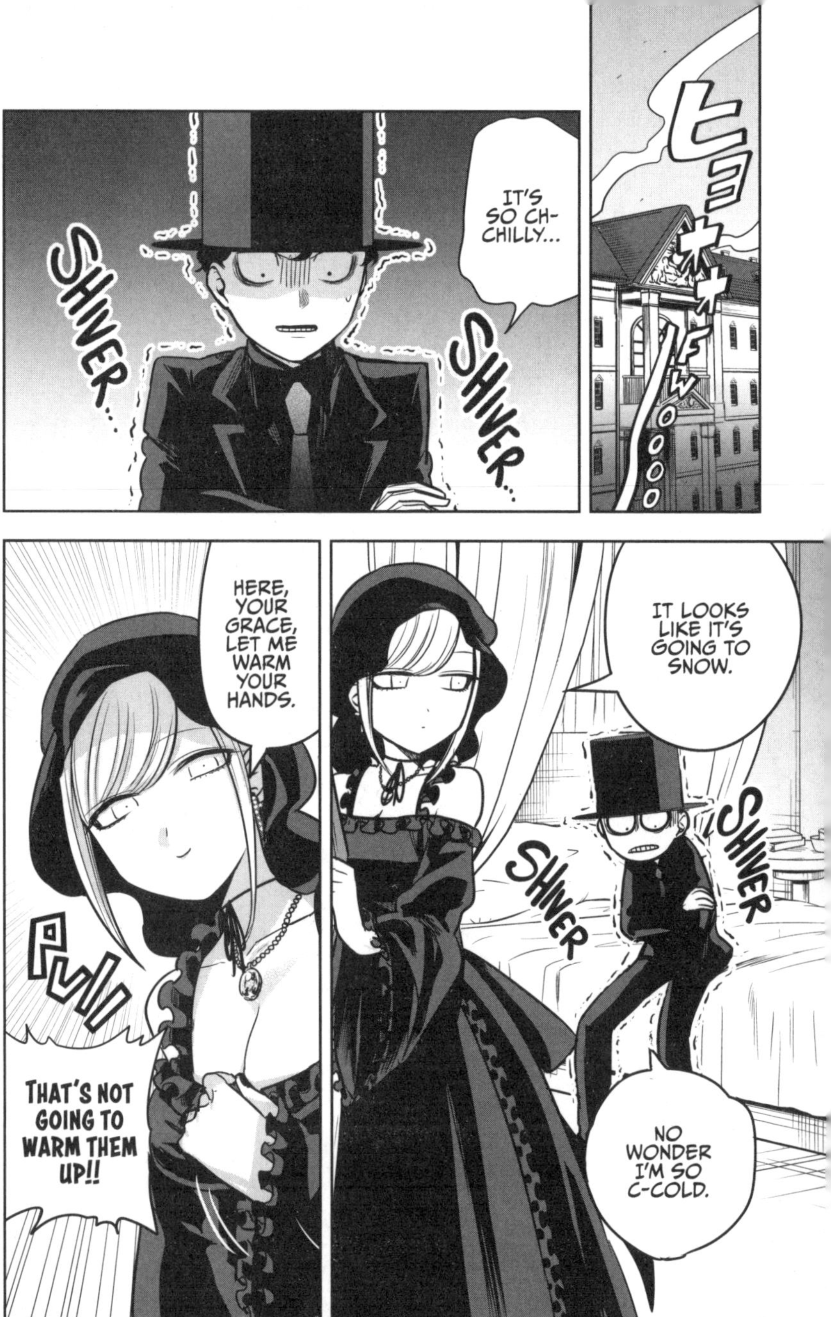
ヒョオオ
FWOOOOO
IT'S SO CH-CHILLY...
SHIVER...
SHIVER...
IT LOOKS LIKE IT'S GOING TO SNOW.
SHIVER
SHIVER
NO WONDER I'M SO C-COLD.
HERE, YOUR GRACE, LET ME WARM YOUR HANDS.
PULL
THAT'S NOT GOING TO WARM THEM UP!!

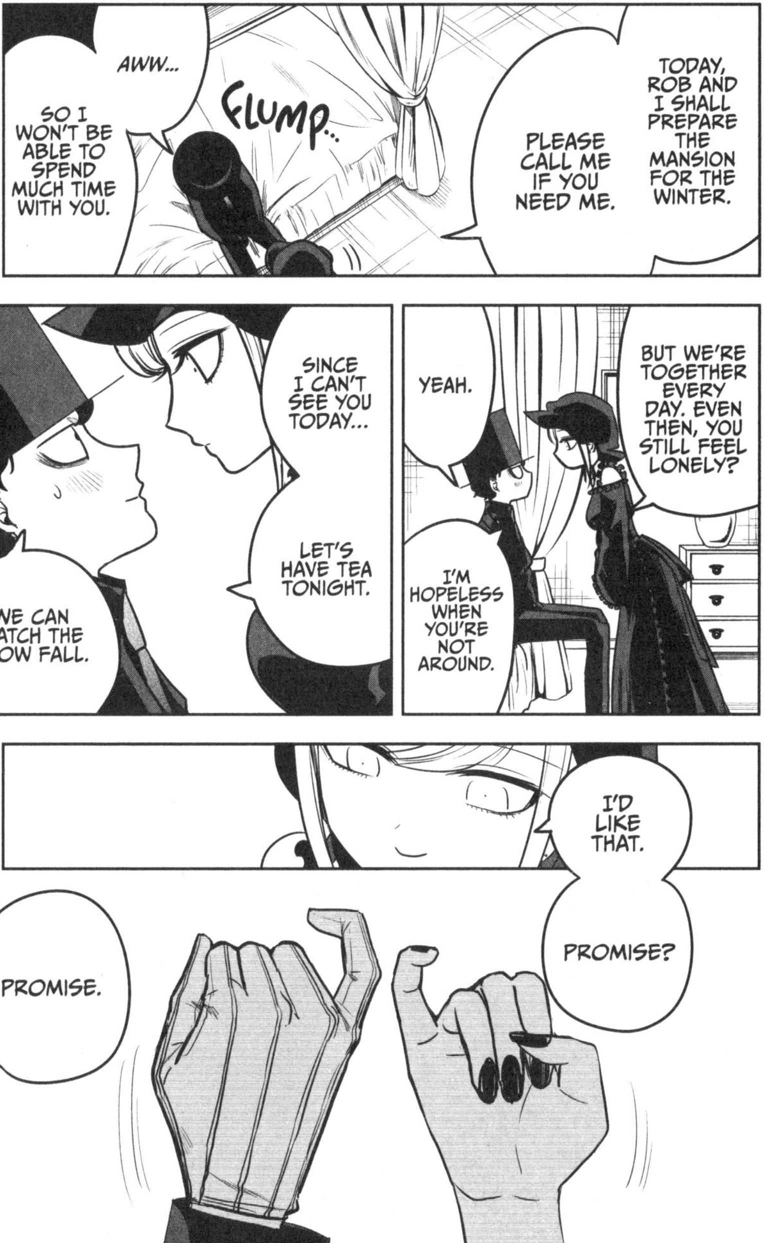
TODAY, ROB AND I SHALL PREPARE THE MANSION FOR THE WINTER.
PLEASE CALL ME IF YOU NEED ME.
FLUMP...
AWW...
SO I WON'T BE ABLE TO SPEND MUCH TIME WITH YOU.
BUT WE'RE TOGETHER EVERY DAY. EVEN THEN, YOU STILL FEEL LONELY?
YEAH.
I'M HOPELESS WHEN YOU'RE NOT AROUND.
SINCE I CAN'T SEE YOU TODAY...
LET'S HAVE TEA TONIGHT.
WE CAN WATCH THE SNOW FALL.
I'D LIKE THAT.
PROMISE?
PROMISE.

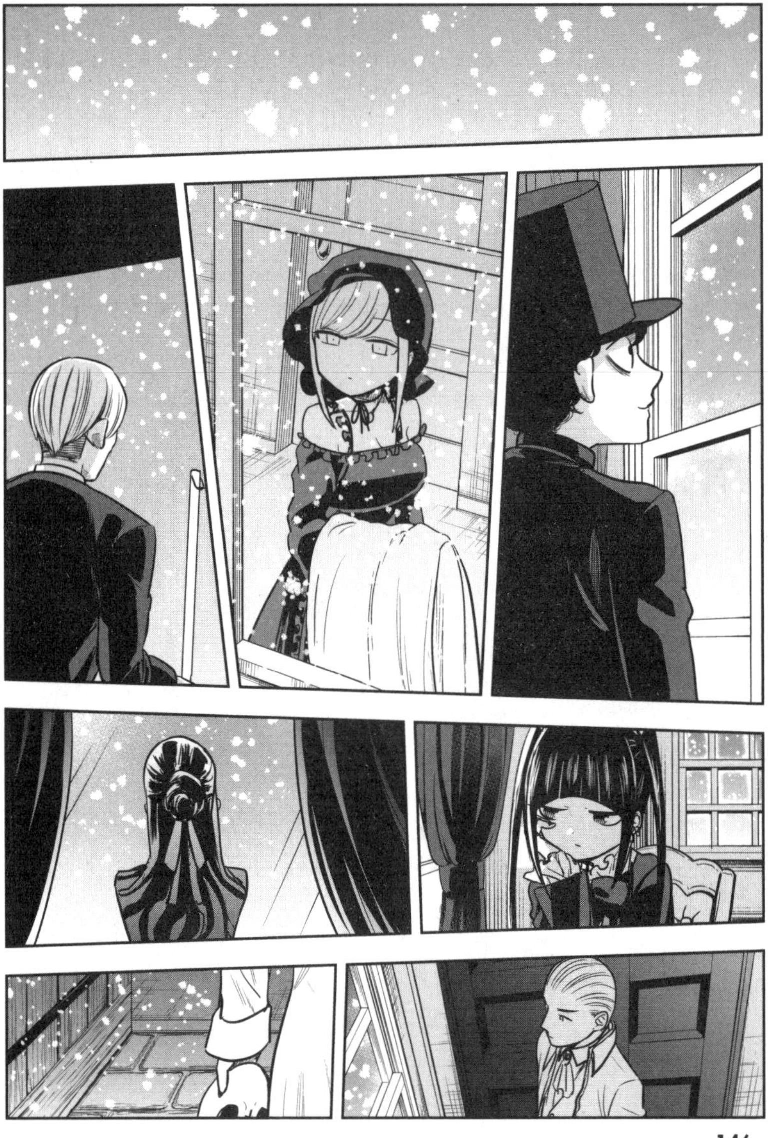

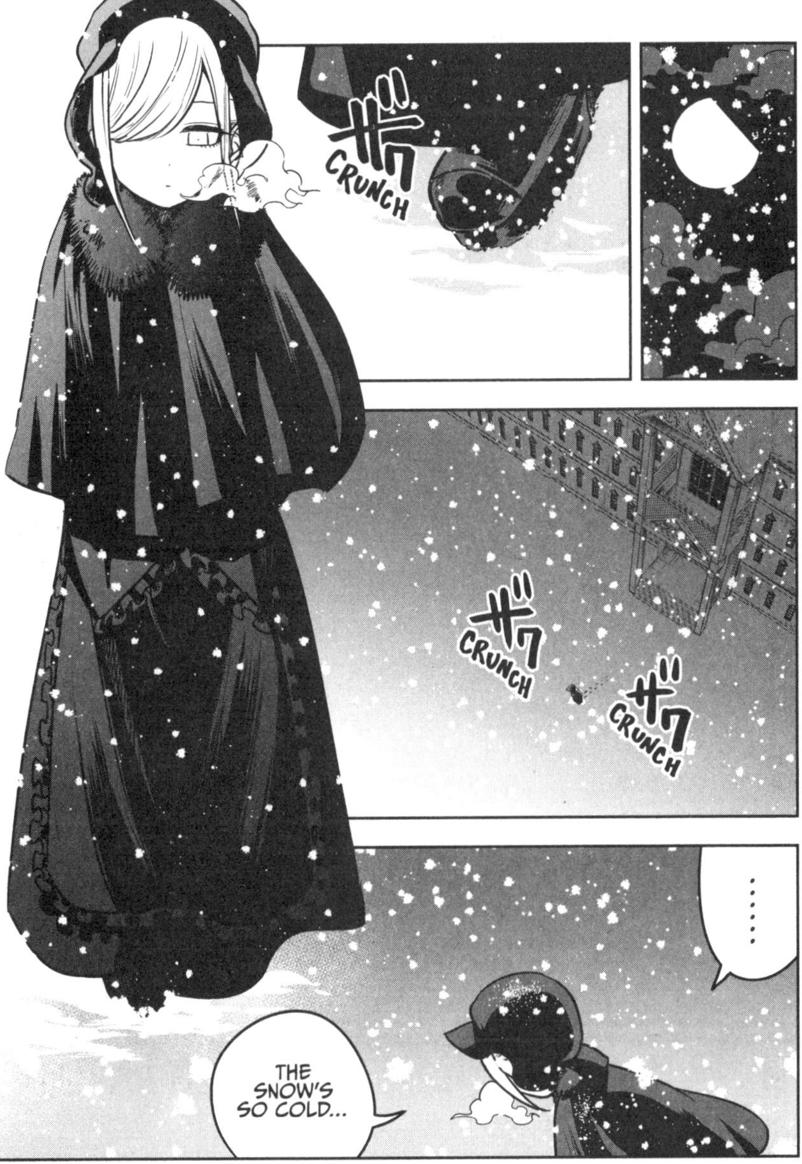

ザク
CRUNCH
ザク
CRUNCH
ザク
CRUNCH
......
THE SNOW'S SO COLD...

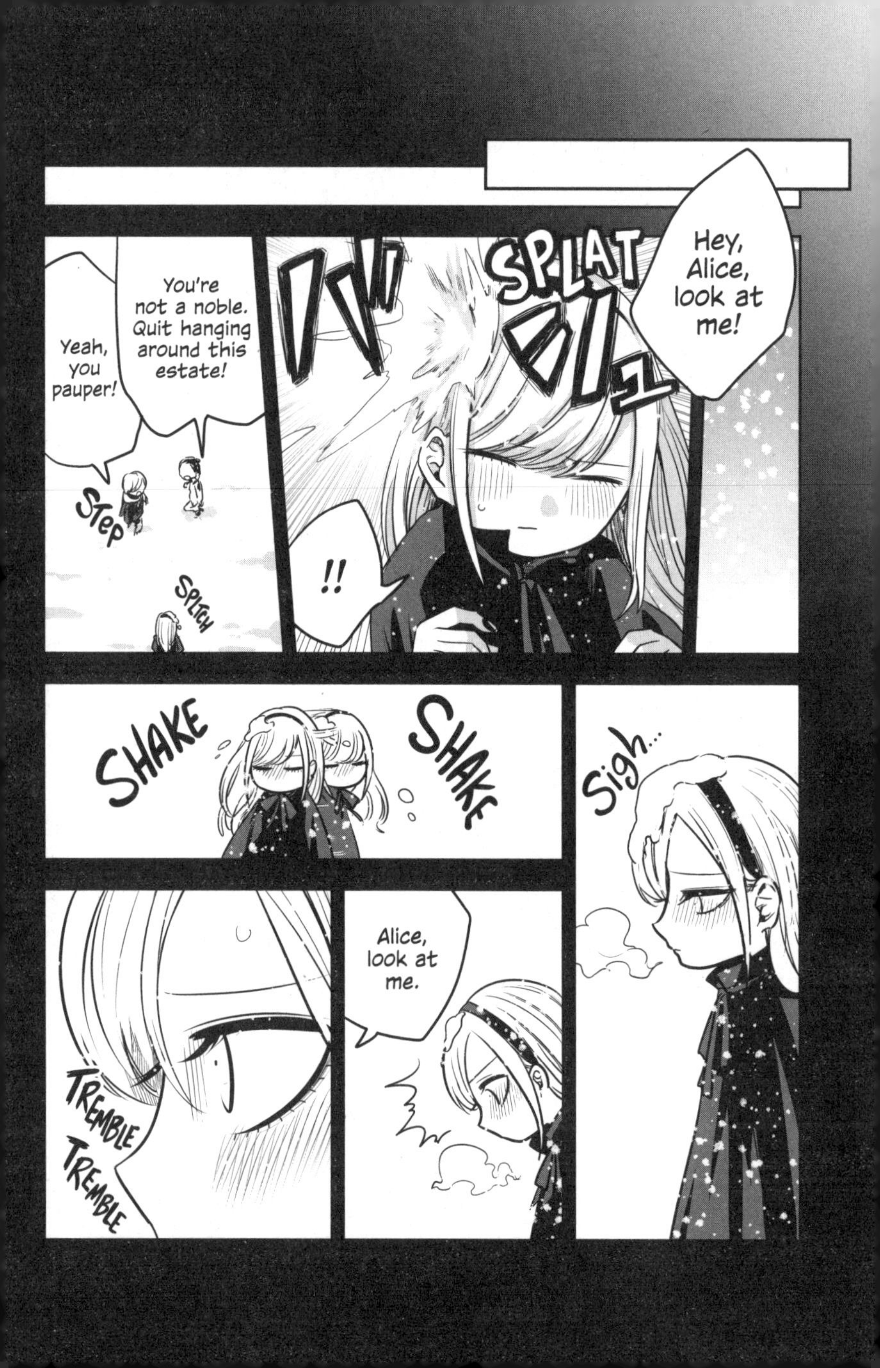
Hey, Alice, look at me!
SPLAT
!!
You're not a noble. Quit hanging around this estate!
Yeah, you pauper!
Step
SPLITCH
Sigh...
SHAKE
SHAKE
Alice, look at me.
TREMBLE
TREMBLE

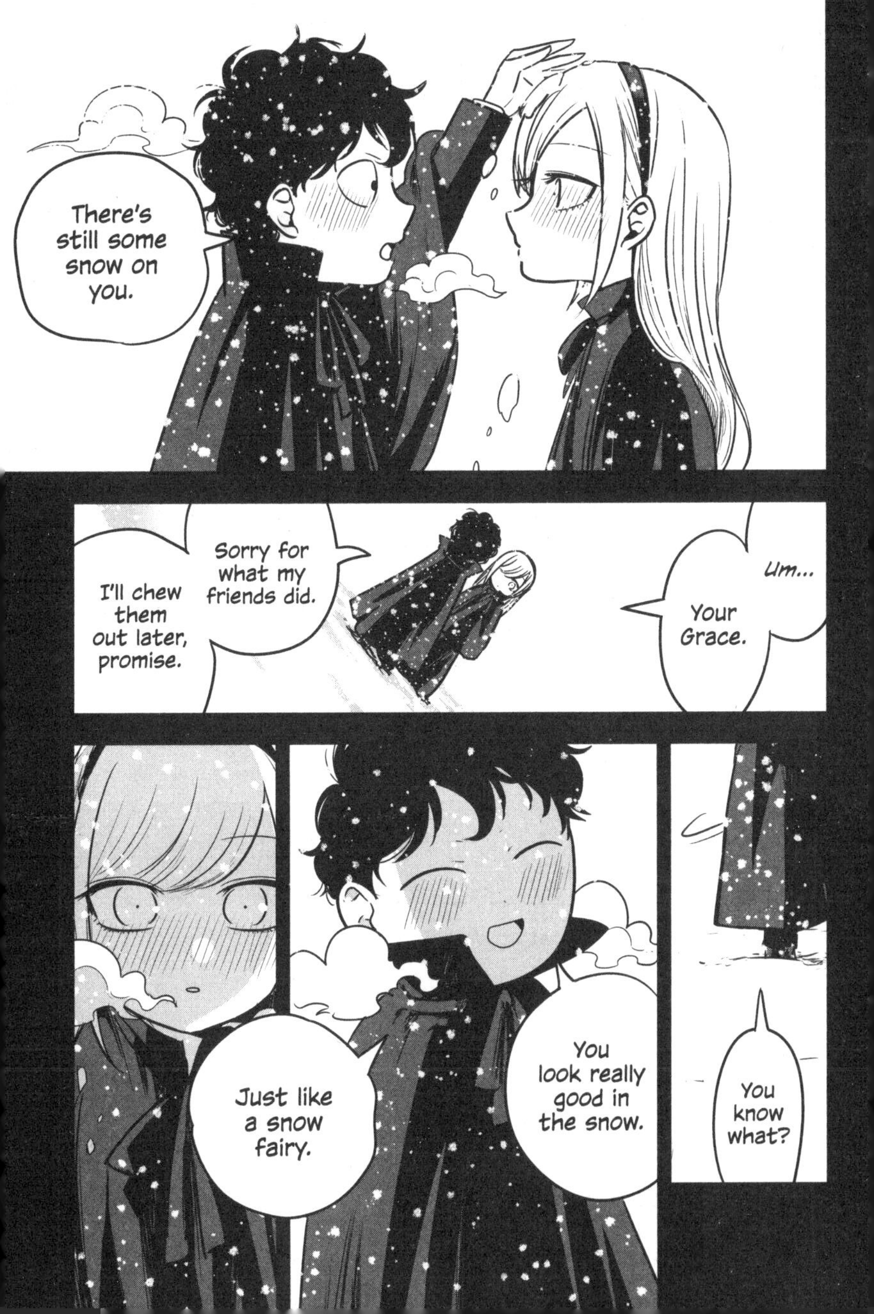
There's still some snow on you.
Um...
Your Grace.
Sorry for what my friends did.
I'll chew them out later, promise.
You know what?
You look really good in the snow.
Just like a snow fairy.

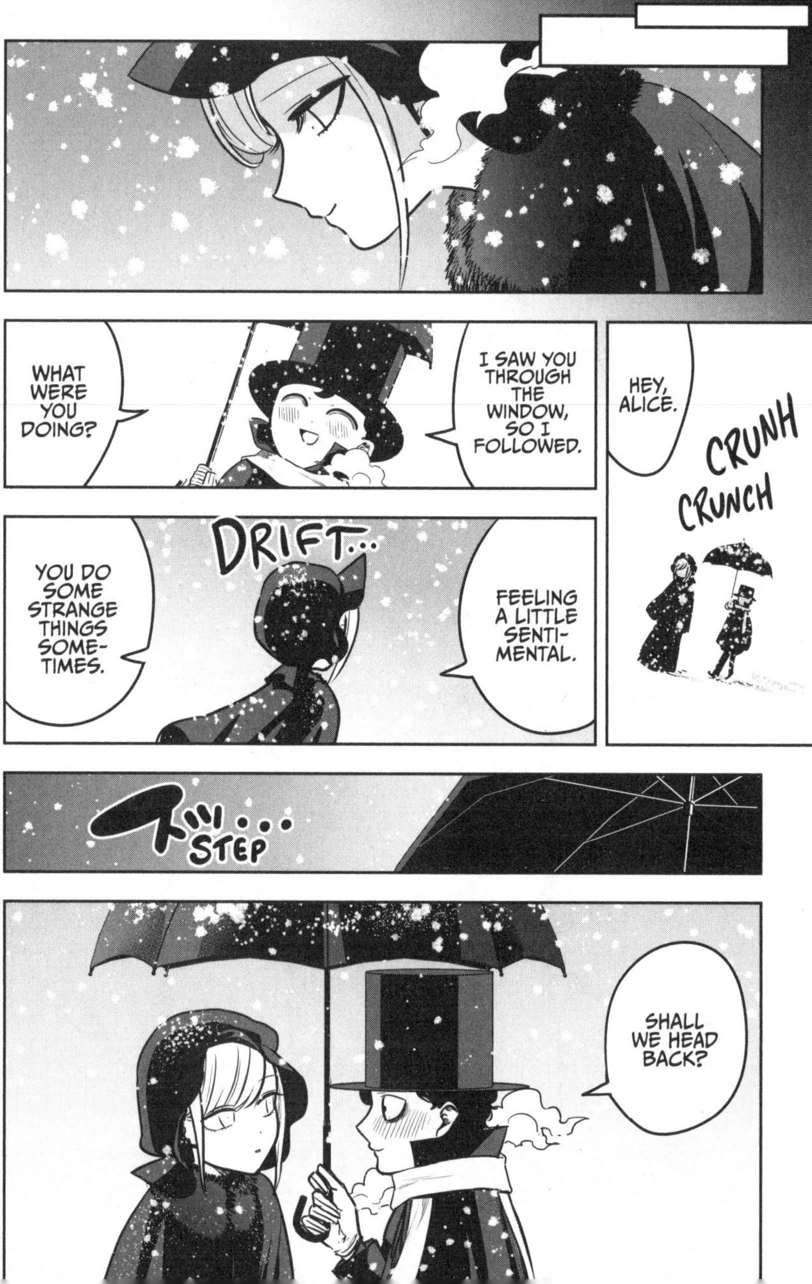
HEY, ALICE.
CRUNH
CRUNCH
I SAW YOU THROUGH THE WINDOW, SO I FOLLOWED.
WHAT WERE YOU DOING?
DRIFT...
FEELING A LITTLE SENTIMENTAL.
YOU DO SOME STRANGE THINGS SOMETIMES.
STEP
SHALL WE HEAD BACK?

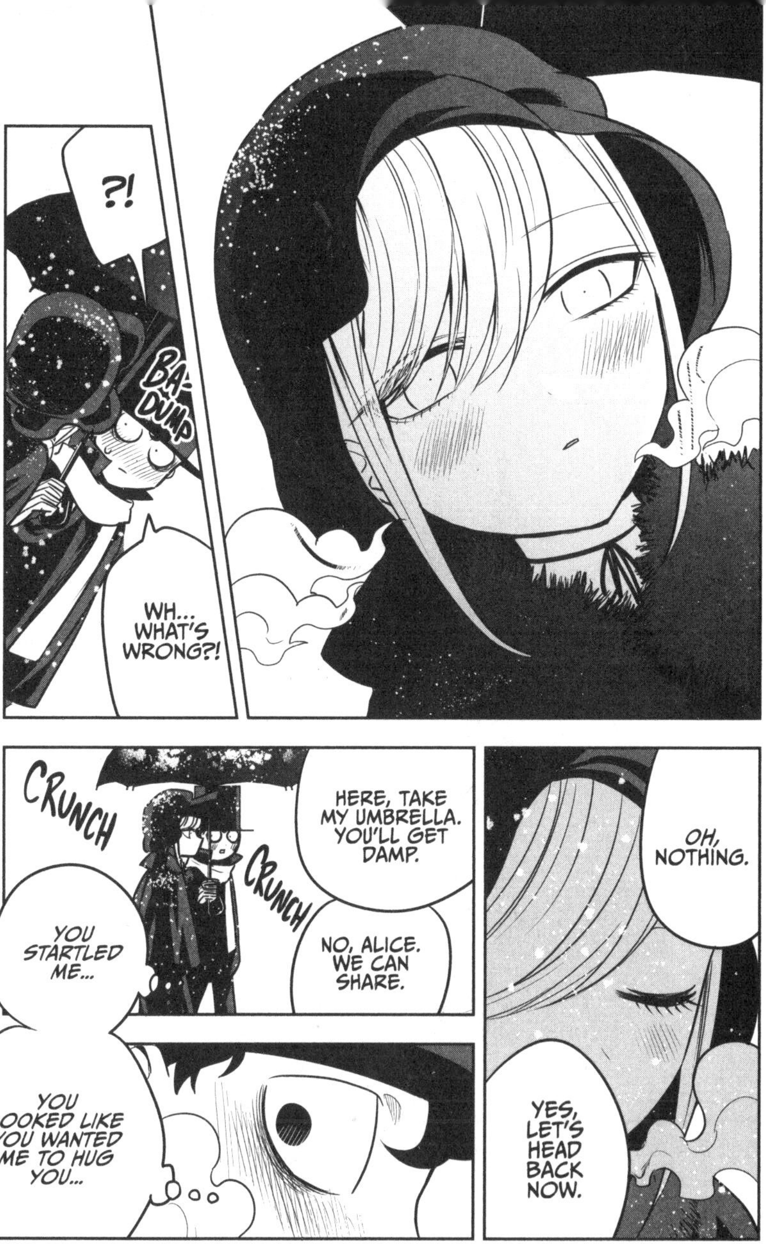
?!
BA-DUMP
WH... WHAT'S WRONG?!
OH, NOTHING.
YES, LET'S HEAD BACK NOW.
HERE, TAKE MY UMBRELLA. YOU'LL GET DAMP.
CRUNCH
NO, ALICE. WE CAN SHARE.
CRUNCH
YOU STARTLED ME...
YOU LOOKED LIKE YOU WANTED ME TO HUG YOU...

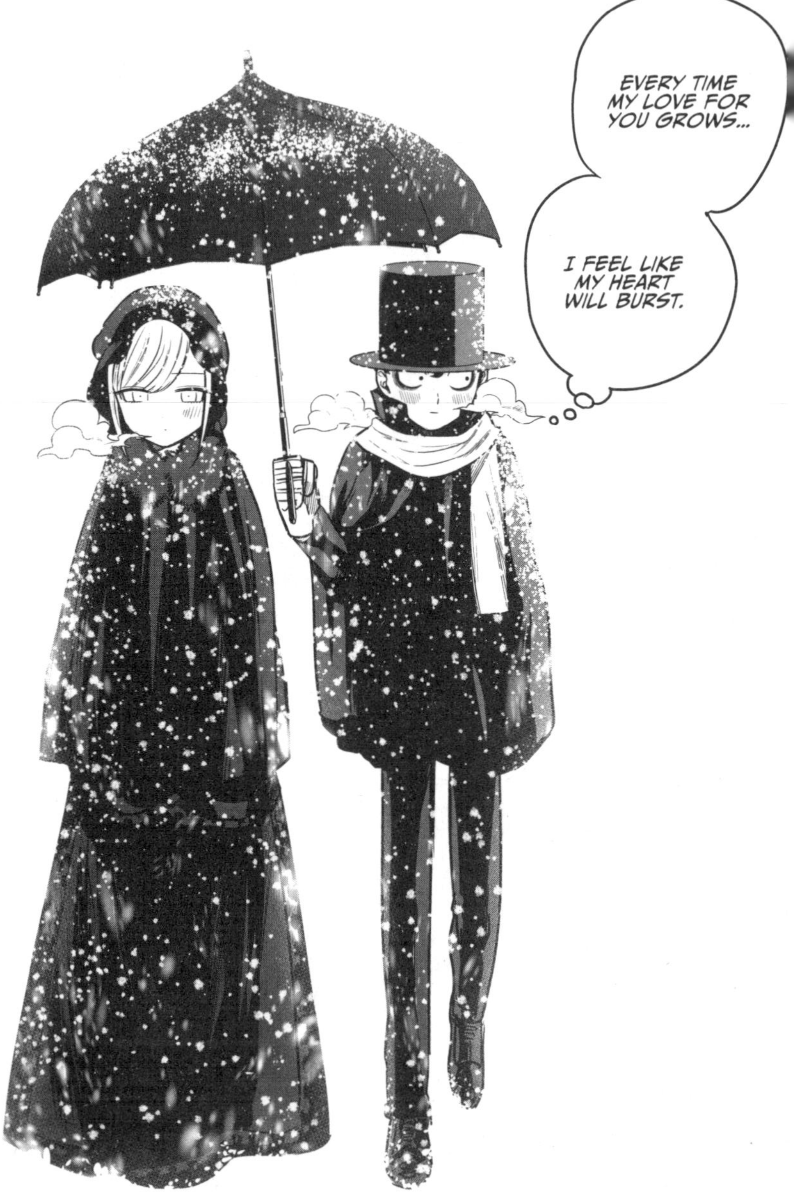
EVERY TIME MY LOVE FOR YOU GROWS...
I FEEL LIKE MY HEART WILL BURST.

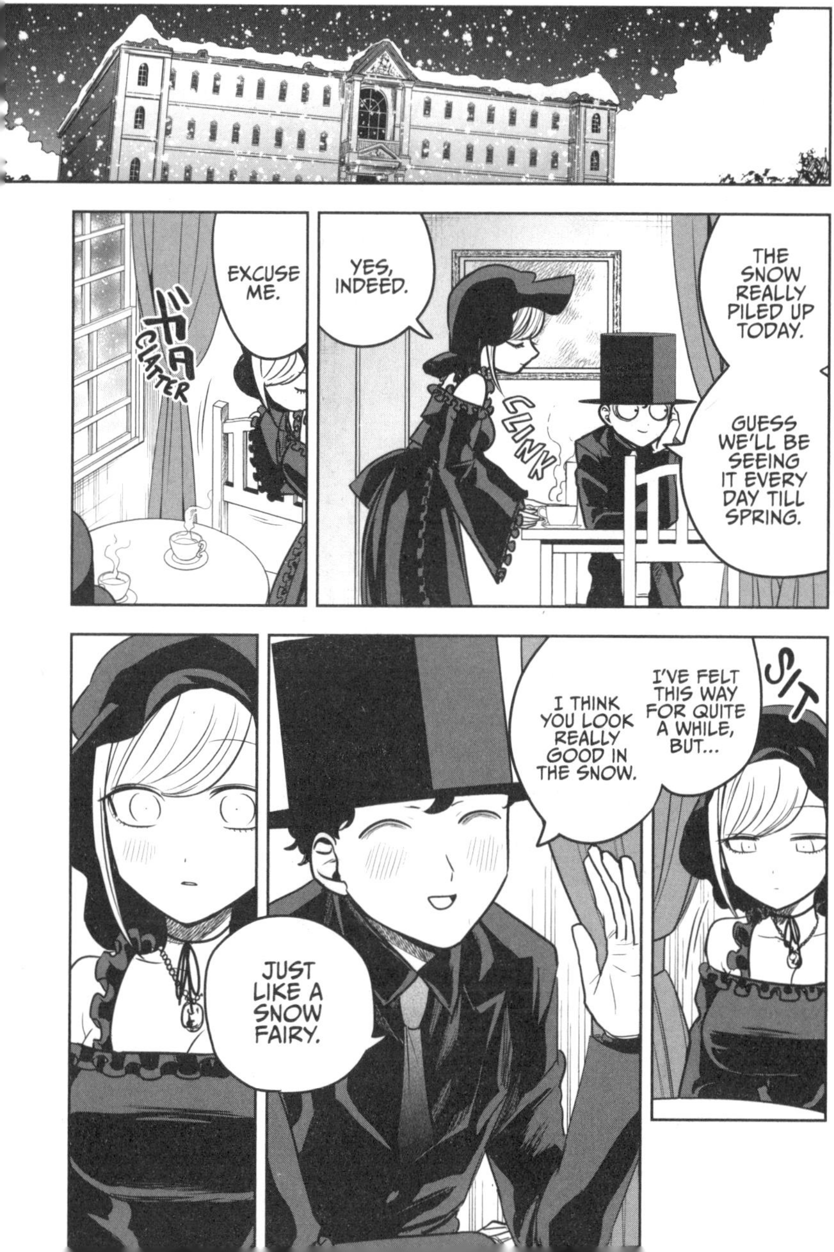
THE SNOW REALLY PILED UP TODAY.
GUESS WE'LL BE SEEING IT EVERY DAY TILL SPRING.
CLINK
YES, INDEED.
EXCUSE ME.
ガタ
CLATTER
SIT
I'VE FELT THIS WAY FOR QUITE A WHILE, BUT...
I THINK YOU LOOK REALLY GOOD IN THE SNOW.
JUST LIKE A SNOW FAIRY.

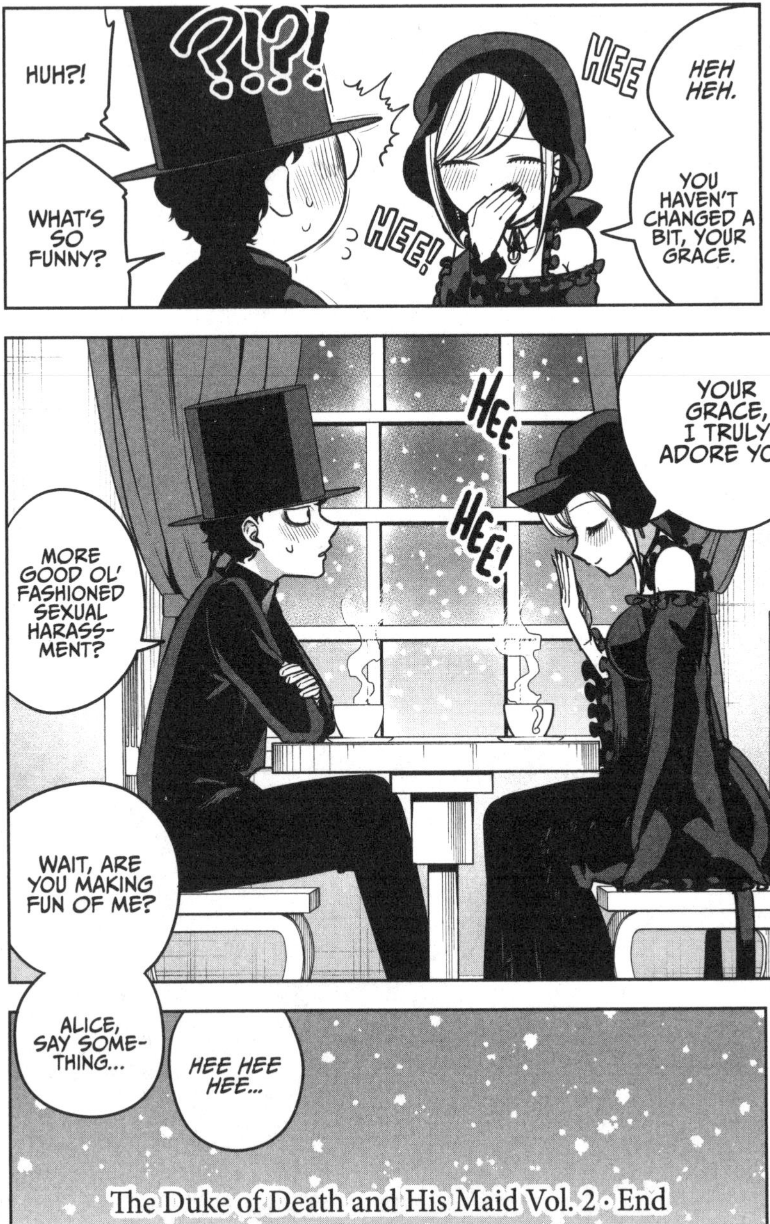
HEH HEH.
HEE
YOU HAVEN'T CHANGED A BIT, YOUR GRACE.
HEE!
?!?!
HUH?!
WHAT'S SO FUNNY?
YOUR GRACE, I TRULY ADORE YOU.
HEE HEE!
MORE GOOD OL' FASHIONED SEXUAL HARASS-MENT?
WAIT, ARE YOU MAKING FUN OF ME?
ALICE, SAY SOME-THING...
HEE HEE HEE...
The Duke of Death and His Maid Vol. 2 • End

The Duke of Death and His Maid

VALENTINE'S DAY SPECIAL

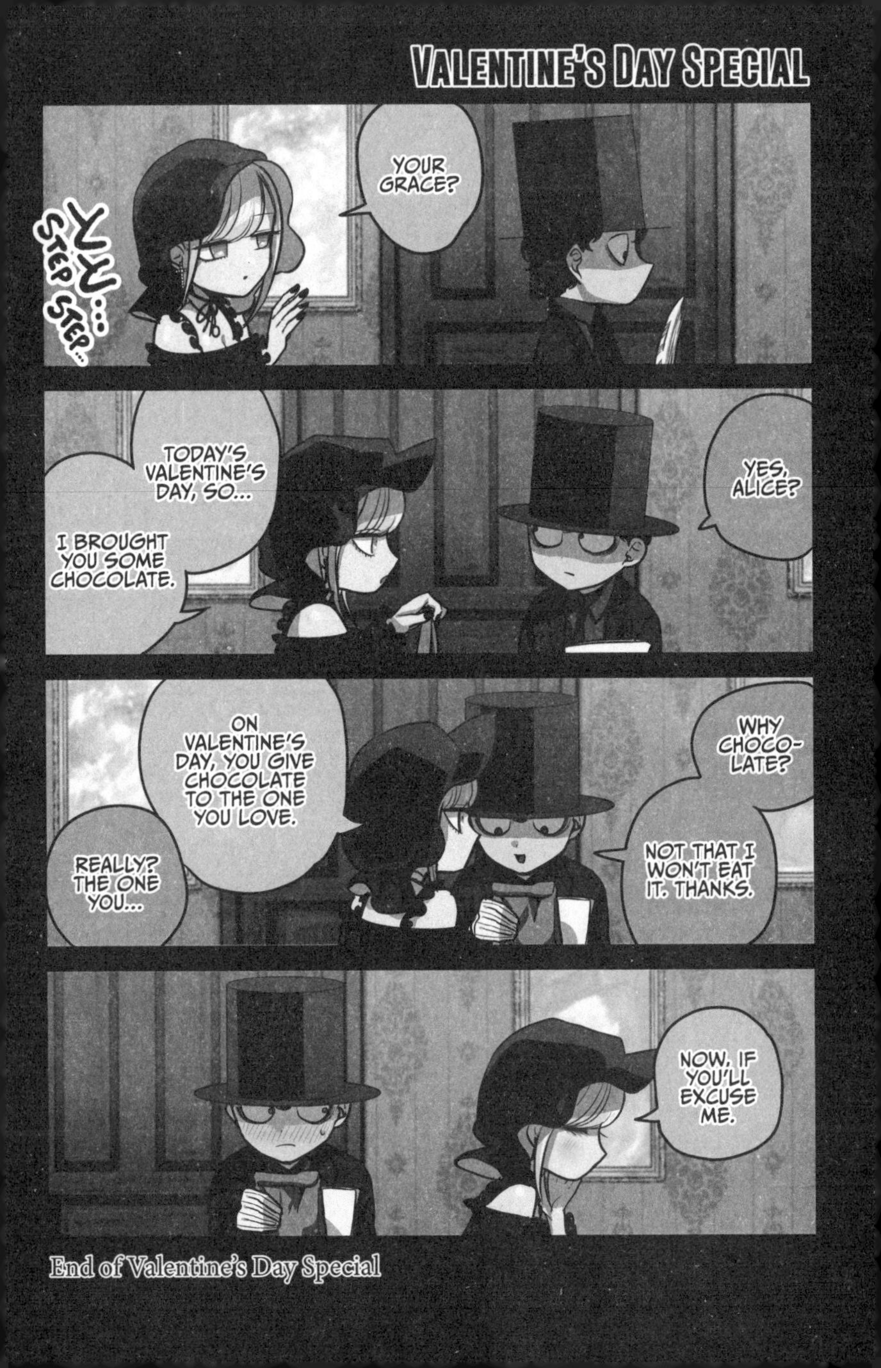
YOUR GRACE?
STEP STEP...
YES, ALICE?
TODAY'S VALENTINE'S DAY, SO...
I BROUGHT YOU SOME CHOCOLATE.
WHY CHOCO-LATE?
ON VALENTINE'S DAY, YOU GIVE CHOCOLATE TO THE ONE YOU LOVE.
NOT THAT I WON'T EAT IT. THANKS.
REALLY? THE ONE YOU...
NOW, IF YOU'LL EXCUSE ME.

End of Valentine's Day Special

THE DUKE OF DEATH AND HIS MAID

THE DUKE OF DEATH AND HIS MAID

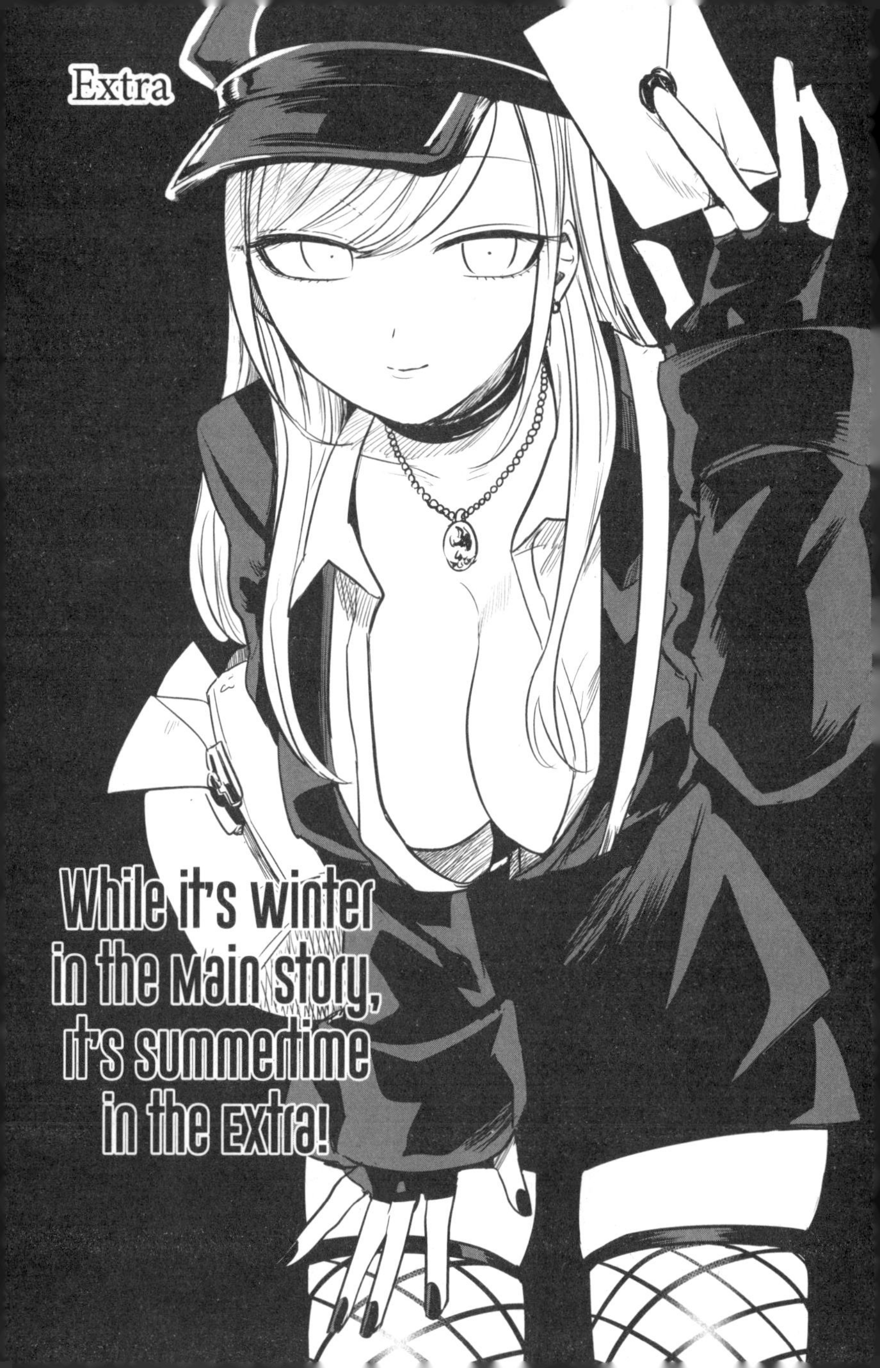
Extra
While it's winter in the main story, it's summertime in the extra!

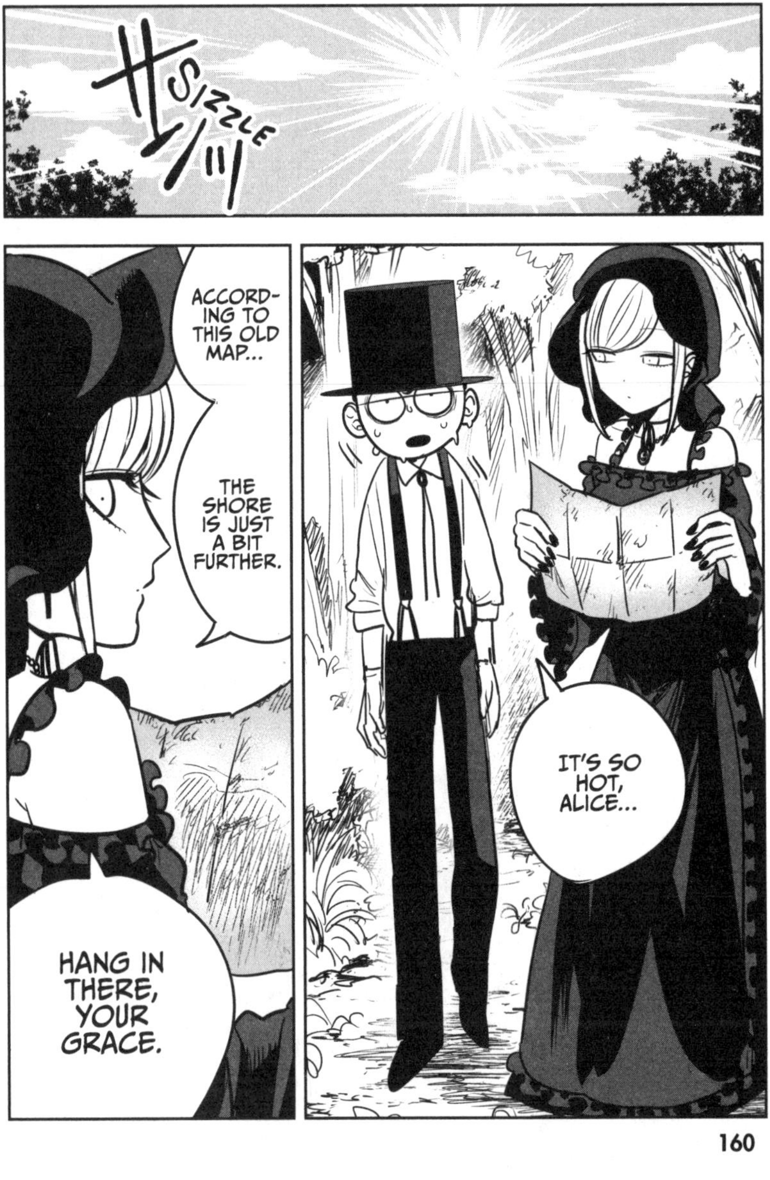
SIZZLE
IT'S SO HOT, ALICE...
ACCORD-ING TO THIS OLD MAP...
THE SHORE IS JUST A BIT FURTHER.
HANG IN THERE, YOUR GRACE.

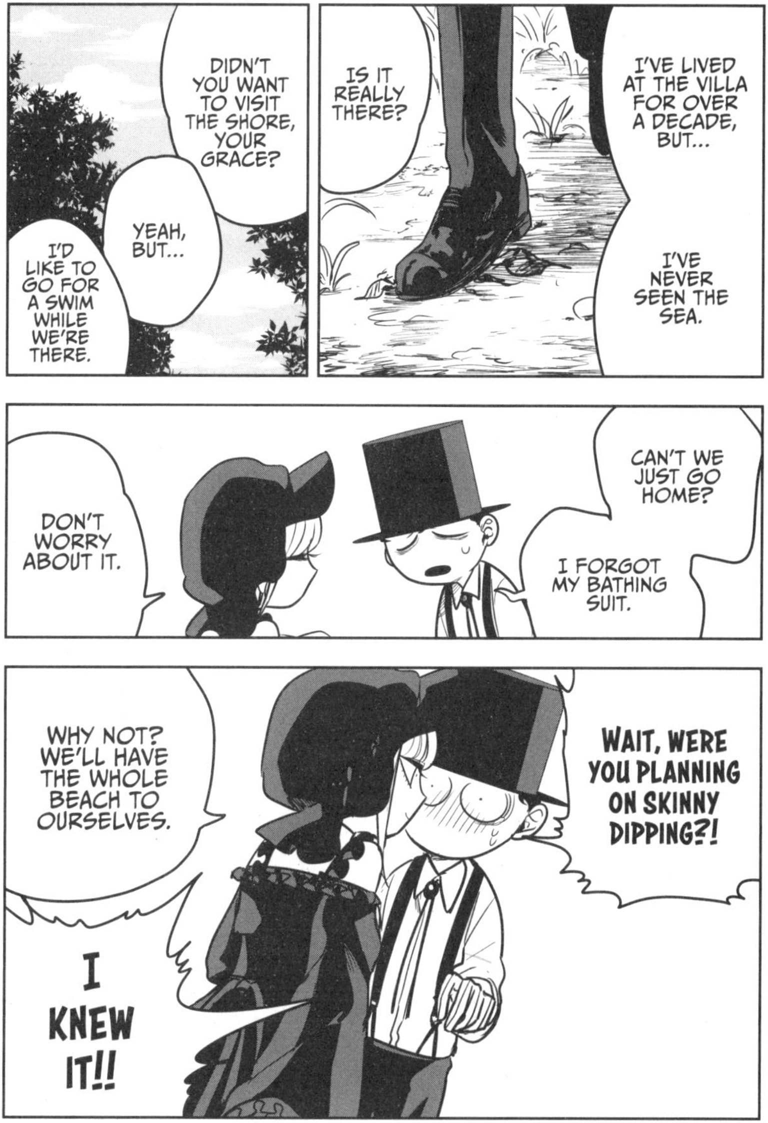
I'VE LIVED AT THE VILLA FOR OVER A DECADE, BUT...
I'VE NEVER SEEN THE SEA.
IS IT REALLY THERE?
DIDN'T YOU WANT TO VISIT THE SHORE, YOUR GRACE?
YEAH, BUT...
I'D LIKE TO GO FOR A SWIM WHILE WE'RE THERE.
CAN'T WE JUST GO HOME?
I FORGOT MY BATHING SUIT.
DON'T WORRY ABOUT IT.
WAIT, WERE YOU PLANNING ON SKINNY DIPPING?!
WHY NOT? WE'LL HAVE THE WHOLE BEACH TO OURSELVES.
I KNEW IT!!

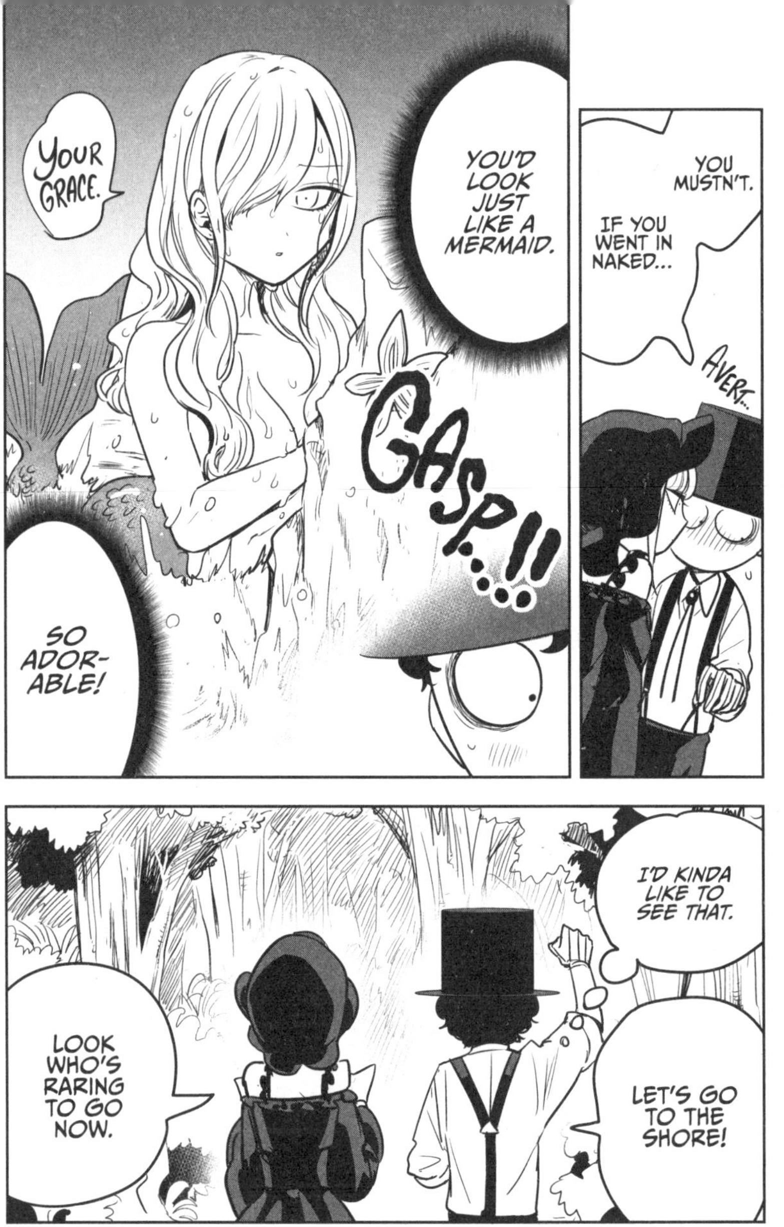
YOU MUSTN'T.
IF YOU WENT IN NAKED...
AVERT...
YOU'D LOOK JUST LIKE A MERMAID.
YOUR GRACE.
GASP...!!
SO ADORABLE!
I'D KINDA LIKE TO SEE THAT.
LET'S GO TO THE SHORE!
LOOK WHO'S RARING TO GO NOW.

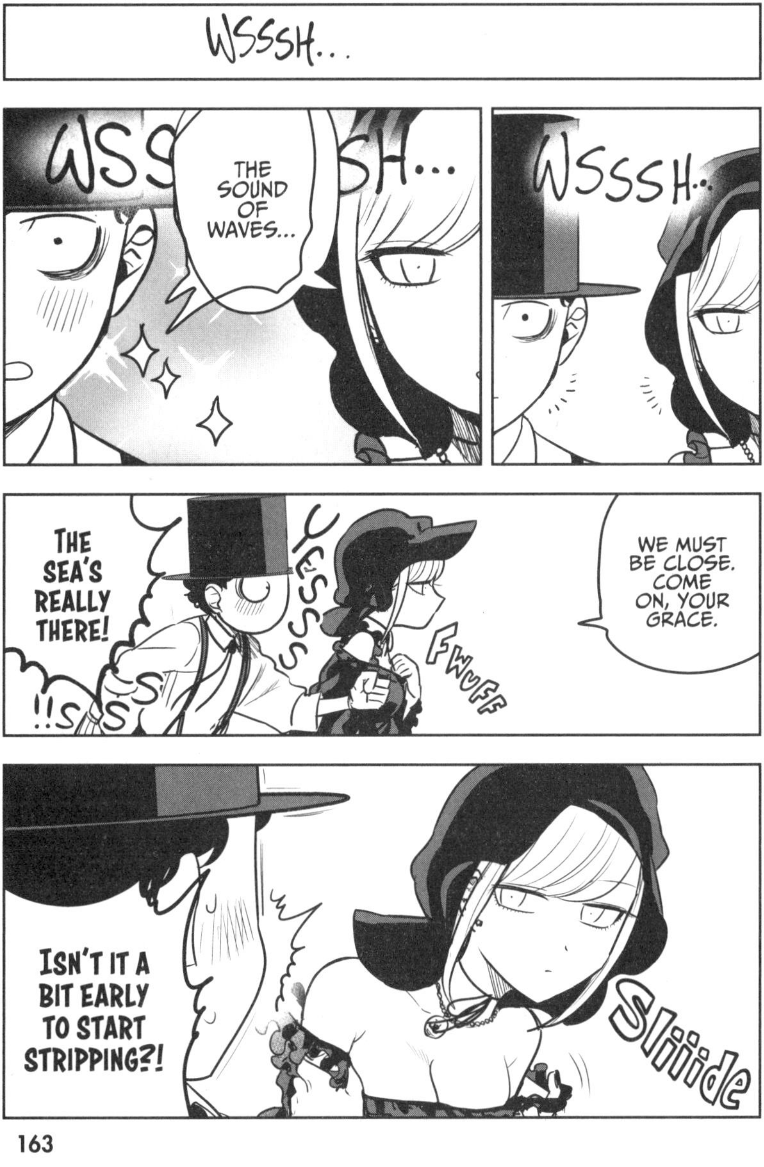
WSSSH...
WSSSH...
WSSSH...
THE SOUND OF WAVES...
WE MUST BE CLOSE. COME ON, YOUR GRACE.
FWUFF
YESSSSS
THE SEA'S REALLY THERE!
SSS!!
Sliiide
ISN'T IT A BIT EARLY TO START STRIPPING?!

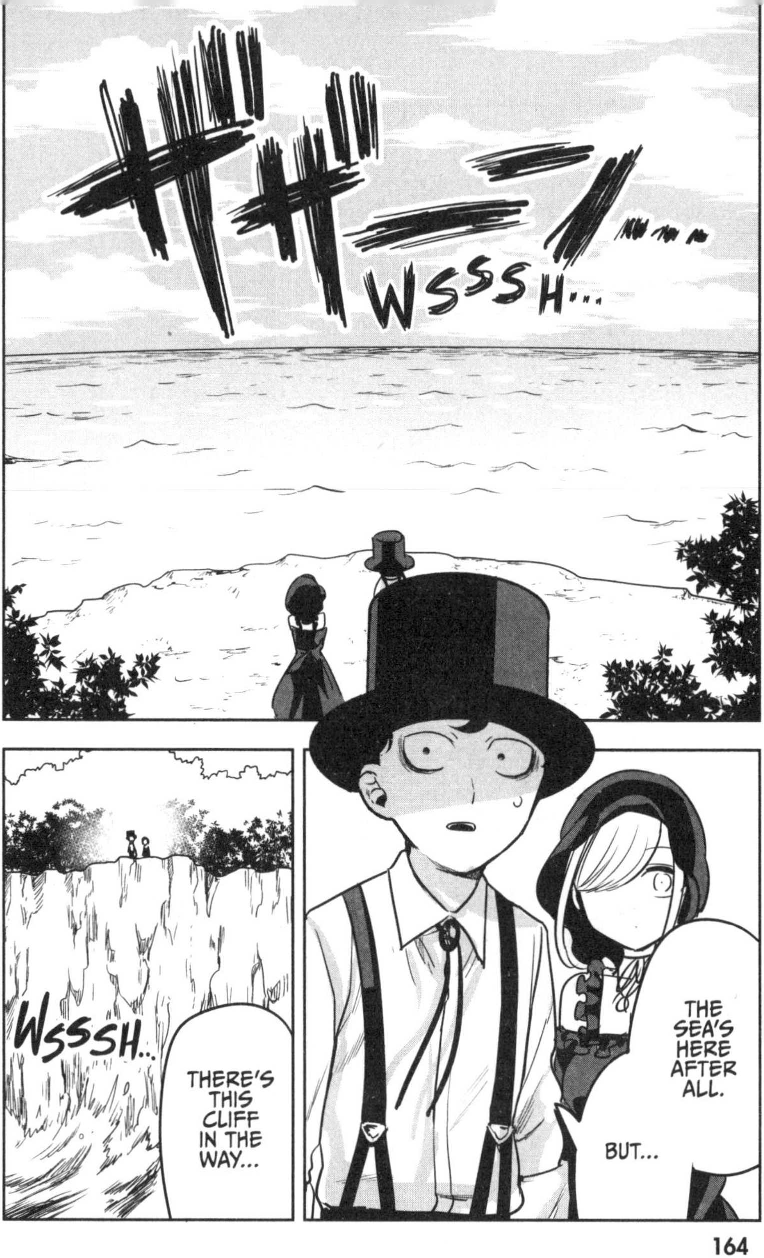
WSSSH...
THE SEA'S HERE AFTER ALL.
BUT...
WSSSH...
THERE'S THIS CLIFF IN THE WAY...

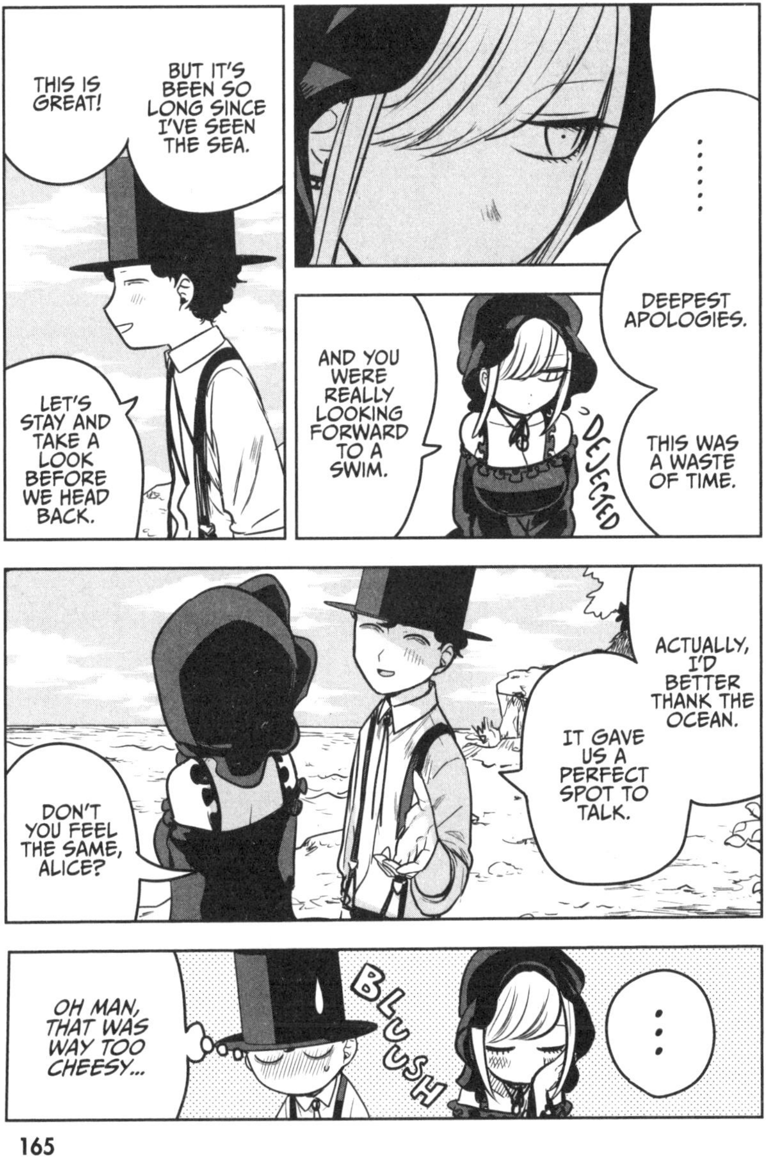
......
DEEPEST APOLOGIES.
THIS WAS A WASTE OF TIME.
DEJECTED
AND YOU WERE REALLY LOOKING FORWARD TO A SWIM.
BUT IT'S BEEN SO LONG SINCE I'VE SEEN THE SEA.
THIS IS GREAT!
LET'S STAY AND TAKE A LOOK BEFORE WE HEAD BACK.
ACTUALLY, I'D BETTER THANK THE OCEAN.
IT GAVE US A PERFECT SPOT TO TALK.
DON'T YOU FEEL THE SAME, ALICE?
...
BLUSH
OH MAN, THAT WAS WAY TOO CHEESY...

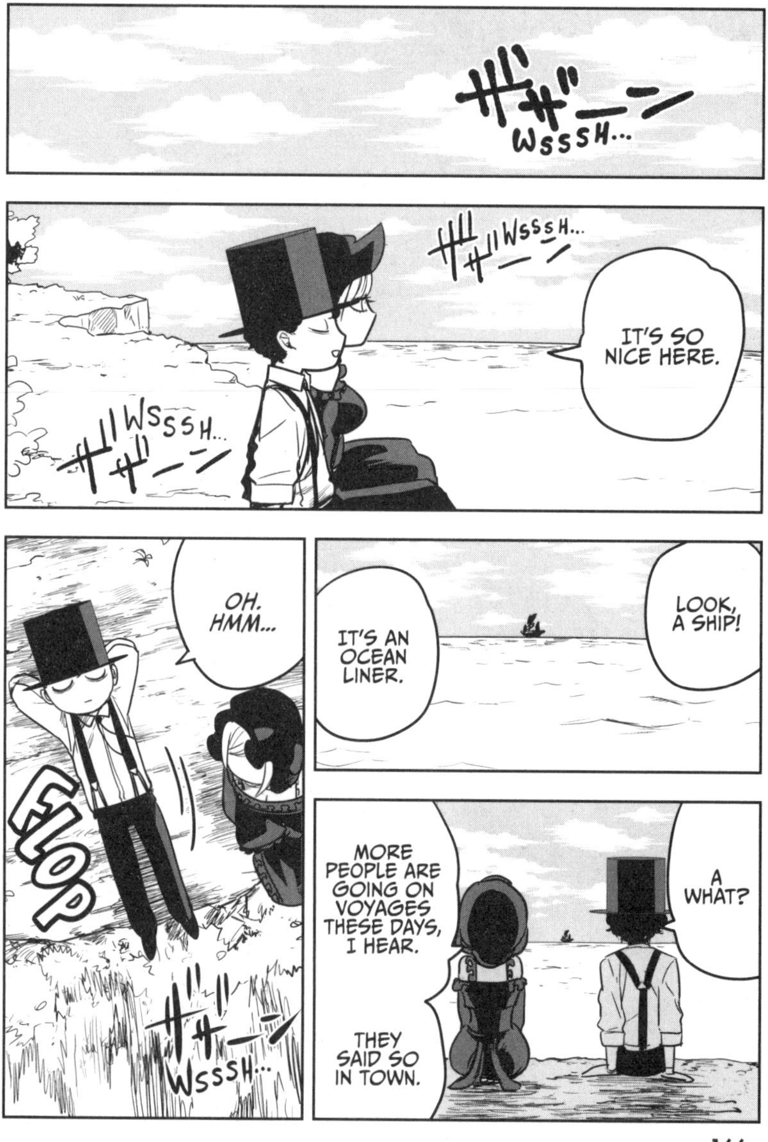
ザザーン
WSSSH...
ザザーン
WSSSH...
IT'S SO NICE HERE.
ザザーン
WSSSH...
LOOK, A SHIP!
IT'S AN OCEAN LINER.
A WHAT?
MORE PEOPLE ARE GOING ON VOYAGES THESE DAYS, I HEAR.
THEY SAID SO IN TOWN.
OH. HMM...
FLOP
ザザー
WSSSH...

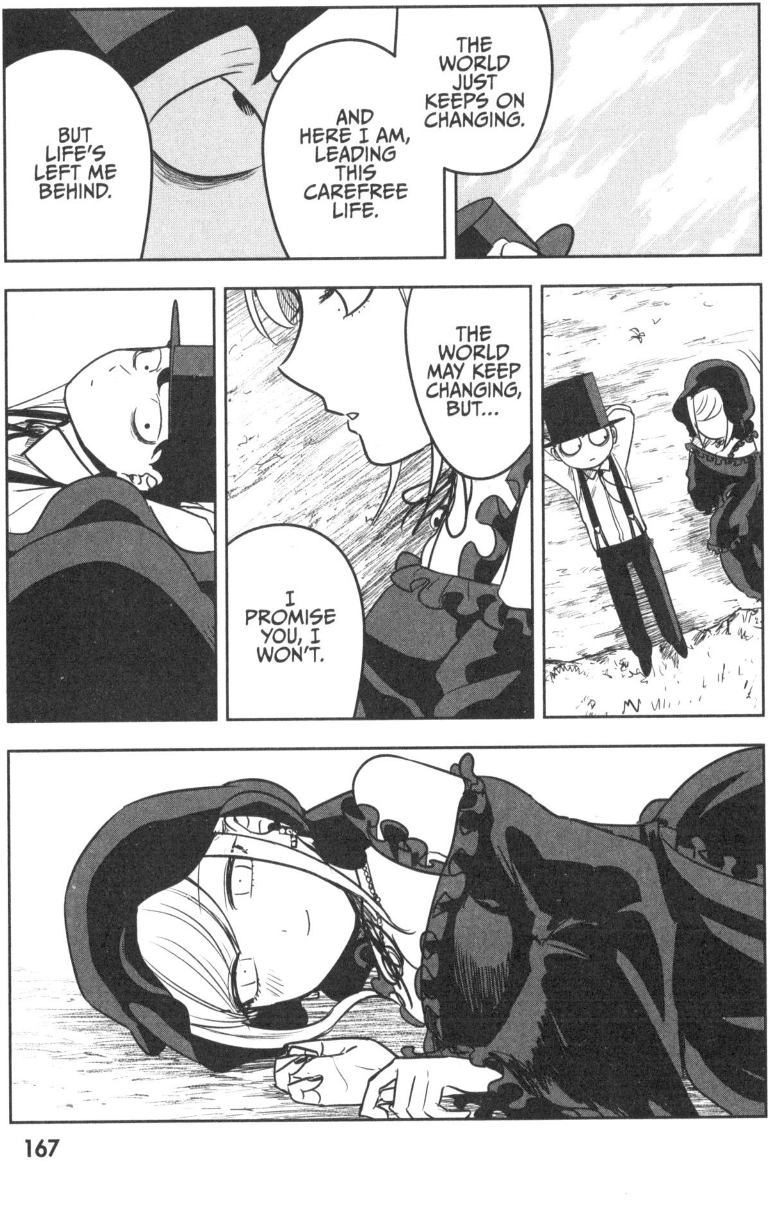
THE WORLD JUST KEEPS ON CHANGING.
AND HERE I AM, LEADING THIS CAREFREE LIFE.
BUT LIFE'S LEFT ME BEHIND.
THE WORLD MAY KEEP CHANGING, BUT...
I PROMISE YOU, I WON'T.

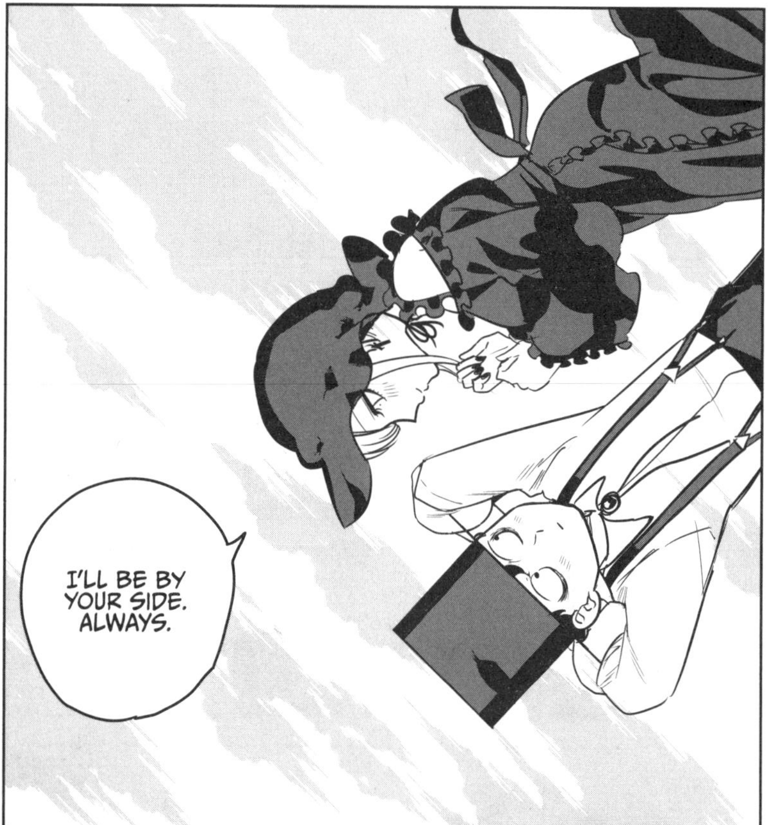
I'LL BE BY YOUR SIDE. ALWAYS.

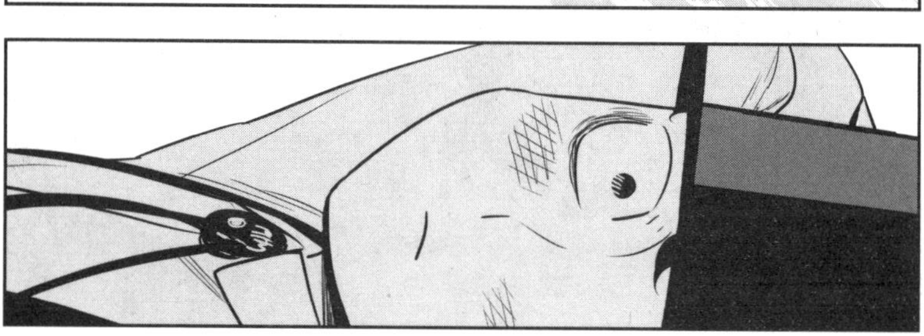

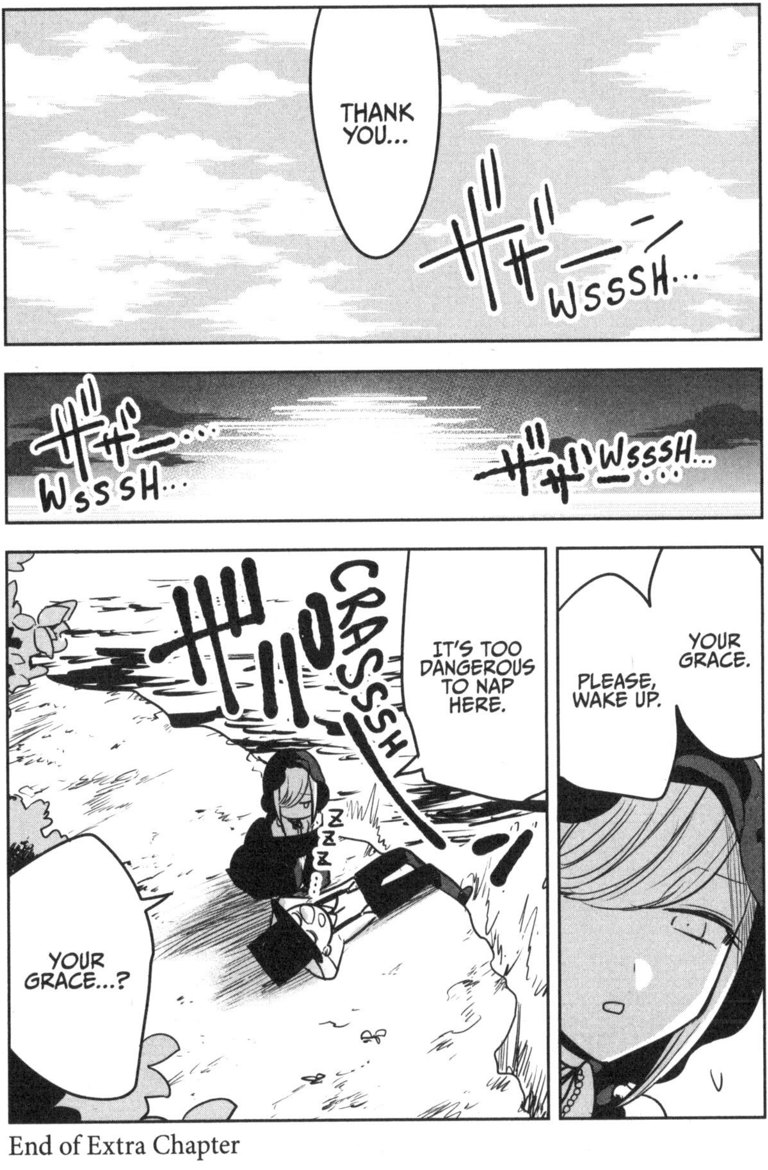
THANK YOU...
WSSSH...
WSSSH...
WSSSH...
YOUR GRACE.
PLEASE, WAKE UP.
IT'S TOO DANGEROUS TO NAP HERE.
CRASSSSH
YOUR GRACE...?

End of Extra Chapter

THE DUKE OF DEATH
AND HIS MAID

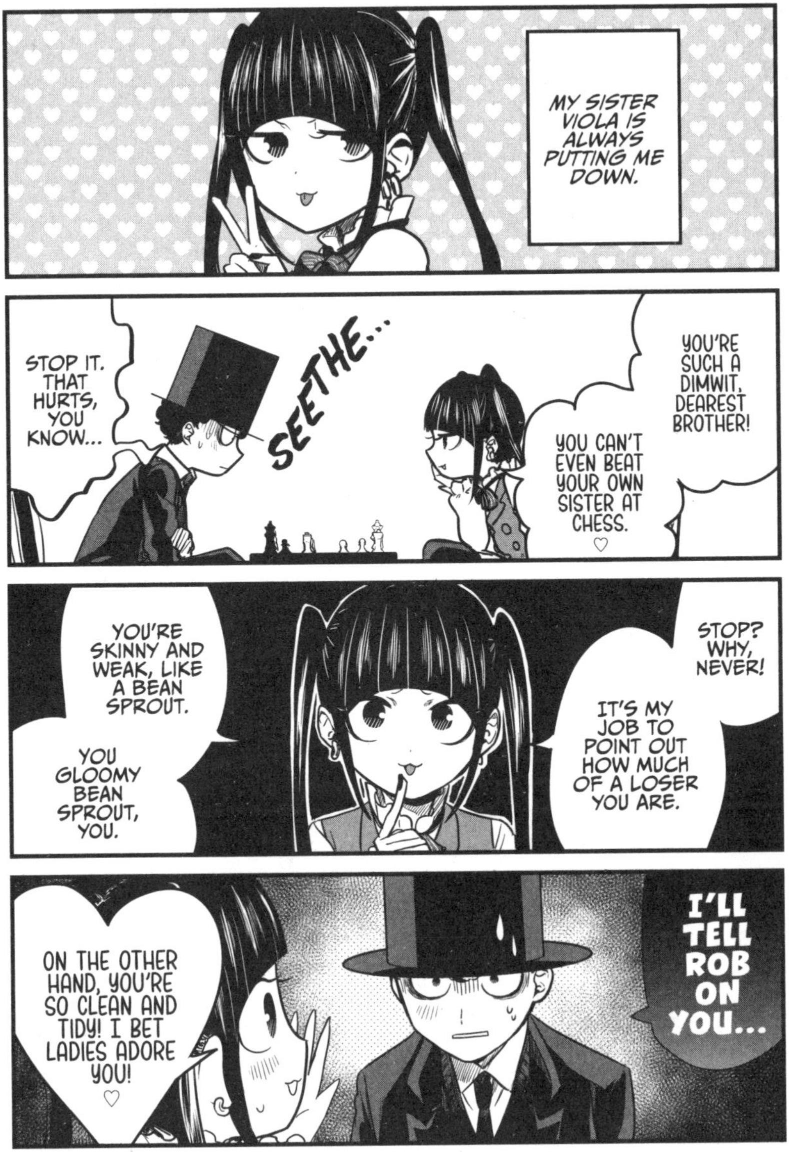
MY SISTER VIOLA IS ALWAYS PUTTING ME DOWN.
YOU'RE SUCH A DIMWIT, DEAREST BROTHER!
YOU CAN'T EVEN BEAT YOUR OWN SISTER AT CHESS. ♡
SEETHE...
STOP IT. THAT HURTS, YOU KNOW...
STOP? WHY, NEVER!
IT'S MY JOB TO POINT OUT HOW MUCH OF A LOSER YOU ARE.
YOU'RE SKINNY AND WEAK, LIKE A BEAN SPROUT.
YOU GLOOMY BEAN SPROUT, YOU.
I'LL TELL ROB ON YOU...
ON THE OTHER HAND, YOU'RE SO CLEAN AND TIDY! I BET LADIES ADORE YOU! ♡

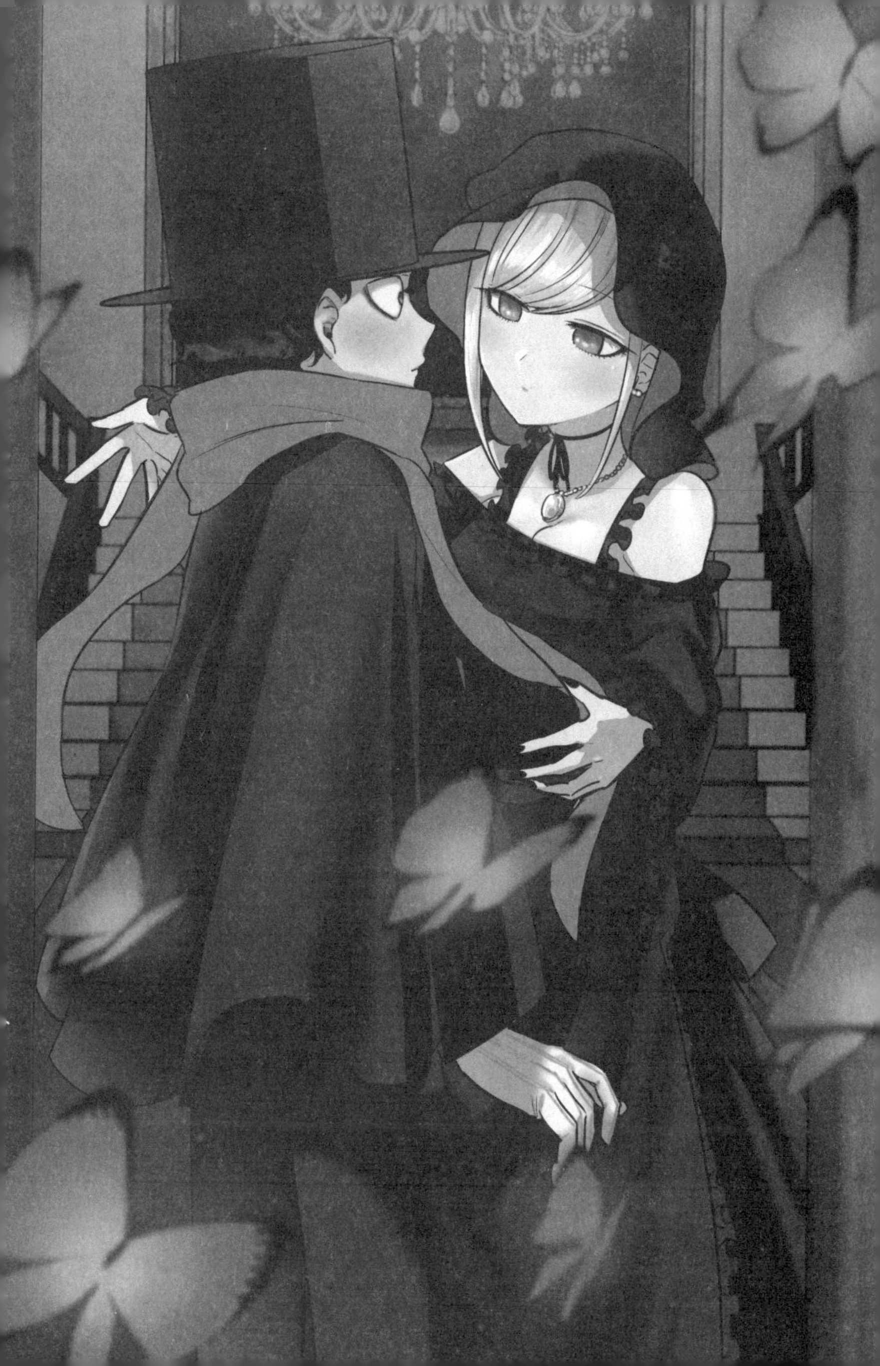

INOUE

For the cover of the
second volume, I redrew a
picture I drew a little over a
year ago. I really liked this
sketch, after all.

THE DUKE OF DEATH AND HIS MAID

A charming story of unlikely companions, available now from Seven Seas!

The Tale of the Outcasts

An Orphaned Girl Meets A Lonely Immortal

What begins as a chance encounter on the edge of the late nineteenth-century British Empire soon becomes a full-fledged journey to find their place in the world.

Seven Seas

STORY & ART BY
Makoto Hoshino

SEVEN SEAS ENTERTAINMENT PRESENTS

THE DUKE OF DEATH AND HIS MAID

story and art by INOUE   VOLUME 2

TRANSLATION
Josh Cole

ADAPTATION
Matthew Birkenhauer

LETTERING
Aila Nagamine

ORIGINAL COVER DESIGN
Yasuo Shimura (siesta)

COVER DESIGN
H. Qi

SENIOR COPY EDITOR
Dawn Davis

EDITOR
Abby Lehrke

PRODUCTION DESIGNER
Christina McKenzie

PRODUCTION MANAGER
Lissa Pattillo

PREPRESS TECHNICIAN
Melanie Ujimori

PRINT MANAGER
Rhiannon Rasmussen-Silverstein

EDITOR-IN-CHIEF
Julie Davis

ASSOCIATE PUBLISHER
Adam Arnold

PUBLISHER
Jason DeAngelis

SHINIGAMI BOCCHAN TO KURO MAID Vol. 2
by INOUE
© 2018 INOUE
All rights reserved.
Original Japanese edition published by SHOGAKUKAN.
English translation rights in the United States of America, Canada, the United
Kingdom, Ireland, Australia and New Zealand arranged with SHOGAKUKAN through
Tuttle-Mori Agency, Inc.

Seven Seas press and purchase enquiries can be sent to Marketing Manager Lianne
Sentar at press@gomanga.com. Information regarding the distribution and purchase of
digital editions is available from Digital Manager CK Russell at digital@gomanga.com.

Seven Seas and the Seven Seas logo are trademarks of
Seven Seas Entertainment. All rights reserved.

ISBN: 978-1-63858-417-9
Printed in Canada
First Printing: July 2022
10 9 8 7 6 5 4 3 2 1

////// READING DIRECTIONS //////

This book reads from *right to left*,
Japanese style. If this is your first time
reading manga, you start reading from
the top right panel on each page and
take it from there. If you get lost, just
follow the numbered diagram here.
It may seem backwards at first,
but you'll get the hang of it! Have fun!!

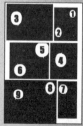

Follow us online: www.SevenSeasEntertainment.com